KNOWLEDGE AND PUBLIC POLICY

KNOWLEDGE AND PUBLIC POLICY

The Search for Meaningful Indicators

Second Expanded Edition

JUDITH ELEANOR INNES

Transaction Publishers
New Brunswick (U.S.A.) and London (U.K.)

New material this edition copyright © 1990 by Transaction Publishers,
New Brunswick, New Jersey 08903
Originally published in 1975 by Elsevier Scientific Publishing Company
as *Social Indicators and Public Policy: Interactive Processes of
Design*, by Judith Innes De Neufville.

Library of Congress Catalog Number: 89-5189
ISBN: 0-88738-810-8
Printed in the United States of America

Library of Congress Cataloging-in-Publication Data
Innes, Judith.

   Knowledge and public policy : the search for meaningful indicators/
by Judith Eleanor Innes.—2nd expanded ed.
      p.   cm.
   Rev. ed. of: Social indicators and public policy. 1975.
   Includes bibliographical references.
   ISBN 0-88738-810-8
   1. Social indicators.   2. Public policy.   3. Knowledge, Sociology
of.   I. Innes, Judith. Social indicators and public policy.
II. Title.
HN25.I56   1989
306.4′2—dc20   89-5189
                                                              CIP

Contents

To Eleanor, Judy, Karen, Kathy, and Chris—whose advise and support have made a real difference.

Introduction to the Transaction Edition: Understanding the Alliance of Knowledge and Policy

If we don't get the data, the decision will just be based on politics.
—A local elected official in California on the subject of whether the county should enact controls on growth.

KNOWLEDGE IN PUBLIC POLICY

When it really comes down to it, there is not much that can be said with confidence about how knowledge influences policy. As a society we must be pretty confident it does have an influence, or we would not keep producing studies and statistics directed to policy. Policy makers and the public, like the official quoted above, widely subscribe to a view that policy making should be well informed—if not, then it will be merely "political." Certainly major public decisions are often surrounded by facts and analyses. But it turns out to be difficult to pinpoint the effects of such information. Why do they persuade or not persuade? What do they communicate? How do they fit into the processes through which public actions are devised and implemented? And if these formal kinds of information are not influential, what is?

This book is about how one particular kind of information—social indicators—can come to be important to public decisions. It is grounded in case histories of the development and use of three widely discussed indicators: the measures of unemployment, living standards, and crime. The purpose was to explore what indicators and decision processes would have to be like for the indicators to play a significant role in deliberate policy choices. The research concludes that, under

1

certain conditions, indicators can be pivotal to policy debates or integral to administrative decision making. Indicators that are influential in resolving policy controversy, according to this research, are theoretically sound and meshed with publicly understood concepts. They are developed and overseen by people representing a variety of interests and knowledge. A process is carefully constructed to require public exposure of the indicators and policy attention to them. The indicators themselves are institutionalized and protected from tampering. To achieve all this takes effective institutional design, communication, and negotiation as well as time, energy, and a major public commitment to addressing a policy problem.

The research I did for this book has been useful as much to show how formal information such as indicators can be tied explicitly into policy as to show that there often are real, practical limits to achieving this direct linkage. For me, the research has been particularly important for the questions it raised even more than for those it answered, and for the intellectual journey it initiated. I have come, fifteen years later, to formulate a different view of how and why knowledge is linked to public action than that which framed my investigation of social indicators. This new model of the alliance of knowledge and policy in no way invalidates the findings of this book. Rather, it provides a better way of understanding much of what was going on.

This introductory essay to the second edition will explore basic features of this alternative perspective. It will draw both on intellectual developments in the growing literature on knowledge in society and on my own historical and field research since this book was published. The essay will illuminate certain aspects of the cases in this book, but it will also provide a more realistic and, I believe, more useful way of understanding how knowledge and public action shape one another. With such a framework we also have a more realistic basis for prescribing ethical and effective ways to inform public choice.

LINKING KNOWLEDGE AND POLICY

The view of knowledge and its links to policy which framed my study of social indicators was one that was widely shared in the social sciences in the late 1960s. It is a view grounded in the positivist conception of knowledge and knowledge use. I will refer to it here as the "scientific" model of knowledge use, though it represents an oversimplified and somewhat mechanistic conception of science. In this

2

form it has become an implicit working model that frames the expectations of the average participant or observer about the role of information in policy. Though experts and those deeply involved may know the reality to be more complex, no one has thus far offered an equivalent alternative view. The "scientific" model remains, if only by default, the principal way in which we understand and prescribe for the use of knowledge in policy.

The key normative and descriptive elements of this model are several. First, the view assumes that policy makers should use formal information, such as statistics or the findings of social science, to aid their decisions in a way analogous to how a scientist tests a hypothesis and is persuaded by the evidence of carefully designed experiments. For this view of knowledge use to apply, policy makers must represent unitary interests and be able to make meaningful, deliberate choices. Their task is to choose options that are likely to achieve goals on the basis of criteria, evidence, and logic. When their actions do not appear to be influenced by the evidence—as is often the case in practice—this view would attribute to the policy makers laziness, duplicity, or undue responsiveness to pressures of special interests.

What counts as knowledge use in the scientific model is explicit information processing, supportive of identifiable decisions. What counts as knowledge includes facts, statistics, theories, and findings of formal research and analysis. Experts who are unbiased and outside of a political process produce such knowledge. Knowledge production and use are, and should be, separate activities. The process of informing policy is therefore stepwise, with a division of labor where policy makers do the goal setting, experts do the analysis, and policy makers make decisions.

The model of the linkages between knowledge and policy that I will develop in this essay is grounded in an interpretive or phenomenological view of knowledge, rather than in the positivist perspective. It is more contextual, more evolutionary, and more complex than the scientific model. It regards formal, identifiable decisions as only a small part of all that leads to public action. It takes a broader view of what counts as knowledge. In fact, I have come to prefer the more inclusive term, "knowledge," over my earlier term, "information."[1] My perspective is that knowledge influences without necessarily being actively used. It contends there is a symbiotic, two-way relationship between knowledge and action.

I have pursued the inquiry through research on the practice of policy making in a variety of contexts and literature, including the philosophy of science, anthropology, political science, and organizational behavior, as well as planning theory[2] and policy science. My own odyssey has been paralleled and informed by others similarly unable to satisfy their concerns about the nature of the policy process within the accepted framework of understanding. A growing literature now seeks a more satisfactory way of explaining and assessing the nexus of knowledge and policy. There is more to do, but a direction and basic ideas have begun to take shape.

ISSUES NOT ADDRESSED BY THE SCIENTIFIC MODEL OF KNOWLEDGE USE

The research in this volume identified a number of issues which at the time of writing I recognized, but whose implications I did not know how to explore. A careful reading of the book will reveal these implications, but now, recognizing their importance and placing them in a new context, I can give them more clarity and development than I could fifteen years ago.

From my perspective this book's principal conclusion is that the most influential, valid, and reliable social indicators are constructed[3] not just through the efforts of technicians, but also through the vision and understandings of the other participants in the policy process. Influential indicators reflect socially shared meanings and policy purposes as well as respected technical methodology. If they were not simultaneously technical and political creations, as I have discussed elsewhere (de Neufville 1978–79), they would not be valid, since the very concept of validity implies a correspondence of measure and meaning.

These basic conclusions challenge the scientific model in several ways. First, they imply that knowledge is not produced only by experts. Nonexperts also have knowledge to contribute, though exactly what that knowledge is or how they contribute it needs to be elucidated. Second, the process of informing policy is not a straightforward, stepwise procedure, with policy makers offering values and goals and with experts providing answers to questions. It is a messier, more interactive process, where the division of labor between technician and politician is not a sharp one. Third, the conclusions suggest we have to know, at least in broad terms, what kinds of policies we want *before* we create indicators. Not only are policy makers unlikely to fund knowledge production that has no relation to acceptable policy,

4

they will not make use of information that suggests policies they cannot support (Tenenbaum and Wildavsky 1984).

The debates over methodology pointed up what researchers and statisticians understand, but often do not publicly emphasize. An indicator is simply a set of rules for gathering and organizing data so they can be assigned meaning. In this respect an indicator is no different from any type of formal research. In both instances there are some technically incorrect ways of ordering and relating the data, but a good many alternatives which are not incorrect. An indicator, like a piece of research, highlights certain aspects of a situation at the expense of others. It allows observers to "see" the world through a particular lens. It inevitably relies on a prior conception of a phenomenon. When the public has the opportunity to discuss methodology in relation to policy issues, they can come to understand the ways in which the structure of an indicator can shape policy.

This reasoning, however, brings us to the most difficult issue. If we cannot rely on our methods to reveal an objective truth, but can only see what our preconceptions, indicators, research designs, and policy preferences allow us to see, what legitimate claim can be made that knowledge can inform the policy process? If knowledge is relative to a viewer or a viewing device like an indicator, is the use of knowledge little more than a circular, self-fulfilling activity?

The problem is aggravated by the fact, demonstrated in the indicator case studies, that indicators must be institutionalized and protected from manipulation once they have been developed, if they are to be trusted and used. While this institutionalization makes them a known quantity and therefore effective for communication among parties to a policy controversy, it also crystallizes a particular conception of a policy problem, containing a particular set of values and understandings. The use of an indicator reinforces that conception and over time makes the conception seem an objective reality rather than a social construction. For example, we come to take the idea of unemployment as coincident with the particular version of the unemployment rate represented by the indicator. This problem is referred to in the sociology of knowledge as reification.[4] Its seriousness lies not simply in the blinder effect, but also in the political role of an indicator, or of any accepted idea, in protecting certain interests. It is virtually tautological to say that the political process that produced agreement on an indicator—or on a popular theory—and institutionalized its use in policy, selected a perspective that benefitted those who had most power at the time. An institutionalized indicator thus not only supports the status quo in knowledge, it supports the status quo in society.

The dilemma is that, on the one hand, we cannot get along without institutionalizing some concepts and information for the sake of communication, trust, and mutual understanding. We cannot allow people to manipulate and alter information at will. On the other hand, we cannot get along *with* institutionalized information if we want to see beyond blinders, grow in understanding, and have some assurance that public actions based on this knowledge are just.

The final question raised in my mind by the indicator research was why information sometimes seemed to move people to act—or at least to change their views—whereas, at other times, it appeared to have no effect. Indeed it is not difficult to find instances where policy action and public opinion seem to fly in the face of all reason and carefully gathered evidence. Whatever it was that made the indicators in these case studies persuasive in decisions, in the infrequent instances when they were, seemed to have something to do with the public debate over methods, where people came to share an understanding and attribute a common meaning to the indicators.

WHAT HAPPENED TO THE SOCIAL INDICATORS MOVEMENT?

At the time of the writing of this book, there was in full bloom a movement whose aim was to make social indicators an essential component of public policy making. Though this movement was soon to lose momentum and was a disappointment to many of its originators, it did leave a legacy in policy science and practice. Some of the misunderstanding of the potential role of social indicators among those who led this movement can be attributed to their being unaware of the kind of dynamics outlined in this book. They thought that creating influential indicators would be simpler and more straightforward than it was. They focused energy on the measurement task, often to the exclusion of the political and institutional one.

As the book recounts and I have discussed elsewhere (de Neufville 1981a), enthusiasm for social indicators was born in the mid-1960s, inspired by the success of economic indicators in influencing policy. The basic idea was that if governments regularly reported on social conditions, these conditions would not only have more salience in policy making, but policies could be more accurately designed to address problems and to be more quickly responsive to social change.

During the 1970s many governments did produce social reports, including the U.S., which produced three in a decade. But the task—at least in the U.S.—was difficult, and the results disappointingly hard to identify. The effort was hampered by lack of commitment from White House leadership on the one hand and, on the other, by involvement of agencies which saw implications for their programs in the indicators and tabulations selected for presentation. Months passed without agreements on the data, and the reports that finally emerged were rather bland compromises, without text that might link the data to policy.

In the meantime, researchers who were studying the impact of the U.S. social reports found that decision makers who had expressed interest in such indicators used the reports, if at all, only as a background reference or for preparing speeches (Caplan and Barton 1976, 1978). Respondents viewed them as out of date relative to other sources, too general in scope, and too lacking in interpretation to be useful. None cited any specific use of the indicators in the reports for making a decision. A study of the Canadian social reports (Brusegard 1978) made a similar finding, arguing that such reports had their primary use in education, giving teachers and students a broader and more quantitative picture of their society.

While other factors in the U.S. helped produce these disappointing results—most notably a government pullback from many domestic activities, particularly social programs—these reports were doomed to failure if their goal was a visible policy impact. The indicators were not selected explicitly to address defined policy objectives, nor were they linked to policy proposals in areas where there was a public commitment to action. The indicators were not designed to characterize issues narrowly or to evaluate policies. They were not explicitly based on accepted theories about social problems or their solutions. The choices of what indicators to include may have represented results of negotiation among agency and social report staff, but the task had not included public and Congressional debate. Thus, the implications of the indicators were neither salient nor known to these audiences. Moreover, there was no public obligation to examine the data during policy debate in a way that might have forced their linkage to issues. The one attempt to establish a system that might have accomplished such a linkage, through legislation establishing a Council of Social Advisors, designed to parallel the Council of Economic Advisors, failed to pass in Congress.

By 1978 the great hopes for social indicators to revolutionize public policy had been tempered. The outpouring of literature using the term "social indicators" dwindled. Policy scientists turned their attention to other topics or found new labels for their interests. The Social Science Research Council closed its Social Indicators Research Center in Washington, D.C. and stopped publishing its newsletter. Many observers decided the social indicators movement was a failure.

The movement was not without outcomes, however, despite the wasted effort and unrealistic expectations. One important consequence was that efforts to measure elusive and important social concepts became more sophisticated. Many of those who worked on this aspect of social indicators continued to do so without necessarily using the term. Some of their work continues to appear in the journal *Social Indicators Research*, but much is routinely published in the journals of various disciplines and professional fields.

A second major legacy has been increasing public attention to country- or community-wide social reporting. A core group around the world maintains an interest in social reporting, and many of its activities are regularly reported in an international newsletter.[5] Territorial indicators which allow comparisons among communities and nations have considerable potential value to governments, international agencies, and the private sector, though many of the composite indices have the conceptual problems of aggregation discussed in Chapter IX.[6]

The perceived failure of social indicators to revolutionize policy has also been part of the legacy. It has helped to make clear that more is required to inform policy than simply producing academically certified data and handing it to policy makers.

THE EMERGENT FIELD OF KNOWLEDGE USE

DISILLUSIONMENT WITH THE SCIENTIFIC MODEL

As the enthusiasm for social indicators was subsiding, a new interdisciplinary field of inquiry—or more accurately, a new stage of an existing field—was emerging. This inquiry responded to many of the same concerns that had led to the disillusionment with social indicators. At least since publication of Lynd's *Knowledge for What?* (1939), a small, but eminent, group of social scientists had focused attention on how to make social science knowledge more likely to improve society. As academics and their ideas became part of the Great Society programs in the 1960s, the group widened to include individuals drawn not only from social sciences but also professional fields. The scientific model became the predominant ideal. Evaluation and program planning, systems analysis, cost-benefit studies, data banks, and large-scale computer models were developed, used, and examined. Schools of public policy were created by the early 1970s, along with journals like *Policy Sciences*, *Policy Analysis*, and *Policy Studies*. The field of policy analysis formally came into being, construed by many of its originators as a profession whose task was to bring social science knowledge into the policy process by advising "rulers."

By the mid 1970s, however, there was a consensus that a lot had gone wrong. Great Society programs were a disappointment because, many contended, social scientists got the theory wrong. Alternatively, critics blamed policy makers for being too "political" to use the information. Many simply contended that the world was too complex for scientific knowledge to be of much help. Whatever the explanation, there was a mismatch between expectations and performance. Along with critiques of the practical value of social science, moreover, voices began to challenge the conceptual foundation of the scientific model— the idea that analytic information could be value-free and unbiased, serving simply the rulers' or public's goals.[7]

The experience with failed policy advising and doubts about the scientific dependability of knowledge were magnified as the social sciences were themselves reshaped by developments in the philosophy of science. These developments challenged the positivist view of knowledge as the unique, or even the primary, one for social inquiry and sought to replace it with interpretive, hermeneutic approaches.[8]

Several widely cited works in the mid 1970s marked a turning point in the acceptance of the view that social science knowledge—particularly statistics and the findings of controlled field studies—could readily affect decision makers' choices through a straightforward, rational calculus. Alice Rivlin, for example, after several years in the White House Budget Office, concluded that cost-benefit analysis was good at comparing costs but not at measuring what works or ultimately saying what ought to be done (1971). Graham Allison's study of the Cuban missile crisis, which quickly became required reading for students of public policy and planning, also demonstrated clear limits to the usefulness of "scientific" knowledge. He showed convincingly that what decision makers do can as easily be seen as bureaucratic behavior or game playing rather than rational, utility-maximizing assessment of evidence and options (1971).

At least one study directly tested the dominant assumptions about decision makers' use of research and found them to be wanting. Because the research offered such a test and because it was to be so widely cited by later analysts,[9] it is worth outlining here. The study (Caplan 1975; Caplan et al. 1975), completed at about the same time as this book, involved interviews with 250 high-level federal policy makers. Its purpose was to find out whether they were receptive to using social science knowledge, to learn what they did use of such formal research for decisions, and to identify the reasons for their use or nonuse.

Respondents had positive attitudes toward such knowledge, but could give little evidence of actually using any of it. They preferred to get information from the people at the Congressional Research Service or from their own staff rather than to use noninteractive, "cold" sources, such as written materials or computer terminals. Those who did say they used social science knowledge meant that they used a social science perspective rather than, as the researchers intended, that they used specific findings for specific purposes. Sixty percent of the use that respondents reported was of concepts, while 40 percent was of data-based or special-purpose studies. Not surprisingly, researchers were unable to measure the degree of impact of the knowledge.

Neither the authors nor others at the time had a satisfactory explanation for such paradoxical results. Policy makers were seemingly willing to use social science knowledge, they claimed an ability to assess its objectivity, and they even perceived themselves as using it—Researchers however did not find use. Even the popular "two-communities" theory (Caplan, 1977a), which contended that the basic reason knowledge was not used was that researchers and policy makers were part of different cultures with different values and incentives, begged the questions raised by these results. How does conceptual use of information occur and what is its importance? Why did policy makers think they were using the knowledge while researchers did not? Why did decision-related use seem to be so infrequent?

Limitations of the implicit framework in Caplan's work, as in much of the contemporaneous work on knowledge use, prevented the answering of many of these questions. Because he was looking for

10

knowledge use of the scientific variety and because he relied on survey methodology, he necessarily focused on explicit processing of information by individuals for decisions they could pinpoint. He could find out only about policy makers' perceptions and their conscious decisions to use or not to use particular information. He could not investigate the organizational or political processes in which this information may play a part. He could not find out how the knowledge users and providers interact, although the responses suggest interaction is an important factor. Finally, Caplan's method did not allow him to examine the information itself. He had to rely on the assessment of policy makers to determine what counts as information. As a result, his interpretation is hampered by a mismatch between the researchers' and respondents' views of both knowledge and knowledge use. The research does demonstrate clearly, however, that the scientific model does not provide a good lens for examining the relationship of knowledge and policy.

The research reported on in this book, and some of the other studies to be discussed in this essay, originated in an intention similar to Caplan's—to identify decision uses of formal information. Because I adopted different research strategies, I have been able to identify some processes invisible in Caplan's and much of the other work up to that time. The focus of my research is not individual policy makers, but the larger organizational and political processes which, over time, produce, use, and are transformed by knowledge.

THE TRANSFORMATION OF THE KNOWLEDGE USE QUESTION

By the late 1970s a number of academics had joined the search for a more useful framework for examining knowledge use. A journal, *Knowledge: Creation Diffusion, Utilization,* was instituted. Academics in professional fields, along with practicing policy professionals, addressed themselves to the issues. Several important insights began to transform the way that observers saw the knowledge use question.

The first of these insights is that social science knowledge has its most important role in "enlightening" policy makers rather than in answering questions, solving problems, or in other ways playing a measurable role in deliberate decision making. In her important research, Carol Weiss (1977) found that policy makers particularly valued studies which made them see issues in a new way—research which challenged the status quo and suggested the need for change. They not only valued their own learning or confirmation of things they suspected but could not say with confidence, they often welcomed the opportunity to use the research to justify reforms.

The concept of enlightenment was to become part of the basic vocabulary of the field of knowledge use. It became accepted that knowledge affects policy in a tacit way by changing the way policy makers understand issues. How or why enlightenment happens, what it is that policy actors actually understand from the research, and how they transform the ideas into practical action remained to be explored.[10] The enlightenment idea was to coexist uneasily with the scientific model, which has no place for so elusive a phenomenon as enlightenment.

A second important contribution was Weiss's (1979) typology of research utilization, which helped the field move to a more complete description of practice and a less confining set of norms. She identified and asserted the legitimacy of six different ways in which research is actually utilized. In the first, the *knowledge-driven* model, ideas from research stimulate new ways of doing things. In the *problem-solving*, or instrumental model, corresponding to the scientific model as I have discussed it here, research use is also a linear, stepwise process, but one where the problem is first defined in the world of practice and the research is then designed to solve it. In the *enlightenment* model, which Weiss contends is the most common way research enters the policy process, decision makers' ideas are framed by social research. The *tactical* use of research is not to learn or know, but to gain legitimacy, build a constituency, or enhance an agency or individual's position. The *political* use of knowledge selects findings that support positions already held to persuade others. Finally, the *interactive* model of knowledge use is a nonlinear process, where ideas of a variety of people are pooled, and where social science knowledge is used along with experience, insight, and communication in a way that has so many interconnections and interactions that the paths of influence of the knowledge cannot be easily traced. Two important implications of Weiss's typology are first, that we have to rethink the meaning of knowledge "use," and second, that a new account of the knowledge-policy link should incorporate all these "uses" of research.

The third insight of importance in the literature was that, while the framing of problems centrally shapes policy action, there is no way of approaching such a task legitimately or systematically within the scientific model. While this model offers rules for problem solving, it offers none for problem defining. The enlightenment idea, moreover, suggests that research itself is a source of problem definitions. No one

12

was prepared to argue that such research was simply uncovering in an unbiased way a fixed form of policy problems. Indeed, as Rittel and Webber (1973) and a handful of others noted in the early 1970s, policy research implicitly makes value judgments and arbitrary choices in selecting and framing the policy problems—choices which have important action consequences.

Rein and White (1977) put it even more directly, contending that the idea of research as problem solving is little more than a soothing fantasy to which policy makers subscribe because they do not want to acknowledge that in commissioning or using research they are delegating the value decisions that are supposedly their responsibility. In practice, the authors say, policy making is not a freestanding activity any more than is the informing of policy making. Rather, both are part of everyday political action. They argue, as I do in this book, that in the policy process, arguments over the structures of meaning and language are used to resolve policy issues. Inevitably, also, a researcher sorts among questions rather than just finds answers. Thus the researcher helps create issues, and the policy maker helps define knowledge. The authors call for a new myth describing the research-policy alliance, one conforming better to the realities.

Rein and Schon (1977) contend that basic tasks of policy analysis are to surface the tacit assumptions and perspectives that underlie problems as defined in public settings, to examine their sources in the culture, and to develop ways of assessing the definitions. They argue that constructive skepticism and questioning is the way to address hidden world views that shape these formulations. This, however, was a proposal that did not fit with norms of professional and academic practice at the time. Its logic was persuasive, but it opened too many questions and offered too few answers for others to follow up its implications a decade ago.[11]

The fourth insight was that we need a broader concept of knowledge to encompass all that is used in policy. Lindblom and Cohen's book-length essay, *Usable Knowledge* (1979), explores what kinds of knowledge are in practice part of social problem solving. They reject the term "social science knowledge," replacing it with a more inclusive one, "professional social inquiry," incorporating the contributions of policy professionals. Second, they argue for the legitimacy and centrality of "ordinary knowledge" and casual analysis in the policy process. They argue that professional inquiry has and should have a relatively limited role, even in problem solving, if only because it is costly. It is, in any case, necessarily incomplete and must incorporate

13

much that is simply ordinary knowledge. As professional inquiry in their view, is inherently partisan, they contend that it should be used within debates, rather than be offered to policy makers as authoritative. While they do not offer an alternative to the scientific model, their plea for further research leads in the direction of a new conception of knowledge use.

Lastly the concept of the "reflective practitioner" has been an important image for a new conception of the knowledge-policy relationship. Schon (1983) makes the case that a practitioner should work closely and interactively with a client rather than take the role of aloof expert. The latter role, he contends, has been discredited as the public has come increasingly to challenge the authority of professional expertise in many fields. The way to serve a client is for the practitioner and client to share their understandings in a cooperative way, to define and redefine problems, exploring assumptions and creating new possibilities until they jointly find a solution. On the basis of detailed observation of leading practitioners in several professional fields, Schon contends such "reflective practitioners" use their knowledge in highly contextual and contingent ways and are prepared to modify that knowledge in response to the client's understanding. His argument, like Lindblom and Cohen's, respects the importance of ordinary knowledge. It is an example of what Weiss referred to as the "interactive" model of knowledge use.

MY RESEARCH

The interactive model is the view that has tacitly framed my own interpretation of the cases in this book and guided my later investigations of the knowledge-policy link. My research since 1975 can be grouped under two main themes. One set of studies focuses on when and how quantitative information can be influential. The thrust of its conclusions are that data can, under certain circumstances, frame action and set the terms for discourse, even when they are not explicitly used in decisions. The second cluster of research studies explores the public meanings that are attached to indicators, to research findings, and to policy ideas and actions. These meanings are seldom articulated, yet they are known and often widely shared. The research demonstrates the key importance of understanding these meanings if we wish to identify the links between knowledge and public action.[12]

14

Under certain circumstances quantitative data and other products of professional inquiry can become powerful policy tools. Occasionally, as is demonstrated by the unemployment indicator, a particular statistic can become crucial in policy decisions. More often, selected indicators can be central to efforts to allocate resources in an equitable and reliable way. The standard budget was used, as discussed in Chapter VI, in many programs to determine assistance levels for families according to need. Similarly, social data are part of formulas which allocate federal funds to states and localities (de Neufville and Stoddard, 1988).

These decision-linked, explicit uses of statistics pale in importance, however, beside a variety of tacit and second-order influences. Statistics and other products of professional inquiry can become part of the framework *within which* action is taken. Their role can be not just to allocate funds, but to allocate power among participants and among policy perspectives. These numbers and ideas can frame policy problems, create tacit boundaries on options, and set the terms of public discourse.

These conclusions emerge from a series of field research efforts between 1977 and 1985 in diverse policy contexts. These studies all focus on cases of public policy making which are accompanied by requirements to produce and publicly debate quantitative and other professional, formally generated information. My purpose at the outset was to confirm whether the findings in this book could be generalized across levels of government and types of policy. In particular, I wanted to find more ways in which data were directly used in decisions. The result was to confirm that decision use of data is rare. The studies also provided a rich and complex picture of the indirect ways that data alter the processes, conditions, and norms of policy making.

We conducted field research in several contexts. The first study focused on local decision making on U.S. Department of Housing and Urban Development (HUD) Community Development Block Grant (CDBG) funds in 1977–78 in five California jurisdictions (de Neufville 1981b; Innes 1988b). Localities had considerable leeway in their decisions, but had to fit proposals within federal guidelines and submit lengthy data-based documents to qualify. The second was a study of the production and use of the U.S. State Department's *Country Reports*, which describe, where possible in quantitative terms, human rights conditions in all nations. Congress mandated this annual report to aid in carrying out human rights objectives in foreign policy. My own involvement was first as a consultant in 1980 to the Carter administration, assisting them in improving the quantitative component of the reports (de Neufville 1982), and then again in a followup study in 1985–86 designed to see what changes had occurred during the Reagan years (de Neufville 1986). The third piece of research involved case studies of the role of environmental impact review (EIR) in local policy consideration of four proposals for large-scale, mixed-use land development projects in California (de Neufville and Solloway 1986; Innes 1988b). For these projects state law requires that large amounts of data and other information on a variety of social, economic, and natural environmental conditions be produced and publicized along with predictions of future consequences of development.[13],[14]

These policy making situations had in common several key elements that parallel the unemployment indicator case in this book. First, in each a legislative body or granting agency required the public agency to prepare and publish information on specified topics related to the policy objectives. Second, a forum for public discussion of the data in relation to policy decisions was in place. A citizen commission debated CDBG proposals and examined the data. A Congressional committee evaluated the *Country Reports* in public hearings, and numerous other Congressional committees used the findings in public debates. The EIR legislation required public hearings before the local legislative body could certify the adequacy of the impact assessment report. In none of the cases was public action legally tied to particular findings or statistical results. It was up to the legislative body whether and how to pay attention to the findings.

Technical Capacity.

The data requirements in these studies increased technical capacity in the implementing agencies in several ways. In most of the cases, filling the requirements obligated agencies to hire or to educate personnel to gather, interpret, and manipulate information. In all but one of the CDBG cases, the only community data analysts on staff were originally hired to prepare HUD reports on CDBG or its predecessor programs. Many of the planning staff developed expertise to oversee and to do some of this work themselves, as well as to interpret and explain data to citizens and legislators. EIR requirements not only had similar effects on local agency staff, they helped spawn an industry of environmental consulting and stimulated rapid growth in professional environmental education. When Congress demanded human rights reports, the Department of State had to educate its foreign service officers to uncover and consistently report abuses.

In each case the requirements also produced permanent and regularly updated bodies of information on the topics— information that was available and used in a variety of ways by participants, not only in the debates in question but also for related issues. These sources became part of the recognized official description of the situation.

Once the data and the expertise were available and the process of examining information was set in motion, organizational learning began and, with it, changes that have gone beyond the mandate of the legislation. Second-order effects were long-term increases in the technical capacity of the agencies. Once on staff, for example, CDBG data analysts conducted surveys, created data banks and computer systems, provided data to answer the questions of citizens and public officials, and advised and educated local participants in the meaning and use of data. In the constrained revenue environment of California, the EIR data were often the only source of up-to-date information on such key planning issues as the local population characteristics, traffic levels, and the economy. These data became the foundation for the required General Plans that communities prepare. Policy makers debated other policy issues, such as regional transportation questions, in terms of the information revealed by the EIR. The Department of State, in gaining access to a large body of information and developing expertise on human rights among its foreign service officers, became more inclined to include human rights information as routine parts of internal policy debates.

Empowerment of Policy Supporters.

Data requirements empower participants in the policy process whose values are congruent with the objectives of the original legislation. Because of self-selection and training, planners, environmental professionals, and human rights specialists are likely to believe in the values of the respective legislation and use their influence for implementing it. In the CDBG case, for example, planners tended to support HUD objectives of directing funding toward housing and low- and moderate-income areas, in opposition to powerful local interests favoring downtown or affluent neighborhoods. In the State Department, foreign service officers working on human rights became believers that these were important issues for foreign policy and advocated for attention to them even when they later moved into other roles. Such experts influence policy, even when they do not explicitly advocate a particular view, by calling attention to issues, framing problems, and defining solution alternatives in terms of the data.

The roles of these professionals as creators and interpreters of data also helped make them more legitimate and authoritative in the view of citizens, policy makers, and other participants. Many times in our interviews legislators and citizens cited these professionals with respect explicitly because of their expertise in data. Some, for example in the CDBG cases, contended that the planners were uniquely qualified to say whether proposed projects would be acceptable to HUD because the planners were keepers of the data. They held this view despite the fact that the required data had little, if any, bearing on project eligibility, and HUD did not use the data as a criterion for withholding funds. The EIR data allowed planners to identify, in negotiations with developers, which aspects of their projects were likely to meet with public opposition or damage the environment, and to specify levels and types of development that would be acceptable. The data helped make planners credible and effective negotiators.

The data also altered power relationships in all the studies by providing "talking points" to those concerned about the issues represented by the data. They provided concrete and unarguably legitimate information with which critics could challenge proposals or identify problems which had to be taken into account. The data gave many groups a basis for argument they would not otherwise have had. For example, in one case a citizen commissioner succeeded in getting CDBG funds allocated to poor neighborhoods and away from middle-class neighborhoods by using need indicators developed for HUD. Thus the data served both tactical and political purposes, in Weiss's terminology.

The data requirements offered, finally, formidable weapons to citizens who wanted to challenge decisions. Because of the legal requirement for data, citizens could and did file lawsuits in CDBG and EIR cases, contending that the data were inadequate, or that policy was made without regard to the data. The suits resulted in changes in policy decisions and efforts to improve the quality of the data. Even when lawsuits are not actually filed, a threat of lawsuit has often been sufficient to give those with concerns related to the policy objective a place at the bargaining table.

The requirement to generate data and present them to the public assures that organization and political attention goes to the issues the data represent. Professionals, managers, and elected officials have to learn about the data because they are accountable not only for the data's accuracy and interpretation, but also for consistency between their policies and the data. Such learning and a corresponding change in norms were evident in all contexts studied, as the actors faced legal or political consequences of ignoring what the data showed.

The process was particularly notable in the State Department under the Reagan administration, where officials at the outset opposed using human rights as a criterion for foreign policy. They were often unable to justify policies, however, on the basis of claims at odds with the *Reports* because its findings were official and highly publicized. They could not report inaccurate information without internal opposition and embarrassing publicity. As a consequence two things have happened. During the Reagan years, for all but a handful of controversial countries, the reports have become more accurate. In addition, many State Department officials have come to believe that human rights issues are essential to U.S. foreign policy.

Terms of Discourse.

Data requirements of the type discussed here change the content and structure of the discourse through which perceptions and understandings are formed and out of which formal decisions and actions emerge. They change the rules about who can participate, what are legitimate topics for discussion, and how the discussion must be conducted. They influence which assumptions the discussion will take for granted and which ones participants will have to justify. They do this, first, by assuring that policy discourse will focus, at least in part, on the topics the data represent, such as affordable housing, environmental protection, or human rights. Second, they help legitimize the participation and increase the capability to debate of groups with interests in these topics. Third, where the data are about communities themselves or problems of broad community concern, public-regarding perspectives gain legitimacy relative to narrow, self-interested ones. Fourth, the requirements help to establish a norm that policy arguments should be supported by evidence and that the better evidence should prevail.

Such changes in the content of the discourse are implicit, gradual, and difficult to observe. Perhaps for this reason, however, they can be particularly powerful. As the data enter the policy language, they become part of problem definitions, they set boundaries on possibilities for solution, and they define the standards for choosing actions and evaluating results. Thus, the data affect policy not so much because of facts they reveal as because the concepts implicit in them become implicit in the discussion.

These new terms of discourse do not eliminate the tendency for some participants to prefer other issues or to choose in self-interested ways, but they do provide a counterbalance. While some may argue that the way one talks is little more than rhetoric covering real motivations, this is an overly simplistic perspective. Forcing participants to conduct a particular kind of discourse can lead many to internalize, or at least accept, values reflected in that discourse.

The processes identified in this research are illuminating examples of what Mary Douglas calls "how institutions think" (1986). Social institutions—whether they are formal organizations like the Department of State, institutionalized processes like the public hearings on environmental impact, or social indicators that are accepted representations of particular concepts—encode and organize information. Sometimes they substitute for individualized decision making because they offer routine procedures, expectations, and norms. Institutions influence individuals' cognition and understanding in many ways, while assuring some potential for collective understanding. Institutions help individuals decide what is predictable and accepted and what is deviant and should therefore be given attention.

NEGOTIATING KNOWLEDGE AND POLICY

Much of this same field research illustrates another kind of process through which knowledge and policy shape one another in practice. Where the opportunity and incentives exist for technical experts, other professionals, and policy makers to negotiate over information, all are likely to alter their understandings. During such discussions, participants internalize the knowledge and give it meaning in relation to an actual problem, transforming it for their situation. In such negotiations distinctions between knowledge and action are blurred because agreement on at least the basic principles of policy is likely to be achieved jointly with agreement on how to formulate information. Later action on the basis of such information is a foregone conclusion.

The debate, for example, over the methods for unemployment statistics, described in Chapter VI, was integral to the debate over unemployment policy. There was no agreement on methods and concepts until there was agreement on the policies to mesh with them. In the other cases, failure to achieve broad agreement on indicators mirrored a failure to identify acceptable policy. In the human rights study, a negotiation among State Department officials over how to define and measure political prisoners or freedom of expression and over what to take as evidence of abuses was, de facto, a process of reaching decisions on policy. The effort forced these officials to consider how they would apply any particular definitional principle in a given country. They had to relate abstract principles to unique contexts and, in effect, to agree on the rudiments of a policy toward a given country.

In the EIR study, the definition and measurement of predicted impacts of development became the primary focus of public debate over a project. Rather than diverting attention away from the "substantive" to the "technical" issues, debates over the adequacy of the numbers were largely, if indirectly, about the substantive issues. They focused on such questions as how much damage a project would do to a watershed or how much economic benefit it would provide. In the course of achieving public consensus on the impact predictions, the agency was likely to renegotiate the design of an offending project, altering its density, location, or mix of uses so that the impacts would be less. Unless there was agreement that the impacts were both correctly measured and insignificant, citizens could bring lawsuits. Since even a groundless lawsuit meant costly delays, public action had, in effect, to correspond to knowledge that was both official and widely shared.

Research on the role of computer modelling in land use decisions in four rapidly growing California counties (Dutton and Kraemer 1984) illustrates a similar phenomenon. Consultants were hired in each county to develop models to determine the fiscal impact of alternative general plans or major development proposals on county revenues or expenditures for services. In two counties where the consultants worked closely with local participants to develop parameters for the models, their efforts resulted in basic policy agreements which had been impossible before that time. That is, during a negotiation over such issues as how much or what type of growth should be dealt with in the model, the important actors agreed on a growth policy. Moreover, they came to understand and trust what the model represented.

In these cases consultants recognized that certain parts of their model design were not technical, but involved choices which could be made in a variety of ways, depending on the community's preferences. They understood the task of getting community input to involve more than just asking how much or what kinds of development citizens wanted. That was a meaningless question until citizens could see the specific implications of alternatives.

Professional inquiry and ordinary knowledge closely interact and reshape one another in all such negotiations. Policy values become embedded in the knowledge itself. Policy making occurs jointly with knowledge production. The effectiveness of the negotiation as a way of resolving a policy concern depends on participants' achieving a common way of seeing issues, as well as a methodology that is both transparent to users and acceptable to the experts. A negotiation over definitions and methods can be a way to focus attention on concrete questions and get agreement on the ambiguous and value-laden issues. It offers a way to get a handle on issues in terms of straightforward questions like "who do we count?" or "what do we measure?" or "have all the factors been incorporated?" While such discussion cannot force agreement where value differences are great, it can be a crucial factor where there is potential for agreement.

MYTHS AND THE DEFINITION OF POLICY PROBLEMS[15]

While much of my research has dealt with the micro processes by which knowledge comes to play a role in policy, another type of research has been directed toward understanding the nature of ideas that are widely accepted in policy. In particular, the focus of this research has been the social meanings of certain policies important in the field of city planning. The objective was first to find out what the meanings were; second to trace their origins and evolution; and third to see how these meanings linked policy to something that might be called values and to the collective motivation required for policy to be adopted.

The task is important because, like widely used indicators, most policies with wide public support are layered with implicit meanings. One consequence is that policy participants agree on actions without explicitly agreeing on their meanings, but disagreement eventually emerges to hamper the implementation process. Another consequence is that policies are often adopted which are contrary to what analysts perceive as rational choice. Much of the mismatch of policy recommendations and public choice can, in my view, be attributed to a lack of shared meaning between analysts and the policy makers or public.

22

To identify shared meanings and how they came to be attached to policies, I chose historical study, using official public documents and the statements of influential thinkers and leaders. After preliminary work in land policy and urban renewal in the U.S. (de Neufville 1983), I concluded that conceptions of symbol and myth provided the most useful lens for interpreting the material because they associate representations with actions through tacit meanings, metaphors, and stories. As Douglas has argued, institutions' most powerful and least obvious influence on public and private actions is due to their incorporation of analogies within their assumptions. These ways of seeing problems and tasks through metaphors help to make certain conventions, routines, and policy proposals seem to fit into the natural order of things. They provide particularly powerful ways of focusing collective action.[16] My colleague, Stephen Barton, and I accordingly developed the following ideas.

The Concept of Myth.

The idea of myth in particular provides important insight into how knowledge and action are linked. "Myth," as I will use the term, fits Webster's definition: "a usually traditional story of ostensibly historical events that serves to unfold part of the world view of a people or explain a practice, belief, or natural phenomenon." Myths are an important source of meaning in modern societies as in traditional ones. They provide analogies which help simplify the world and make sense of events. They are created from the repertoire of shared images, symbols, characters, and modes of action in any particular culture (Swidler 1986). They have a moral component imbedded in them, referring to good and evil or simply providing object lessons. Because they are well known in a community, they provide shared reasons for people to act collectively. Because they take dramatic form and touch on deeply held values, they evoke strong emotions. These mythical stories give belief systems life and transmit them from one generation to the next.

Stories with mythic qualities exist in every area of modern life. In our personal lives, myths offer us an image of the proper form of a family and the responsibilities of its members; in our professional lives, myths tell us how scientists should gather information and reach conclusions; and in our public lives, myths tell us the meaning of events and of policies.

The term myth is appropriate to the present discussion rather than a more neutral term such as stories, because it carries implications which are important to understanding the policy experience. These include the taken-for-granted (and therefore often unnoticed) quality of myth, the sedimentation of meanings myths acquire over time, the cause-and-effect relationships embodied in myth, and their normative function in showing how things ought to be. Moreover, several social science disciplines, particularly anthropology and sociology, offer insights into the role of myth in a community.

We do not use the term myth in its popular version as "false or ill-founded belief." We mean the term to imply nothing about literal truth or falsity of a story. Some myths are well grounded in historical fact or correspond closely to knowledge generated through the scientific method, while other myths are largely invented. The important point is that myths represent ideal types of people and situations, and members of a community take them to express truths, whether or not they believe them to be literally true. Myths express ideas and emotions which resonate in their listeners. Their correspondence to facts or other notions of truth is a matter for investigation in particular cases.

Myths provide an important link between knowledge and policy because knowledge that is acted on generally comes packaged with a story (though often one that is not explicit) that has a meaning to the actors and that links actions to valued things and to expected results. The scientific form of knowledge is too abstract to transform directly into practice in a particular situation, or to stir the emotions necessary to motivate change. Even when policy is changed as a result of an indicator, as in the case of unemployment, the action is a response not just to the numbers, but also to the collective understanding of their implications, developed over years of discussion. Myths may be tacit baggage associated with professional inquiry, linking it to ordinary knowledge. They are also likely to be, at least in part, themselves a product of such professional inquiry.

Myths are particularly important for defining public problems because any formulation with popular appeal reflects a shared image of what is wrong and of how the future might be different. A myth provides just such an image, serving as a common metaphor for all to make similar sense of events and similar evaluations. A myth offers a useful shorthand for leaders both to define an issue and to justify public concern. They can quickly communicate a way of seeing a policy question to a wide audience, while also delivering a complex and

24

emotionally charged message. This capability is particularly important because collective agreement to act requires strong emotions to overcome normal resistance to change and objections by groups which will be harmed. Moreover, formal theory and existing information seldom provide certainty about the results of future action. A myth helps overcome doubts and provides a source of faith that a risk is worth taking. Ultimately, it is merely tautological to say that all stories which inform widely accepted definitions of policy issues must to some degree have the qualities of myths.

Myths and Home Ownership.

Home ownership is perhaps the most durable of all U.S. domestic policies, in great part because of the mythological baggage it carries with it. This example is one which shows the potential power of a myth that is deeply embedded in a culture, and it illustrates the tremendous difficulty in adopting policies which cannot be justified through such a myth. There is little doubt that strategies other than home ownership would have been more effective ways to house the population. But home ownership as a policy is not just about housing. It is popularly seen as a way of maintaining a free, stable, democratic society because it is associated with myths that were an early part of the formation of the nation. The persistence of this policy can only be understood in the light of the evolving myths that give home ownership its tacit public meaning.

The public rhetoric of home ownership can readily be traced to the myth of the yeoman farmer, propounded most notably by Thomas Jefferson. He visualized, as the ideal citizen of the emerging nation, the yeoman farmer who owned a modest piece of land and who, with his family, worked the land and was self-sufficient. He was close to the purifying influence of nature and not dependent on powerful, wealthy people for his livelihood. Accordingly, he was politically independent and responsible, economically productive and morally respectable. A society largely composed of yeoman farmers would differ fundamentally from Europe, where inevitable conflict between those with property and those without prevented the development of democracy. Thus, if the majority of people had modest amounts of property, U.S. society would be egalitarian and stable. Property ownership would assure that citizens had a stake in the system.

The influence of this agrarian myth on policy began in the early years of the republic as Jeffersonians called on the moral primacy of the farmer in their debates with the Federalists. The myth then provided the basis for the strategy of developing the continent. Individual settlers were accorded priority over large landholders through limitations on parcel size, requirements to build and live on site, and preemption rights for squatters. Even today, when small farmers represent only a tiny proportion of the population, agricultural subsidies continue to be justified in public rhetoric by the need to protect the endangered family farm.

By the early nineteenth century this myth had become, in the words of Hofstadter (1956:92), "a mass creed, a part of the country's political folklore and its nationalist ideology." The small farmer was a large enough part of the electorate at first (particularly as only property owners were accorded the vote) for the myth to constitute a plausible and flattering description of American society. The myth persisted as cities and manufacturing employment grew, perhaps as a counterbalance to new conditions that threatened existing ways of life and beliefs. The cities were perceived in American thought as sources of corruption, alienation, and harmful speculation (White and White 1962).

By the end of the century, a new version of the myth began to be formulated—one better suited to the reality of an urban, industrialized society. This version, which can be found throughout the public statements and writings of political leaders, businessmen, and housing reformers from the Progressive period to the present, attempts to retain the values of the earlier myth in a more modern form. The yeoman farmer was transformed into the suburban home owner. He was the head of a family, living in a single-family house, physically separated from its neighbors and surrounded by a private yard with grass and shrubbery. While this new version recognized the owner would no longer make his living from the land, the visual image and property ownership dimension linked it to the predecessor myth. The single-family home continued as the symbol of independence, civic virtue, family life, and personal success.

The myth brought old meanings to the new realities of the period. Street railways had opened the suburbs to development, while city governments were often seen as corrupt. A move to the suburbs could be justified as a return to the virtues of the rural life. There continued to be a commonsense notion that property owners would be more conservative and stable members of the community than those with less financial stake. The myth evolved along with changes in urban form. By the time of the landmark *Euclid vs. Ambler* Supreme Court

26

decision in 1926, the view had evolved to say that single-family houses should be located in a neighborhood of similar houses, well separated from workplaces and multifamily housing. This decision validated the constitutionality of single-family residential zoning, referring to apartment buildings as "mere parasites," which could destroy the "residential character" of the neighborhood.

Though the myth dominated public rhetoric of housing policy for many years, home ownership did not actually become the principal form of U.S. housing until after World War II. In the 1920s many alternatives to the single-family house seemed viable. Rental apartments were popular with middle- and upper-income people as they offered easier housekeeping and more modern facilities than most single-family units. The well-to-do often favored residential hotels in central cities which provided services still wanting today in the suburbs, such as meals, house cleaning, and child care. These housing arrangements offered a different vision of family life, however, and were in conflict with the popular mythology. As President Hoover expressed in an address to a 1931 Conference on Home Building and Homeownership:

> "Those immortal ballads, Home Sweet Home [and] My Old Kentucky Home ... were not written about tenements or apartments ... they never sing songs about a pile of rent receipts. To own one's own home is a physical expression of individualism, of enterprise, of independence, and of freedom of spirit. ... It makes for happier married life, it makes for better children, it makes for confidence and security, it makes for courage to meet the battle of life, it makes for better citizenship. There can be no fear for a democracy of self-government or for liberty or freedom from homeowners, no matter how humble they may be ... " (Hoover 1952:257)

This view of the remarkable consequences of home ownership was widely shared among political leaders and reformers, who promoted home ownership and detached housing while attacking tenancy and other types of housing. One of the most prominent of these said, for example, that the then residential luxury hotel, the Waldorf Astoria, was as bad as a tenement in its "destruction of civic spirit and the responsibilities of citizenship." The myth was so widely accepted that though many hailed home ownership as a protection against socialism, some socialist reformers even supported it.

During the interwar period the institutions were established which made single-family ownership the most advantageous housing choice. Zoning to protect these neighborhoods became a popular tool for municipal government. The New Deal set in place legislation restructuring housing finance to make available guaranteed long-term mortgages for home ownership, set up federally backed mortgage-lending institutions, and established a secondary mortgage market. Along with the tax deduction for mortgage interest and wartime prosperity, the policies were to increase nonfarm home ownership from 41 to 51 percent in the five years between 1940 and 1945. The federal highway program opening up the suburbs, in combination with loans to veterans, produced nonfarm home ownership of 61 percent by 1960.

No comparable protections, subsidies, or encouragements were offered to other types of housing. No rent deduction was made available. Rent control offering tenants security or stable housing costs after World War II continued only in New York City, where the single-family home was virtually nonexistent. Federal mortgage protections were not extended to cooperative housing. Public housing became an inferior choice for an underclass, rather than a model for housing the population, as it was in Europe.

Public/Private Partnerships.

Myths do not always have so decisive an influence in directing or precluding policy alternatives, but those who have even limited success in framing policy agendas necessarily draw on popular myth. In a second study of policy emergence and evolution, which I will not recount here, we found that those who, in the 1970s, worked to legitimize the idea that many urban development initiatives could and should be taken with a much larger role for the private sector and less control from the public sector, did so in great part by reworking popular myths. They created the notion of public/private partnerships to a great degree in order to rationalize the withdrawal of the federal government from the cities and to legitimize new forms of relationships that were spontaneously developing to fill the void. The policy documents and other literature about the idea consisted mainly of two types of things: storytelling about "successful" partnerships and relating of these activities to familiar myths about the efficiency of business and the role of government in protecting the public interest. The effort was to create a new concept of "partnership" suggesting harmony and commonality of purpose, while glossing over the issues of who controls the development activities and who benefits from government investments. These were the very issues that could have been sufficiently divisive to have been an obstacle to the widespread public support this idea was to garner.

Consequences of Myths in Policy.

Both the home ownership and the partnership myths are typical of policy myths in having a variety of functions and consequences which point in opposite directions. They helped motivate many creative policies for encouraging ownership and generating public benefits. They also were obstacles to systematic consideration of higher-density and rental housing options or to full evaluation of the consequences of allowing public benefits to be provided through private means. The home ownership myth excluded alternatives such as hotels which provide crucial services and amenities that the suburban housing pattern makes virtually impossible. Myths in both cases provided frameworks acceptable to both political parties, to unions and to corporations, representing as they did shared societal concepts.

The existence of myths in policy making has a number of other problematic consequences. For one thing, myths change more slowly than the world. A story which may have once been a productive way to make sense of events, applying relevant, contemporary values and theories, is apt to persist long after conditions have changed. The myth may thus encourage the pursuit of anachronistic policies like the pursuit of home ownership in the mobile and increasingly crowded urban society of the U.S. in the 1980s. The myth merely confuses the owner of the condominium who may own his home, but is far from independent of neighbors (Silverman and Barton 1984).

The logic of myths, moreover, is magical. They offer analogies which persuade simply by demonstrating in a vivid, emotionally charged way what the world is like. Cause and effect in a scientific sense are not at issue. Because the myth does not spell out cause and effect, the listener can neither evaluate the reasoning nor consider critically its application to the case in point. The belief that good citizenship goes along with self-sufficient farming can be transformed into a parallel belief about home ownership without challenge partly because the logic is inexplicit.

This skipping of explicit logic makes certain relationships sacred. In this sense modern myths continue to serve the same function they have throughout history. We know that home owners are better citizens and therefore we do little systematic research to evaluate the assumption. We do not debate the question. Interestingly, the little research that has been done suggests there are serious flaws in the myth. Survey data in the U.S. show that home ownership has little influence on political participation and does not predict the likelihood that someone will be conservative or liberal, once other factors are held constant.

A myth typically provides rationalizations which cover contradictions inherent in the structure of a community (Berger and Luckmann 1966). Indeed, such rationalization is one of the primary functions of myth. Myths turn attention away from thorny issues, uncomfortable realities, and discrepancies between public values and actual conditions. They help maintain the social order by providing soothing explanations of phenomena that otherwise might be alarming. Thus, myths enabling us, for example, to "blame the victim," allow us to maintain a value of caring about the poor without having to change a social system that permits poverty. Such covering of contradictions can, however, lead to policies that will not work or that are unjust.

A myth is a self-fulfilling vision. Like a social indicator, it provides a lens through which to see. But a myth is more powerful than an indicator in that social agreement on it can encourage people to act out its imagery. For example, the more predominant is the view that home ownership is the solution and tenancy the problem, the more it is likely that public policy will increase the disparities between the attractiveness of owning and of renting and between the people who own and those who rent.

The tacit quality of myths, their magical logic, and their inherent contradictions make it difficult for policy analysts to apply the scientific approach. Some ignore myths, as many housing analysts have done, and go about proving that policies promoting home ownership are neither efficient nor equitable housing policy. This proof, however, is unpersuasive to those who know housing is not the issue. Other analysts simply embrace the myth as part of the given value system and develop policies to promote home ownership. Few do the one thing they are best equipped for—examine critically the assumptions of the myths to determine whether the policies promoted in their name really accomplish what the myth implies.

Policy analysts have difficulty using techniques based on deductive logic when policies are myth-based. Because a myth combines descriptive and normative information, it is hard to disentangle wishes from cause-and-effect assumptions or problem statements from particular solutions. The procedure of comparing policy options to value criteria is meaningless; home ownership is both option and value. Tradeoffs among values cannot be done when values and alternatives are simultaneously defined.

Finally, the policy analyst normally assumes that policy making is simply about solving problems and selecting policies. It is, however, also about myth making, myth interpreting, and myth maintaining. Because myths legitimize and rationalize a political and social system, in practice the construction, maintenance, or alteration of a myth may itself become the crucial policy problem—more important than providing housing or redeveloping the cities. As Bennett (1980) has argued, one major function of public policy is "to help create and stabilize social reality in terms that conform to the dominant myths that produced them." Thus, rather than the myths offering reasons for implementing particular policies, policies may be designed, as in the case of home ownership, to keep the myths in place.

REFLECTIONS ON THE RESEARCH

The accounts that emerge from all this research contrast sharply with the expectations of the scientific model. Knowledge that is influential in these examples is not unbiased and produced by value-neutral experts; it is constructed through a social process. It partakes in part of "politics" and, in part, of professional inquiry. Data and politics are not as dichotomous as the city councillor's statement quoted at the beginning of this essay suggests. Data are shaped by politics—whether it is the politics of science and science funding (Knorr-Cetina 1981) or of the local community.[17]

The use of knowledge that does occur is not policy makers' explicit application of information to their questions and problems. Much of the important use of knowledge is not visible to the user. Most often knowledge has its influence when it has been internalized by the actors and has created frames of reference *within* which discourse and action occur. Knowledge influences much of the time by enlightening the actors. The processes of knowledge production and use in these examples are not distinct, stepwise activities with different norms and practices for each. Knowledge producers include policy makers and other participants, and knowledge has some of its influence *during* knowledge production. Knowing, valuing, and acting are interactive, ongoing processes.[18]

TOWARD A REDEFINITION OF THE KNOWLEDGE-POLICY ALLIANCE

A more useful and realistic description of the relationship between knowledge and policy can be built on the ideas drawn from an interpretive rather than a positivist view of knowledge. The ingredients of such an account are implicit in this essay. I will identify here some key ideas from this philosophy which lend form and legitimacy to an interactive model of knowledge influence and which illuminate the case material. To develop a prescriptive model for the practice of the policy professional, we will need to look beyond the interpretive view to ideas drawn from pragmatism, critical theory, and other normative perspectives on knowledge, discourse, and action.

THE INTERPRETIVE TRADITION

Several concepts useful to the present discussion distinguish the interpretive from the positivist view of knowledge.[19] Most importantly, the interpretive perspective is that knowledge is grounded in everyday understandings and does not solely take the abstract and "objective" form of facts, theories, and statistics. The interpretive view takes as central the subjective notion of meaning and regards socially shared beliefs to be "constitutive" of reality. That is, in the social world we cannot know what a phenomenon is until we know what it is believed to be. While the view does not require us to accept a shared meaning as the only way to understand something, such meanings are essential "data" for any analysis. The interpretive view thus is distinctive in saying that knowledge is not the exclusive province of experts, and in accepting a subjective element in all knowledge.

A corollary is that no knowledge is free of the bias of an observer or of a method. The expert "knower" must use his own subjectivity to understand that of others, trying as much as possible to set aside his own personally unique reactions, in much the way a psychotherapist does. Knowledge represents a negotiation between the more "expert" knower and the participants in the world. The process of knowing and learning engages the expert knower deeply in everyday life.

Knowledge in this perspective is situational, grounded in particular contexts. It need not be generalizable to count as knowledge. Moreover, this knowledge is about whole phenomena rather than simply about relationships among selected variables or facts in isolation from their contexts.

32

Interpretive knowledge may take the form of a story which can make sense of a complex set of components and link actions to contexts in ways that scientific knowledge cannot. Much everyday knowledge is in the form of ideal/typical stories which tacitly organize our understandings of the world. The validity of interpretive knowledge depends on how much sense the stories make, on how well they link to what is already understood in a community, and on how well they persuade.

CRITIQUE AND COMMUNICATIVE ACTION

This account of knowledge remains unsatisfying to many, however, without some touchstone for truth, some way of assuring that what is regarded as true is not merely circular, relativistic, self-reinforcing, and even deceptive. The most promising ideas for building an approach which leads to the improvement of knowledge, and which offers a basis for an ethical stance in practice, grow from the work of the Frankfurt school of critical theory, particularly Jurgen Habermas, and from the American pragmatists, particularly John Dewey.[20]

There are two key questions. First, how can we assure that what we take as knowledge has some correspondence to a world of life and action and is not simply a construct of our minds, concealing the important dimensions of that world? Second, how can we assure that what we take to be knowledge is just? That is, how can we assure that the biases and assumptions do not reinforce power relationships and that knowledge is not a tool of oppression, but rather of emancipation?

These are the central questions for many contemporary philosophers and social theorists, and their work is drawing increasing attention from those who study and teach in the policy professions. The questions strike at the heart of the task of professionals. The literature of fields such as public policy, urban planning, and education have already begun to find key ideas from these literatures around which to structure their own critical research on practice.[21] Work on these topics remains exploratory in its application to policy making, but it is rich in possibilities for new or modified forms of practice.

The first set of ideas I will term "social learning"; it derives primarily from the pragmatists, though it has a close kinship with interpretive epistemology. In this view knowledge is developed through a *community* of self-critical inquirers. They bring to their cooperative inquiry not only their formal knowledge and their abilities to think and reason, but also their lived experience. They use a process of discourse to reconstruct experience and gain understanding and

33

control of their environment. Learning occurs through a combination of doing, discussing, and creating new understandings. A transformation of individual perspectives and even of values may occur in such a process. The knower in a social learning context is an agent in the world rather than a passive observer, and part of a community rather than a lone analyst. Means and ends are inseparable, so those who learn must take practical as well as moral responsibility.

Two concepts embedded in this social learning model have received particular attention in the critical approach to practice. One is praxis—the notion that practical action is an important component of knowing, a way of guarding against the possibility that what we think we know is only a form of thought rather than a reflection of any external reality. The second concept is that we can improve public discourse to assure ourselves a better chance of arriving at a kind of truth. Inquiry on discourse has examined rules for discussion, validity claims for knowledge, involvement of participants, modes of reasoning, and argumentation. The ideas range from ways of making public discourse correspond more to logical, deductive thinking (MacRae 1988) to the idea that such discourse should be in the form of narrative, because it is through narrative that people in everyday life make sense and evaluate action (Fisher 1984, Kaplan 1986).

The notion of critique is, in my view, the central concept for a new prescriptive model of practice, but it is also the most difficult to apply. Critique implies it is the knower's responsibility to surface and challenge assumptions, to be self-reflective, examining her own biases. This may mean incorporating into public discourse those who have a real stake in action or finding ways to represent their interests. It may require the professional to take a stance herself against the status quo. Emancipatory knowledge requires critique to avoid the intellectual straitjacket of reification and the potential for knowledge to become a tool of oppression.

Habermas (1984) has offered an overall view of this critical, social learning approach, calling it "communicative action." This perspective is one useful way to conceptualize the policy making process. The key idea is that action and communication are so closely intermeshed that they cannot be conceptually distinguished. In communicative action participants negotiate definitions, values, and mutual understandings as they join in discourse around a task. They bring to this not only formal kinds of knowledge, but also experience and interests. Communication and action are thus different sides of a common enterprise. Well-designed communicative processes can transform understandings while reshaping action.

34

In Habermas's view, however, we need not reject one view of knowledge in favor of another. Indeed, there is a place for each kind of knowledge, corresponding to the nature of the task. He contends that we have three kinds of cognitive interests: technical; practical and emancipatory. The technical interest is an instrumental concern to know how things work—to solve problems. For this the scientific form of knowledge is best adapted. The practical interest is in understanding situations, communicating, and making things happen. For this, the interpretive form of knowledge is appropriate. Finally, when the task is to uncover what is hidden or to challenge the status quo, then the method of critique is essential.

AN ALTERNATIVE VIEW OF THE KNOWLEDGE-POLICY ALLIANCE

My proposal therefore, is, to replace the scientific model of knowledge use with a more encompassing, interactive model of knowledge influence. Five main tenets of this model are central.

- Knowledge that is influential is socially constructed, at least in part, in the community it influences.
- Knowledge influences as it becomes internalized in the shared understanding of a community. It influences more often as part of taken-for-granted assumptions, which frame problems and put bounds on the solution options, than as a result of explicit information processing in relation to policy questions.
- Just as objective and subjective knowledge cannot be sharply differentiated, professional inquiry and ordinary knowledge are intermingled. All are informed by the others, and all are jointly required for knowledge to be both valid and influential.
- Knowledge that motivates collective action is often in the form of stories and myths which are part of a shared, usually tacit, repertoire on which those in a community rely to make sense of events and to point in the direction of desirable actions.
- Knowledge, particularly in its mythic form, packages facts, theories, and values, and means and ends in ways that cannot be disentangled.

There are times in the policy process when the scientific model offers an accurate description and a useful set of norms, but these are special cases. This model is appropriate where a number of important conditions are met.[22] These include: basic political and social agreement on the nature of the issues, on the definition of a specific problem, and on the values that should be applied in resolving it; a known and generally accepted technology for resolving the problem or answering questions pertinent to it; a unitary policy maker who has the power to make a decision, the inclination and time to use information, and the willingness to respond to unexpected recommendations; information which can be gathered and analyzed in time for a decision; and methods and types of expert knowledge which mesh with the way the policy maker thinks about the issue.

When these conditions are met, the roles of value-neutral expert, problem solver, or neutral evaluator are appropriate. It is in these conditions that analytical methods based on neoclassical economics are useful, with their emphasis on measurement, optimizing known values, and assumptions of the "rational economic man" who makes logical choices based on evidence and self-interest. Within a framework of social agreement on certain values, assumptions, and understandings, this approach can work very well to identify "best" options, in the decision space that is left. Cost-benefit analysis, for example, can be an effective criterion for issues where monetary cost is the primary concern. When cost-benefit studies attempt to monetize the value of human life, however, they become too controversial to be usable decision criteria.[23]

The conditions for decision use of the information are not met for the great majority of policy issues. In most policy debates there is no agreement on values, no accepted definition of the problem, nor any readily available or well-understood methods of action.[24] Even more likely, there is no agreement on what concepts should describe the situation. These uncertainties are so typical in policy making that where the conditions do exist to apply the scientific model, we are likely to regard the issue as a technical or administrative task rather than a policy question. A major purpose of policy making is to achieve agreement on the slippery issues so that a more scientific approach can later be applied.

In the more typical cases where values and knowledge are uncertain, effective policy professionals like the consultants in the California cases and the statisticians in the Bureau of Labor Statistics become interactive, "reflective" practitioners. They develop usable knowledge with the intended clients and publics and with those who understand the situation in a direct, experiential way. They take different roles according to the nature of the task. If policy making consists largely of conceptualizing, problem framing, and formulating and agreeing on values, then it is for these tasks that knowledge for policy should particularly be directed. It is for these tasks, however, that we as policy professionals are least prepared.

Peattie's account of the planning of the new town of Ciudad Guayana (1986) illustrates how professionals can fail who do not take the interactive approach under conditions of high uncertainty. It also shows how this failure was closely associated with their role in supporting the existing power structure. Planners, architects, and economists did their work in Caracas offices, hundreds of miles from the "site" and its existing population. They used concepts and forms of representation—architectural drawings, site plans, columns of numbers—that fit their professional way of organizing ideas. They planned for a hypothetical population that would correspond to the objective of the development corporation and the powerful economic interests supporting it. Peattie, as staff anthropologist, could not carry out her assigned task of telling the planners what the people's values were. She simply could not fit people's concerns into questions of "open space needs" or "amenity." Explaining the life of the community was not possible, given the way the professionals worked and represented knowledge. The basic rationale for the city grew out of economists' view of the national economy and not out of the realities of the region or activities of its people, and thus did not change during planning or implementation. The infrastructure of the new city was built and subdivisions laid out, but twenty-five years later the expected level of industry and commerce has not materialized. Much of its population lives in the unplanned city on the other side of the river.

Interactive professionals not only recognize that their concepts need to mesh with those of everyday life, and that they need to challenge existing assumptions, they also know that community goals and values are generally not known until community members understand options in terms of very specific outcomes. Among city planners it is well known (and often bemoaned) that the public gives far more attention to proposed developments than to the general plans which are supposed to define desirable development patterns. Citizens discover their values in the context of real and comprehensible situations.

Interactive professionals try to embed knowledge in an organizational and policy process so that it will make a difference. They do this not just by providing knowledge, or even by making sure it is understood, but also by taking responsibility to develop institutionalized forms for its use. One task is to assure that the knowledge gets incorporated in the daily work of an implementing agency. This involves face-to-face communication among policy professionals and other actors and joint development of the application. For example, when I was asked to provide social indicators for the *Country Reports*, I worked with the foreign service officers in charge of the reports to select the indicators, carefully working through how the indicators would be incorporated into the arguments they would have to make about individual countries. We then jointly developed model reports for officers in the field and guidelines for discussing the indicators (de Neufville 1982).

Knowledge providers who want knowledge to be influential may have to do more than interact in an ad hoc way with clients and knowledge users to negotiate concepts, develop procedures, and explain issues. They may also have to design what have been termed "forums, arenas, and courts" (Bryson and Crosby 1989) in which the knowledge can be debated in relation to the policy issues. Examples include the Council of Economic Advisors, congressional hearings on the *Country Reports*, and formal procedures for challenging environmental impact assessments. As a society, we have been inventing many other models for knowledge assessment and decision, from science courts and community dispute resolution boards to condominium management associations.

Social scientists not involved in the daily activities of policy making can make their knowledge more influential in several ways. One is to assure that their research concepts can mesh with those of policy makers. Social scientists must understand the world of policy making and how its participants think and act. They have to pay attention to what is not said, as well as to what is said, and be aware of the "culture of policy deliberations," (Bell 1985) so they can relate their research to the concepts and myths actually in use in policy processes. At least some should do research on such important and elusive topics as the nature and meaning of values in policy practice and community life.

Professionals or social scientists who simply accept community concepts or generate consensus among those who happen to participate, however, are likely to reinforce misinformation and support the political status quo, rather than enlighten. The work of social scientists which challenges given knowledge, reframes problem definitions, or critically examines the assumptions of accepted myths in the light of empirical evidence is valuable. Equally essential is research focused on the interests which are poorly represented and underserved by existing policies, and which examines how assumptions in the policies create injustices that are not recognized in policy debate.

Policy professionals can give voice to such unrepresented groups, including them as legitimate and, as far as possible, equal participants in policy arenas. They and academics in policy-related professions can be reflective and self-critical about the ways their professional knowledge may routinely serve certain interests at the expense of others. They can themselves take a stance against the status quo, recognizing that from that stance they can develop new understandings. They can engage in action research designed not only to produce findings but also for the research "subjects" to learn and change (see, for example, Comfort 1985). Finally, both social scientists and policy professionals should participate in direct and personal ways in action from time to time outside of their professional roles as part of their own learning.

For developing knowledge under conditions of uncertainty—knowledge that can be influential on action, emancipatory in breaking through accepted frameworks, and ethical in representing the interests of the least powerful—it is my contention that we must aspire to a model of knowledge development and use which has the following characteristics: all important stakeholders are involved; all have equal power; all have equal information; all are able to communicate jointly in some kind of arena; their communication is organized around a task; each participant brings experience to the task. The discussion should address the assumptions and interests of stakeholders and not be bound by existing statements of the problem. The goal is to achieve group learning and if necessary a transformation of perspective which allows a solution satisfactory to all stakeholders (Marshall and Peters 1985).

Such an ideal learning process is potentially long and arduous and is only justified where the task is important, controversial, and has proved intractable to more routine methods. Many of its conditions are hard to achieve—particularly where key stakeholders are without power in the world or where information distribution is highly unequal. The ideal is not achievable in full, any more than is scientific objectivity. But this reflective learning model can, like the scientific model, serve as a template against which to evaluate policy knowledge for the difficult and controversial issues.

PRACTICAL ISSUES: CAN IT BE DONE?

The institutional and conceptual problems of creating and regularizing the activities outlined here are considerable. The biggest obstacle is that we, as a society, have become accustomed to the idea of the value-neutral expert, and we need the "soothing fantasy" of the division between politics and knowledge. An expert, after all, is said to be defined as someone who lives more than 500 miles away. Politicians need to act as if they are relying on unbiased data; professionals and social scientists need to believe they are not political; and the public needs to know who is responsible for what. The myth of value-neutral expertise serves important purposes in practice, as any professional knows who has made her political opinions public or given the appearance of favoring one interest over another.

Elements of the old myth must then be maintained, but transformed. The new myth should be about expertise involving the linking of ordinary and expert knowledge, about knowing when and how to challenge the given knowledge of experts and of everyday life, and about knowing how to guide stakeholders in developing new ways of understanding and new forms of action.

Despite the old myth, policy professionals often have successfully taken on interactive roles which may help to define a new exemplar[25] and a new myth for policy practice.[26] Professional inquiry similarly has expanded increasingly into interpretive and even action research—though most of the latter remains undocumented. Forums for interactive knowledge development and use have also become more common in policy settings, including workshops, retreats, task forces, mediation, and negotiation. Examples of interactive roles beyond those discussed in this essay include the policy advisor who understands the political context in which the ruler operates (Meltsner 1976), planners who take the role of problem framing and managing the relationship of various actors through the nature of their dialogue with them (Forester 1989), and consultants who work on retainer to governments and know their situation in depth. Group processes involving stakeholders and efforts to surface and challenge assumptions are also increasingly common.[27]

Interactive roles for many policy professionals may be actually more common in practice than the more conventionally recognized ones. A study in the late 1970s of urban planners, for example, showed that while some identified themselves as primarily technicians, and others as primarily political in their professional style, nearly half had to be classified as "hybrid." Neither the researchers nor the respondents had the language or the model of practice to understand this "hybrid," which had both technical and political elements (Howe 1980). With the benefit of several years more research on practice, this role seems likely to have been an interactive one, where the planners mingled their technical, knowledge-producing activities with their communicative ones, and where they consciously took positions on particular policies.

We can learn a good deal about these interactive roles from examining the practice of policy professionals in fields which antedate the emergence of policy analysis, with its emphasis on the scientific model. Fields such as urban planning, public health, and social welfare never fully embraced this model, continuing to teach and practice in a variety of ways which are better understood through the lens of an interactive model.[28]

Interpretive, qualitative research is gaining respectability in the social sciences, refining its methods and developing more explicit criteria for high-quality academic work. A few social scientists, moreover, have begun to examine the value and ethical premises that we need to understand to move to a new phase of the practice of providing policy knowledge. (See, for example, Callahan and Jennings 1983; MacRae 1976, 1985; Fischer and Forester 1987).

The obstacles to interactive policy practice and interpretive inquiry in the social sciences are largely in getting recognition and in the regularization of many current practices. This will involve elaborating the practices and developing norms, principles, and standards. There will have to be ways of assuring that the practitioners can maintain some degree of distance from the political process while still being involved enough to facilitate understanding and debate.

The more difficult challenge is to create and regularize practices and roles for the critical policy practitioner or academic. Indeed, the very idea of regularizing such a role is virtually a contradiction in terms. The critical practitioner must challenge the institutions and power arrangements which support his practice. Both practitioners and academics have to be willing to let go of the assumptions on which their own roles may depend.

Efforts that could fit this model, like the Office of Economic Opportunity's program designed to empower the poor, met with at best limited success, in great part because they challenged existing power. The advocacy planning movement of the 1960s, which sought to increase the power of the poor by improving their access to professional knowledge and offering them professional advocates, foundered in part because of the inability of the poor to pay for and therefore to trust these services. Yet such models offer lessons, as we compare them to the ideal outlined above, for how to design critical processes for practice. There are more strategies worth exploring which can shift practice in the direction of critical learning processes, at least in the cases where power differentials among stakeholders are not too great.

If there is to be a viable alternative model of professional expertise, several basic tasks lie ahead. The first is to identify existing roles and possible exemplars for interactive policy professionals through research on the practices of knowledge development and use in policy. The second is to invent new roles and, along with them, strategies for incorporating these roles into the political and institutional processes of policy making. The third is to develop criteria and principles as guides to effective, accountable, and ethical practice of informing policy. The fourth is to incorporate these ideas explicitly into professional and social science education. The fifth is public education. The expectations of the public and of the policy makers about social science and the contributions of policy professionals will have to change if they are to accept the knowledge purveyor as partisan in some basic way and imperfect in knowledge, and yet as having a special contribution that they, as citizens, can use. This education should also be directed at encouraging citizens to accept greater responsibility in the creation and application of knowledge and to apply a greater degree of reflectiveness about their own and others' assumptions. In short, we need, as Rein and White (1977) have said, a new myth to define the knowledge-policy alliance and a new model of practice to guide academics, practitioners, public officials, and citizens who want knowledge to serve policy.

NOTES

1. At the outset let me clarify several terms I will be using, which are frequently used loosely and inaccurately in the literature. These definitions are all drawn from Webster's *New Collegiate Dictionary*, 8th edition, 1977. The term "data" refers to "factual information (as measurements or statistics) used as a basis for reasoning, discussion, or calculation." In other words, data have no meaning in themselves, but only in relation to the context of argument, where the arguer assigns them meaning. The term "fact" is problematic, as this essay will suggest, but Webster's fourth and fifth definitions best fit my usage: "an actual occurrence" or a "piece of information presented as having objective reality." "Information" is a higher-order concept: "knowledge obtained from investigation, study, or instruction" or "something (as a message, experimental data, or a picture) which justifies change in a construct (as a plan or theory) that represents physical or mental experience or another construct." In other words, information is data organized to have a meaning and a purpose, which may be to change ideas or actions. "Knowledge" is both "the fact or condition

of knowing something with familiarity gained through experience or association," and "the sum of what is known: the body of truth, information, and principles acquired by mankind." Thus, knowledge is again a higher-order concept than information, including it, but going beyond the specific quality of information to an understanding of a whole ensemble of data, information, and experience.

2. Planning theory is a body of loosely related ideas routinely taught in urban planning, which focuses on the processes and justifications for public planning and policy. It draws heavily on decision theory, welfare economics, systems theory, institutional analysis, and the philosophy of science.

3. See Chapter IX on how indicators are constructed.

4. See Berger and Luckmann, 1966 for further understanding of this concept.

5. *SINET Social Indicator Network News*, Abbott Ferris, ed., P.O. Box 24064, Emory University, Atlanta, GA 30322.

6. For an excellent discussion of the conceptual problems in the design of aggregated quality of life indicators, see Landis and Sawicki, 1988.

7. One of the earliest and still among the most powerful such statements is in Tribe, 1972.

8. For an excellent overview of these developments see Bernstein, 1978.

9. Research by Zhang (1987) on citations in the journal *Knowledge* found this to be the second most cited article over a period of seven years.

10. A new book by Weiss and Singer (1988) sheds light on one aspect of the linking of social science ideas and public action, as it explores the way the media report these ideas.

11. See also Rein's more recent piece which develops the notion of "frame-reflective discourse" (1986).

12. Reich (1988) offers a powerful new contribution to this effort in his collection on how ideas come to have power in policy contexts.

13. Our findings were parallel to those of Weiss and Gruber (1984a, 1984b) who found that federal civil rights objectives were furthered by data requirements through mechanisms similar to those described here. Another study with some comparable findings on environmental impact assessment is Taylor, 1984.

14. This whole section is adapted from Innes, 1988a.

15. The following section is drawn from de Neufville and Barton, 1987.

16. See also Schon, 1979 on the role of "generative metaphor."

17. See the collection by Alonso and Starr (1987), which provides many examples of this interface of politics and statistics.

18. Dunn and Holzner's recent review of the literature on knowledge use (1988) indicates that many others are reaching conclusions that are compatible with these points. They indicate there is consensus on four points: the subjectivity thesis—that all scientific and professional knowledge is construed subjectively by the individual and collective actors; the corrigibility thesis—that such knowledge can be improved according to nonarbitrary standards; the sociality thesis—that the production, transfer and utilization of scientific and professional knowledge are social processes, influenced by social arrangements, structured according to power, status, etc.; and the complexity thesis—that knowledge mandating, production, distribution, utilization and all the functions and products of knowledge are part of an interrelated system.

19. For some further elaboration of the nature of interpretive knowledge, see Bernstein, 1978, Callahan and Jennings 1983, and Healy 1986.

20. Bernstein (1978) also offers an accessible account of these intellectual developments.
21. Forester, 1989 and Fischer, 1980 offer examples of this kind of work. A conference on Critical Theory and the Professions held in 1987 at the University of San Francisco demonstrated a high degree of interest among academics in such professions and new ways of reflecting on practice.
22. Both Sabatier (1978) and Caplan (1977b) outline basically parallel conditions for knowledge use in general.
23. Hird (1988) has illuminated this point clearly in his case studies of the use of cost-benefit analysis in federal agencies. It was most persuasive as a criterion in the Transportation Safety Board regulatory process where it applied to bumper standards, and least for airbags. In the former case, cost was the main issue as little injury was involved, whereas the latter was an issue of saving lives.
24. This discussion relies in part on Christensen's work on the role of uncertainty in planning (1985). She argues persuasively that technology and/or goals are often unknown factors, though planning has to proceed nonetheless.
25. An exemplar in this context is the model of practice around which the ideas and principles of a new paradigm could be built.
26. Dryzek (1987) and Sabatier (1988) offer notable efforts to reframe the model for practice, along some of the lines suggested here.
27. For example, Mason and Mitroff (1981).
28. For insight into the differences between those educated as policy analysts and those educated as planners, see Alterman and MacRae, 1983.

REFERENCES

Allison, G. (1971). The Essence of Decision. Boston: Little Brown.

Alonso, W., and P. Starr (Eds.). (1987). The Politics of Numbers. New York: Russell Sage Foundation.

Alterman, R., and D. MacRae (1983). "Planning and Policy Analysis: Converging or Diverging Trends?" Journal of the American Planning Association, 49, 200–215.

Bell, R. (1985). The Culture of Policy Deliberations. New Brunswick, N.J.: Rutgers University Press.

Bennett, W. L. (1980). Public Opinion in American Politics. New York: Harcourt Brace Jovanovich.

Berger, P. L., and T. Luckmann. (1966). The Social Construction of Reality: A Treatise in the Sociology of Knowledge. Garden City, New York: Doubleday and Company.

Bernstein, R. (1978). The Restructuring of Social and Political Theory. Philadelphia: University of Pennsylvania Press.

Brunner, R. (1982). "Policy Sciences as Science," Policy Sciences, 15, 115–135.

Brusegard, D. (1978). "Rethinking National Reports," Social Indicators Research, 6, 261–272.

Bryson, J. M., and B. Crosby. (1989). Design and Use of Strategic Planning Arenas. Minneapolis: H.H. Humphrey Institute of Public Affairs, University of Minnesota.

Callahan, D., and B. Jennings (Eds.). (1983). Ethics, The Social Sciences and Policy Analysis. New York: Plenum Publishing Co.

Caplan, N., and E. Barton. (1976). Social Indicators 1973: A Study of the Relationship Between the Power of Information and Utilization by Federal Executives. Ann Arbor: Institute for Social Research, University of Michigan.

Caplan, N., and E. Barton. (1978). "The Potential of Social Indicators," Social Indicators Research, 5, 427–456.

Caplan, N., et al. (1975). The Use of Social Science Knowledge by Decision Makers at the Federal Level. Ann Arbor: Institute for Social Research, Center for Research on the Utilization of Scientific Knowledge, University of Michigan.

Caplan, N. (1975). The Use of Social Science Information by Federal Executives. Social Research and Public Policies (G. M. Lyons, Ed.) (Chap. 2). Hanover, NH: The Public Affairs Center, Dartmouth College.

Caplan, N. (1977a). "The Two-Communities Theory and Knowledge Utilization," American Behavioral Scientist, 22, 459–470.

Caplan, N. (1977b). "A Minimal Set of Conditions Necessary for the Utilization of Social Science Knowledge in Policy Formulation at the National Level," Using Social Research in Public Policy Making (Chap. 13). Lexington, Massachusetts: D.C. Heath and Company.

Christensen, K. S. (1985). "Coping With Uncertainty in Planning," Journal of the American Planning Association, 51, 63–73.

Comfort, L. K. (1985). "Action Research: A Model for Organizational Learning," Journal of Policy Analysis and Management, 5 (1), 100–118.

de Neufville, J. I., and S. E. Barton. (1987). "Myths and the Definition of Policy Problems: An Exploration of Home Ownership and Public-Private Partnerships," Policy Sciences, 20, 181–206.

de Neufville, J. I., and M. Solloway. (1986). The Role of Environmental Impact Review in Land Use Planning: Four California Case Studies. American Planning Association Conference, April, Los Angeles.

de Neufville, J. I., and S. Stoddard. (1988). "Formula Allocation as a Policy Tool: Politics and Measurement," Planning Outlook, 31, 95–102.

de Neufville, J. I. (1978–79). "Validating Policy Indicators," Policy Sciences, 10, 171–188.

de Neufville, J. I. (1981a). Social Indicators. Handbook of Applied Sociology: The Frontiers of Contemporary Research (M. Olsen, and M. Micklin, Ed.) (Chap. 1). New York: Praeger.

de Neufville, J. I. (1981b). Data and Planning at the Local Level: Case Studies of the Community Development Block Grant Program. San Francisco: U.S. Department of Housing and Urban Development, Region IX.

de Neufville, J. I. (1982). "Social Indicators of Basic Needs: Quantitative Data for Human Rights Policy," Social Indicators Research, 11, 383–403.

de Neufville, J. I. (1983). "Symbol and Myth in Land Policy," Values, Ethics and the Practice of Policy Analysis. (W. Dunn, Ed.) (Chap. 12). Lexington, Massachusetts: Lexington Books.

de Neufville, J. I. (1986). "Human Rights Reporting as a Policy Tool: An Examination of the State Department Country Reports," Human Rights Quarterly, 8, 681–699.

Douglas, M. (1986). How Institutions Think. Syracuse, New York: Syracuse University Press.

Dryzek, J. (1987). "Policy Analysis as a Hermeneutic Activity," Policy Sciences, 14, 309–329.

Dunn, W. N., and B. Holzner. (1988). "Knowledge in Society: Anatomy of an Emergent Field," Knowledge in Society: The International Journal of Knowledge Transfer, 1, 3–26.

Dutton, W., and K. Kraemer. (1984). Modeling As Negotiating: The Political Dynamics of Computer Models in the Policy Process. Norwood, New Jersey: Ablex Publishing Co.

Fischer, F., and J. Forester (Eds.). (1987). Confronting Values in Policy Analysis: The Politics of Criteria. Newbury Park, California: Sage Publications.

Fischer, F. (1980). Politics, Values and Public Policy: The Problem of Methodology. Boulder, Colorado: Westview Press.

Fischer, F. (1983). "Ethical Discourse in Public Administration," Administration and Society, 15, 5–42.

Fisher, Walter R. (1984). "Narration as a Human Communication Paradigm: The Case of Public Moral Argument," Communication Monographs, 51, 1–22.

Forester, J. (1989). Planning in the Face of Power. Berkeley, California: University of California Press.

Habermas, J. (1984). The Theory of Communicative Action: Reason and The Rationalization of Society (T. McCarthy, Trans.). Boston: Beacon Press.

Healy, P. (1986). "Interpretive Policy Inquiry: A Response to the Limitations of the Received View," Policy Sciences, 19, 381–396.

Hird, John (1988) Use and Quality of Cost-Benefit Analysis in the Federal Government. Ph.D. Dissertation, University of California, Berkeley.

Hofstadter, R. (1956, April). "The Myth of the Happy Yeoman," American Heritage.

Hoover, H. (1952). The Memoirs of Herbert Hoover: The Cabinet and the Presidency, 1920–1933. New York: MacMillan.

Howe, E. (1980). "Role Choices of Urban Planners," Journal of the American Planning Association, 46, 398–409.

Innes, J. E. (1988a). "The Power of Data Requirements," Journal of the American Planning Association, 54, 275–278.

Innes, J. (1988b). "Effects of Data Requirements on Planning: Case Studies of Environmental Impact Assessments and Community Development Block Grants," Computers, Environment and Urban Systems, 12, 77–88.

Kaplan, T. J. (1986). "The Narrative Structure of Policy Analysis," Journal of Policy Analysis and Management, 5, 761–778.

Knorr-Cetina, K. D. (1981). The Manufacture of Knowledge: An Essay on the Constructivist and Contextual Nature of Science. Oxford: Pergamon Press.

Landis, J., and D. Sawicki. (1988). "A Planner's Guide to the Places Rated Almanac," Journal of the American Planning Association, 54, 336–46.

Lindblom, C., and D. K. Cohen. (1979). Usable Knowledge: Social Science and Social Problem Solving. New Haven: Yale University Press.

Lynd, R. S. (1939). Knowledge for What? The Place of Social Science in American Culture. Princeton: Princeton University Press.

MacRae, D. J. (1976). The Social Function of Social Science. New Haven: Yale University Press.

MacRae, D. J. (1985). Policy Indicators: Links Between Social Science and Public Debate. Chapel Hill: University of North Carolina Press.

MacRae, D. (1988). "Professional Knowledge for Policy Discourse: Argumentation versus Reasoned Selection of Proposals," Knowledge in Society, 1, 6–24.

Marshall, J., and M. Peters. (1985). "Evaluation and Education: The Ideal Learning Community," Policy Sciences, 18, 263–288.

Mason, R. O., and I. Mitroff. (1981). Challenging Strategic Assumptions: Theories Cases, and Techniques. New York: John Wiley.

Meltsner, A. (1976). Policy Analysts in the Bureaucracy. Berkeley: University of California Press.

Peattie, L. (1986). Planning: Rethinking Ciudad Guayana. Ann Arbor: University of Michigan Press.

Reich, R. B. (Ed.). (1988). The Power of Public Ideas. Cambridge, Massachusetts: Ballinger Publishing.

Rein, M., and D. Schon. (1977). "Problem Setting in Policy Research," Using Social Research in Public Policy Making (C. Weiss, Ed.) (Chap. 16). Lexington, Massachusetts: D.C. Heath and Company.

Rein, M., and S. H. White. (1977). "Policy Research: Belief and Doubt," Policy Analysis, 3, 239–271.

Rein, M. (1986). Frame-Reflective Policy Discourse. [Inaugural Address]. Leyden: Leyden Institute for Law and Public Policy, Working Paper 3.

Rittel, H., and M. Webber. (1973). "Dilemmas in a General Theory of Planning," Policy Sciences, 4, 155–169.

Rivlin, A. (1971). Systematic Thinking for Social Action. Washington, DC: Brookings.

Sabatier, P. (1978). "The Acquisition and Utilization of Technical Information by Administrative Agencies," Administrative Science Quarterly, 23, 396–417.

Sabatier, P. A. (1988). "An Advocacy Coalition Framework of Policy Change and The Role of Policy Oriented Learning Therein," Policy Sciences, 21, 129–168.

Schon, D. (1979). "Generative Metaphors in the Setting of Social Problems," Metaphor and Thought (A. Ortony, Ed.). Cambridge: Cambridge University Press.

Schon, D. (1983). The Reflective Practitioner: How Professionals Think in Action. New York: Basic Books.

Silverman, C., and S. Barton. (1984). Condominiums: Individualism and Community in a Mixed Property Form. (Working Paper #434). Institute of Urban and Regional Development, University of California, Berkeley.

Swidler, A. (1986). "Culture in Action: Symbols and Strategies," American Sociological Review, 51, 273–286.

Taylor, S. (1984). Making Bureaucracies Think: The Environmental Impact Statement Strategy of Administrative Reform. Stanford: Stanford University Press.

Tenenbaum, E., and A. Wildavsky. (1984, November). "Why Policies Control Data and Data Cannot Control Policies," Scandinavian Journal of Management Studies.

Tribe, L. (1972). "Policy Science: Analysis or Ideology?," Philosophy and Public Affairs, 2, 66–110.

Weiss, J., and J. Gruber. (1984a). "Deterring Discrimination with Data," Policy Sciences, 17, 49–66.

Weiss, J., and J. Gruber. (1984b). "Using Knowledge for Control in Fragmented Policy Arenas," Journal of Policy Analysis and Management, 3, 225–247.

Weiss, C. H., and E. Singer. (1988). Reporting of Social Science in National Media. New York: Russell Sage Foundation.

Weiss, C. H. H. (1977). "Research for Policy's Sake: The Enlightenment Function of Social Research," Policy Analysis, 3, 531–545.

Weiss, C. H. (1979). "The Many Meanings of Research Utilization," Public Administration Review, 426–431.

White, M., and L. White. (1962). The Intellectual Versus the City: From Thomas Jefferson to Frank Lloyd Wright. Cambridge: Harvard University Press.

Zhang, X. (1987). "History and Core Literature of Knowledge Use Studies," Advances in Knowledge Utilization Conference, University of Pittsburgh, October 8–10, 1987.

PREFACE

This book is about quantitative measures and their role in public decision-making. It addresses the twin questions of how to design indicators that can be useful to policy and how to design processes to make better use of such information. The concern grows out of my education in urban planning and social policy and experience on a congressional staff. I was struck by the tremendous gulf between the processes of public choice and those of information production. On the one hand, data and the capacity to manipulate it were growing rapidly, and, on the other, most public decisions continued to be made with minimal information. The fault seemed to lie with both the information producers for failing to deal with the style, objectives and constraints of decision-makers and with those in the action arena for not establishing the systems which would permit them to choose the information they needed and to make use of it.

One way to cut into this problem was to begin with the most fundamental question in quantitative analysis, that of measurement itself, and to look at the most straightforward uses of measures. The problem of social indicators was a case in point. There was growing public and academic interest in designing quantitative measures that would serve as indicators of the magnitude and direction of change of important social phenomena. Yet despite the expenditure of considerable effort and money on the problem in the late 1960's, new and useful indicators were not emerging.

We already had some indicators that we used regularly, however, on housing, employment, poverty, crime. and many other topics. They were not ideal measures nor were they always used as we would wish them to be, but they have become part of the vocabulary of public decision-making. If we could understand more about the roles these measures play and how they came to play them, then perhaps we would get some insights into how to develop and use new measures. I decided, therefore, to look in some detail at the origin, uses, and evolution of three indicators that have been around a long time, the unemployment rate, standard family budgets, and the crime rate.

The analysis is based in large part on the notion that you can have no meaningful measure without a theory. In science this means one must at least have a hypothesis about how the phenomenon one wants to measure is related to its environment and to the things we observe directly. In public policy it becomes an issue of how to decide whose theory to use, as a measure based on one analysis suggests one policy and one based on another an entirely different policy.

The intended purpose of making a measurement then has to play a role in the process of designing it, and the design process becomes part of a political process. In fact, for successful indicators there is an interaction between design and use, and therefore such measures can and should evolve over time, and, when used for public decisions will often be controversial as they represent a particular perspective and theory. The case studies illustrated these principles well.

The design of an indicator and its environment interact in other significant ways as well. Not only are the concepts necessarily based on a particular perception of reality, but also the practical constraints of data collection methods partially determine the concept ultimately measured. Subtle distinctions in structuring the data for presentation also affect the concept. Since there is no single correct way to design an indicator though it may have considerable effect on the allocation of public resources, there will be both incentive and opportunity for interested parties to alter an indicator to suggest what they want it to. It becomes clear that if an indicator is to have a continuous and trusted meaning, its concepts and methods require some institutionalization. The uses of the indicators are widely varied and sometimes inappropriate, but as they come to have an impact on public decisions, they also come to be understood and challenged and redesigned. Though this iterative process is slower than we might wish in producing measures or responding to new needs, the slowness may serve a useful function in assuring the indicator's relevance.

The findings of the book reflect, as one should expect, much of what I set out to look for. One's research design, awareness and selectivity are inevitably influenced by one's prior assumptions. Nonetheless, I feel confident several conclusions will hold up under the scrutiny of other approaches. One is simply that the measures have made a difference to public decisions. Another is that the development of indicators that will be sufficiently understood and respected to be used will require a matter of many years for the iterative process to occur, if past experience is a guide. Finally, the process of indicator design and presentation is itself a critical factor in a measure's acceptability for public policy. The institutions for its production and use must be as

50

carefully planned as the indicators themselves. One useful model for indicator production is the U.S. Bureau of Labor Statistics, with its balance of professional expertise and structured relations to decision-makers. For indicator use and education of the public, the Council of Economic Advisers and Joint Economic Committee perform critical functions.

The conceptual framework of the book arises largely from my teaching of a course in measurement for public policy, and it allows a critical look at the case material. I have explored the problems in turn that confront those who wish to design, use, or evaluate indicators for public decisions, or to set up to systems for their design or use. Topics covered are the role of quantitative measures in that first critical step of public policy, problem definition; the setting and context for future systems of indicator production and use in U.S. statistical policy; the problems and constraints on creating concepts; the criteria for choosing among data collection processes and recognizing how they may change concepts; choices for structuring data and their implications; ways of institutionalizing indicator production and creating public acceptance; the range of uses, from high-level public discussion of goals and policy to criteria for the allocation of program funds, and the effects of letting data become manipulable for short-term political considerations. The discussion draws on the three cases as well as other examples of American and British indicators. The book is an exploratory step in the direction of understanding how technicians, politicians, and the public can use more information to aid processes of public choice.

The book is aimed at teachers, students, and practitioners of public policy, and the users and creators of data and analysis for public decisions. It tries to suggest ideas about the processes of information development and use in public policy that may be worthy of further research, to provide a conceptual framework for some hitherto little analyzed experience, and to present these in a way that will make a good reference or text for those intersted in developing or using indicators for public policy.

Many people have contributed to my efforts and I am grateful to them for their time and advice. Hayward Alker and Martin Rein helped me formulate the original conceptual scheme. Robert Aaron Gordon, Robert Fogelson, Aaron Fleisher, Daniel Bell, Raymond Bauer, Lester Thurow, and Paul MacAvoy all read and provided valuable criticism of portions of early drafts of the manuscript. Numerous individuals in government and international organizations in the U.S, U.K. and France gave time and careful thought to dicussing their work and problems with me. There are far too many to thank individually but needless to say this study would not have been possible without their help. I do owe Helen Lamale a special debt for her advice and perspective.

Rosemary Carpenter, who patiently and efficiently typed through two drafts of the manuscript saved me countless hours by her accuracy, interest and care. The Institute of Urban and Regional Development of the University of California, Berkeley typed the final manuscript, and I am grateful to the staff there for their efficient, careful work.

The greatest debt of gratitude, however, I owe to Richard de Neufville, for his professional advice, for the hours he spent reading and commenting on various drafts and for his infinite patience and encouragement which made it possible for me to get through the grueling process of creating a book.

Judith E. Innes
Berkeley, California

Chapter I

Measurement and the Identification of Problems

"...It is the changes in both the world and the perceptions of the world, as communicated by the citizenry to politicians and bureaucrats, that drive the processes of democratic government." (Duncan, 1972)

Open a newspaper any morning and you will find it littered with statistics. Almost every article refers to numbers of something. *The Times* of London on a typical morning,* contained the following items on its front page:

270,000 miners are going to vote on whether to strike for their pay claim of £8 to £13 a week, and a 55% majority is required.

The Israelis are trying to clear 750,000 mines in Egypt and have returned 300 wounded Egyptian soldiers.

A table shows the oil sales income of oil-producing countries in the previous five years and projected income for 1974 under four different pricing situations.

An opinion poll shows a 4% Conservative lead in popular support has been changed to a 3% Labour lead.

London Broadcasting Company will get £500,000 in new capital and it has an average weekday audience of 385,000. Sixteen percent of the listening population hears LBC, 13% hears Radio London and 55% BBC 1.

Most major newspapers contain similar data and more because figures represent an efficient way to communicate information to a wide audience. The reporter can potentially convey more information less ambiguously with a number than with a term like

---

* Thursday, January 24, 1974.

"many" or "few" which depends on the reporter's viewpoint and may not coincide with readers' views. If he did not use figures, one newspaper could say "The miners are asking for a great deal of money" and another would say "The miners are asking for a small amount of money", instead of stating the amount and letting the reader judge.

This is the potential strength of quantitative information in public discussion and decision-making — it can allow us to refer to commonly understood phenomena and to agree on their levels without intervening value judgments. It is then possible to go on to discuss the more complex questions of priorities and problems.

However, data does not always fulfill this attractive function. Many members of the public, governmental leaders, and analysts regard numbers with suspicion or find most of them irrelevant to the important issues. Indeed they feel statistics distort or conceal critical factors and, accordingly, ignore them. Those who take this view may be wise because the data has, more often than not, been collected, tabulated, categorized or otherwise manipulated with little purpose. As a result it may represent phenomena or concepts that are far from central to policy-making. It can also be presented in a misleading way, suggesting a significance which it does not have. Because measurement is such an integral part of problem definition processes these problems cannot be ignored. The processes are poorly understood but their results place major constraints on later decision-making, and may even predetermine them. Therefore it is important to understand problem definition both for general policy-making and the specific planning of measures to use in policy.

MEASUREMENT IN THE DEFINITION OF PROBLEMS

It is the conventional view that decision-making starts with a problem or an objective and proceeds from there to generation of and choice among alternative actions. However, an important insight is beginning to gain currency among policy analysts. Moynihan (1970a) puts it succinctly, that "the crucial phase in solving a problem is the process by which it comes to be defined". Horst Rittel and Melvin Webber (1973) put it in another way. In defining the special difficulties with planning or policy problems they say that "the information needed to *understand* the problem depends on one's idea for *solving* it", and "the process of formulating the problem and of conceiving a solution ... are identical, since every specification of the problem is a specification of the direction in which treatment is considered".

In other words, problems are not simply givens that policy-makers must accept; rather they may be defined in quite different ways, each of which contains the seeds for a different solution. If we agree there is a problem of hungry people, then food is the answer. But we might decide that the problem is low-income and if so, we look for a way to supplement income. Another observer of the same situation might say the problem was ignorance, and clearly education is the answer. Once we recognize this interdependence of problem perception and solution, we must also recognize that the policy-maker has a responsibility to begin analysis with the definition of the problem and not after, with an unsuitable problem definition forced upon him.

This starting point becomes even more important when one recognizes the power of clearly defined problems. Once it is perceived and accepted, that the current situation diverges from a desirable situation in some specified way, in other words, once a problem is defined, then it becomes psychologically necessary to try to do something about it. As Moynihan (1970b) put it "The setting of future goals no matter how distant, drains legitimacy from present conditions. Once it is established and agreed upon that the future will have to be very different from the past, it becomes absurd to be content with the present".

Although the specification of problems is so critical, we know very little about how it happens in practice or how it should happen. One element which does play a large part in the process is statistics. Numbers provide a simple way of specifying a discrepancy between present and desired circumstances. It is an easy step from many of the numbers reported in *The Times* headlines to a specific problem. London Broadcasting should try to get a bigger share of the listening audience; the Conservative party needs popular support. One could define the questions in other ways, but the numbers suggest these formulations.

Moreover, the numbers provide a ready way of formulating a goal or defining a norm. Values, from which goals presumably flow, and norms, which represent socially agreed upon standards, do not flow from innate human instinct any more than problem definitions do and they are not simply constraints on the planner. They are created on the foundation of what we know to exist and believe possible and the policy-maker can never have much to do with creating this picture. Values are abstract, somewhat contradictory concepts, like freedom and order, equality of opportunity and freedom from want. Norms represent a level of these which approximates what is attained by many in society or can reasonably be expected to be attained by society as a whole. They provide specific content to the terms we think of as our values, and change over time as society changes (Vickers, 1973). A goal tends to be defined as either achievement of the norm for all or achievement of a level just beyond the current actual level.

It should not be surprising then that the things we measure and the way we measure them contribute to the formation of both norms and goals. The number of children per classroom is one such measured item that becomes a norm and goal in policy, and it has an interesting way of varying from country to country according to the actual ratios. The characteristics of standard housing in the U.S. include indoor plumbing, heating and lack of crowding, and these are goals for all U.S. housing now. Some other unmeasured qualities may be equally important, however, like ambient noise levels or environmental hazards, but will have to await measurement to become norms and goals.

The number of standards created by our measures and implicitly used in policy is tremendous. A two percent inflation rate is considered normal; more is alarming and requires action. Since 1946, 3 to 4% unemployment has been an explicit target for U.S. economic policy. The potency of this norm to force policy actions is made obvious by attempts since 1972 by the Council of Economic Advisors (CEA) and other Administration officials to convince the public that the norm had become unavoidably higher. It is an interesting example as well of how a sophisticated policy-making body may try to change the norms instead of accepting them as given.

The norms and related measures can also be powerful triggers for policy, and as parts of the distribution formulas for government or other funds. The most obvious are the price indices, movements in which may trigger automatic wage increases and affect the ceilings for increases when wages are under government control. Agricultural parity indices have determined the distribution of millions of dollars in farm subsidies. Local unemployment figures and numbers under a specified poverty line have determined the allocation of federal funds for manpower and economic development, education, and numerous other purposes (Wickens, 1953). Crime rates now provide a criterion for disbursement of

Law Enforcement Assistance funds. Other statistics have been used to trigger programs into action. The Emergency Employment Act of 1971 was to provide funds for public employment to localities with more than 6% unemployment rate, for example.

An important question then for any policy analyst or decision-maker who wants to have flexibility in identifying the options for society is how do norms come to be defined? A superficial response is that the statistics that happen to be available form the basis of the norms. It is true at the margin that a particular statistic focuses attention in a particular way, but it does not explain how that topic was selected nor how the discrepancy between ideal and actual was defined.

PROBLEM-FINDING MODELS: THE INTERPRETATION OF STATISTICS

Some useful insights into this question come from a study by Pounds (1969) on the processes by which managers "find" problems. In an effort to understand the cognitive processes and decision rules that lead managers to identify certain situations as problems and to devote time to their solution, Pounds interviewed executives in a large company. He points out that the definition of a problem depends on the existence of a model (usually not explicit) of the expected or good situation against which to measure the actual. He tried to characterize the models managers used, and the result is strikingly comparable to what policy-makers seem to do.

The principal sort of model is historical. The manager expects that the present should look approximately like the past, and, when it does not in some respects, there is a problem. For example, the percentage of defective products might increase or the expected extra sales in April over March might not materialize. Policy-makers found a problem when the number in poverty increased in 1970 instead of continuing its historic decrease. If unemployment fails to decrease in September, when we expect it to, it is a problem. Indeed we have incorporated the expectation into our figures by doing a seasonal adjustment, which assumes historical continuity. A historical model is obviously simple, but not so obviously ideal. Discrepancies (problems) often appear because the model is so simple, and these may not be the most appropriate discrepancies to try to alleviate, since doing so will not necessarily make things better, just more like the past.

Another type of model is what Pounds terms the planning model. Norms are the targets that managers hope to achieve. These are ineffective as problem finders as the managers deliberately set targets low enough to assure their achievement. Planning models can be ineffective on the other hand because they are also likely to be unrealistically high (which of course they are only likely to be when the target setters are different from the implementors). The disastrous Chinese experience in 1958 with an attempt to use a planning model to spur workers on to great achievements illustrated that problem well. The central government set production targets and each successive lower unit of government was expected to set a target exceeding that of the unit just above. The result was a massive deliberate distortion of statistics and an embarrassing miscalculation of national production (Li, 1962). Clearly there is a tendency, in effect, to drop norms which are unachievable.

Other kinds of problem-finding models Pounds identifies are "other people's models" and "extraorganizational models". The Federal government provides the "other people's models", to define problems for states and cities. To get federal funds they have drawn up "workable plans", employ particular kinds of staff and meet specified standards. For nations, or the equivalent, models might be imposed or suggested by the experience of other countries. International organizations giving aid or loans to developing countries almost inevitably use an implicit model based on the experience of developed countries. This then becomes also the operative problem-finding model for countries interested in aid.

Pounds' preferred model for problem-finding or norm setting would be a "scientific" one analogous to models engineers use to build an electronic control system. The model is far more complex than the others and based neither on history nor on a simple application of experience, but on a theoretical model established and tested by others. Managers use such models occasionally for inventory control systems or distribution systems. Policy-makers attempted to use such models to design poverty programs* (that is, to define the problems that the programs would solve, which was tantamount to defining the programs). But unfortunately, the models were not well enough established and tested for this ap-

---

* Various theories were involved concerning the culture of poverty and, most notably, the relation between delinquency and opportunity. For two divergent accounts of the role of social science models in this policy effort see Marris and Rein (1967) and Moynihan (1969).

proach to be much improvement over the simpler models. Current experiments on housing allowances, income maintenance, and school voucher systems represent attempts to develop scientific models. Problems and norms derived from such models in future should provide more productive ways of understanding our situation. Use of such models will also imply that we cannot simply look at measures in isolation from one another but only in a context of their likely interrelations.

We identify problems then through some combination of implicit model and measurements that relate to it, and therefore we have difficulty identifying problems clearly where we have no measurements. Moreover it is generally true that governments do not take actions on problems before they learn to measure them. They prefer to concentrate efforts on matters where they can demonstrate progress, and they are often able to ignore matters where demands for change are unfocused.

THE TASK AHEAD

Those who are interested in improved public policy are confronted with a problem themselves. Statistics are increasingly easier to collect and more readily available in this computer age. They are simple, forceful means of communication. They help define the problems we are impelled to address and help determine the shape of the solutions we produce. Sometimes the measures and the models behind these societal "problems" do not coincide with the kind of analyses and values we would like to use. Sometimes models and data are lacking altogether. This situation suggests that decision-makers cannot reasonably ignore either the process by which statistics are created and used or the models that enter implicitly into our calculations. It also presents an opportunity for planning and analysis to deal with basic questions and eliminate some of the artificial constraints under which they normally work.

What is needed is not just statistics like most of those reported in *The Times*, but indicators — statistics which reflect directly on matters of public concern. Statistics on the number of union members or the number of radio listeners do not suggest much to us in the way of a potential issue, though related information might. The fact that 100 miners a day leave the pits in Britain is frequently used as an indicator of the inadequacy of pay. The weekly increase or decline in listening audience would be an indicator of the radio station's quality. A measure may or may not adequately reflect what it is presumed to, but that is a further issue. The immediate problem is how to see that statistics can be developed and presented in a form which has some significance in terms which we recognize, and which those concerned with public policy can use.

A few social statistics turn out to be relevant almost by accident. They may have been the product of a generalized data gathering effort without much guidance from specific objectives — very basic data may fit in this category like population movements, age distribution, and births. However, even this must be structured to have meaning, as for example with rates of population increase, or birth rates.

A number of measures, however, have been deliberately designed to be indicators of specific phenomena. The unemployment rate in the U.S. is based on data collected specifically to calculate the rate and designed to reflect on how well the economy was doing for the working population. It has been collected and used in public policy since 1940. The standard family budget is another deliberately designed and widely used indicator. It attempts to reflect a societal norm for consumption levels, and dates back to the turn of the century. The poverty line is of a similar antiquity and was specifically designed and measured to quantify and identify the poor and estimate the scale and type of remedial programs. Crime rates, life expectancy, housing quality measures, fertility rates, price indices, and many others are also measures deliberately designed to indicate change in significant aspects of social life. The process by which they came into being, came to be accepted and to be used was a long and complex one wherein prevalent theories, norms, problem perceptions, and practical constraints fed into the measure's design, which, in turn, affected and altered these creating forces.

As has often been pointed out in recent years, we are lacking measures for many important subjects, particularly in the hard-to-define aspects of life quality. Indeed, a whole intellectual movement for social indicators has grown up in recognition of this need. It is perhaps less recognized that even outside the explicit social indicator efforts, there is growing up the basis for a number of new indicators, indicators which should ultimately have a similar degree of consensus behind them and relevance to accepted definitions of problems. For instance, the discussion which began with the massive survey known as the Coleman Report (U.S. Department of Health, Education and Welfare, 1966) and continued in the courts across the U.S. and in several reassessments (notably Jencks et al., 1972) may ultimately produce indicators of racial imbalance in schools and of school contributions to equalizing opportunity. A related intellectual controversy based on statistical analysis has stirred up widespread public interest and may help determine whether IQ is used as an indicator of racial superiority (Jensen, 1969; Herrnstein, 1971; Bowles and Gintis, 1973).

The present study is based on an examination of some of these measures, the long-established ones and the developing ones. Topics explored included motivations and situations that prompted the creation of measures, influences on the choice and design of the measures, ways which the measures influenced the definition of problems and norms, ways in which the measures were used, and finally ways the indicators evolved in response to a changing environment or perceptions. The object was to find out if there were some common features to this development and evolution for indicators that have achieved some public acceptance. It is also suggested where there might be pathologies that would make for misunderstanding or misuse of a measure or that would present serious obstacles to the development of an acceptable measure.

While I do not expect to prove that there is any particular right way to develop or use indicators, hopefully the experience with indicator design and application can suggest some strategies that are likely to be successful and others that could backfire. The research has covered methods of data collection and design, institutions and processes of dissemination, institutions, processes and models for use, and interactions among all these. Hopefully these topics will give those interested in creating new indicators some guide as to the kind of questions that may require attention and the kinds of alternatives that may be open. The study is not designed so much to provide answers as it is to raise questions.

There has been relatively little systematic study of the design and use of information in decision-making, and at this stage, it seems appropriate to do an exploratory analysis like this, trying to identify classes of problems and types of solutions. While one can draw no definitive conclusions about particular processes causing particular outcomes, the combination of this study of a number of indicators with the observations and hypotheses of others on policy-making processes and the role of information and bodies of experience in statistical method and measurement theory, will perhaps open a seam of ideas that will be suggestive to others.

The broad conclusions of the study are several. The design of a measure that will be used and accepted as an indicator is a far more lengthy and complex process than many who advocate new indicators recognize. There are false starts and many years between the conception of a new measure and its collection *and* use, and usually a tremendous impetus is required to get it going. The measures themselves can be potent, an almost independent force in public decision-making, rather than a supple tool of the unscrupulous few if they become institutionalized. If they are to be used and effectively convince people, they must represent concepts and fit into models that are generally accepted. This puts measures that are designed empirically, with little basis in theory, at a considerable disadvantage. Finally, measures which are not coupled with a policy perspective and an institutional arrangement for considering them publicly are unlikely to have much impact.

Chapter II

Traditions of Social Measurement

"Social indicators" is a popular new term of the 1960s and 70s, but social indicators themselves are far from new, and there is much to be learned from the experience with them. The practice of quantifying societal phenomena for public decision-making goes back to the 18th century, and the idea back at least to Sir William Petty and the Political Arithmeticians of the 17th century, whose interest was the "Art of Reasoning by Figures upon Things Relating to Government". The term "statistics" refers to "matters of state", and the earliest were simply outputs of governmental record-keeping systems.

New statistical efforts were seldom undertaken without specific purposes. The U.S. population census was required by the original Constitution to provide the basis for determining Congressional districts. The French Constituent Assembly in 1791 ordered a census and statistical accounting of resources to help them with their unfamiliar task of governing. These initial steps rapidly led to wider inquiries. The first censuses involved simple population information, head counts or family counts, age, sex, and color data. Other statistical inquiries covered economic phenomena as these were the principal concerns of government, and they were not only useful but also relatively easy to obtain and straightforward to describe. By the early 19th century, the U.S. was collecting data on production of goods like iron and gold, on acreage devoted to important crops, on currency, public land sales, balance of trade, and more.

It was not long, however, before governments began to collect data that we would identify as primarily social or political. Immigration was a dominant fact of U.S. life and, accordingly, the census gathered data on it from 1820. By the 1830s some states in the U.S. and a number of European cities had begun to gather a variety of social statistics and by 1840 the U.S. Census covered work activity and physical disabilities. Social statistics gathering began in earnest in 1850 when the census involved inquiries on schools, libraries and newspapers, as well as on religion, criminals, paupers and wages. It not only asked new questions of individuals about marriage and literacy, but also called for a compilation of social data from political subdivisions.

The impetus to this effort was the industrial revolution and the rapid immigration and urbanization that it entailed. Society was changing and the old government roles would no longer work, nor the old perceptions be accurate. While the specific uses of each type of data were undoubtedly not clear in the minds of those planning the census, the collection of the new data was an effort to get a perspective on social change. It should be noted, however, that virtually all the data collected had bearing on activities in which government was already involved. Information on the work force was often related to questions of foreign trade relations and protective tariffs and, only towards the end of the 19th century, to humanitarian considerations.

Government responsibility for statistics gathering became a firmly established principle. In the U.S., gathering statistics was often the only action the Federal government would take on social questions. For example, the agitation after the Civil War for a Department of Labor to represent the interests of the worker in government resulted in the establishment of the Bureau of Labor whose only function was statistical. The pattern was that statistics often preceded policy commitments, though at least an imprecisely defined but significant problem perception preceded and motivated their collection.

THE EMPIRICAL TRADITION

While governments were gradually accepting wider responsibility for social statistics, research and practice among statisticians was rapidly developing in the latter half of the 19th century and setting patterns which persist even today. Statisticians in Europe and the U.S., mostly in the pay of governments, gave form to the modern school of practical statistics, expanded governmental commitment to statistics, and defined an empirical approach to data. Though surveys had been done in the previous century, it was the work after 1850 which pioneered large-scale sampling and interviewing and established modes of classification and tabulation. It is true that 19th century statisticians had little concept of most potential sources of bias, and their sampling methods were based on judgment as to representativeness and convenience. They had to overcome considerable resistance to questioning in a population unused to the idea. Their interviewing methods were unsophisticated, and one presumes, unreliable, but they began the long course of development of interview techniques that today are quite dependable. They also established ways of organizing data and categories of classification that would guide (or hamper) thought processes of later analysts.

In social statistics a major effort was in family consumption studies, though there were studies as well on employment, wages, and health among others. The most notable researcher was a Belgian, Ducpétiaux, who did studies in the 1850s, emulated in other countries, on family expenditure patterns, collecting data from hundreds of working class families on their income and expenses in such categories as housing, fuel, and food. The topics were broad rather than deep and the information somewhat superficial as a large survey inevitably requires.* Though the pattern of data gathering and analysis has evolved since Ducpétiaux, current consumption studies have many fundamental commonalities with his.

The purpose of the studies was to get a view of working-class life styles, and an idea of the adequacy of wages. It was motivated by such objectives as social reform, the specification of the condition of groups such as women and children, or the demonstration of the causes of hardship of worker families. (Were they squandering money or simply underpaid?) The first official U.S. consumption studies were designed, in part, to compare the living level possible on U.S. wages to that with European wages. The statisticians approached the questions with virtually no specified hypotheses to explore the relationship, for example, between social conditions and individual life styles. Rather they gathered quantities of data on the general topic, tabulated them in a convenient way, and presented them with little comment or interpretation.

It is not surprising that these masses of information did not clarify the ongoing debates. They were not structured to do so, but rather were presented in the tradition of so much social data, on the assumption that if you have it all in front of you in more or less raw form, you will suddenly see what it implies. It is seldom

---

* For a survey with abstracts of virtually all consumption studies to 1935 see Williams and Zimmerman (1935).

the case that one can find anything interesting in data unless one has an idea of what to look for and collects and organizes them with the idea in mind. However, the empirical approach of amassing data on the general topic of public concern was popular then, as it often is now. It involved no requirement for the statisticians to spell out assumptions, problem definitions, policy alternatives, or presumed causality. The volume of data would make it difficult to accuse them of any particular bias, and they could leave the conclusions (if any) to the reader. This approach kept them well out of politics and allowed them to go on working without interference.

This situation exemplifies a basic dilemma of all research, in that there are two fundamentally different approaches to dealing with a broad, poorly specified problem (Duncan, 1969, pp. 7—10). They are not so much associated with time periods as with particular habits of mind. To oversimplify somewhat, one strategy, the empirical approach, is to gather data first and find its meaning later. The other view demands that one have some sort of *a priori* model* before selecting or interpreting data. The empiricist says "let's get on with it and measure something", though he may not know exactly what it represents or how exactly it fits into any analysis. The theorist says this attitude is likely to produce useless or meaningless data and to permit the neglect of critical variables. Each has a point as one usually requires at least some data to devise a theory, while at the same time, masses of data are uninterpretable without the aid of a theory, however rudimentary. The empiricist's structuring of the data into categories and choice of questions, whether consciously planned as part of a test of a hypothesis, or not, will preclude some analyses and predispose towards others.

Most empiricists are influenced in their study design at least subjectively, by prevailing theories and their own suppositions about relationships, however vague. They do not collect all possible data and do not make random choices. The theorist, on the other hand, who does do any data collection, particularly on behavioral questions, usually finds that theory does not take him far enough to define every variable in detail that he requires and he too must rely on intuition. From a practical standpoint, one has to

---

* See pages 62—67 for the usage of the term "model" in this study.

think of the process as an iterative one, and purists on either side of the argument are oversimplifying.

Although masses of data on family expenditure had been accumulated by 1900, there was little restudy and analysis. Researchers on family living have bemoaned this neglect of a rich data source. But perhaps this was no oversight; perhaps the data source was not so rich. Indeed, close perusal of the tabulations is unlikely to evoke much interest from a reader. It is vaguely edifying or perhaps sobering to know just how little the 19th century workmen had for pleasures or to see how small were the quantities of meat in his diet. But if one asks "why?" the data is silent, and mostly one can think of no questions at all.

One exception to this neglect of the data for analysis was in the search for "laws of expenditure", but this was, like most of the consumption studies, sharply separated from theoretical analysis (Stigler, 1954). Ernst Engel, chief of the Prussian bureau of statistics, examined groupings of consumption data and produced several empirical propositions about the relationships of particular categories of expenditure to total outlay and income (Zimmerman, 1932). The most famous of these, which is still widely accepted and is the basis for the U.S. poverty or low-income line is that "the greater the income, the smaller the relative percentage of outlay for subsistence". It is an empirical law, a rule of thumb, well suited to the kind of data on which it is based. It is perhaps the only kind of law one can draw from such data. It may hold true under many conditions, but it is not testable objectively, nor does it contain any explanation for why it might be true or when it might not be. In any case, others, most notably the U.S. labor statistics chief, did spend much effort trying to explore the propositions. However, the efforts never bore any fruit and faded out after a few years, though the "laws" persisted in the conceptual vocabulary.

It seems obvious from this vantage point that the pure empiricism of these 19th century statisticians made it difficult, if not impossible, for others to use or build on their work. However, many statistical efforts today are guided by little more in the way of hypotheses and important questions. The data seems also destined for oblivion. The empirical tradition is still strong in social statistics, but the excuse is far weaker now that we have so many more ideas about the workings of society.

The controversies we have today over new data are many of them old, familiar issues. It is instructive to examine the origins of one of the oldest types of social data, now the best understood and most reliable that we have — population data. Looking back to when there were no population statistics, we can inquire why people thought the data would be useful. The perspective on what now are obviously odd ideas and misapprehensions will hopefully help us to view with a skeptical eye our own arguments for and against gathering new information.

In the mid-18th century population figures became the subject of considerable controversy and speculation in England.* A complete census had never been done, and vital registration was neither legally required nor regularly practiced. However, for a variety of reasons, it had become a popular contention that population had been declining. The reason may have been the prevalence of wars and disease, the increasingly evident misery of the poor in urban places, or possibly just a general inclination to believe that times were always better in the past. The conviction was certainly not based on data. But the supposition of a population decline was a matter of some importance. The mercantilist theory of national wealth demanded a substantial population to produce as much as possible for trade. A declining population could also mean a lowered capability to muster troops. The implications and supposed implications were many.

Fifty years passed, however, after the beginning of the controversy before a complete census was done in England and more than 80 years before registration of births and deaths was legally required. It was not that such data gathering concepts were unknown. Iceland had done several censuses already, and Sweden had established a vital registration system. The idea was known to the British as well, since a bill was introduced into Parliament in 1753 to do an annual census including broad age data and to require registration of all births and deaths. Such an act would have brought together many of the ingredients for a fairly sophisticated population analysis. The bill was not passed, and was strongly opposed in the popular press. In spite of continuing agitation during the rest of the century over population figures, census legislation was not passed until 1800 and then only with a number of additional motivations.

---

* The account is drawn largely from a study by D.V. Glass (1973).

Today it is obvious, even to the most anti-quantitative among us, that population data is necessary to government actions, if only to predict taxes, social benefit payments, or the requirements for schools. The data is also important to the predictive models of demographers and actuaries which provide us with indicators of life expectancy and fertility and ultimately permit planning for the longer term.

Though population data could have helped make government more effective in 1753, even the proponents of the bill were not perceptive about its potential. Thomas Potter, who introduced the census bill, listed some of the advantages in a speech to Parliament. The results would, he said, make it possible to estimate how large an army might be raised, provide evidence about desirability of emigration and show correctly the burden of the poor to the kingdom. It is not clear, however, that the census, as proposed, would have answered any of these questions or that Mr. Potter had thought them carefully through. He perhaps belonged to the category of person who believes implicitly in the value of data to settle discussions. He might not be able to specify exactly what data was needed for precisely which questions but felt sure the presence of the data would somehow clarify things. Such individuals often make a considerable contribution to furthering the cause of improved data for policy by being fervent spokesmen for the cause at a time when others are waiting to be more certain of the reasoning. Intuition is not necessarily a false guide and may be the only one at an early stage of development of a subject.

The opponents of the census, on the other hand, seem to fit into the category of those who are permanently disposed against statistics as an ingredient of argument. Perhaps their view reflects an inability to understand figures, or perhaps it is simply a recognition of the gaps in the logic of the proponents of the data. There were unique arguments in 1753, such as the fear of divine anger. Opponents could not see any counterbalancing advantages to the expected resistance. The *Gentlemen's Magazine** covered the debate in detail, including an attack by William Thornton on the whole concept of the census, which sounds familiar. He saw no useful role for numbers. "Can it be pretended, that by the knowledge of our number, or our wealth, either can be increased?" Accordingly he was convinced of ulterior motives on the part of the bill's proponents, saying "the hope of some advantage to

---

* November and December, 1753 and supplement, 1753.

themselves can only urge them to perpetrate such evil to others; for, not to set any value upon the reputation or peace which they risk, it cannot be imagined that they would molest and perplex every single family in the kingdom merely to set a beggar to work or determine any questions in political arithmetic."* In short he assumed the bill was a fundamental threat to English liberty.

It is remarkable how perspectives change and we accustom ourselves to new patterns, yet how the same kinds of fears regularly arise with new data proposals. When registration of births, marriages and deaths was proposed in 1836, the arguments were not dissimilar. It would be a nuisance and a threat (noncompliance involved a penalty) to the ordinary person, and the only beneficiaries would be the statisticians. It was doubted that the "statistical fancies of some few philosophers" might aid in dealing with matters of public interest. There was considerable protest at the invasion of privacy as well, though today we no longer question the right of the state to record the birth of a child. The change may in part be due to the fact that children are considered less as property now than people, but it is certainly also due to our acceptance of the practice as normal and recognition of its value.

When the population census finally was approved in England in 1800, it was after a lengthy controversy over the figures in which the estimates for the midcentury population ranged from 4½ millions to 7½ millions. Both the amount and direction of change in the previous fifty years were in dispute, with some claiming a decline of over a million, others a similar increase. There were sources of data, mostly based on taxes, published bills of mortality or parish records on baptisms and burials. All were incomplete, however, unrepresentative of the total population, and suffered from the usual problems of administrative byproduct data in bias and incompleteness. Poll tax was not levied on beggars and children. Window tax was not applicable to windowless cottages of the poor, and the count, in any case, was highly inaccurate. Vital registration in parishes excluded the substantial group of dissenters.

The controversy and the wide variation in estimates helped define the problem of a lack of population information and set up a situation where reliable data would be seen as necessary. The perception was to take many years to become widely and firmly established, and the lesson should not be lost on those who are so

---

* Glass, 1973, page 20.

regularly frustrated in efforts to institute new data series today. The squabbles between the analysts on fine points of estimation procedures suggested the data would serve to clear up questions of concern only to statisticians. This too is a contemporary problem. The specialist becomes involved in the unique puzzle of his own discipline and sometimes forgets to look outward toward the public who wants to know what it means to them (Rein, 1970).

The controversy and what it represented — a demand to know whether the population was declining — was only one of the factors in the approval of the census by Parliament. The local enumerations conducted without incident in connection with the controversy calmed fears and made a census seem more feasible, furthering the iterative process of design and practice. However, other specific motivations appear to have played a role as well. The British were waging a war and with a bad harvest that year, had tremendous relief costs for the poor and military dependents. The M.P. who introduced the Bill in 1800 spoke of the "urgent pressure of circumstances" and said "in times like these when the subsistence of the people is in question, this knowledge (of the state of the population) becomes of the highest importance. It is surely important to know the extent of the demand for which we are to provide a supply."* But war and food shortages were recurrent events, and one has to look still further for reasons.

The attitude toward population increase was becoming less and less favorable at the end of the century as the poor seemed to increase and food had to be imported. Mercantilism was on the wane and Malthus and his "gloomy" science were becoming more convincing. But most importantly several other nations had begun to take censuses for administrative purposes, and this fact cannot have escaped Parliament. One of the major stated objectives of the bill was to learn whether population increase was the reason the country had ceased being an exporting country, and whether agriculture should be increased. Another was a more research oriented concept, a responsibility to posterity to collect population statistics. Clearly a mixture of motivations was involved, some not too different from those for present day "social indicators" — most notably, the objective of helping those who come after us understand their society better.

---

* Glass, 1973, page 97.

Chapter III

Statistical Policy:
The Setting for Indicator Development

The structure of the statistical system of the U.S., all appearances to the contrary, is the result of some conscious policy choice. Policy has been debated in government and among academics repeatedly over the last 80 years. While the recommendations of experts have not always been heeded, many issues have been laid out and the political decisions taken with them in mind. One reason it may appear that there is no policy is that the decision has often been to let the system continue decentralized and relatively uncontrolled. Another reason is that the policy has concerned principally the organization of statistical production, the presentation and dissemination of data, and more recently, coordination and avoidance of duplication and the assurance of data quality. The policy has not, however, said anything about what *kind* of data *ought* to be collected or what procedures might be established to identify new data needs.

This laissez-faire approach has been both a strength and weakness of American statistical policy, but it makes planned development of a system of social indicators virtually impossible. Some statistical functions have been performed by special agencies closely tied to policy and operational aims of government so they have been able to work closely with analysts and respond with useful data. Other more general purpose functions are performed by the Census Bureau which has developed considerable expertise in data collection. Other statistics are little more than byproducts of administrative activities. There are mismatches and duplications; there is no overall plan nor opportunity to have one, but there is vitality, relevance and methodological work at the forefront of statistics.

An issue that confronts those interested in social indicators is how to introduce a concentrated effort to develop and put to use a new range of measures in the context of existing statistical policy. New institutional arrangements will be needed, but long-established arrangements for statistics are not likely to be turned upside down. The reasonable approach would be to build on the strengths of the system we have. It is essential therefore to understand this system and the options that may be open.

THE DILEMMA OF THE OFFICIAL STATISTICIAN: THE EMERGENCE OF LABOR STATISTICS IN THE U.S.

The case of labor statistics provides a graphic illustration of the way a fundamental philosophical question about the relationship of official statisticians to policy has been dealt with. The story is worth recognition here because labor statistics are the earliest and probably the most successful systems of social indicators in the U.S. (U.S. Department of Labor, 1922 and Clague, 1968). It was in the labor statistics bureau that many effective patterns of interaction with policy-makers were established and where well accepted social data were first produced. Although "labor statistics" may sound as if they would interest only those in business and economics, the tradition is otherwise. Labor statistics covered the human condition broadly, including not only productivity, wages, and employment, but also family budgets, poverty and health. The purpose was only occasionally to improve the state of business. It was usually to investigate living conditions of workers and families.

Labor statistics as a government activity emerged after the Civil War in a climate of labor unrest, during a period when labor organizations were becoming vocal and Marxism was gaining adherents.* Manufacturing industries were growing, hours were long, and factory conditions little regulated. Labor reformers called attention to the miserable lot of the workingman, while other social reformers produced graphic descriptions of urban slum life. The answers varied widely. Labor reformers laid the blame on the capitalist system and proposed a range of redistribution approaches. The conservative view was that alcohol was the cause of

---

* This account draws primarily on reports of the Bureau of Statistics of Labor of Massachusetts, and the Bureau of Labor (later Department of Labor and finally Bureau of Labor Statistics), as well as on the excellent volume by Leiby (1960).

working-class poverty and crime, and prohibition laws were the answer. Some thought wages too low; others contended that workers would only squander higher wages. Groups agitated for ten-hour and eight-hour days. Prostitution seemed to increase. Child labor and lack of education came to be defined as problems. Huge fortunes were amassed, while poverty became increasingly visible.

Against this backdrop, the state of Massachusetts in 1869 created the first Bureau of Statistics of Labor. It was a response to an incoherent, but profound, discontent among the people, and its mandate gave it no precisely defined problems to attack nor clear-cut role to play. The legislature established it as a concession to labor interests, but apparently hoped the agency would define, or even settle, the problems they could not articulate. Some may have thought of the bureau as a harmless way of circumventing immediate action. Labor organizations were unimpressed and uninterested in the new bureau, and they continued agitation.

The Bureau's mandate specifically was "to collect, assort, systematize and present in annual reports to the legislature ... statistical details relating to all departments of labor ... especially ... to the commercial, industrial, social, educational, and sanitary condition of the laboring classes, and to the permanent prosperity of ... productive industry".

This vague directive laid the ground for the Bureau's chief to establish the style and process of operation. Indeed the Bureau's director was to set a permanent mark, not only on labor statistics production, but ultimately on U.S. statistical policy more generally, as he came to be much admired. Often individuals with a special vision and a competence crystallize issues in a particular form and transform vague discontent into specific action. Carroll Wright was to play such a role in the development of labor statistics, helping to assure that they would receive respect and attention from all parties to disputes.

INFORMATION AND ADVOCACY

Before he was to be involved however, a different philosophy guided the Massachusetts Bureau. It was an advocacy approach to the role and diametrically opposed to the professional, nonpartisan stance that Wright was to establish. The first chief was a former school constable who was known for his labor reform views. His deputy was president of the Boston Eight-Hour League. Their implicit mandate was to promote a point of view, and they hastened

74

to do so. They sent for public documents from England where labor discussion was considerably further advanced in the hope of "surprising and shaming" the legislature into making reforms. They collected statistics (in a very inadequate fashion) only because the act required them to.

They believed that their role was to find answers to the "labor problem", which would not be done "by any tabular array of figurate statistics alone". The first report included vivid descriptions of particularly bad tenements with names and earnings of owners. It won the bureau notoriety, and produced action against the landlords. In seeking to prove the inadequacy of wages they examined the growing workers' deposits in banks, to which many pointed as proof that the workers were doing well. Their report concluded that deposits were too large to be from workers and that capitalists were using these accounts as a tax dodge. The accusation infuriated the bankers and was quoted in the national press and on the floor of Congress. Although a legislative investigation did not exonerate the banks, the incident brought opposition to the bureau to a peak, and it was nearly dissolved.

The objectives and strategy of the bureau officers may have been effective for advocates of particular views, but they were disastrous for a statistical agency. Such openly partisan reporting was not likely to be tolerated long by the politicians who had set up the agency, nor were the statistics themselves likely to be trusted.

THE DILEMMA OF PROFESSIONALISM VERSUS POLITICS

It was at this point that the governor appointed a new director, Carroll Wright, who introduced a different style and won bipartisan support for his activities. His guiding creed was to "be free of partisan dictation" and "the seductions of theory" in order to have support of the press and the public. He would, in other words, stick to "facts", avoid theorizing, and keep out of politics.

His concept was deceptively simple, and even now statisticians and technicians of all sorts take this view of their role. However, as we will discuss in Chapter VII, there are no facts without theories, and the only way a statistician can keep out of politics is to collect irrelevant data. If a statistician does the barest minimum — compose a questionnaire and tabulate the returns — he is defining the terms of the problem. This is only possible in terms of some theory, no matter how subjective or poorly perceived, about what data to collect, how to elicit it and why certain answers should be classified together.

In fact, Wright did much more than the minimum. He selected topics and ways of studying them. He used the questions suggested by his predecessors. His reports, however, showed figures with little commentary or explicit conclusion. The result was that either the conclusion was obvious, or in the effort to give "facts" without a framework, the data was not very edifying. Long lists of consumption items and prices do not necessarily convey any message. One exception, however, was the comparative study of wages, hours, and prices in Massachusetts and England which was organized to show that American workers were better off. Wright came around to seeing the Bureau's role as twofold, to answer specific questions posed by the legislature, and to provide general education to decision-makers and the public.

Though Wright was to stick to his effort to keep statistical analysis and policy separate, he was eventually to recognize the basic ambiguity in this concept. At one point he said that statistics bureaus responded to a "general demand" for "specific, well-classified" information. While the bureaus might be impartial to particular reform schemes, they could help create popular sentiment for reforms and "crystallize" the discussion into well-directed investigations. In other words, where the legislature might be worried about child labor, the statisticians would define the problem more precisely as a question of hours, or health or income. And sometimes they could create perceptions of needs where none had existed before. It was a modern view and a perceptive one.

In any case, Wright's large surveys (based in part on European advances in method), painstaking procedures, and his occasionally interesting results, won him a worldwide reputation as a statistician. He was a natural choice for the chief of the federal Bureau of Labor set up in 1884.* He brought to the job the same meticulous avoidance of politics, and set important precedents for future directors. He soon gave the bureau the reputation it maintains today of an agency applying the best available methods, remaining out of politics, and trustworthy to all parties. The data he gathered did not have many identifiable impacts, but Congress did not feel it was a wasted effort. In 1888, Wright managed to inject into a debate on tariffs some of his figures on comparative living stan-

---

* Eventually to become the Bureau of Labor Statistics.

dards, which encouraged the Congressmen to request more detailed data. But the results were little used.

Wright confronted the dilemma that all statisticians must if their work is connected to policy. He participated in no policy questions and his reports made no reference to policies under discussion. Meanwhile he quietly set the terms for the next discussion as he mapped out a new study. He fervently hoped to design data that would be used, and he continually looked for evidence of its impact. His massive presentations had so little focus that few could make use of the data for an argument. The compromise he chose may not have been ideal, but it ensured the survival of the BLS. His foresight assured it the public confidence that was essential. In recent years it has been possible for the Bureau to produce far more pointed information and to provide analysis and explanation without risking its own existence. The exercise is not completely without risk (see Chapter XII), and the basic ambiguity of the statistician's role remains. It will perhaps be helpful ultimately to both statistician and politician for both to be able to spell out more clearly the symbiotic nature of their relationship.

DATA PRODUCTION AND POLICY

Every major department of the U.S. government compiles statistics, either in the course of its other activities or as part of a separate statistical and research function.* The responsibility to collect and publish statistics is frequently part of the legislation establishing the agency, and may even antedate the agency itself, as the BLS antedates the Department of Labor. The variety of data is tremendous, ranging from crop reports to characteristics of welfare recipients. Some data are primarily for management and control and some for public consumption. Some are limited in their applicability or intended audience and others are designed to fill the requirements of Congress. Moreover statistics collected in different departments are often related, or even overlapping, as the departmental functions reflect the incremental growth of government. For example, due to the priority and funding the U.S. has long given to agricultural research, the Department of Agriculture

---

* An excellent account of U.S. statistical policy issues describing producers, users, and systems of coordination is in U.S. President's Commission on Federal Statistics, 1971, Vol. I.

has been involved since the 19th century in collecting food consumption data, and its researchers did much of the groundbreaking work on dietary needs before nutrition was even an accepted field of study. Therefore, though the National Institutes of Health or the Public Health Service might be the logical location for nutrition statistics, the Agriculture Department is still heavily involved for historical reasons.

The U.S. Census Bureau dominates the statistical scene as the largest and most skilled collector and processor of statistics. Although it is today technically under the aegis of the Commerce Department, it is in many respects an independent agency with a separate budget. It is not only responsible for censuses on a variety of topics, but it also provides the expertise and staff to design and conduct surveys and tabulate results for other agencies. Thus it has varying degrees of cooperative relations with agencies.

Much of our national data are gathered at the state or local level, either for local consumption or as part of a cooperative, federal-state or federal-municipality program. Some are part of an effort which exists purely for the statistics, such as the cooperation between local police districts and the FBI, which produces the quarterly crime index figures. Others, like the insured unemployment statistics, are a byproduct of a joint state-federal program to distribute unemployment insurance. Private groups also produce data in considerable volume. University survey research centers, and organizations such as the Russell Sage Foundation, or the Social Science Research Council, have sponsored essential research for new social statistics. A private group can often risk failure, or the production of lower quality statistics more easily than government and can mount investigations on subjects that as yet arouse little public interest without first having to win the assent of Congress. Profitmaking groups also collect data, notably the opinion pollsters, and numerous consulting firms. The topics range widely; the quality is highly variable, but the data nonetheless forms part of the total statistical "system" of the country and the sources must be considered along with all the others in any statistical policy.

CENTRAL GUIDANCE OF STATISTICAL AGENCIES

This brief outline should suggest the difficulties involved in any overall policy for production of statistics. The existing statistical functions are strongly institutionalized, integrated into the departments, and jealously guarded. Introducing change may be difficult, even undesirable. No mechanism exists for guiding state or city statistical activities of a uniform basis and control over private data sources is usually only possible through incentive public funding. For many topics on a federal level, policy can potentially be made at budgeting time, at least in the broad sense of setting priorities, changing relative funding, levels and styles of operation. For statistics, however, such distinct policy planning is not possible, as most are tied to programs which must be considered on other grounds.

Policies and programs on many subjects benefit greatly from the expertise of the small group of Congressmen who regularly consider legislation in committee, but responsibility for statistical activities is spread over many committees and few Congressmen are experts on statistical programs. One exception is the Subcommittee on Economic Statistics of the Joint Economic Committee which ranges in its investigations over many statistical issues that bear on economic policy. Its deliberations have served an educational function for many Congressmen on principles of statistical design and use and it provides a model for how one might (and might not) design future Congressional statistical policy groups. The Census Subcommittee is, of course, also expert about certain data collection processes. The substantive committees give little attention to statistical programs as they are peripheral to their main concerns. In practice, the only Congressional attention given to many statistical programs is in the appropriations process and, as the Appropriations Committee does not meet as a whole, statistical policy cannot be considered in perspective.

At the executive level statistical policy is the responsibility of the Office of Management and Budget (OMB). They have a role simply by virtue of their power to veto any appropriation request from a department before it gets into the President's budget, as submitted to Congress. Sometimes programs do get funding from Congress anyway, but lack of Administration backing is a handicap. OMB has further and more effective roles, however, in that their permission is required for all new questionnaires and surveys. Also, they can and do set up interdepartmental committees which determine compatible concepts and methods for many statistics. As of 1974, for example, an interagency task force in OMB is trying to produce a "poverty" definition for common use, and resolve considerable dispute. These activities, however, are at the margin and do not add up to a positive, creative policy which would allow substantial innovation.

OUTLINES OF THE POLICY

The fundamental characteristic of U.S. statistical policy is that the processes of creation and use of data occur without central planning. The situation is likely to persist as it is one which has been publicly considered and implicitly endorsed on many occasions. Time and again in response to Congressional dissatisfaction or other complaints, a commission has been set up or an agency designated to examine the organization of statistics production.* The motivating issue almost invariably has been whether statistical operations should be centralized. The concerns were for inefficiency, duplication, and failure to make use of existing data. While some commissions did recommend more centralization in, for example, the collection of general purpose data, the only actions taken by the federal government to further this end have been in coordination, changes in definitions, and an occasional shift of responsibility between agencies. The Subcommittee on Economic Statistics has investigated the problems of coordinating and integrating statistics (for example, U.S. Congress, Joint Economic Committee, 1967 and 1969). Nonetheless the policy has been to accept the fundamental decentralization of the system and the pattern of incremental development of statistical activities and to modify them as much as possible by central coordination and veto power.

The reasons for such a policy go to the basic character of U.S. governmental philosophy, antithetical to centralized, positive planning, which is popularly equated with totalitarianism and manipulation by elites. Centralized statistics provide no great advantage without centralized decision-making. Indeed they may be a disadvantage, as a central agency is likely to produce data that responds poorly to the needs of decision-makers. None of the task forces has thought duplication was a major problem. In any case, it is not unreasonable strategy to allow some undirected development and even duplication. Statistical programs which grow out of the needs of the operating agencies can be the most relevant and usefully

---

* See "Commissions on Statistics, Statistics on Commissions," article in vol. 2 of U.S. President's Commission on Federal Statistics, 1971.

formulated of any data. Overlap may help to insure that we do end up with some that is useful. The unplanned strategy may produce a confusing result to the outsider but it permits considerable flexibility and vitality.

Other topics which have been the subject of statistical policy include the quality of the data, the relationship of the statistical function to the political one, methods of presenting data, timeliness and dissemination to users. Congressional committees have heard testimony and taken action on these subjects. Special commissions have considered them either in connection with an overall view of statistical policy or in connection with individual statistics that had become important to public decisions. Thus Presidential Commissions have covered, for example, crime statistics, cost of living indices, housing quality statistics, and unemployment figures.

ACCESSIBILITY TO USERS

These inquiries produced consensus on the importance of data accessibility. In practice major U.S. statistical agencies not only disseminate information about data widely, but they also have regular meetings of user groups in which they explain changes and in turn learn about problems users have with data. The Federal Statistics Users Conference performs such an intermediary role, as do the Business and Labor Research Advisory Councils to the BLS. These groups provide an opportunity for serious exchanges which lend strength to the whole statistical system. The members and associates are more likely to use data and use them properly, and the agencies are inclined to be responsive to criticisms, as the users provide essential lobbying support when they go to Congress.

PRESENTATION OF DATA

The policy on the presentation of general use statistics is to provide clear explanation of concepts, methods, and limitations of the data. As the statistical agencies have gained greater public confidence, they have also published more about their investigations into various problems, like the uncounted blacks in censuses (Taeuber, 1969) and the reliability of housing data (U.S. Department of Commerce, 1967).

The agencies, particularly the BLS, have gone to considerable effort to package the data in various useful compilations like The Annual Handbook of Labor Statistics, the BLS monthly publication, Employment and Earnings, some special studies pertinent to discrimination (U.S. Departments of Commerce and Labor, 1971), and the series on the poor (U.S. Department of Commerce, Series P-60). They also provide quick summaries of most interesting points and send out press releases on many topics. They cultivate a relationship with the media. It is reasonable for them to do so as they may need allies at some time, but it also furthers awareness of the data and its potential significance.

Finally the usual policy is to present data in an apolitical context with technical comment, but none on current policy issues. Releases may call attention to trends or draw comparisons with previous years (which is a form of problem definition but not an obviously political one). For regular statistics like price indices, or unemployment, presentation must be on a timetable fixed months in advance with no announcement ahead of time. All these requirements are designed to protect the indicators from giving the impression that they are partisan political tools.

TIMELINESS

There is no single policy for timeliness, as the meaning of the term depends on the context. The techniques and system now exist for rapid data processing if necessary, but it is expensive. Statistical policy is just beginning to recognize the tradeoff of cost and benefits in timeliness and precision of data. Both can be obtained at great cost, but for many purposes we cannot make use of improvements. One example of this argument was President Nixon's proposal to collect unemployment data weekly instead of monthly. The Administration's purpose was to cancel more of the random variations that confused the public in periods when all eyes were on the unemployment rate. However, the idea was not implemented as its marginal value did not justify its cost.

DATA QUALITY

The regular public scrutiny and openness about methods encourages statistical work to be as sound as possible. Regular consultation of academic experts and non-government statisticians through committees and congressional hearings, helps to insure that up-to-date methodology is used to uncover problems. Several professional organizations, like the American Economic Association and the American Statistical Association pay close attention to statistical developments. The recent Commission on Federal Statistics (Wallis Commission) in 1971 recommended an outside professional review committee for federal statistics (Kruskal, 1973) which was rapidly set up. Finally, statisticians in the more respected agencies have been encouraged to publish in professional journals and to maintain their standing professionally.

DATA PRODUCERS

An important note introduced into the discussion by the Wallis Commission is the identification of characteristics of data producers that make a difference to the type and quality of statistics. They discuss the effect of funding processes, performance measures and users of the data on the type of output. For example, their report asserts that agencies whose primary purpose is gathering, processing and dissemination of statistics like the BLS and the National Centers for Health Statistics and Education Statistics (and presumably any agency producing general social indicators) receive separate consideration by Congress and accordingly require public backing. The quality of the data is particularly scrutinized in such contexts. Moreover the fact that such figures are often used in policy places a great premium on accuracy and reliability. The result of these incentives is that:

"1. The agency is likely to seek to be 'objective' in the sense of avoiding commitment to explanatory theories of behavior that may generate controversy with users.

2. Since it is viewed as a producer of a 'free good' (i.e., users do not pay directly for production of the data), the agency is likely to be bombarded by requests from special interest groups for new and detailed data of limited interest. In response, the agency will try to find a consensus of users, and will seek to produce 'general purpose' statistics which can be used by many, although what is produced will not be completely tailored to the demands of any particular group.

3. To maintain its quality, the agency will strive to achieve accuracy even at the cost of timeliness. It will not administer surveys if the expected rate of response will make the statistics 'unreliable', or if the time allowed for the survey is so short as to preclude careful planning and analysis. Advanced

methodologies will be sought or developed, but innovations will be adopted only after extensive testing greatly reduces risk of failure.

4. To reach the broadest possible audience, the agency will concentrate on publication while discouraging requests for special tabulations or for provision of tapes or tape services which reach isolated or individual researchers.

5. The agency will pay great attention to making sure that data supplied to it will not be released for purposes detrimental to any supplier.

6. The agency will concentrate its resources on meeting its primary responsibility of informing the public, and functions such as administering surveys on contract for other agencies will be subordinated to this primary responsibility.'' (U.S. President's Commission on Federal Statistics, 1971, pp. 47–8.)

If we can understand such incentives and institutional structures behind the pathologies and strengths of our existing system, we should be better able to work toward systems that may produce the sort of output we want.

The Commission went on to describe some features of other statistics producers. For example, agencies which process other people's data have to interpolate among data sources and play a useful role in discovering incompatibility among data series. Statistical offices of operating agencies, like the Office of Research and Statistics in the Social Security Administration, work closely with their client, the department, and do not have direct contact with Congress on funding. Their data tends to be tailored to particular issues and to be based on their own special definitions. Statisticians in such roles have conflicting motivations to serve the public and the program manager, and the latter may have to come first in times of a limited budget. Strictly management information systems give even lower priority to outside requests for data.

DATA USERS

Different kinds of users such as policy-makers, program managers, program evaluators, industry, local government, exploratory researchers, and the public make different demands on the system and are served with varying adequacy. For example, policy is usually made in a state of crisis, when the precise problem is not well defined and certainly appropriate data is not available. Though planning can improve the data for policy, it can never assure that needs will be met. Program evaluators seem to have a vast appetite for data. They can seldom define program objectives narrowly and instead try to look at everything. Exploratory research requires data in a fairly raw form and is seldom served well by statistical services.

It is heartening to see that those interested in statistical policy are prepared to go beyond the now familiar platitudes about the need for data accessibility, usefulness, quality, and compatibility, and look for some of the underlying forces shaping production and use. Hopefully this volume will continue the process.

NEW METHODS AND STATISTICS

The U.S. statistical system has been shaped, to no slight degree, by the introduction of new methods. These can completely alter the structure of a statistical system and its uses. We should understand the dynamics of such developments, and be prepared to create or to take advantage of new opportunities. However, the significant breakthroughs in methodology which potentially affect the statistical system and its uses in any basic way are very few. A number of techniques have been developed, such as the construction of price indices and ways of dealing with the aggregation problem, but these have not had a pervasive effect on the design and use of statistics. Gimmicks seldom provide basic answers.

One technical achievement, sampling methodology, has had a major impact. It has made possible inexpensive, timely, accurate, and reliable data on virtually any topic for which one knows how to elicit information. Before the method was developed, data was either expensive and slow to obtain, or limited in topic, coming from an administrative process. Today we are just beginning to explore the new freedom the sample survey gives us to delve into untouched topics and to change our policy-making procedures so we can respond to frequent information.

The computer promises to provide another such breakthrough for the design and use of social statistics, although its capabilities have scarcely been tapped. The methods of statistical manipulation and the structure of statistical use in policy have as yet altered little to take advantage of the new analytic opportunities offered by the computer. Policy-makers and many statisticians are still doing more or less what they did before the computer, using it to help them at the margin only. A computer may serve as a filing system, as a faster way to check for errors or as a way of doing the same calculations statisticians used to do on their calculating machines. No doubt these capabilities have improved the quantity and quality of data, but in themselves, they have not produced the fundamental change in the character of policy analysis that could eventually result.

A popular proposal is to use computers as massive banks of data and give decision-makers on-line access to them so they can check a fact or figure any time. The proposal seems premature at best, and represents a misunderstanding of the decision-maker. He or she is unlikely to know what data would be useful. A research social scientist may have plenty of ideas, but such ideas are his speciality. The decision-maker specializes in action and seems likely always to prefer data manipulated into a form with immediate relevance to his problem. Data banks will undoubtedly serve those who are making basic and innovative studies, but it still leaves missing links between data and policy-making.

The computer's great virtue is its capability to perform endless repetitive tasks fast and accurately, and this power has only begun to be tapped to improve decisions. The computer, for example, made feasible the seasonal adjustment to monthly economic data, which has made it more meaningful to the general public. The testing of hypothetical or simulation models, helping us to explore the implications of the assumptions we use in day-to-day decision-making is another important possibility. If we can stop focusing on the data storage characteristic of computers to think more about the manipulative potential, we can more likely exploit the full potential of computer systems.

A third breakthrough that has been little recognized is one made possible by the computer — geocoding (U.S. President's Commission on Federal Statistics, 1971, Chapter 3, Part C). This is a system for placing address-coded data onto a map. It will permit the assembling of a range of information according to any desired geographical area. This will begin to fill a vacuum in local area data, and quite possibly change radically the way cities and towns can use information and plan. Nation-wide samples are not big enough to give results for cities and towns, which have not the funds, expertise or inclination to run their own surveys. Their proposals and planning documents tend to be filled with data from the last census — superficial and out-of-date in many ways by the time it is available. Such tabulations appended to the documents get little attention and impress no one.

Geocoding will permit the combining of police, welfare, and school data, for example, to give a broader picture of small areas and permit some better guesses as to the definitions and causes of problems than city or statewide aggregates do. Such data may prove to be relatively inadequate as much would be by-product data (see Chapter VIII). However, in combination with the increasing state responsibility for dispensing federal funds in revenue sharing and the inevitable demands for accountability, it seems likely that more geocoding programs will be developed. The use of a little data even if it is poor, is likely to create a habit of argument and increase the demand for and use of data at the local level. This dynamic of a little data creating its own increasing demand for further data has occurred many times at the national level. The process is bound to have an effect on the local decision-making patterns which, in the absence of reliable numbers, have often been a private affair of the politicians and the "experts". In other words the use of geocoding could have a substantial impact on who makes what decisions for what kind of reason in the cities.

Thus far geocoding has fulfilled little of this potential, though it has been available about ten years. Many have proclaimed their disappointment with it. But ten years is a short time in the typical process of introduction of and adaptation to innovation. Moreover, no one has yet spent the time to set up the interactive process between the geocoding system and its potential users that could produce new patterns of information collection and use.

Future developments that may radically change our current patterns of statistics development and use are likely to occur in two directions (Kendall, 1968). One is in the increasing application of measurement techniques and scaling methods* developed by psychologists for measuring subjective phenomena. A substantial body of methodological work exists and is adaptable to attitude measurement. The stimulus increasingly exists for such work as we grow as a society more dissatisfied with the purely monetary and physical measures of welfare and benefits. The logical direction to seek new criteria for decision-making is in public attitudes.

---

* The term "scaling" here refers to efforts to place observations on an objective scale, showing their quantitative relation to one another, even if this relation is only an ordinal one. See Torgerson (1958) for a basic account of this procedure.

There is likely also to be the increasing development of predictive, causal, or exploratory models of social phenomena (with the aid of the computer no doubt) which will drastically alter the way we use data in the future, and alter the type of data we demand. Quietly but deliberately in many areas of sociology and political science work continues to define social theories in quantitative, testable forms. Once formulated in this fashion, the translation into policy is likely to be easy and even inevitable. A quantitatively defined theory can specify tangibly the objectives for a policy and the means to implement them. For example, a theory might say the cause of low black achievement in school is the loss of self esteem that comes from being in segregated schools. We might then specify measures of achievement and segregation and relate them in a mathematical model showing say, that some increments of achievement are related to particular levels of segregation. It becomes obvious that we have to cut back on segregation. This is not to say the model is causally correct, but as we said in the first chapter, the measurement of phenomena and the specification of how they may diverge from some better condition is a powerful force creating demand for action of specific kinds.

While it is true that those in power may not be swayed by theories which do not jibe with their preconceptions or preferences, there are vast areas where they have few preconceptions about the nature of a problem or the best way to solve it. In these cases a theory can be highly influential, as it can in others where the decision-maker recognizes the limitations on his own understanding and feels the public considers the matter one on which the experts know best. The degree to which a particular subject is considered technical may, of course, vary over time and in different places. Inflation is usually considered a technical problem; the alleviation of mental illness sometimes is and sometimes is not; and fluoridation of water supplies, which sounds offhand like a technical issue, has usually been defined as a political one. Recognizing these variations in practice, however, does not mean that causal theories will not have considerable power in many situations to define problems and solutions, nor that politicians and decision-makers will fail to seize upon the opportunity they present.

If models are to become a principal mode for use of statistics, the demands on the production system will change from largely general purpose and management data to more focused, analytical statistics. The median income of a population for example, is less

88

likely to be interesting than the average income of some specific groups over time or before and after the introduction of a new policy. Users will be less inclined to think of indicators individually without recognizing their interconnections with others. Policy will be less likely to focus on optimizing one dimension without accounting for damage in another — just as we have become painfully conscious in recent years that unemployment and inflation are inversely related when we apply our usual remedial measures.

It is important to recognize that innovations can change our whole perspective and avoid designing a statistical system or social indicator system which is too inflexible. At least we should take account of the immediately incipient innovations that are likely, and keep alert to other technologies and ways of analyzing problems that may radically alter the quality and type of statistics we demand and are able to produce.

THE DEVELOPMENT OF SURVEY SAMPLING

To understand the process of developing and implementing new methods and applying the results, we can take a brief look at the history of sampling. It is revealing in showing the interaction between the development of a method and the perceived requirements for information. Prior to the development of the survey, existing data on unemployment did not serve the purposes for which it was demanded. This demand proved a major stimulus to the development of the method. On the other hand, the existence of efficient sampling methods has opened new horizons and created further demands for data and improved methods.

The concept of sampling is probably as old as man. Even a small child knows that a taste of a vegetable is sufficient to tell him he does not like the rest of it. The idea that the sample must be representative is presumably old as well. Certainly the 18th century statisticians tried to argue that their particular sampled town was representative, but they had no criteria by which to judge. Two basic approaches have been applied. One is to use judgment about what is representative and what extreme. In the 19th century consumption studies this meant excluding the poor and the rich to survey only the working man with family. In other cases one might simply choose the town that seemed to represent the desired cross-section.

The second is to select one's sample according to some arbitrary rule, like choosing every nth unit on a list. A researcher did this for a survey of Norwegian workers as far back as 1895. The method does not provide foolproof randomization, however, unless the list itself is random. The practical idea of using a random number table goes back at least to 1906 though such a table was not generally published until 1927 (Stephan, 1948). Gradually the theory and practice of sampling was advancing though the pace was slow. A systematic sampling of 1% of workers in the British unemployment insurance system in 1923 produced administrative and policy information at a relatively low cost (Hilton), but other government bureaus did not imitate the method. A quick sampling of 1 in 1000 after the Japanese earthquake in 1923 had its accuracy confirmed when the full census results eventually arrived. Learned papers were presented at statistical meetings, but procedures were not widely adopted. The general view would remain well into the forties that a complete census was the only reliable process.

It was to require the pressures of the Depression to get sampling adopted widely as a principle for data collection and to develop the selection procedures which would make small, efficient samples possible. The sweeping new policies of the period escalated the demand for data, both to help plan programs and to evaluate the results. In addition, the WPA had to find ways to put hundreds of thousands of people to work. Statisticians and academicians were regularly enlisted as advisors for many of the new activities. The obvious answer was to give people work collecting data, and the projects were often guided by considerable expertise.

The result was a vast array of statistical studies, each of which helped advance the knowledge and practice of sampling. A huge survey of consumer purchases covered 783,000 people (the present U.S. expenditure survey covers only 17,000). A comparable National Health Survey was done, along with a series of experimental studies of unemployment in different cities. The important principle was being established that samples could be chosen hierarchically, among units, and then subunits to decrease the sample size required for a given likely error. Never again are we likely to sample 783,000 people.

The basic outlines of an efficient sampling methodology were in existence in 1940 in the context of the Monthly Unemployment Survey*. Improvements were made in the forties and even fifties in

---

* Later the Current Population Survey (CPS).

the method of drawing the sample for greater accuracy (Hansen and Hurwitz, 1944) at the same or less cost. Full public confidence in the method was to take much longer in coming. A difference between CPS results and the 1950 census was at first feared to indicate that the sampling method was wrong. Testing eventually showed the census to be at fault because of less skilled interviewers and a greater bias in those left out. Today well-informed people generally accept that surveys can provide accurate estimates. But it has been a long time since Quetelet proposed that probability methods could be usefully applied to population sampling, a long time since the first practical efforts to do so, and even a long time since 1940, when the full-fledged survey went into the field. It was to take time and motivation to solve the problems of drawing an economical sample and time and education for the statisticians, analysts and laymen to grasp what had happened.

A POLICY FOR INDICATORS

The U.S. has a statistical policy of deliberate laissez-faire and the encouragement of incremental growth. Minimal central control is exercized in negative ways like coordination, standardizing definitions and vetoing duplicative efforts, but no positive force exists to create new measures or get a general perspective on the statistical system and plan for its future. Centralized planning has seldom been done in the U.S., and this fact is unlikely to change. A policy which will encourage the development of indicators in more or less the same decentralized way they do now may be the most sensible, taking advantage of the modes in which statisticians have learned to cooperate with policy-makers and the reputations and expertise various agencies have built up. New agencies focusing on particular subject areas might be built on similar models. Some new institutions will certainly be required. For a start, better arrangements for Congressional oversight of data seem essential, as does an executive agency with expertise and power to formulate, produce and publish new data. Processes providing more open flow between the world of ideas and the world of politics should help speed up adoption of innovations and create the understanding necessary for effective measures and models to be developed.

Chapter IV

The Social Indicator Movement

Sometime in the 1920s the idea began to take shape that a society should produce a quantitative picture of itself and its changes. A Presidential Committee, appointed in 1929, set about the task and produced a massive report, entitled *Recent Social Trends* (1933). The work and the concept behind it are forerunners of the present social indicator movement. Statistical policy in the U.S., as the previous chapter has indicated, has been merely regulation and coordination. The unique concept behind "social trends" or "indicators" was that there should be an active, deliberate effort to select and present an array of measures of social change.

The idea was not extraordinary for 1933 though some who have recently "discovered" social indicators may be inclined to think so. A large collection of social statistics already existed, or were under consideration, including demographic data, unemployment rates, crime rates, and consumption levels. These were not just figures someone happened to gather in the course of doing something else, but measures designed to illuminate particular phenomena of social concern. Deliberate design of indicators for policy was a familiar concept.

Moreover society and life styles had been radically transformed since before the first War. The standard of living had risen dramatically. Crime was a dominant question and urban sprawl had begun in earnest. Women's suffrage, race riots, and child welfare had become issues. In retrospect, the study seems a predictable response to the situation. In a time of rapid change, specific problems and answers are not obvious, and often the reaction is to survey everything in the hope the problems will come into focus.

The Committee's report consisted of 13 monographs by eminent social scientists on such topics as race and ethnic groups, education, women, health and environment, communications, and leisure activities. If the list sounds familiar, it is not surprising, as the topics are approximately the same in present compendia of indicators. The monographs covered the authors' conceptions of principal issues and directions of change, using data where available. The Committee also produced reports on existing statistics and the systems of collection and processing, touching on such issues as confidentiality, data comparability, user accessibility, centralization of functions, the need for impartial statistical agencies, and the conflict between administrative and public interests in data. It even proposed something which we have only begun to consider seriously today, now that we have the technology, the idea that the government should keep longitudinal records of individuals as they pass through public systems like the schools or the criminal justice system.

The report had little impact. The success of its concept of defining and maintaining a complete, coherent set of social measures for public analysis depended on the existence of a central planning function. Indeed, the Committee recommended developing one. In 1933 the time was ripe, as suddenly the national government was called upon to provide for massive new needs the states could not fill. Roosevelt did establish the National Resources Planning Board in partial response to the recommendation, but preferred to keep power to himself, giving the Board only advisory responsibilities. The Central Statistical Board, established in the same year, was not in any better position to take positive action.

Although during the war much official statistical activity had to turn to the immediate needs of mobilization and scarcity, the social indicator idea did not die. The 20th Century Fund compiled a vast study of "America's Needs and Resources", which it later repeated (Dewhurst, 1947 and 1955). They were massive volumes of data, and analysis on trends in such areas as consumption, income, housing, and medical care. In the United Nations, international meetings and discussions about levels of living defined them in a broad sense including many dimensions, and comparable to the 1974 term, "quality of life" (U.N., 1954). The measures were intended as a counterfoil to the exclusive focus on economic growth of developing countries.

These continuing efforts suggest how fundamental is the need in modern society to measure itself and find out what direction its life is moving. It is a simple, inchoate kind of purpose. The authors of these compendia did not know precisely how the data might be used, but they felt they would somehow help to improve society. The philosophy was empiricist: "We know certain situations are unsatisfactory. If we collect a lot of data maybe we will know just what those things are and have an idea what to do."

ORIGINS OF THE CURRENT MOVEMENT

When the idea of social trends revived in the U.S. in the 1960s it was, to begin with, motivated by concerns almost as unfocused as before. This time, however, the idea caught on, and it has evolved into many lines of inquiry. The setting was more appropriate for systematic social measurement than before, and now the movement has developed a momentum which it is unlikely to lose. Some nations have already begun regular production of compilations of social indicators and international organizations are pressing forward with projects which will produce increasing social statistics in developing countries. The U.S. government, and private foundations have committed millions of dollars to research on social indicators. Scholars in virtually every field of social science and professional practice are giving explicit attention to indicators and holding discussions in meetings about them. A recent bibliography (Wilcox, 1972) found over 1,000 articles and books pertinent to the subject. To put the present volume in perspective, it is worthwhile to look at the meaning and reasons for this flourishing social indicator movement.

The recent interest in social indicators was triggered by a rethinking of priorities in American society in the late 1950s and early 1960s. Earlier Russian successes in space had led to a massive U.S. space program and concentration on scientific research and education. President Eisenhower appointed a commission to study national goals (1960). NASA commissioned a study of the impact of the space program on society, which resulted in a book which popularized the term "social indicators" (Bauer, 1966). To pursue "second-order consequences", the unforeseen effects on the broad range of social, political, and economic life would require a broad set of measures, rather than simply those derived for particular, previously agreed-upon problem areas.*

---

* A statement by the Committee on Space Efforts and Society explained this view lucidly (American Academy of Arts and Sciences, 1963).

Although the study group did not have the resources to do the vast data gathering project that was implied (Bauer, 1969, pp. 7—10), a book of essays on problems and purposes of making social measurements emerged, entitled *Social Indicators*. It was not long before the phrase became a familiar catchword, and an umbrella under which a wide assortment of interests was to gather. In particular, it fitted well with the developing interest in and commitment to potentially far-reaching social programs in the period. Soon after the book's publication, President Johnson set up a group in the Department of Health, Education, and Welfare to "develop the necessary social statistics and indicators ... With these yardsticks we can better measure the distance we have come and plan for the new way ahead". And a year later, in 1967, a bill was filed in the U.S. Senate to set up a system of social accounts.

Thus the present social indicator movement began, like the earlier efforts, as a general groping for a handle on problems still only vaguely perceived, at a time of questioning of basic national values. The original purpose was simply to describe society quantitatively along various dimensions. It was analogous to the idea of a doctor giving a check-up. He would check temperature, white count, breathing, and a number of other factors that he had some reason to suspect would be associated with ill health. He would hope that if there were an illness, at least one indicator would show some peculiarity. On the other hand, to decide what course to take, he would have to take a number of indicators into account in some complicated and often intuitive way. This medical analogy is appropriate because a diagnosis is often the product of experience rather than well-evolved theory. Certainly social theory is not yet well-developed at any practical level, and social diagnosis proceeds in an exploratory and intuitive fashion.

Despite grand phrases that soon appeared about the possibilities of using indicators for forecasting, analysis, prediction, understanding causes, and evaluating policy, the original idea was only suited to this general check-up kind of purpose. The theories and the political processes permitting the choice and use of the data for more specific purposes had not been thought through. Enthusiasts of indicators foresaw, however imprecisely, that social data could contribute to solving some specific problems. These early writers tended to promise much for indicators that they could not readily deliver. The achievement of fundamentally new modes of thinking takes a long time and ideas only gradually become understood and put to use. Unfortunately "oversell" was somewhat to discredit the idea of social indicators among policy-makers, who looked for immediate impact. They failed also to recognize that measures alone do not provide answers or settle issues. The problem definition, analysis and commitment to action would have to evolve along with indicators if they were to make a difference.

Today the impetus created by the conception of social indicators has dispersed through the social sciences and taken many new, almost unrecognizable guises, all concerned with the improvement of social measurement in analysis. Some have been concerned with measures themselves, others with the analytic structure into which they fit, and still others with their policy implications. The broad interest in indicators for general societal monitoring continues alongside the others. Although its generality may be too great for it to have any identifiable policy impacts, it may be useful as a starting point, a way of arousing interest in particular areas and opening up discussion from a self-perpetuating consideration of the problems we already recognize.

ECONOMIC INDICATORS AS A MODEL FOR SOCIAL INDICATORS

Another idea behind the original social indicator work besides this general pulse-taking one is reflected in the term "social indicator". 1963 and 1964 were years of tremendous success for economic indicators. Economists using indicators (and models) prescribed a tax cut to revive the sagging economy, and President Kennedy took their advice. This somewhat counterintuitive proposal, about which many were dubious, seemingly had the intended effect, as GNP increased by something close to the predicted amount. It was not a great conceptual leap to say that social measures could also be indicators and help "rationalize" social policy in a similar way. Indeed one of the pioneers in social indicators, Bertram Gross, visualized a whole system of social accounts analogous to economic accounts (Bauer, 1966, Chapter 3). Two major obstacles to the implementation of the idea did exist — one that social theory was not as developed as economic theory and the other that no institutions existed for social advice, planning and control as they did in the economic sphere. However, the analogy has been useful in suggesting approaches and frameworks to begin to address the general problem of improving social measurement.

96

In addition, the relative ease of analysis for economic objectives in part due to the indicators was giving economic criteria what many felt was too high a priority. We were solving the problems we could measure or set targets for and ignoring those we could not. We were maximizing GNP but probably not social output. We were producing more things but also more pollution and perhaps more disorder and dissatisfaction. Gross termed it "economic philistinism".

For those who demand immediate results from social indicators it is worthwhile to note that economic indicators began in the 1920s. Some specific indicators existed before then, like price indices and employment measures, but in the twenties the National Bureau of Economic Research (NBER) amassed hundreds of economic measures, and followed them over time. The object was to predict the movement of the business cycle by identifying the leading indicators. They were eventually able to provide some short-term forecasts about downturns and improvements, although they could not use the measures to suggest or predict the results of policies. The sophisticated use of a subset of economic indicators to make precise predictions of the outcomes of policies, was to await the development of econometric models on the basis of Keynesian theory. This was 30 to 40 years after the creation of the economic indicator system.

INDICATOR WORK — A TYPOLOGY

While any effort to categorize or generalize on a subject as complex as the social indicators work is bound to oversimplify, it is necessary if one is to get any perspective. Many of those who claim interest in indicators are actually beginning with entirely different problem definitions, objectives, and methodological context or inclination. The result is that someone who looks at indicators from one vantage point may feel that another's proposals or solutions are obviously wrong, when in fact they may not be in the other person's frame of reference at all.

CREATING A COMPENDIUM OF MEASURES

One mode, which is most recognized as a social indicator effort, is to regard the problem as one of choosing or designing the best set of measures for a society. The precise uses for the measures normally are undefined; the principal effort is rather to determine what problem areas or aspects of society are important and then how best to measure these. The planning seldom extends beyond publication of the measures. The use of the statistics becomes a problem for someone else, or a problem that will solve itself. Sometimes there is an implicit assumption that the mere existence of well-chosen measures will be enough to assure their use.

There are a number of steps, however, in this process, selecting the topics, analyzing the issues and trends, assessing available data, and devising new measures, and the various efforts have emphasized different ones. The HEW report (U.S. Department of Health, Education and Welfare, 1969) begins with seven broad categories like income, public order and learning, and devotes most of its attention to analyzing what the principle existing indicators suggest about the directions of change. It takes no stands on the issues and makes no specific recommendations for how to make the next steps. It was a disappointment therefore to government activists hoping for answers and definite statements. But if the report had tried to do much more, it would certainly have been premature in terms of the thinking about problems, policies, and processes of integrating the data into the decision-making system.

A later U.S. study, intended as a follow-on to the HEW report (U.S. National Goals Research Staff, 1970), had almost no numbers. Raymond Bauer, the consulting director, recognized the enormity of a task of choosing indicators or making projections on a wide range of topics with a small staff and only 7 months. He chose to organize the book as a series of essays on various problem areas with the common theme of how to combine growth with other goals. It is the kind of preliminary discussion that is needed before we can settle on what to measure (and what to aim for), but its immediate impact was slight.

Privately sponsored studies attempted similar, but more ambitious things. The Russell Sage Foundation sponsored two major compendia of essays on various aspects of social change in American society, one dealing with structural and institutional changes in topics like knowledge, labor force, population and leisure (Sheldon and Moore, 1968), and the other (Campbell and Converse, 1972), with similar topics but focusing on subjective measures. The essays, which discussed trends, issues, data, and analytic approaches, were all written by experts in their fields and were frequently perceptive summaries of basic questions. However, they contained no common methodology or approach, and anyone

98

reading them for guidelines about how a social indicator should be designed would be mystified.

The United Kingdom in 1970 took hold of the problem a different way. The Central Statistical Office surveyed existing data and selected and published in an annual volume, *Social Trends*, the data that seemed most pertinent to the concerns of British society. They bypassed the complicated stage of defining the issues explicitly to concentrate on selecting among available statistics. France has followed suit with a similar volume (Institut National de la Statistique, 1973).* The data are largely the byproduct statistics of such programs as the Supplementary Benefit scheme or National Health. Insofar as the programs cover a large portion of the relevant population, they are reasonably indicative of the state of society.

The figures appear with some description of their sources but no further explanation or analysis of their implications. This idea of avoiding "theorizing" about causality even in the simplest way and never drawing the most obvious policy implications from the data is in the tradition of successful government statistical agencies everywhere. It creates an impression of impartiality. It may be a political necessity if such agencies are to ply their trade, but it is fundamentally (though seldom deliberately) deceptive to imply that such indicators are somehow passive "facts" for all to deal with as they wish. The statisticians have made selections of measures and designed the presentation format, inevitably suggesting certain problem formulations rather than others.** The very choice of measures relating to existing programs encourages the observer to think in terms of the established problem definitions and solutions and not to recognize possible new analyses. The mere design of a table involves a considerable array of choices each of which affects our perception of the nature of the problem. The statistician chooses the title of the table, the categories to apply and the relationships to feature. Unless we suppose the choices are random, we have to assume that the statistician applies his own perceptions of what is important and his own analyses of the issues.

The U.S. government has finally, in 1973 produced its social indicators volume (U.S. Executive Office of the President) much later than the others despite an early start. The reason for the

---

* See also Germany (1973), Japan (1974) and Canada (1974).
** See Chapters VIII and IX for a detailed account of the sorts of choices statisticians can make and their various implications.

delay was the greater ambition of the effort to explicitly point up issues and suggest causes. Significantly, it was not sponsored by a statistical agency, but by the OMB, which is directly and politically responsible to the White House. Even in that context, however, the effort to combine anything remotely resembling a polemic with indicators was not feasible. Measures alone or polemics alone are apparently acceptable, but the two together provide too potent a combination. After considerable work had gone into the project, the political decision was made to present only the data, without comment. The book, as it finally appeared, represents a much more selective set of measures than the others, and includes relatively more measures from focused surveys like the crime victimization or National Educational Assessment studies. These are not only more suggestive of issues and problems than unmanipulated administrative byproduct data, but they also are more appropriate as indicators of the state of society. The book also has an emphasis on visual efforts like charts, to make a more immediate impact on the wide range of readers, and not just those already tuned in to the technical questions. It is likely to have some effect on the prevailing ways that its readers think about or define public issues, but it is unfortunate that the process of putting the book together was not the open and interactive one that could produce consensus on these problem definitions. However, if we are interested in getting a discussion going about such questions, one must start somewhere. If the book helps to start a discussion, it will have served a useful purpose.

The Organization for Economic Cooperation and Development (OECD) is, however, going methodically through a mapped-out process of selecting issues, choosing topics for measurement, and designing indicators. It will be interesting to see whether this produces radically different results from the more casual approach. A first phase involved selecting social concerns common to member countries. A second phase, in progress now, is to select variables, and the third will be to choose the actual measures and, finally, to collect them (OECD, 1973a, b). Each decision is based on the results of discussion and negotiation among country representatives so that choices should represent some kind of consensus. The problem is that the process will take a long time — 10 or perhaps 20 years.

These compendia may focus attention on important topics and measures, and hopefully the efforts will merge with the analytic ones so that gaps or inadequacies of the data will be remedied. The difficulty is that, with the exception of the OECD effort, the work has no criteria for where to start, which subjects to choose, nor how to define problems. If the criterion for data selection is largely the availability of the information, or even if it is also the judgment of one, two, or a group of experts, there still is a certain arbitrariness. Even an expert's choice depends on his personal and professional perspective. For example, on a topic such as income, a sociologist might want indicators relating it to social status over the long-term to study social structure, the social psychologist might want indicators to reveal the effects of income dependency, and the economist would like to know income in relation to consumption or employment. These differences in objective will affect not only the variables they choose to examine, but also the definitions they assign to them. A measure of income requires a decision about what sources and types of benefit will be included as well as about what period will be considered and whether individual or family income is the object.

This problem of choice cannot be solved by simply limiting indicators to matters of known policy concern, as the time scale for developing and following measurements is far greater than it is for most policies. Moreover, many likely problem areas would have to be ignored. To choose indicators on the basis only of previously specified need would be a circular and unedifying process. This study is in part addressed to the need of thinking through some more productive process for selecting indicators.

NEW CONCEPTS AND METHODS FOR MEASUREMENT

A second approach to social indicators is to work on new methods for measuring the hard-to-quantify. These efforts are numerous and many are not labelled "social indicator design" but are simply done in the course of experimental or analytical work in one field or another. Economists work at producing measures of poverty with the aid of production functions (Morgan and Smith, 1969), sociologists search for the best proxy measure for socioeconomic status (U.S. Dept. of Commerce, 1963), and labor statisticians look for ways to measure the underemployed. Countless manipulative techniques like cluster and factor analysis are applied to data to choose indicators (UNESCO, 1972). Experimental and conceptual work is proceeding in measuring things like work and housing satisfaction, housing and neighborhood quality and in structuring indices of concepts like pollution or inequality.

This effort is important as many topics have been neglected by public policy in part because of an inability to measure them. In particular, the obverse of all familiar objective measures, the subjective issues of satisfaction, have been neglected. Some of the efforts may be criticized for being gimmicky, the result of a researcher's interest in applying a particular method rather than of a carefully thought through analysis of what was needed. On the whole, however, these explorations are a critical creative element in the production of meaningful social statistics. Unfortunately the efforts tend to occur in somewhat isolated contexts, and methodological or conceptual advances may take considerable time to be recognized by others interested in the problems.

DESIGNING FRAMEWORKS

A third kind of social indicator study begins even further back than the OECD effort, with the design of theoretical frameworks for indicators. These efforts are based on the conviction that it does not make sense to design indicators without a structure into which to fit them and through which to interpret them. One of the most interesting is embodied in a manuscript by Mancur Olson outlining the problem of incorporating what are now considered externalities (the economist's term for most social or political problems) into the conceptual framework of economic analysis. The objective is to evaluate overall performance of society, perhaps with a new general measure of social output to replace or supplement our more usual economic output measures.

The best known kind of framework is that of social accounts suggested by Gross (1966) and worked out in some detail by, among others, Terleckyj (1969), Stone for the U.N., and currently proposed for U.S. health statistics (U.S. Department of Health, Education and Welfare, 1973). The model is the vast input-output tables of economic accounting and the idea, to oversimplify somewhat, is that the inputs and outputs of social programs can be measured and laid out in a matrix showing their interactions to help determine how best to allocate scarce resources. The difficulty is to find a common metric for such diverse topics as education and health, and fill in all the elements when some are very hard to measure. Both must be done for the system to work analytically.

Others, like Kenneth Land (1972), propose that indicators should fit into a specified model of the social process. The variables and their form should be chosen because they work in some descriptive or causal model. One desirable result of such a rule is that movements in the indicators would not have to be evaluated in isolation, but could be jointly interpreted with movements in the other phenomena to which they are connected. Wrong interpretations should decrease and certainly the behavior of the measures will help to confirm or deny the correctness of the model. Most interpretations of indicator movements are based on some implicit model in any case, but an explicit one is easier to examine and reject. Unfortunately, there are few adequate models for significant issues. Population questions are among the few exceptions as most of the important measures do fit into demographic models.

All these approaches share certain virtues and difficulties. It is true that one cannot interpret individual pieces of data without some framework nor rationally decide what information out of the infinite possibilities to collect without some general guide. However, to posit a completed framework first can put an unrealistic strain on data production capacity. If one has to wait for this to do any analysis, the wait may be very long indeed. Moreover, theorizing about structure without much application of data to problems may lead an author astray from a realistic or useful approach. While my view is that such efforts are important for the long run, it is also possible that genuine, if somewhat halting, progress may be made in a more iterative way. Some partial models using available data may help us to reach the fuller models and more respectable level of analysis.

REPLICATION

Replication studies represent a fourth kind of social indicator effort, with yet another perspective. The argument is that social indicators are supposed to measure social change but that really we know very little about how to do that. Most studies have looked at one-time surveys, not at long-term time series data. What is needed is a set of measures collected in a carefully controlled way over time. To save time, the effort is to replicate studies that have already been done at least once. The purpose is both to learn more about how to collect and interpret indicators over time and more about the social processes themselves. A prominent example of such an effort has been described in a recent volume entitled Social Change in a Metropolitan Community (Duncan et al., 1973).

The orientation so far has been one of sociology and basic research, as it addresses the issues in a broad way rather than one aimed at a policy. Though such basic research can certainly provide the foundation for problem definitions and policy ideas, the topics involved are those which happen to interest the researchers and seem amenable to quantitative study. There is no deliberate effort to fit the indicators into a whole set of social indicators. The disciplines themselves provide a sufficient framework for the effort. The precise selection of the measures is relatively less important than the study of the results over time and the design of the indicators is likely to be more pragmatic than ideal. Thus while such studies are important and should feed into work on devising total systems of indicators, they do not address many of the general issues that are pertinent to such efforts.

This method seems an unexceptional way to build a foundation for future indicator collection and analysis methods. One hopes that the findings will make their way into wider practice and government statistical policy. It will be unlikely to happen without a deliberate strategy, however, and it is to be hoped such will emerge.

OTHER OBJECTIVES FOR INDICATORS

A number of other concerns often come under the heading of social' indicators reflecting a variety of different methodological issues and objectives, some of which are not well thought through, as much of the work is speculative. There are those interested in indicators for forecasting or prediction, or futurology, for example. While these terms may imply any number of specific kinds of analyses, forecasting is likely to be some kind of trend extrapolation. Prediction more often implies a warning of a unique event or results of an intervention. Futurology is the study of alternative futures, often in the long-range. Each of these modes has its context and purpose and demands quite different forms of data — so different that to term them all indicators can be highly confusing. For example, forecasting requires long time series and aggregated data, while prediction may require more focused data fitted into well-defined models, and exploratory, wide-ranging indicators.

Analysts and policy-makers often demand that social indicators be designed for the evaluation of policies and programs and perhaps the measurement of performance. Such analysts want measures that can be related to programs. This view is partly a misinterpretation of the idea of social indicators and creates some confusion. Indicators that are collected regularly over time, on a general population (the usual kind meant in discussion), are not useful to tell us whether particular public actions have or have not had an effect. Such indicators can give us an idea whether things are improving generally along the dimensions that interest us, but cannot provide evaluations of specific programs. Evaluation requires specific analytic structure, controlled conditions, and special data collection before and after on the target population and on a control group. A change in the general population can be influenced by many other factors than the policy, and a rise or decline cannot be attributed to the policy unless the affected group is isolated and the data collected to correspond closely in timing to policy impacts.

Performance or output measures may indeed be more significant indicators than many we now use, but this does not imply that they are the only appropriate indicators. We also need measures related to causality and to inputs if we wish to make applications to policy. We need, not only measures of performance like community health, but also measures that allow us to associate them, however vaguely, with the instruments we use like the number of doctors, or hospitals per capita.

Data banking, the collection and filing by computer of data, is often associated with the concept of social indicators. The problem that interests such researchers is the difficulty of getting access to the vast quantities of existing data, particularly in its raw form. Data banks can make access easy and make it possible to put together a wider variety of tabulations for analysis. Whatever the merits of this form of research, it does not seem useful to think of it as social indicators as it innately involves no selectivity and no concept of what the data is for. If some social indicators emerge from this effort, it will be because someone with more specific interests has worked with the system to create them.

Although these efforts are motivated by an interest in improved measurements for social analysis, each represents an attempt to get hold of the problem in a different way. The starting points are different, problem definition, emphasis, and criteria for success all differ. It is not surprising that in recent years there has developed some controversy among these researchers as to just what an indicator was and the appropriate strategy for its selection and use. But much of the controversy is beside the point if one accepts each of the efforts in the terms in which it is done. Most of them can feed back into a general effort to get better overall measures, and many will also lend strength to studies in a wide range of disciplines and subjects.

INDICATORS IN USE

The last category is small and heterogeneous. It includes those who are primarily interested in indicators in their political and organizational context. For these analysts the problem is how to design information and institutions for its collection, dissemination, and use in decision-making. The topic is not so much the characteristics of information as the process by which it is generated and used and its potential effect on decisions.

Although interest in the politics and institutional framework of information is rapidly developing, only a few major studies have addressed any part of the problem. Topics that have been explored are, for example: the types of intelligence function within organizations and the effectiveness with which they can inject information into decision-making (Wilensky, 1967); the impact on media, interest groups, the public, and the politicians of a statistical and analytic study of the Negro family (Rainwater and Yancey, 1967); the use of scientific information by the public in water fluoridation controversies (Crain et al., 1969) the difficulties of getting community leadership to accept quantitative indicators of school output (Wynne, 1972); information use by legislators (Beckman, 1971, Barker and Rush, 1970) and by the President (Flash, 1965 and Lyons, 1971); and newsmen as gatherers and filterers of information (Carter, 1958 and Hale, 1968). At least one analyst is attempting to look at a broad range of political aspects of indicators, but the field itself remains relatively unexplored (Henriot, 1970, 1971).

As for practical efforts to develop indicators within a context of their use or along with a set of institutions for their use, there are relatively few. They include two efforts in the U.N. and one in the U.S. Senate. The two U.N. efforts are relatively small, but are both working in slightly different ways towards similar goals of finding indicators that will help redirect some policies of developing countries and the international organizations that influence them. Neither is simply trying to design indicators on a theoretical level, but both are working pragmatically with researchers and analysts in the countries themselves. Both have a strategy of design for indicators, as well as some strategy of implementation and objective for use.

106

Currently organizations such as the World Bank and UNCTAD give loans and aid to nations at least in part in relation to their performance on certain indicators. For example nations ranking among the lowest 25 in GDP (Gross Domestic Product), literacy levels, and percentage urban population are eligible for special aid. International loans tend to be given for projects which are seen to be likely to increase GDP. Clearly such a practice is likely to influence the direction of planning and priorities in such countries, but not always in the way which makes most sense for the country in terms of its own internal problems. One answer may be to develop new indicators that will produce different results.

One effort in UNRISD (1973) involves exploratory research to develop measures growing out of local realities rather than convenient national aggregates. For example, national school enrollment figures may conceal the real problem of attendance at harvest time in rural areas. In UNESCO (1973) another is concerned with promoting the use of new sets of aggregate indicators that lead toward or suggest different analyses than those in current use. They hope to expand the concept of GDP to include more on human relative to physical resources and to explore new concepts that will mesh with the framework of economic planning, but contribute to altered priorities in the direction of social programs.

Though one may find fault with certain aspects of either of these projects, they are worthwhile attempts to design and implement new measures to achieve some policy ends. They are relatively small efforts compared to many others in the U.N. and elsewhere. They lack the glamor and imaginative appeal of massive data banks or glossy books of social indicators, but they seem to me to be on a useful track.

In the U.S. legislation proposed several times since 1967 by Senator Mondale* also is an effort to confront the question of getting indicators into use. The proposals have dealt, not with the

---

* The bills include
Full Opportunity and Social Accounting Act, S.483, in 1967 with hearings before the Senate Committee on Government Operations, the
Full Opportunity Act, S.5, in 1969, hearings before the Senate Committee on Labor and Public Welfare, the
Full Opportunity and National Goals and Priorities Act, S.5, in 1971, hearings before the Senate Labor and Public Welfare Committee, the
Full Opportunity and National Goals and Priorities Act, S.5, in 1973.
The last three bills all passed the Senate.

design of measures, but with the institutions for their promulgation and use by Congress and the Executive, setting up a Council of Social Advisors parallel to the CEA and an annual social report. This will be discussed in more detail in Chapter X, but at this point we should note that though it received enough support to pass the Senate, it never had support from either a Democratic or Republican Administration nor a hearing in the House.

PERSPECTIVE OF THIS BOOK

This study attempts to do what no one has thus far — to look at the entire process of indicator design and use as a piece to find out how the requirements of one may affect the other. The purpose is to try to identify some of the interactions that may occur, the kinds of institutions and styles of information production and dissemination that have worked in the sense of producing acceptable information that plays a role in public decisions. It will look at how the character of data gathering and analysis affects the resulting indicators and the ways indicators are regarded, the types of uses and misuses and their feedback on the design of measures. It will also explore how indicators have become part of decision-making processes and how it may be possible to institutionalize measurement efforts and use of such information.

The object is to define some of the problems, steps and pitfalls in designing indicators which may have an impact. It defines indicators as political and social phenomena as well as technical outputs of social science and recognizes that the mere collection and presentation of data does not assure its use or usefulness. The study is based on the premise that data are most likely to be used and beneficial in public decisions where their collection and design were done in relation to a purpose and theory about the nature of certain public problems. Moreover it is only likely to be used when organizational structures and institutions have been created to mesh with real decision processes. In short, the contention of this book is that design of social indicators is something that cannot be considered in isolation from their application in decision-making nor from the prevailing perceptions of public problems. On the contrary, in the cases of measures widely accepted as satisfactory, the design and application process are at least to some degree integrated.

108

Chapter V

Method and Assumptions of the Study

The two interrelated contentions of this book are that the way we measure things does make a difference to the way we think about problems, and that the design and production of measures must therefore be integral to the processes of public choice. If we wish to have control as a society over what we do and maximize opportunities for choice, we should incorporate the problem definition process into our analyses and decision-making. As measurement is a key factor in this, as well as in many of the ultimate ways we implement our plans, it follows that we should try to understand and control the choice and design of indicators.

Many of the characteristics we want in a measure depend on how it functions in the context of public decision-making and what kind of process we want. Information provides a critical lubricant to decision-making and its quality makes a difference to its effectiveness. Good decision-making can of course be judged by good outputs. It is virtually impossible, however, to agree on such judgments. An outcome desirable to one group may not be to another. The seemingly simple answer of judging a policy on the basis of whether it produces the intended results does not work either as, normally, intentions are ambiguous, if mentioned at all, and they tend in any case to change in the course of implementation.

Therefore the criterion I will apply to define good decision-making is informed decision-making, where all those who have a potentially useful perspective on the problem or a necessary role in the decision can participate with accurate, commonly understood information relevant to their concerns. In different political systems, views of who has a legitimate analytic or decision-making role may differ, but this makes no difference to the basic principle that those with a role should be talking in terms of similar high quality information. The use of such information will still not necessarily produce ideal results even in the terms of the participants, as they may not be able to put the pieces together well nor to find a satisfactory way of making tradeoffs or going through the political and social process of choice. It does seem evident, however, that to try to do any of these things in the absence of information or with ambiguous information or information in dispute is even less likely to produce the desired benefits.

The following propositions about good decision-making processes seem relevant to the qualities we will look for in indicators and the steps by which they should be designed:

— Participants can agree on some basic concepts and facts, and go beyond these to consider issues and values.
— Information is appropriate and sufficient to analyze at least the simplest level of the problem, but preferably more.
— Problem definition is done deliberately and with a degree of consensus.
— Available information does coincide with perception of issues and analyses.
— Communication among participants is good.
— Information is available to participants so they may take appropriate stands and make their arguments effectively.

Following closely from these propositions we can posit some general criteria about what makes a good indicator to use in public decisions:

— The measure must be pertinent to questions of concern.
— The concepts underlying the measures must be clear and agreed upon.
— The measure must relate to the concept which it is assumed to, and do so in a well-understood way.
— The methods to produce the measure must provide reliable results, measuring what they purport to without hidden or unexpected bias.
— The measure must be understandable and understood in its concept and limitations.
— It must be known to essential participants.
— Major parties to discussion on opposite sides must accept the measure.
— It must be appropriate to its uses.
— It should relate to more complex analytical models.
The fundamental assumption of this book is that to achieve

these qualities we cannot develop indicators in isolation from actual processes of public action and decision. We need rather to find ways of integrating the technical requirements of data collection and analysis with political realities and public perceptions.

Hopefully this study will provide convincing evidence that the assumption is well founded. In a sense it is the hypothesis that these studies of indicator development and use are intended to test. However, I am dubious of such formal sounding statements of research design. One tends often in social research to find what one is looking for. A hypothesis is somewhat self-fulfilling, especially where many factors are causally involved. However one hopes that at least the completely wrong notions will become obvious in the analyses, that partly wrong ones will be altered, and that the case will be duly convincing for the more satisfactory ideas.

CAPITALIZING ON EXPERIENCE

The principle research effort behind this book has been to examine the origin, development, use, and evolution of some indicators with which we have had considerable experience. The measures examined are primarily ones that have a general role, though they may have been originally designed for some specific purpose. They are of interest to the public and those who set broad policy, and therefore they already have a few of the desirable features of indicators in that they are known, pertinent to questions of concern and at least partially accepted. The study will examine the extent to which the measures meet some of the other criteria, and look for explanations for their success or failures through comparisons among them and with the aid of some basic observations about the nature of measurement and of decision-making.

Attention will be focused on the processes through which measures which meet these criteria may be produced as well as on the qualities of such measures themselves and their applications in decision-making. A basic hypothesis of the book is that measures which are used with some degree of effectiveness along the dimensions listed grow at least in part out of perceived needs and fit some prior conception of a problem. Moreover, their methods and concepts evolve in response to changing requirements of society.

111

Equally, the measures themselves affect the perceptions of problems and their existence may open up possibilities for uses which will require some restructuring of decision-making processes. This interactiveness, with measures affecting processes, perceptions, and values and perceived needs affecting the measures in turn, is essential to a measure's utility.

Clearly the definitive testing of a particular proposition requires a structured study, such as a set of carefully selected comparisons or an experimental study where the presumed relation is introduced in a test situation and not in a control. To *prove* measures do change perceptions, or that interactiveness of measure and environment makes a difference, a study would have to explore similar situations, with and without measures, or situations with an open interactiveness and ones without. Occasionally one can take advantage of the introduction of an innovation to do a quasi-experiment (Campbell, 1969) or existing comparable, but slightly different situations (Blalock, 1961). I have tried to bring out the similarities and differences where possible and identify key factors, but it is unclear that one can find sufficiently comparable situations to do a very structured study. Social experiments are time-consuming, expensive and difficult to set up and conduct without so many intervening influences that they cannot be interpreted as experiments.

Moreover, to take either of these approaches to a problem requires some very specific propositions for testing. One might test the question of whether complex or aggregate measures serve the requirements of an open, informed policy process better than simple unitary measures by looking at numerous examples of each. Or one might test whether lobbying groups gain or lose power after the introduction of new measures into decision-making by looking at some before/after situations. Such questions are potentially interesting and useful to those planning for better public information. But they might also turn out to be uninteresting or unimportant. If one sets out in a structured study simply to test one of these, one is unlikely to discover anything else.

At this stage in the development of an understanding of the relation of information to decision-making an open-ended study seems more appropriate. This is why I have chosen to look at past and current experience in a broad way. The study does explore some selected comparisons and does proceed with some hypotheses in mind (one is unlikely to discover anything if one does not look for it), but its objective is exploration of some comparatively uncharted ground. The conclusions from such a study are not definitive but hopefully may suggest further questions for research. The observations may fit with experience of others and help them to identify patterns that may be common to other situations or define more usefully the problems they confront. An account of what we have done so far cannot of course tell us what to do next or predict the effects of our efforts. Each event in the past or future is unique and depends on unique circumstances. However, history can show us what has been possible, and what has created difficulty.

After years of thought and proposals, the social indicators movement still has little to show in terms of new indicators in use or new systems for indicator production or use. We could benefit by examining some indicators that have been widely used, particularly if we do so with the objective of understanding:

— how and why they came into existence in the particular form they did,

— under what circumstances they came to be known and used, and

— how their use, misuse, or perceived failings came to bring about changes in the design or other aspects of the measure.

While these accounts will not provide a blueprint for the future, they are likely to contain much that can help us to shape the future better than we now seem able to. For example, we do not even know *one* way to produce new measures that will be used, much less the best one. We can perhaps identify some obvious mistakes and begin to think through strategies to assure both development and use of indicators in particular environments. If history is to help with this it must be structured and interpreted, and this book tries to provide a coherent explanation for events. While it may be wrong in some respects, hopefully it can provide a working hypothesis for others and some organization to an account of past experience.

MODELS AND MEASURES

A basic guide to the interpretation of events is my view of the nature of measurement and the importance of prior models in dealing with public problems. This view integrates many of the seemingly disparate questions and conclusions of this study. Measures and models are inseparably intertwined* in a way few social analysts explicitly recognize. The interrelationship is a central problem of designing measures for use since use is also integrally related to models, which may or may not mesh with measurement models.

DEFINITION OF A MODEL

At the outset I should define the term "model" as it often is used in different and specialized ways in various fields. In the terms of this book a model is any representation of reality which abstracts important elements from it and reassembles them for more convenient analysis and manipulation. It may be a 100-equation, mathematical formulation of the workings of the economy, a cardboard mock-up of a proposed shopping center, a hypothesis about the causes of poverty, or even an idea about how to roast a piece of beef. A model can be called a theory, though usually that term is reserved for the more complex and explicit models which purport to define causal relations.

Models exist on a continuum from very simple and intuitive to highly complex and abstract. However, it is models ranging from middle range social theories to the implicit guides for everyday actions which are most pertinent to the kinds of indicators we will be examining. The most complex models currently available to help the formulation or interpretation of indicators are those dealing with such problems as how social stratification occurs, the determinants of minority group relations. Other more specific models might be of the influences on a Congressman's vote or motivations for worker's job choices. Such models are in some cases well specified in mathematical terms, but they may as often exist only in verbal form. For example the statement "A Congressman votes to please his constituency primarily, and when he does not know their views, he relies on trusted colleagues" is a model providing the basis for a prediction of the behavior of a Congressman. It may not be correct, but it does provide a guide for action if one wants to influence Congress.

All purposeful action is based on a model of some sort, no matter how inexplicit or imperfectly defined. One must have some

---

* For a lucid discussion of many of these points on concepts, measures and models in social analysis, see Kaplan (1964), especially Chapters II and V, and Blalock and Blalock (1968).

114

presumption about the result of one's actions. This requires deciding which features of the environment are important, and how they may interact and respond to possible actions one may take. Even if one's perception is wrong or very simplistic, it amounts to using a model of one's environment. A normative model describing, at least partially, the desirable end state is also involved. Thus the cook who sets the oven at a certain temperature and cooks a roast longer the larger it is, is using a model which says, perhaps, "meat cooked at this temperature does not dry out" or "bigger pieces of meat take longer to be heated" and one which defines the color of the meat if done to perfection. The models may be simple, based on experience or possibly on some understanding of thermal mechanics, but without them action makes no sense. Even turning the knob of the oven requires a model which says this will cause the heat to come on.

MEASURES INTERSECT WITH MODELS

Thus, in public decision-making each participant has some model, though it is usually implicit and often concerns quite different aspects of a problem than someone else's model. It may be a simple forecast, "the future will resemble the past", or a complex analysis involving the non-intuitive conclusions of many researchers. The important point is that these models can be influenced and shaped by the measures available, as Chapter I suggests. The measures available, on the other hand, may simply fail to coincide with the models at all and be unused or confusing and disruptive to discussion.

The indicators cannot simply be absorbed into models of decision-makers if they are not well-chosen because measures themselves are based on models which may not mesh with those of would-be users. Even the most straightforward of measures depends on some assumptions and on how one defines a problem — which brings us full circle. Imagine, for example, a classroom full of chairs and tables. The professor would count the number of places to sit, the janitor would count the pieces of furniture in categories demanded for his inventory, perhaps the number of each type of chair or table according to which department owns it, and a junk dealer might simply want the weight of scrap metals and wood.

Even to classify the simplest item requires a model and a purpose. To identify a chair, for example, you must know that a chair is for sitting and have some idea how people sit and what is the range of items others accept as chairs. There may be some border-line cases like benches, stools, and couches, and the way you classify them depends on whether you are setting up an elegant drawing room or just trying to find places for everyone to sit. But if you classify things according to one purpose and use the count for another, the conclusions can be misleading. Much of the data we do use for social analysis is classified for one purpose and used in some other, and we must be conscious of this. Much data is collected without any direct purpose and this too should arouse suspicion. To collect it for no particular purpose is arbitrarily or unconsciously to choose or imply a purpose. And merely to col-lect it in the first place implies some model and value judgment.

MODELS AND MEASUREMENT INSTRUMENTS

Measures also depend on models in another way. Our observa-tion of reality is mediated by many things about which we must make assumptions. Even the most direct measure, let us say a count of chairs, depends not only on our correct classification but on the light, how good our eyes are, and whether we do the counting correctly. Most indicators are likely to have been collect-ed by someone other than the user, and so we must make all the assumptions we did for our own efforts, but also assume that the enumerator understood our request and that he is neither lying nor in error in reporting. The assumptions multiply when we get to information that must be elicited by interview, as the oppor-tunities for misunderstanding or deception increase. To interpret the results we must have a model defining how the subject will react to the questions. The model may just be that he will react as we would, but it is a model nonetheless and can be wrong.*

We measure many items even more indirectly, and, accordingly, a more elaborate model must intervene. We may measure only a portion of the phenomenon and assume it varies in the same way as the phenomenon.** For example, using annual income as a measure of poverty includes an implicit assumption that income,

---

* Basic references on the potential for error in assumptions about instruments of data collection, and on some strategies for alleviating the problem are: Webb et al. (1966) and Morgenstern (1963).
** An excellent typology of the ways measures can fail to represent the intended phenomenon is provided by Etzioni and Lehman (1969).

116

wealth, needs, and expectations for the future are all approximately similar in individual cases. The choice of measure depends on our model of what poverty is, what is bad about it and what causes it (Townsend, 1970). Most phenomena that are of concern to social policy are difficult to define precisely and require an extensive model. To measure the number of people who are ill, for example, we must have a model of illness and a model defining how the observer will recognize it. Sometimes we want to measure an abstract concept never directly observable, such as social status. No one has ever seen it and the only reason we suspect it exists is that it is an explanation for some observed patterns of behavior. The attempt to measure it requires an entire social theory, and the only way to test the result is with the aid of that theory.

OPERATIONAL MEASURES

One of the pitfalls of measurement which is done empirically without reference to theory has been termed "operationism in reverse". Operationism is the effort to measure something without defining precisely what it is or perhaps even knowing if it exists. One suspects there is a phenomenon of some importance, perhaps something one needs to estimate for an analysis, and one collects and structures data in various ways to find some combination that behaves in the way the phenomenon might. An operational measure is often an essential starting point for an indicator where no other is likely to be available.

The IQ is the best known example of an operational measure. It is based simply on the results of asking people a set of more or less arbitrarily selected questions and it is widely thought to reflect in some way the concept of intelligence. Although that concept has yet to be defined, the IQ measure does predict achievement to some degree (though far from perfectly) and may well have some bearing on a phenomenon that could be called intelligence. However, it is still not established what phenomenon if any, the measure does correspond to so it is difficult to interpret the results of its application. In fact, the tremendous dispute over the relationship of IQ scores to heredity and race is partially due to the basic difficulty of defining what underlying phenomenon IQ reflects and in what way.

The danger in using operational measures, particularly in analyses of public problems, is that their divorce from theory or models makes them difficult to interpret as a guide to action or an aid to understanding. The worst problem, however, is that we tend to assume the measure does represent the concept we are concerned about, such as intelligence, and in the absence of a good definition we, by default, accept the measure as the totality of the concept. We then proceed to assume the concept behaves in whatever way the measure happens to and contains no subtleties that the measure does not. If we had defined a concept first and tried to measure it second, we would be far more aware of the ways in which the measure fails to capture the concept. We would also be more conscious of the peculiarities of the measure's behavior due to the measurement instrument. These are important caveats to keep in mind as the unrecognized peculiarities can lead to serious distortions in analyses and choices of public actions.

SCALES FOR MEASUREMENT

Models and problem definitions also enter into the basics of measurement when we chose a scale. One may not recognize one is using a scale when simply counting heads, but to do so implies a decision that each individual is equal to one unit. There are other choices, however. In some societies some individuals clearly count for more than others, and for the analyses of some types of problems individuals may be more usefully weighted by the amount of money they have or their distance from a particular facility.

For other topics scaling issues are more obvious. To make an index which aggregates, say sulphur dioxide pollution with particulate pollution, you need a model (perhaps no more than a normative one) defining how much of the first is equivalent to how much of the second. If one is measuring waiting time in a hospital, the first hour might well be assigned a different weight than the fifth hour. It depends on your model of how harm to a patient is related to waiting time. Money has a diminishing marginal utility as one becomes richer. Many social phenomena that we count in units corresponding to common functional usage may be more appropriately counted on some other scale. It depends on what we want to learn and why. There is no particular reason why we should accept for measurement and analysis the fact that the world happens to be divided into units like cities, or that income is normally computed in dollar units. If these concepts do not connect with our models, we may want to find new ways of dividing them and new scales.*

* On scaling and determining the dimensionality of phenomena for measurement, major works are Torgerson (1958), and Coombs (1967). There is a considerable further literature, primarily in psychometrics.

118

Finally, one has many choices about structuring and presenting data each of which depends on what one wants to show and how one believes the world is organized. One can show distributions, percentages, rates, averages, rates of change, and many others. The choice should not be considered arbitrary. A Marxist economist may look at the change in the distribution of income from upper to lower levels, whereas the market economist may look at the growth in averages. Even within the question of distribution is one that allows considerable leeway depending on what one thinks are the dynamics of income.

MEASUREMENT WITHOUT THEORY

This whole question of whether measurement without theory is meaningful or useful in economics has been debated before, but most notably in Koopmans' (1947) now classic criticism of Burns and Mitchell (1946). They amassed vast quantities of economic "indicators" which were widely used to measure the business cycle. They did not select data on the basis of any theory about the nature of the economic processes. Koopmans believed that the empirical approach had sometimes served as a partial foundation for theory, citing the example of Kepler's systematic but apparently empirically selected measurements of the positions of the planets. Koopmans said the data helped inspire Newton to formulate his laws of the attraction of matter, but he also pointed out that Newton had made use of Gallileo's experiments. Economic theory was far more developed in 1946 than physics in Kepler's time, and Koopmans asserted that the shorter and, perhaps the only, path to understanding business cycle dynamics was to incorporate the concepts and hypotheses of economic theory into the processes of observation and measurement. He argued that measurement without such theory would not further understanding or policy.

Burns and Mitchell had set out merely to describe the mechanical behavior of business cycles with their measures (time between turning points, amplitudes, etc.) and not to uncover the forces at work generating it or its effect on society. The prime objective of economic analysis, he said, was to guide policy, which would not be possible without some *explanation* of economic phenomena rather than simply an arbitrary mapping of some conveniently measurable aspects. Without explanation one could not predict the effect of a policy intervention on the movements of the variables.

119

His contentions were prophetic. A few years later, economists had selected a subset of the measures and some new ones, that would mesh with Keynesian economic theory to explain events and predict the effect of interventions. These econometric models do even simple forecasting with greater precision and less data than Burns and Mitchell required. Their business cycle mapping has not led to further theory or understanding.

Social analysis today is probably in a state somewhat comparable to economics in 1947. Although it is doubtful any social analyst is quietly producing a parallel to the comprehensive, explanatory theory of Keynes, we do have a good many lower level theories explaining more limited issues which we still do not exploit in most of our efforts at measurement. In fact, the data collected now still fits into a highly empirical tradition. It is time, however, for us to collect statistics that will help us to test a theory of the causes or effects of welfare dependency instead of simply describing welfare recipients along some obvious dimensions.

DESIGNING MEASURES FOR PUBLIC ANALYSIS

The viewpoint of this book is then that social indicators will be most useful to us if they are chosen and designed deliberately and on the basis of the best conceptions and theories we have about the dynamics of the social process. Such measures will save effort and confusion, and help us to do more sophisticated analysis and develop more sharply focused and successful policies. Creating such measures will require considerable analysis and identification of assumptions and models. Some of them will come directly from social science research, but some will only exist in primitive form in the minds of policy makers. The "scientific" analysis of many social questions is still in its infancy, but that is no reason to proceed without models — we must make do with the best we can.

Such reasoning implies that the process of measurement has to interact with the perspectives and views of participants in planning as well as with the findings of social science. Over time as theories, problems, and values change, in part no doubt because of the interpretation of the movements in an indicator, a continuing interaction is needed to produce changes essential to its continued relevance. The present study concerns mostly indicators which have had considerable use over a long period. If the above contentions are correct, then some of this interactive process will be evident in their history and their usefulness will correlate at least in part to the responsiveness of their design process to the perceptions and models that are prevalent. Though this sort of historical analysis cannot fully prove the contention, the study does provide evidence that indicators which make a difference are indicators which mesh with our models and values.

Chapter VI

Sagas of Three Indicators

Much of this book is organized around tasks and problems in indicator design and use, but it is important to be conscious of the total process into which they fit and the ways in which design considerations intertwine with policy models and uses. The discussion of each topic will try to make the context clear, but there are patterns and phenomena one can only see in an overview of the system which creates and uses an indicator. Therefore this chapter covers the origin and evolution of three long-lived and widely used indicators that will be referred to throughout the book: unemployment rates, standard family budgets and crime rates. There are basic similarities and equally fundamental differences in these stories, which can hopefully be accounted for at least in part. An appendix at the end of the book has tables describing these indicators and their chronological development.

THE UNEMPLOYMENT RATE: A SUCCESSFUL INDICATOR

The U.S. unemployment rate is currently one of the two or three best recognized and most influential indicators in the country. Its monthly oscillations receive front page attention and Presidential advisors and even Presidents feel called upon to account for its behavior — and to seek remedies for its misbehavior. The persistently high unemployment rate in 1971, in combination with the equally sticky inflation rate, were major factors in the first peacetime institution of economic controls on wages and prices in that year, and in the enactment of public employment legislation, very much contrary to the philosophy of the governing Republican party.

The monthly household survey to collect the data is one of the most elaborate and expensive in the world and it continues despite the bad news it often provides the government that sponsors it, and despite the fact that its results have often occasioned great public dispute.

Many others outside of the Presidency refer to and use the figures. Economists use them in predictive and analytic models of the economy. Congress, the media, and the public use the statistics to judge economic policy and Administration economists use them to help guide such policy broadly and to set targets for it. But the measure is not simply an economic one. It was originally designed as a social measure of people wanting work. It was less an index of the health of the economy, but more designed to assess the remedial effort needed to relieve the problem of families without income. Since its inception it has been used in connection with discussions of social as well as economic policy.

THE WILL WITHOUT THE WAY

National attention focused on the measurement of unemployment just after the First World War. The Federal government had tried to count unemployment in censuses as far back as 1880, but a sustained national commitment to measurement only began in 1921, when President Harding called a conference of business leaders to consider the problem of unemployment. The country was in a depression, and unemployment was obviously high, though there were just guesses about the numbers. A principal purpose of the conference was to inquire into the volume and distribution of "needed employment" and to recommend measures to deal with it and encourage business recovery. Economic dislocations were frequent and disruptive to business, and concern for the lot of the working man was growing, along with the labor movement. Public feeling was that worker and job should be more firmly attached, and in Europe social insurance programs for unemployment, for example, had already been enacted.

But the U.S. was not Europe and both the President and Chairman Hoover made it clear that the responsibility for remedying unemployment should not fall on the Federal Treasury and that Federal legislation for unemployment was "paternalism that will undermine the whole system". The Conference should limit itself to finding the facts that could aid businessmen to keep in business and help states plan relief programs. Even the task of information collection and analysis was not to be a governmental function. The studies that the Conference requested and planned were conducted in the 1920s with private funds (NBER, 1923 and 1929).

123

The only responsibility the Federal government accepted was to mobilize the nation's intelligence. It had often happened before that the Federal response to a social concern was to gather statistics and try to remain neutral about a policy. The commitment to some sort of employment policy, however, would be essential to the establishment of an indicator as this would require both time and money no one was yet prepared to spend.

As the Conference set to the task of measuring unemployment, they drew attention to the inadequacy of the information: whereas their Economic Advisory Committee estimated 3,500,000 out of work, exclusive of farm labor, the Commissioner of Labor Statistics had produced a figure of 5,735,000 for the Congress only two months earlier. This discrepancy led the Conference's Committee on Unemployment Statistics to do its own study of available data, producing an estimate of between 3,700,000 and 4,000,000 unemployed. In what must be one of the lowest points in the history of social measurement, the Conference *voted* on the number to announce as unemployed, choosing a suitably high range of figures to attract the nation's attention. It became painfully obvious that if responsible statisticians confronted with available data could produce estimates differing by 60%, then the data was inadequate.

The data available for unemployment statistics in the 1920s were incomplete and scattered; the total estimates were based on interpolation and guesswork about hidden biases. For example, the data consisted of 1) estimates of unemployment in 182 cities made by various local or state agencies; 2) monthly reports of the employed in a selected group of manufacturing industries collected by the BLS; 3) quarterly reports of trade union unemployment in Massachusetts; 4) estimates of reduction in mining employment based on U.S. Geological Survey data on output; 5) monthly numbers of railroad workers collected by the Interstate Commerce Commission; and 6) preliminary tabulations of the number in different occupations in the 1920 census. Obviously the estimates varied according to how much credence one gave to each source, how one adjusted for the different time periods of the data collection, assumptions about how well the data collected represented the data not collected, and the assumptions one made about what had happened to those employed in a particular occupation.

Not only were the data sketchy and the methodology undefined, but the concepts were fuzzy as well. Employment and unemployment were not precisely defined in the Conference Report, but the assumption seemed to be that the unemployed were people who had worked, but now could not find jobs. No agreement was reached on how to deal with the borderline categories (on strike, sick, old, unwilling to take certain jobs), but in some sense it was not necessary. The methods of estimating were so approximate, and the available information on sickness or job preferences so poor, that a decision would have been pointless.

The Administration, researchers and businessmen wanted the data very much but did not have a clear view of why. They certainly did not foresee the later uses. The main thought was that data could alleviate the continuous boom and bust problem by helping inform businessmen on economic conditions so they would make better production decisions. Other uses cited in 1921 for unemployment data were measuring the welfare of working classes and planning expenditures needed for relief. Accurate unemployment data was a high priority item in 1921, a focus of national attention. People in many segments of society viewed unemployment as serious and unlikely to solve itself. Most agreed data was essential to beginning the solution, but exactly how it would be used was still unclear. So the motivation existed for getting the data, and there were some potential uses, albeit vaguely defined.

Several ingredients were missing, however, which were not to come together until 1940, when the first reliable figures were obtained. First, there was no real commitment to do anything in particular about unemployment and thus little idea about how it should be defined and analyzed. Second, there was no methodology to produce even reasonably accurate data with sufficient speed to be of any use. Sampling had developed very little since the 19th century and provided no alternative to censuses or ad hoc uses of byproduct data. Third, the concepts were still too poorly defined for measurement.

From 1921 to 1930 research on the statistics continued. The NBER sponsored work and the American Statistical Association appointed a Committee in 1922 to study the problems. The issues and possibilities of unemployment measurement began to emerge. As a period it may provide a parallel to the current one for social indicators.

Congressional interest, which would play a critical role later, was awakened in 1928 when estimates of unemployment in the wake of a severe recession ranged tremendously, and the press became highly critical. Critics were claiming unemployment was about 4,000,000, far more than the Administration would admit.

The Senate Education and Labor Committee held hearings on unemployment, the first in a long series in Congress, which were to educate legislators and the public and help focus issues. No special legislation was involved; federal action on unemployment would have to await experience with the Depression. The hearings were broadly investigatory and focused in part on the various indirect methods of estimating unemployment.

The Chairman was conscious of press agitation about the quality of the figures and expressed concern that there seemed no way to resolve arguments in Congress without better data. The Committee recommended that questions on unemployment be included in the census to give benchmark data for better estimates. Most important, however, they expressed a firm principle that the opportunity to work was a fundamental right. They considered the protection of this right as the responsibility of individual members of society and employers, but the belief was to guide the design of statistics and be an incentive and continuing theme for later employment policy.

CREATING A MEASURE

The advent of the Depression assured the inclusion of unemployment questions in the census, and launched an intensive search for an adequate way to quantify unemployment. The search was to require ten years of experimentation with methods and concepts, the effort of numerous groups and individuals, and many mistakes and misjudgments before a satisfactory solution was found. Ironically, accurate national figures were never available during the period of greatest unemployment (Nathan, 1936). The massive work relief programs and unemployment insurance were enacted essentially without data on the size of the unemployment problem, much less on the characteristics of the unemployed. However, there was a rising chorus of demands for better data, and ultimately this steady pressure did produce a measure.

The questions on unemployment on the 1930 Census were the first of the many mistakes (Arner, 1933, Van Kleeck, 1931). Statisticians were unprepared with concepts or questions, despite a year's work done by an ASA committee on the problem. The Census Bureau bypassed the difficult step of defining unemployment and proceeded directly to measurement. They included questions to fit people into 7 categories, and hoped someone else would decide which were the unemployed. Unfortunately, many thought the unemployed were unknown percentages of the tabulated categories. This ambiguity was the reason for the furor when the government announced the official unemployment figures including only one of the 7 groups. The press was filled with cries of "politics" and the statistics were thoroughly discredited.

Further problems were that the questions allowed ambiguous replies, the untrained interviewers were unable to elicit accurate responses on such personal topics, and the coding and tabulation turned out to be a tremendous problem. A special check census a few months later only added to the confusion, as differences could not be attributed unambiguously either to methodological difficulties or actual changes in the population. Finally the concept that previous censuses had used, identifying the work force as those with previous gainful occupation (gainful workers) turned out to be sadly inadequate. Formerly, these data were not obviously inadequate as they had been collected for general information. Now, however, they had the specific purpose of providing a benchmark for estimating unemployment in the future, and they did not do this. They left out the young or women who were looking for their first jobs and they included the old who were already retired. Moreover, the census made no count of employment to be compared with the BLS reported totals that would be used for later estimates. The numbers were, accordingly, useless.

The next major mistake was an effort to count the unemployed via voluntary post-card registration in 1937 with predictably inadequate results (Dedrick and Hansen, 1938; Myers and Webb, 1937). This mistake had a salutary effect in convincing Congress and the public that sampling was the better way to proceed in future. Throughout the decade business organizations, labor unions, and economists had produced widely varying estimates of unemployment, based on the regular BLS employment reports and various assumptions about the number of unemployed in 1930. The estimates differed by as much as 2 million and reflected the bias of the estimates. Significantly, the government made no estimates. President Roosevelt had resisted repeated Congressional demands for an unemployment census, insisting it did not make any difference whether unemployment was 5 or 8 million. He presumably enjoyed the freedom that the lack of data gave him to pursue policies as he wished. Congress recognized this as well and finally authorized the National Unemployment Census.

Although the WPA and private groups had been gradually developing sampling methods, concepts, and interview techniques in local unemployment surveys throughout the country, neither the expert advisors nor Congress seriously contemplated depending on a sampling for information at that point. A full census was too expensive so a voluntary registration of the unemployed was selected. Researchers managed, however, to tack on a sample survey to check the post-card returns. The random selection of postal routes was not the ideal survey design, but it left little doubt that the registration results represented 70% or less of total unemployed, undercounting women and others irregularly employed, and overcounting a few enthusiastic groups like emergency workers and others who were organized and coerced to fill in the cards.

The census then settled nothing, but raised more questions, particularly as unemployment rates continued to change and even rise again. The media gave little credence to the results and disputes over figures rose to a crescendo in early 1940. The Administration had been seizing on the lowest possible figures, and the anti- New Deal business groups on the highest ones. Prominent newspaper columnists began to pick sides (see Lindley, 1940; Thompson, 1940). Finally, with the onset of war in Europe, WPA director Corrington Gill was anxious to convince Congress that unemployment was still high to maintain his agency. He responded angrily to low unemployment figures, with larger ones of his own. The data, of course, provided no assistance with the basic issues of relief policy, and confused the discussion even more.

INCEPTION OF THE MONTHLY SURVEY

Interestingly enough the WPA had already, in late 1939, quietly instituted a monthly survey of unemployment, which provided reasonably accurate national estimates and became the Current Population Survey (CPS) on which we now base our dependable unemployment figures. Doubts remained about the new procedure, however, and it received little publicity and remained unrecognized as a source of accurate information for some time. It was assumed that the 1940 Census (which contained the same questions as the survey) would give the definitive answer. There was a discrepancy between the census and survey results which cast doubt on the survey for many years until census failings were established as the source.

Although improvements were to be made in the sampling procedure and interviewing process, the survey was in fundamental respects that of today. The concepts are basically the same, and the methodological changes have been at the margin. The critical ideas were developed in the thirties by WPA researchers in combination with social scientists and statisticians. They developed the essential concept that permitted objective measurement, that of defining unemployment or employment primarily by current activity rather than a state of mind (see Table 4). In other words, the unemployed are defined as those looking for work, not just wanting it. They also developed the critical notion of a "labor force", which was the population at risk against which to compare the number of unemployed. The idea of stratified sampling was established along with the basic questionnaire and interview techniques.

The measure reflected the perspective of the Depression. It focused on active job seekers, but recognized that some would be quite reasonably discouraged and inactive. It made no effort to measure the factors that might affect the size of the labor force, as the assumption was that it would remain a fixed proportion of the population. Finally, it counted as employed all with any type of work, as during the Depression remedying partial unemployment was of far lower priority than full unemployment. These issues have only begun to come to the fore in the changing labor market of the sixties and seventies.

Ten years may seem a long time to develop a measure, but it would very likely have taken even longer if it had not been for the continued pressure of high unemployment and the peculiar situation which gave the WPA vast funding, considerable freedom to operate and an able staff. Future measures may be able to rely more on developed methodology, but the lack of sound, measurable concepts is likely to be a continuing obstacle.

The war had two main effects for the indicator. First, it deflected attention from unemployment and gave statisticians the opportunity to iron out the remaining major difficulties. When the WPA was dismantled, the survey was switched to the Census Bureau, where the experienced statisticians were put to work improving the sample (Hansen and Hurwitz, 1944). The second impact was indirect. The need for more labor in war industry led to a change in the questionnaire to uncover potential workers. Instead, however, it uncovered uncounted workers who had been previously tabulated "out of the labor force" due to vagueness in questions. An improved schedule in 1945 reducing ambiguity and removing the inactive unemployment category (which was a tiny group at the time) was the last major discontinuity in the series, giving a sharp jump of 2,500,000 in the estimates of the employed (Ducoff and Hagood, 1947; Bancroft and Welch, 1946).

1946 was the critical year for the unemployment indicator, the year when it became officially and permanently part of public policy. It was the initial step in a process which was to institutionalize the measure and make it a force on its own, highly visible and widely used. It was the year Congress passed the Employment Act, which established for the first time *a policy* for employment (not just a relief program) in the U.S. and, more importantly, the machinery to implement it. An essential part of the machinery was the requirement for the Administration to produce data on unemployment levels and give predictions about future levels and a plan for any remedial action.

Congress did its about-face for two reasons, a fear of another depression in the wake of the war, combined with a growing recognition of the implications of Keynesian economic theory that first an economy could reach equilibrium at a low level of activity, and second, government intervention could alter the equation. Sir William Beveridge (1945) had produced an influential paper defining for a popular and government audience a concept of full employment, a level of economic activity providing jobs for all but those frictionally unemployed, in transition from one job to another. Though there has always been disagreement about precisely how to define the level of unemployment corresponding to full employment, the basic idea captured the attention of the industrial countries that a government should have a target of full employment.

The Employment Act called upon the government to "use all practical means. . . to foster and promote free competitive enterprise and the general welfare, conditions under which there will be afforded useful employment opportunities, including self employment for those *able, willing and seeking to work* and to promote maximum employment, production and purchasing power".*

The statement seemed to embody the concept of unemployment measured in the survey. The Act's requirement for annual data on unemployment has meant that the report has depended on the unemployment rate from the survey for its analysis and predictions. If it diverged too far from expectations, the Administration was forced to take action. So the measure was not only to be used,

---

* Public Law 304, 79th Congress, 15 U.S.C., 1021 (italics added).

the legislation virtually guaranteed its continuance no matter how badly it might reflect on a government.

The Act also established two other institutions which were to ensure and expand the use of the measure as well as keep it under scrutiny and demand its continual improvement. One was the Council of Economic Advisors (to the President) which, according to the legislation, was to be made up of persons whose "training, experience and attainments" give them exceptional qualifications to "analyze and interpret economic developments, to appraise programs and activities of the Government and to formulate and recommend national economic policy. . .". This mandate produced council members, primarily economists, who found the data essential for the kind of analyses they would rely on and who, in addition, demanded great reliability in the data. The other group created by the Act was the Joint Economic Committee in Congress, which was first solely to evaluate the economic report, but over time was to focus on a broad range of economic policy in a way unique in the Congress. It became a redefiner of problems, providing some alternative to the more privately conducted analyses of the Council and, as a user of statistics, it became a watchdog. Its subcommittee on Economic Statistics, set up in 1954, became very expert over the years about the methods and concepts and alert to problems.

It is remarkable how this Act without establishing any new powers, but simply declaring a policy and setting up institutions to implement it, produced so significant a change in the direction and style of U.S. policy. The Act did provide for the use of a new tool, however, statistics — statistics in combination with analysis. Although social indicators had been used in policy before, their precise role was less specific and they had not been incorporated into an institutionalized framework.

Setting up the institutions alone would probably not have assured the indicator the degree of confidence and attention it came to enjoy. Other factors undoubtedly were relevant. First, the debate over defining full employment brought the indicator to center stage. It might be the level of unemployment where job seekers and vacancies were equal — but then there was no job vacancy measure. It might also be measured by the unemployment at some prosperous, non-wartime period. Most accepted this as a practical definition, but it is a continuing issue today as to what is a normal reference period and whether conditions have changed. The exact level was very important as governments would be unwilling to heat up the economy more than necessary and risk inflation.

A second important factor in gaining acceptance for the indicator was the openness of the whole process of design and use of the measure. Government statisticians published their work in professional journals, and over the years the agencies themselves published an increasing amount of information on the methods, concepts and reliability of the results. When there were problems casting doubt on the quality of the data (like the major discrepancy in the results of an old and a new sample in 1954) outside experts were called in to evaluate and report on the problem, publically.

The Budget Bureau was instrumental in setting up in 1956 the Federal Statistics Users Conference which involved principal labor and business data users in regular meetings to exchange questions and criticisms about the data. The Department of Labor, which took over the analysis and presentation of the survey results, instituted Labor and Business Research Advisory Committees, made up of analysts in both areas who were given the opportunity to comment on proposals for changes in the data and make suggestions themselves. Working relationships were to develop between users and statisticians and an atmosphere of trust grew.

The indicators became even more public after 1959 when unemployment figures began to be announced in press conferences. Congressional hearings in 1954 and 1955 provided an open forum for complaint, discussion, and mutual education of statistics gatherers and users. Minor changes in the concepts and methods were recommended by the Joint Economic Committee after public consideration, a report of a technical committee, and testing of the proposals against user views. This kind of gradual development of a public consensus was cautious but proved wise.

THE INDICATOR WITHSTANDS A CHALLENGE

In 1961, the indicator emerged into general public view, under a severe attack which was to reveal the indicator's strength and show how valuable was its informed interest group. It began with James Daniel's article in the *Reader's Digest* (1961), which attacked the concepts, methods, and integrity of the agencies responsible for unemployment figures. Though academic discussions had considered these issues, this was the first commentary to appear in a mass magazine on the implications of measurement decisions. Remarkably for such a seemingly dry topic the article instigated articles and editorials nationwide, and a massive official evaluation of unemployment data, entailing two sets of Congressional hearings, quantities of position papers, analytic pieces, speeches by agency personnel and finally investigation by a Presidential Committee.

The *Digest* article could catalyze this chain of events because of a combination of political and economic circumstances. Unemployment had been "stuck" at over 5% since 1958, and national attention had been focused on the causes for this high rate, unusual in otherwise prosperous times. President Eisenhower's benign regime had just been replaced by the administration of the liberal John Kennedy. Conservatives feared he would try to implement the Employment Act with public spending programs to lower the unemployment rate. If anyone had any doubt about the connection between the official figures and justifications for programs, it was dispelled by Secretary of Labor Goldberg. He had begun to hold press conferences personally on the release of the monthly unemployment figures and to combine them with policy proposals. Mr. Daniel armed himself with many facts, and his criticisms were sharply pointed. Finally, the *Reader's Digest* is one of the most widely read magazines in the U.S.

It should not be surprising that the attack on the indicator came from a conservative publication, nor that it struck a responsive chord in many readers. Daniel's article suggested bluntly that there was a conspiracy in Washington to inflate the unemployment figures as an excuse to set up more federal programs. To support his argument he cited lower European rates, elimination of the inactive worker category in 1945, the vagueness of the questions identifying who is looking for work, the sampling discrepancy in 1954 and the inclusion of some who are not actively seeking jobs among the unemployed. He spoke disparagingly of the sampling approach as a method of getting accurate information and concluded that, since the censuses of 1940 and 1950 showed less unemployment than the survey, the survey interviewers were deliberately inflating unemployment data.

Although the account contained inaccuracies and outright misrepresentations (it claimed, for instance, that the enumerators asked respondents "How many people here want a job?" instead of the more specific questions they did ask about job seeking), Daniel brushed against some fundamental issues. He did not know the exact questions that were asked, but he was correct that there was a vagueness in the concept of unemployment and in questions

133

about who was unemployed. The elimination of the inactive unemployed category was not done deliberately to conceal the figures as he implied, since there were so few in 1945. However, the move was a clumsy attempt to gloss over the technical problems of getting accurate information on the reasons for not working or not looking for work.

Significantly, too, he attacked the definition of unemployment, raising issues that had long been troublesome about who "ought" to be included among the unemployed. First he sneered at the permissive attitude in the decision to include among the unemployed those who do not look for work because they think no work is available. Then he pointed out that many counted as unemployed did not deserve to be because they had quit their jobs to find better ones or needed only pin money and part-time work. He disagreed with the value judgment that ignored such considerations to count all those who look for work as unemployed.

Although the article raised basic and ultimately unanswerable questions about concepts and values, these were put to rest in the ensuing investigation as completely as the unjustified criticisms. Within two months Congressional hearings had been called and Kennedy had appointed a committee of noted economists and statisticians, chaired by Robert Gordon, to investigate the allegations. Representatives of unions, the Chamber of Commerce, the National Industrial Conference Board, the Chairman of the Federal Statistics Users Conference and academics rushed to defend the indicator and the statistical agencies. They wrote letters to newspapers and the Joint Economic Committee, testified at the hearings, and conferred with the Gordon Committee personnel. Their faith in the integrity and professionalism of the agencies was virtually unanimous. As proof they cited the openness of the process by which decisions are made and the qualifications of the staff. Although interest groups desired changes in the indicator, which they took the opportunity to describe, they supported it in all its basic respects. They accepted the fundamental ideas that a sample survey could be representative, that accurate information could be elicited by interview, that the questions were appropriate and certainly not deliberately misleading, and that unemployment was suitably defined by the activity of seeking work, with minor exceptions for the difficulties in finding work but not for need. These supporters presented an almost impregnable front. Who would believe a journalist when so many distinguished individuals of different political views contradicted him?

The concepts and values represented "open covenants openly arrived at", as all confirmed. Daniel was too late. The concepts issue could be dismissed. The Gordon Committee touched on the problems of eliminating some ambiguities in concepts but confined its primary attention to methods. Disposing in short order of the criticisms of the article, the report (U.S. President's Committee, 1962) went on to suggest many improvements in the measure quite unrelated to the criticisms. The Committee concluded "unanimously" and "categorically" that "doubt concerning the scientific objectivity of the agencies responsible for collecting, processing and publishing these data is unwarranted". Congress echoed the words.

The effect of the dispute was to bring the indicator center stage, to inform many more people about the issues and problems of designing measures for policy and to reveal graphically the degree of consensus behind this particular measure. The indicator was strengthened both by gaining public respect and attention and by getting a rich source of talent, funds, and impetus to improve and expand.

NEW DEMANDS ON THE INDICATOR

The stickiness of unemployment at high levels in the late fifties, the search for the meaning of full employment and the recognition of poverty amid affluence were factors which would combine to create a new set of demands on the unemployment indicator — demands which it probably will not be able to meet. New and parallel indicators may have to be the answer.

High unemployment in the late fifties hanging on despite economic growth led to an extended debate among academics, the Administration and Congress as to whether the causes were structural or due to inadequate demand (U.S. Congress, Joint Economic Committee, 1959 and 1961). The inadequate demand theory was derived from Keynesian analysis and suggested that the cause of unemployment was too little demand for goods. The solution to such a definition of the problem is for government to create demand through spending or stimulate it through tax cuts or monetary policy. The structuralists, on the other hand, said that the cause was a change in the composition of the labor force to include greater percentages of the difficult-to-employ. The solution to this problem is manpower policy, or programs to train people for jobs and economic development in areas especially hard hit.

Both types of solutions were tried in the following years, with the structural approach in The Manpower Development and Training Act and the fiscal approach in many ways, including the novel one of a tax cut. Each analysis had its followers and each made different demands on the data. To conduct economic policy and respond to changes in the economy with fiscal and monetary solutions quickly to avoid recessions, there was an increased pressure to produce figures quickly and to make seasonal adjustments to try to cancel out short-term or random fluctuations. The indicator now appears within a few weeks of its collection and has been seasonally adjusted since 1959. The structural discussion demanded far greater detail in the data on the characteristics of the unemployment and duration of unemployment. The CPS in the early sixties gradually expanded its questions to gather much more of this kind of information.

During the Johnson Administration with its concentration on poverty and the alleviation of its causes, the unemployment figure began to get some serious reappraisal. The Manpower Administration decided the CPS concepts and methods were inadequate for its purposes of understanding employment problems in poverty areas. The criterion of seeking work did not necessarily locate those who genuinely wanted work but had quite reasonably given up looking. The employment concept which included all those with even an hour of work a week as employed may have been conveniently objective, but it classified many blacks incorrectly for any policy analysis that tried to determine the amount of work needed in an area. The CPS, like the Census, apparently had missed many blacks, and the questions did not succeed, in any case, in eliciting comparable information in white and poverty areas. New questions on motivations and work histories, new techniques of interviewing and new concepts were needed. Economists were developing theories of dual labor markets and human capital, focusing on situations confronting the poor. Concepts like "hidden unemployment", "discouraged workers", and "underemployment" began to gain currency.

The Manpower Administration contracted with the BLS to produce some special employment surveys in poverty areas (U.S. Department of Labor, 1969a, and 1969b). The 1970 Census also conducted similar studies in the Census Employment Survey. Although the precise definition for subemployment was not settled (just as unemployment definitions were left open in 1930), the early results suggested that depending on the definition, the percentage underemployed in some areas was 20 or 30%. These figures were unpleasantly high and obviously suggested the need for some action, which the Republican Administration was little inclined to take. In the election year of 1972, they discontinued the survey, amidst considerable criticism, on the pretext that the sampling base was out of date. However, the issue seems certain to raise its head again. When it does it will be interesting to see whether the conventional unemployment statistics, more or less unchanged since 1940, will give way to the new ones or whether the two will co-exist.

The fluctuations in the size of the labor force (the total employed and unemployed) in the late sixties and early seventies began to confuse the public and the analysts as well. Unemployment might remain stable while employment grew, or, on the other hand, as unemployment was growing the total labor force could also decline, presumably as discouraged workers dropped out. The speculations about the causes for these shifts cannot be settled in 1974 because there is no independent concept of the labor force and little information on the circumstances for entering it or leaving. Clearly its great variability will have to be accounted for if the figures are to be used in analyses and predictions.

The precise unemployment measure became increasingly important in the early sixties as the concept of the Phillips curve took hold of economic policy. This was an observed relation between inflation and unemployment suggesting that fiscal policy involved a predictable tradeoff between the unemployment rate and the inflation rate (see p. 201). It became increasingly important to get accurate figures to try to achieve the precise balance.

In 1970 economists began to conclude that to produce the same diminution in unemployment would occasion a larger inflation rate than before. The answer, given the high unemployment of 6% in 1971, was to institute price and wage controls to artificially break this relation. Economic controls had never been introduced in the U.S. in peacetime and clearly the Administration had to feel under tremendous pressure to take this step. One of the sources of that pressure was clearly the unemployment rate. Administration anger was directed at some of the bearers of ill-tidings, the statisticians, and it was in 1971 that there were reorganizations in the BLS and cancellations of press briefings.[*] However, the system of openness and the scrutiny of the measure and the informed interest groups have thus far protected it from manipulation and forced general recognition of the story the measure was telling.

---

[*] See pp. 234—235 for more details.

SUMMARY

In retrospect, one would have to say that the unemployment rate has been a successful indicator. It has been institutionalized as part of a continuing policy and reconfirmed time and again as representing the consensus view of the appropriate concepts. It has a loyal group of users who understand it and feel a need for it. Its methods have weathered the inevitable criticism that came whenever the rate became uncomfortably high. In fact, the methods have been at the forefront of statistical research. The indicator's movements have received intensive attention and have been a major factor in public action. It has set to rest arguments about the number of unemployed and permitted a wider group than before to engage in discussion of appropriate policy. The question now is whether the indicator or the system in which it exists can be flexible enough to recognize that the concepts and values on which the unemployment definitions and methods are based have changed and that something new is needed to measure the 1970's perspective and reality.

THE STANDARD BUDGET:
A MEASURE WITHOUT A THEORY

An indicator which is less known but almost as influential in its own way as the unemployment rate, and considerably older, is the standard family budget. It is an official U.S. statistic which has been widely used in wage negotiations, program design, and more recently, in policy discussions. It is difficult to state precisely what it represents; the concept behind it is a matter of some disagreement. The measure itself is a list of goods and services that a family of a particular size and composition would require in a year to live at some specified level. It is usually given as the total cost of the list, and then this is used to compare with annual incomes to give an idea of the adequacy of a level of income for a family type.

If this description sounds fuzzy, it is because this indicator is an attempt to measure a poorly specified concept — the societal norm for the level at which people can or should live. It is hard to specify because it is subjective and because, even if it is possible to get at such subjective information, there may not be any consensus norm. The budget turns out to be a pragmatic compromise

138

that confronts none of the issues squarely, but is probably a ball-park estimate for the norm.

Why should a government produce such a statistic, the reader may well ask, if it is not even clear what it means? The answer is that for close to a hundred years the vague idea it tries to measure has played a significant role in the thinking of decision-makers. In spite of purist's objections to so empirical an approach, those involved in public decisions have demanded the measure time and again. Without this indicator, they use their own even more subjective measures, but without the aura of impartiality that an official statistic provides. In European countries, where the governments do not produce standard budgets, other even less justifiable measures come to be informal measures of income adequacy. In the U.K., for example, the Supplemental Benefits level provided by the social insurance program is a commonly used reference level for minimum living requirements, which turns out to be circular reasoning.

How does a measure work which is designed on the basis of a fuzzy concept and without theory? What are the drawbacks and positive functions of such a measure? The issue is important because today many are contemplating just such measures to define standard housing or acceptable pollution levels. Such measures are unlikely to be based on a concept definable except in operational terms.

The standard budget, like many other proposed measures, presents a further problem because it incorporates by definition the target level of the variable, and thus involves more judgments. The unemployment indicator, in contrast, only defines the scale on which to measure the quantity. Later analysts or the political process can decide the norm or target level. Whether such measures are more desirable than none depends on if they will further one's objectives or not. The story does suggest that a conceptually unambiguous measure, if it had been possible to agree on one, would have been far less controversial and more useful. The reasons for the lack of agreement, however, reflect fundamental indecision about the goals of social policy.

ORIGINS

The first standard budget was probably that designed by Seebohm Rowntree in 1901 to identify poverty in the British town of York, but the roots of the idea go back even further.

Rowntree canvassed families in the town for information on incomes, family size, rent and various expenditures. He then decided what was the minimum quantity or expenditure in each of several categories which would maintain a family. He combined nutritionists' recommendations with actual diets supplied in workhouses to determine quantity and cost of a minimum adequate diet. Rent he took to be the actual expenditure, on the assumption that one had little choice and was unlikely to be extravagant in this respect. For most other items he determined quantities and costs by asking experts, the poor, what was the lowest price for the least quantity they could manage with. He then put the prices together to provide a poverty income line. Budget designers since then have developed more complicated procedures but follow the basic idea of selecting quantities for a specific family type, according to criteria which differ for each category of consumption.

The idea of a budget goes back to the empiricist social statisticians of the 19th century and their studies of family expenditure (see Chapter II). Its particular formulation owes much to their approach. The categories of consumption are those tabulated in 19th century studies of family expenditure. (For example, U.S. Bureau of Labor, 1891, 1892.) The idea that there is a "normal" family of husband, wife and some average number of children also is a product of the way these studies were tabulated and the subpopulation they selected. Their focus on working classes rather than on population averages or some other subgroup was also mirrored in the latter budgets. These were important value judgments, with considerable implications for what the budgets would mean but which were selected by empiricists as a matter of convenience rather than purpose. The choices would create a dysfunctional element when the budgets were used. Because of the implicit way in which they originally entered into the calculations, it was particularly difficult to identify the source of the problem. (See Chapter IX for a further discussion of these issues.)

A variety of budgets began to appear, particularly in the U.S. in the next few years (National Industrial Conference Board, 1921, Bureau of Applied Economics, 1920). The designers' objectives were both research and social reform. They sought to draw public attention to the plight of certain groups; they well recognized the considerably greater power of figures to command attention than generalities or opinions. The early U.S. budgets were sponsored by governmental agencies, organized charities or private foundations.

Their additional purpose was to provide a standard against which to measure wages or relief benefit levels, or on which to base sliding fee scales according to income for private charitable services. U.S. budgets never attempted to represent a bare subsistence standard like Rowntree's; rather they focused on a somewhat higher level appropriate for a respectable working class family. Even the budgets designed to set levels for relief payments were above subsistence and included minor comforts like tobacco, a variety of diet, and perhaps money for things required to make a good citizen, such as a newspaper. Although U.S. welfare payments have never been notably generous, the philosophy behind them has not been the punitive one of the British Poor Law, at least since the poorhouse was abolished in the 19th century.

CONGRESS ASKS FOR BUDGETS

As relief and many other functions were decentralized in the U.S., the Federal government was relatively late in getting into the budget design process. Its well-established statistical agencies like the Census Bureau, and BLS, were also reluctant to risk their professional, nonpartisan reputation in work that was highly normative, potentially controversial, and for which there were no accepted statistical procedures. However, in 1911 the Bureau of Labor Statistics produced a report for the Senate on the condition of women and child wage-earners (U.S. Congress, 1911) which quietly included a standard budget against which to measure the adequacy of the family incomes of the poorly paid textile workers. The ostensible purpose was to discover whether low income or squandering of income was the cause for their observation that many families were underclothed and underfed. It seemed natural within this context to decide what was a reasonable level of consumption and see whether income would cover it.

Though Congress had not specifically ordered the design of this budget, it had implied it. Congress was normally the source of demands for new standard budgets. No member of the Executive took an initiative in this direction until 1966. The first Congressional requests for budgets specifically were in connection with wage determination. Before and during World War I the budgets were used increasingly in wage discussions — either as a criterion for wage levels of, for example, city employees in Dallas, or before National Boards set up to adjudicate wage demands in the controlled war-

141

time economy. Although there was a cost of living index* against which they could judge the justice of certain percentage increases after 1918, budgets were used as an indicator even then for the level below which wages were "substandard" and should not be controlled. When Congress was faced after the First World War with the need to redesign the salary structure of governmental employees, it requested the BLS draw up a standard budget for white-collar workers in Washington.

The use of budgets in wage determination would always present the fundamental conceptual difficulty that a budget was designed for a family, whereas wages were given to an individual in payment for work done rather than to support a particular size family. But the budget concept did provide an attractive norm, as many believed wages should be adequate to support a family in principle. Moreover, a budget would get the Congress off the hook in providing, if not an objective standard, at least an impartial, external one. The problem of defining a reasonable wage was particularly urgent in 1919 as the war had raised prices dramatically and in differential ways which contributed to new life styles that emerged after war's upheaval. It was difficult to get a bearing on this situation simply by making incremental adjustments to past perceptions. Official budgets were often to be produced in periods of major social or economic change.

In any case the BLS produced a "Health and Decency Budget" for a family of five in Washington and later generalized it to the first national standard budget (1919). The methods were more elaborate and less subjective than any previous budget and they had the advantage of data from a large survey of family expenditures conducted to get weights for the cost of living index. Budgets were never to be considered important enough to warrant the expense of special data gathering activities, but would usually be done conveniently after a survey was conducted for price indices.

The BLS budget was distinguished by the fact that it was the

---

* A cost of living index is a figure which combines price changes on the goods people buy, weighted approximately according to the relative percentage of family expenditure that goes for each group of items. Its value is taken as 1 for some arbitrary year and it rises or falls according to percentage changes in prices. The absolute level of the figure has no meaning, only its relative level, unlike the standard budget which can be compared to annual family expenses or income. The index sets no norm, but simply reflects price changes, while the standard budget incorporates a norm. The two indicators are related but fulfill different functions and both often seem necessary.

first budget in which all items were given in terms of quantities (instead of some in terms of cost only), and it could therefore be priced in any city or any year. It represented the most comfortable standard yet in a budget, though it was not luxurious. The elements were determined by a variety of techniques, which combined *a priori* standards and standards based on usual behavior. For example, the diets, which were given in great detail, were based on actual food quantities consumed in a group of families of the type in question, modified by the results of nutritionists' studies on dietary needs. Food quantities represented some average consumption pattern with slightly less meat (for economy) and more milk, fruit and vegetables (for nutrition). Clothing quantities were meant to be the minimum consistent with warmth, cleanliness, comfort, neatness, and self respect and were also based on actual clothing purchases. These actual expenditures were modified in some unspecified way with the aid of interviews and studies of fabric quality and replacement materials. Housing was defined by detailed qualities of ventilation, light, sanitation, rooms per person, floor space, and separation of sexes, among others. It was far more specific than present definitions of standard housing. The total budget also included health maintenance, domestic help, car fare, tobacco, and a telephone.

While it is quite impossible to sum up the living level such a budget represents in a sentence or two, it becomes obvious enough when one sees the pieces. The standard is defined by the measure itself. Though the values involved, like health and decency, are stated at the outset, one has to see the full budget to see what it means concretely. This largely operational definition of budgets has made them difficult to understand and use. Few people would take the time and effort to explore the elements of the budgets and uncover their methods. The result was that few knew whether they accepted the standards even if they agreed income adequacy was the issue. Moreover, with such a complex of methods combining subjective and objective criteria, the validity of the measure is difficult to judge.

NEW BUDGETS FOR NEW NORMS

Interest in budgets declined during the next years, though some research continued*, but revived in the depth of the Depression.

---

* For an account of the hundreds of budget studies before 1935, see Williams and Zimmerman (1935). Many simply explored family spending patterns but many also involved the design of a budget standard.

Once again life styles had changed radically. Once again government was confronted with the difficulty of setting salaries in an objective way. The 1920 Health and Decency budget was out of date not only because it was unrealistically comfortable for the depressed economic conditions, but also because during the interim products and living patterns had changed. Transportation costs evolved with urban settlement patterns, clothing became lighter with the advent of central heating, while fuel bills rose. Electricity and indoor plumbing increasingly became necessities. If a budget is to mirror societal norms, experience suggests it should change at least every 10 or 15 years, as do weights for the cost of living index.

Therefore in 1936 the WPA produced the Maintenance and Emergency Level Budgets for families of four. The former was supposed to represent minimum needs of a family and few comforts, while the latter was designed for temporary existence only, involving little for such needs as health care or replacement of household items. The purpose of these budgets was to aid in setting WPA salaries around the country. The methods of design are apparently undocumented except for a brief description (U.S. WPA, 1936) and a search of the National Archives reveals nothing further — as perhaps one might expect of an agency whose principal purpose was not to produce statistics, but to employ people.

As usual the budget was designed as an afterthought to an expenditure survey conducted for other purposes, and the budget design was only a small additional expenditure. The survey was made possible like Depression unemployment surveys, largely by the need to employ vast numbers of people and the desire of several government agencies for an idea of new patterns of consumption and new indices they would need for their own programs. Several agencies combined to do a massive survey of about 800,000 families.

During World War II the concept of the budget was to get a considerable boost in public attention and understanding. As in the First War, boards were established to keep a control on wages, and wages were generally allowed to increase along with the cost of living, except for substandard wages, which could increase at any rate until they became standard. The low-paid textile workers, in a protracted disagreement, demonstrated successfully that they were paid substandard wages by repricing the WPA Emergency Budget and showing their annual income to be below its very low standard (Textile Workers, 1944).

144

After the War once again there was a disorientation and a feeling in Congress that strong actions would have to be taken to right the injustices in wage levels that had been neglected and to make plans to protect the economy from postwar depression. Revision of the income tax was one high priority and Congress demanded that a budget suited to postwar prosperity be produced to aid in the analysis. The idea was an old one, going back into the 19th century, that taxes should be levied in such a way as to affect only a surplus and not income required for necessities. A budget would be one way of determining this level for various family sizes.

PROFESSIONALIZING BUDGET DESIGN

The BLS, somewhat reluctantly, produced the City Worker's Family Budget (CWFB) (Kellogg and Brady, 1948) based on the obsolete data of the 1934—36 surveys with some interpolations for changes since then. The Social Security Administration produced a parallel budget for an elderly couple. The budget methods were similar in basic outline to the 1920 budget, but they were finally completely routinized (though one could not say rationalized). In other words, the Bureau managed to find ways to avoid introducing its subjective judgment inexplicitly into the design and to specify some of the previously indeterminate design methods. It would be possible for any other agency or group following the instructions to produce essentially the same budget. They used Public Health Association standards for housing and Medical Association standards for health care. They established a statistical formulation based on the income elasticity of actual expenditure patterns to choose the quantities for items where no outside standard existed (Brady, 1949). Where they had to make some choices, they did so explicitly and in a way communicable to others. They documented the material thoroughly (U.S. Department of Labor, 1948). It was still a composite, empirical sort of measure, but at least its methods were available for examination.

The BLS budgets were, like others before them, adjusted to fit the circumstances of different U.S. cities (transportation, housing, and fuel got particular attention), and they were priced in the major cities. Their values in each city receive headline attention annually and are used as an indicator of relative living costs by location. Many private groups which had designed budgets for their own areas stopped doing so, accepting the BLS methods and budgets as now adequate. New York and Boston's united charitable funds used BLS methods as an aid to design budgets that would mirror local needs even more clearly.

USES OF THE BUDGETS

Throughout the next 15 years budgets, both official U.S. ones and the privately designed ones, were used approximately as they had been in the past, and unobtrusively, except for the annual reports on local living costs. Unions used the cost of the CWFB as one argument in wage negotiations, though the cost of living index was more influential. It was mostly useful as an argument where the absolute level of a worker's wages were particularly low, rather than where they had failed to keep pace since the Consumer Price Index (CPI) was more suitable to that issue.

Budgets were part of administrative decisions and analyses. The Treasury Department used them somewhat inconclusively in their study of equity of income tax levels (1947) and the Social Security Administration used them to analyze benefit adequacy. State welfare agencies used them in planning benefit levels. Although the actual benefits did not always correspond to a budget level, scales for relative needs by family size were often used. Private and public agencies offering services on a sliding scale of fees based on need increasingly used budgets to calculate payment formulas. Colleges used them to calculate grant levels according to income and family size. Businesses used them as a factor in location decisions reflecting living costs in particular areas or to determine pay differentials for executives who move.*

Notably misssing was use in research and in the public arena of policy discussion. The reasons for this had much to do with the way the measure was designed with no correspondence to a definable concept and because there really was no policy for income adequacy in which budgets would play a role. Discussions of the two main policy questions, prior to the 1960s where income adequacy was an issue, social insurance and minimum wage, failed to make much use of budgets as indicators. The reasons were partly that the measure was difficult to understand and seemed to conceal many value judgments, and partly that the provision of adequate incomes was not really the objective of either program. Possibly an indicator with greater clarity and consensus behind it

_____

* The accounts of these uses are widely scattered but the best summary is in U.S. Department of Labor (1963) and see also Chapter XI.

might have helped to refocus the programs and provide a different objective.

The minimum wage, as it turned out, was a program to benefit organized and higher level workers. Its results are now widely recognized as having eliminated some marginal jobs entirely, which are now either not done at all or done by the higher paid. Social insurance for unemployment and old age was meant to provide dignified assistance to those who had worked and paid into the fund. It was assumed unemployment would be temporary and that the elderly would have some savings. The amount of the benefit was determined largely by fiscal analyses and a pragmatic view of how much people would be willing to contribute. Even the Aid to Dependent Children, the non-contributory element of the social security legislation, established no adequacy criterion but left it to the states.

THE BEGINNINGS OF INSTITUTIONALIZATION: BUDGETS IN POLICY

These patterns of use were different from those of unemployment figures and meant that the measure did not become institutionalized in the same way. The budget figure was only produced sporadically at the will of Congress. Some years it was repriced according to the price index to update it, but repricing and redesign was not a continuing responsibility of any agency in spite of the budget's wide use and the vast sums of money that were allocated because of it.

The users were a geographically and otherwise varied group with little in common beyond an interest in budgets. Union leaders, business managers, local bureaucrats, and charitable groups were unlikely to come together as an interest group to support and lobby for continuance of the budgets, particularly as the BLS made in the 50s little effort at first to encourage them. Without researchers to use it in policy models and without a policy for adequate incomes, there was little chance for the budget to win national public attention.

The situation changed in the early 60s with the official "discovery" of poverty in the U.S. The budgets were launched into a new prominence and suddenly the possibility of their becoming institutionalized societal measures loomed large. Ultimately their methodological and conceptual ambiguities will very likely prevent such a development, but it is instructive to examine how the possibility came to exist. In 1964 the Council of Economic Advisors

147

produced in its annual report tabulations on the number and characteristics of the poor in the U.S. with the clear implication that something should be done. Though researchers had been studying poverty for some time and the JEC had conducted studies and hearings on the low income population before (1949, 1955 and 1959), this was the first indication of an Administration commitment to action. It was evidence of the proposition that once a government officially measures something and recognizes where it falls short of an ideal, then action is virtually impelled.

There was at the time, however, no accepted measure of poverty. The Council, under pressure of time, decided a simple criterion would be a round income figure of approximately half the median income, which happened to round off to $3000 a year. They tabulated all families with this income or less according to size and race. This crude poverty line came under prompt attack from many quarters as not reflecting equivalent living levels for different family sizes.

No budget existed at the time which purported to represent a minimal or poverty standard, but Mollie Orshansky of the Social Security Administration had been using a related concept for her research (1965). She had developed a poverty line based on an empirical "law of expenditure" developed by Engel in the 19th century (see page 15) which said that the proportion of income a person spent on food was a measure of welfare. In other words, someone who spent a higher proportion on food was likely to be living at a lower level of consumption than one who was spending a lower percentage on food. Miss Orshansky transformed this concept into a poverty criterion by taking the cost of the cheapest adequate diet plan for a given family size published by nutritionists in the Department of Agriculture and multiplying it by about 3 to get a poverty level income which differed by family size. (In 1955, the average family spent close to one-third of its income on food, U.S. Department of Agriculture, 1957.) The results were a set of income levels in the vicinity of $3000 and a total tabulation of poverty which included more children and fewer elderly. It was soon adopted as a semi-official poverty index and tabulations were increasingly often given in terms of this measure. It disposed of a major objection and, perhaps, incidentally (perhaps not), had quite different policy implications.

As the poverty program advanced in the mix-sixties, and researchers and policy-makers began to ask more penetrating questions about the nature and causes of the increase in poverty, objections came to be raised against the poverty line. Unlike the original conception of half the median income, it was essentially fixed, though it was revised upward annually with the Consumer Price Index. It contained no recognition of rising consumption standards of the society, a changing availability and price structure of consumer goods, and new, unavoidable demands on income. For example, as poor housing was eliminated, one could less likely live in the same sort of housing. One had instead to move into a new type of housing altogether — while the price index would only account for a change in price of the old housing. Food became relatively less expensive, jobs moved into the suburbs and accordingly transportation cost more, but that was not accounted for. The original formula for the poverty line grew out of the observed life styles of 10 or 15 years before.

The result was that while food was requiring an increasingly lower proportion of the average person's budget, poverty lines were calculated on the same multiple of the food expenses. Housing began to take a relatively high portion of actual expenditures. The poverty line was increasingly lower relative to the popular view of what it should be. Gallup polls questioning all income groups on what it took a family to maintain themselves in the first part of the decade corresponded fairly well to the poverty line, but went well above that line by the late sixties. According to this criterion, it began to appear that poverty was declining. The conclusion was contrary to impressions of analysts and certainly contrary to the interests of those who wanted to see a continuation of poverty programs.

By 1968 the poverty line was quite thoroughly institutionalized. Reports began regularly coming out of the Census Bureau, counting the poor on this basis (U.S. Department of Commerce, 1970, 1971), and many federal programs used this criterion or something close to it to allocate funds to states and cities. It was used in numerous analyses which were the basis of influential conclusions about the nature of poverty. A lot was invested in the measure, and it was showing improvement in the situation so the Administration was not interested in changing it, despite the vast array of imaginative and technically competent measures proposed by poverty analysts.

There was one alternative official statistic, however, by the end of the decade — a low level budget. It was to cause considerable embarrassment to the Administration and demonstrate graphically the power of the right (or wrong) statistic at the right time —

particularly if it was an official measure as this was, collected by a highly respected, nonpartisan agency like the BLS. This budget had come into existence with little active support from upper Administration levels. The director of the BLS, who had established a good working relationship with Congress, came to them in 1966 with a request to produce a lower level budget along with a new version of the CWFB (which at his request the BLS revised in the previous year). Congress was favorably disposed to handing out considerable sums for poverty programs, and another low-income criterion could be useful for evaluation. The Bureau was responding in part to the opportunity to get one of its measures used in important policy and, in part, to the growing discontent of many agencies with a uselessly low poverty criterion. Many programs were aimed at people with higher incomes. Congress approved the request, along with two higher budgets as well for businesses to use, and made the program for the first time a line item in the BLS annual budget. It would no longer have to be fought for anew each time — instead it would become a problem for anyone to put a stop to it.

In 1969 the new budgets and prices were published (U.S. Department of Labor), and the lower budget soon began to provide strong, unwelcome competition to the poverty line in the major new policy questions of the 1970s. It is important to note that while the budget was being developed, the Administration changed from the liberal Democratic one which was the architect of the Poverty Program to the more conservative Republican one bent on dismantling it. In late 1969 President Nixon announced his proposal for a Family Assistance Plan, something like a negative income tax, designed to keep all family incomes above some minimal level, through an automatic payment/taxation system that would replace basic cash welfare payments.

In the debate that ensued, the arguments revolved around formulas maintaining work incentives, ways of equalizing benefits in different states, and determining minimal living standards, and what the nation could afford. Income adequacy was a prominent value in the discussion in the Senate Hearings of 1970, and mayors, social analysts, and representatives of minority groups and social agencies testified that the minimum levels in the Administration proposals placed benefits too low. As evidence they called upon the BLS low-income budget — an official U.S. statistic. The budget was, of course, never intended to be a minimum subsistence level, and these spokesmen felt that its level provided something closer to the kind of life they felt should be the goal. At that time the lower budget level for a family of four was about $6960 as compared to the equivalent poverty line of $3968. The debate subsided inconclusively, buried first in election activity and then in Watergate, but clearly the budget had been a thorn in the Administration's side, and they started making proposals to abolish the measure.

BUDGETS BECOME TOO POLITICALLY POTENT

Administration resolve was hardened by another series of embarrassing events illustrating how a government indicator may be used against the government, at least in a country like the U.S. where power is widely diffused. In 1971 President Nixon astonished the country by invoking dormant wage and price control powers. It was the first peacetime effort to control the economy and was not greeted with overwhelming enthusiasm. Clearly the Administration had much to lose if the policy failed to cut inflation. Congressional committees hastily reassessed the enabling legislation and passed some amendments including one to exempt substandard wages from any control.* Their report specifically defined substandard as equivalent to the cost of the BLS lower level budget. The Cost of Living Council, which was empowered to carry out the policy, however, ignored this stipulation and defined a substandard wage level of $1.90 an hour instead of the $3.35 level many claimed the budget criterion implied. A tremendous dispute ensued since using the higher level would exempt 50% of workers, and, the Council thought, endanger the whole program. Congressmen joined union leaders in picketing.

Eventually, a Federal judge ruled that the Council had acted against the intent of Congress in setting the $1.90 figure. It then revised its substandard definition upward to $2.75. The result was a compromise, accounting for the view that a family was likely to have more than one breadwinner. The problem reflected the fundamental conceptual difficulty that continually gave trouble — that although the budget purported to measure needs according to some standard, it was for a particular family type and to compare it with any wage proposal would produce an ambiguous result, as the wages would go to people in many different circumstances.

---

* Economic Stabilization Act Amendments of 1971, Public Law 92-210, 85 Stat. 743.

In any case, Administration determination to abolish the budgets became stronger by 1972 (Moore, 1971). A new BLS director was appointed, a macroenonomist with little interest in the microperspective of the budget, and, in 1972, the principal spokesman for budgets inside the BLS retired. However, new support for the indicator emerged from many sources. Congress had found it useful and was not prepared to abolish it. Business liked the interarea cost index function, which for technical reasons a price index could not fulfill. Social analysts and economists acknowledged the limitations and arbitrariness of the budget's design, but as of this writing it continues to be repriced and published annually by a reluctant BLS.* The reason seems clear enough, that it is the closest available measure to the concept many have in mind. It may not be ideal, but it does try with some degree of success to represent a societal standard. A recent study by Rainwater (1974) provides one possible validation to the measure. It compares budget levels to perceived needs, using Gallup questions, shows that the lower budget level does approximate the income most people think it takes to "get along" on. Thus somehow through the ad hoc complexity of the budget's methods the statisticians have produced a measure which does have an approximate relation to an important concept.

One other factor must enter into any prediction about the future of the standard budgets. In 1970, according to the Orshansky index, poverty increased for the first time since the index was used. This created considerable furor and unsurprisingly, the bearers of bad tidings in the Census who produced and published the information were removed from their positions. Since then the poverty line has been renamed the "low income" line amid considerable Administration effort to bury the issue of poverty. An interagency task force was called together in the Office of Management and Budget to plan a new poverty line. It is a complex technical question as well as a highly political issue as the choice can affect the structure of programs and distribution of funds as well as the perspectives one has for policy. It is likely that the budgets will ultimately lose out in this process as a low-income criterion due to their complexity and their arbitrary elements, but until a replacement is found,

---

* One interesting account of Labor reaction to the abolition of budgets is in the minutes of the LRAC Committee on Consumer and Wholesale Prices (U.S. Department of Labor, 1971).

it seems just as likely that the budgets will continue to exist and be used as they have for the last 75 years.

The standard budget has not been found to be as useful as the unemployment rate in policy-making and basic analysis in part because of its lack of theory. However, it has represented the only effort to measure income adequacy, and as such in practice it has not apparently been far off the mark. It has filled a basic need for a measurement of such a concept and done so well enough where administrative decisions were at issue. Without it, it seems likely that benefit levels would have been very likely lower than prevailing mores would condone. Without it more public decisions would have bogged down in arguments over the meaning of adequacy.

THE CRIME RATE: AN INADEQUATE INDICATOR

Crime measures are among the most visible indicators in U.S. society. There is a tremendous public response to them, and accordingly they play a role in elections and public appeals of many kinds. President Nixon focused his 1968 campaign on the law and order issue and made extensive use of crime figures in speeches. Crime figures are used to attack mayors and police commissioners and to defend policies to the public. They play a role in public anxiety about the safety of streets and homes. As few of us actually experience crime, we must rely on the indicators to tell us it it is getting better or worse. Largely on the basis of such statistics vast sums of money have been committed to new programs of research and assistance to law enforcement in the U.S., and laws about treatment of criminals and suspects have been changed.

Unfortunately, crime indices in most countries, particularly the U.S., have been inadequate on many counts. Though unemployment rates may not include precisely the groups that all users would like, they have been developed with great care over the years incorporating consensus views, criticisms and a high methodological standard. The standard budget failed to satisfy everyone and was confusing in its design, meshing with no clear theory, but no one had a better method to offer and few quarreled with the basic concept. Both have made some positive contributions to public decision-making — unemployment rates to the effective management of the economy and budgets to the application of some generally acceptable standards of adequacy where otherwise

153

none would have been applied. The U.S. crime index, however, is so poorly related to what the public normally means by crime and what they tend to assume the index measures, and its movements are so dependent on circumstances which have nothing to do with crime, that any policy or attitude growing even in part from the measure is based on false premises. In particular, the crime index in recent years has shown a dramatic and almost certainly spurious rate of increase, while at the same time it has failed to account for more than probably 20 or 30% of all crime.

There are several reasons why the indicator is inadequate. First, the U.S. crime index, like those in most developed countries, is based on police statistics — crimes known to the police, and only those crimes. It has always been recognized that many kinds of crime are poorly reported and others virtually never. Recent surveys suggest, however, that the figures represent not more than half of actual crimes, even in the categories included. Second, the police reports are subject to such variation in operation and record-keeping practices (see Chapter VIII) that figures have been known to double in a year or two after a change in management. Third, in the U.S. at least, the returns are incomplete because of a failure of many of the locally controlled police forces to cooperate. No information is presented on how the nonreporting group differs from the reporting groups to evaluate the extent of bias. Fourth, the index represents not all crimes, not a representative group of crimes, not the most serious crimes, but a selection of the presumably serious crimes that happen to be most accurately reported. There is no reason to assume that these particular crimes move in the same way as crime generally, however.

Moreover, weighting in the index is a serious flaw as it simply combines bicycle theft with homicide, giving equal weight to each. The inflation in the figures in recent years is largely due to events of the former type. Homicide has decreased since the index was begun and, in any case, crimes of violence are a comparatively small part of the total. Finally, the level of prosperity and inflation as well as population change, have produced spurious effects on the rate. As stealable goods, particularly cars, have increased and as the category "larceny over $50" has not been altered in 40 years, the opportunity for theft and the chances of a given theft being eligible for the index have both increased without any necessary relation to public morality. Population growth has caused some of the increase, as has the changing age structure of the population, with currently a large group in the age category most likely to be involved in criminal activity.

154

These criticisms are not simply my observations, but they have been echoed and reechoed since U.S. crime measures were first designed in 1930. Despite the fact that they suggest that the measure is highly unreliable, and despite the fact that there is virtual unanimity among the analysts on most of these points, the indicator has remained fundamentally unchanged for 44 years. Just now, in 1974, plans are being set in motion to make use of some better measures, but the crime index is still widely cited.

Why, one may ask, does so imperfect a measure develop in the first place and remain in the second, and how might such problems be avoided? One part of the answer is that the process of setting up the measure failed to develop any consensus or incorporate the best insights and methodology. Another part is that the wrong sort of agency came to be responsible for the measure. There was a fundamental problem that the agency viewed the data as primarily a source of management information for the police departments and weapons for them to use in convincing the public of their needs. The public and many specialized users regarded the data as broad indicators of a social phenomenon, however. The two types of intended use produce measures with different qualities and different presentation styles, not readily interchangeable. Crime data in the U.S. has been inadequate as social or analytic indicators in great part because it was developed for the police and used by the public.

But, in the last analysis, the reason the measure was permitted to persist in such an unsatisfactory form is that it did not make much difference anyway. It is true that the rising crime rate was used to exhort the public and politicians to add to police budgets and support various programs billed as anti-crime, but no actual program depended on the indicator. This seems to be the key since the advent of policies and programs in the last four or five years directed specifically at bringing down the rates is accompanied by a considerable impetus to improve and change the measure.

ORIGINS

The idea of measuring criminality is a fundamental one in many societies. Since the object of societal organization is to preserve order, criminal activity is a serious threat to its fabric. That societies fear this threat is evidenced by their repeated efforts to develop crime indicators. The difficulty is that the exact way in which crime is a problem for society is not unambiguous, nor is it clear

155

precisely what aspect to measure, nor how to go about doing it as a practical matter. The object could be to discover if people in society were becoming more or less moral, to find out whether the impacts of criminal activity were changing, or to uncover the causes of the problem for future prevention.

No matter what one wanted to measure, the problem remained of trading off among the various data collection methods. In the 19th century, and until quite recently, administrative byproduct data rather than survey data has been the only type considered. Perhaps because criminals do come in contact with the system so regularly, it did not seem necessary to do a survey as it did for living cost or unemployment data. However, each of the possible administrative sources had considerable drawbacks. Judicial statistics, from the court system, concerned only those crimes for which offenders were found and evidence was available. Jail population data was relatively easy to get, but difficult to evaluate, as sentencing practices vary according to offender characteristics, jail capacity, and views of the usefulness of incarceration rather than according to crime levels. Data from police records cover only crimes that come to police attention and they are subject in any case to considerable variations in reporting due to the numerous statistically untrained enumerators and variations in police practices (Table 9, Appendix).

None of these issues has been resolved, but the discussion goes back at least into the 17th century when political arithmeticians like William Petty proposed to collect data from official agencies on offenders punished "as a measure of vice and sin in the nation". The French in 1827 initiated the first annual criminal statistics report, using data from the judicial system, with the ambitious object of determining the causes of crime and testing theories and assumptions behind policies to reduce crime. It was not long before statisticians like Quetelet had begun to use the statistics in analytic studies of criminality. Shortly after the French, several U.S. states began to collect similar data, as did several European countries. In the mid-19th century the British were the first to begin collecting data on crimes reported to the police. Although they clearly stated that such data were unreliable, they continued to publish them as a counterbalance to the more limited, but more accurate, data on those who came before the courts.

Although the potential of crime statistics to aid in understanding social behavior and the analysis of crime and its causes was

156

widely recognized, the statistics in the U.S. did not develop primarily for these purposes, and, accordingly, they were not suited to them. They were developed at the instigation of police chiefs, who began asking for crime statistics at the Police Association convention in 1871. They ultimately were responsible for instituting the only series of U.S. crime rates in the past forty years, the Uniform Crime Reports (UCR). The police chiefs saw two functions for crime statistics, management tools and public relations devices. The collection of the data provided a means of monitoring and perhaps controlling the individual policeman's activity, and resulting indicators would show the public how essential police work was and provide an argument for greater funding. The police were not concerned with causes of crime, like alcohol, poverty, or home environments, about which they could do very little. They were not competent with nor concerned about statistical technique for high accuracy and freedom from bias in results. They did not care about data on characteristics of offenders or on situations leading to crimes, though they could use information on types of crimes and locations. Most important the only source they would advocate would be police statistics, as any other type would not fulfill their principle objective.

Other U.S. efforts to collect crime statistics failed time and again largely because of the great decentralization of goverment. There were several efforts by the Census Bureau and other federal agencies to collect data on prisoners and data from the court system. In the U.S., however, unlike most European countries, both courts and jail systems are complex, and there is no central authority over them to insist on cooperation. They are not hierarchically structured, nor could the Federal government readily identify all of them. The process of collecting data on prisoners systematically has begun recently with a simple survey to locate all places where people are incarcerated. There are city and town jails, county jails and Federal jails. There are short and long-term institutions and simple lock-up areas associated with courts and police departments. The courts are equally complex with civil and criminal, municipal, county, state and federal systems, which have different configurations in different states.

The key reason for the difficulty in gathering the byproduct statistics, however, was not the complexity of the system so much as the federal nature of the government. Even today when the national government collects the majority of the taxes and pays for much of local and state public services, states retain an autono-.

my unfamiliar in most European countries. Functions not given by the Constitution to the Federal government are reserved to the states, including virtually everything, in theory, apart from defense and interstate commerce. While the idea has been somewhat eroded in practice, it does mean that Federal control of such things as public services can only be exercised indirectly through grants which states can choose not to accept. In any case the theoretical independence of states from Federal control is an emotionally charged and fundamental tenet of American political doctrine. In general even statistics cannot be gathered through state agencies without their voluntary cooperation.

If statistics generally are difficult to collect nationwide because of decentralization, police statistics are doubly so. Traditionally, most police functions are vested, not even in the states, but in local government in the U.S., with many small towns employing a police force of two or three. This is not an accidental situation, but an expression of the desire to keep the control of the police as close as possible to the community. The idea has prevailed from the inception of the U.S. as a nation along with a fear of a national police force. One effect of this has been to delay the development of police statistics as a national crime indicator for many years after European countries had begun the effort. It would take sixty years after that 1871 police convention before the statistics would be collected.

There were, of course, other reasons for the delay, not the least of which were the conceptual and practical problems of gathering the data on a uniform basis. The laws of each state classified crimes differently and the practices of police departments in recording, or not recording, them varied even more. To develop uniform classifications and get cooperation from thousands of separate police forces was a formidable job. No federal authority was either in a position or particularly motivated to do this as responsibility for protection against crime was not federal. Moreover, the lack of clear purpose and model of what to do with the data once it was collected did not provide much guidance to making the classification in a conceptually clear or useful way.

The police chiefs talked at almost every meeting about the need for statistics but made no progress until the late twenties, when a rise in visible crime with Prohibition and gang wars called public attention to the inadequacies of statistics. Crime surveys at the state level in the period gave evidence of this rising concern. Accordingly at the International Association of Chiefs of Police

158

(IACP) meeting in 1927, a Committee on Uniform Crime Records was established to work toward setting up a national system of criminal reports. They saw the only means of collecting data on crimes to be through the police, and the first priority was to improve and standardize record-keeping.

A major obstacle was a reluctance of police forces to publish such data for fear it would be used to show they were not doing their jobs. Clearly a task of persuasion was in order, particularly as police forces would be involved in new work and who better to do it than the police chiefs' organization? Ultimately, they were able to persuade most police forces that the data could work more in their favor, to demonstrate the need for their services, than against them, laying the blame for crime rates on them.

*A NONCONCEPT**

Crime measures had fundamental conceptual difficulties in great part because of the way they were developed. The police chiefs' focus at the early stage inevitably was on getting uniformity of records and cooperation and not on choosing the ideal concept of crime. Because there was no effort at the outset to define the phenomenon of crime or to relate it to a normative or descriptive model of crime in society, the object of the measurement process was obscured. The measure was conceived of by the police as a reflection of police activity rather than a coherent concept that could be used in policy analysis. If a general principle had been applied to define crime like illegal or socially unacceptable behavior, public conceptions of crime, morally bad or socially damaging actions, then it might have been possible to use the measure in analytic models. Practical decisions about measurement could have been consistent in terms of this concept. As it was, however, research concentrated on comparisons of laws in various states and ways of classifying legally defined crimes on the basis that would require least marginal effort. The result was a measure with no obvious meaning.

The concept behind the index, if any could be said to exist, was one that was there only by default as it was very much an operational measure. The inclusion of the index of only crimes that are serious *and* happen to be well reported is one example, since that

---

* See Chapter VII for a discussion of the fundamental importance to measurement of a prior definition of a clear concept.

group has no particular reason to correlate with general crime trends. The decision that the police would collect the data and do it through the reports they filled out in the course of daily activities already limited the possible concepts that might be measured. For example morally bad behavior would require knowledge of motivation, which the police are seldom in a position to have. The decision was not made deliberately that the index should not measure moral turpitude, but was rather a necessary implication of the data collection method, which was determined before consideration of concepts.

The idea of using the law as a principle of classification of events was also to determine the concept by default. The law is structured for different reasons than an index should be, clustering, for example, activities for which there is the same objective evidence, like rape or larceny. But the question of intent or degree of damage which an index or morality or effect of crime would necessarily incorporate was not necessarily an implicit criterion in these categories. Statutory rape, for example, which is often with the cooperation of the victim, was originally included with rape generally, and borrowing a car for joy-riding with professional car theft. Accepting classifications designed for one purpose may make it impossible to develop an index reflecting on another objective.

THE WRONG AGENCY

Another factor entered into the process that was to prevent the development of a sound, widely acceptable crime index. This was the FBI.* Most of the successful indicators which have existed over a long period and been used for very specific analyses have been the product of a primarily statistical agency such as the Census Bureau or Bureau of Labor Statistics (BLS). Such agencies have had professional statisticians and a primary concern for quality in data. They have turned to outside experts for advice and legitimization or improvement of their methods as well as for public relations. Most importantly they have not had any axe to grind or policy to promote. But such an agency was not chosen to have the national responsibility for the data primarily because the FBI was the preferred choice of the IACP.

---

* Then Bureau of Investigation.

The FBI was the highly respected federal police force that was then dramatically fighting organized crime. It had a reputation for integrity and was making heroes out of policemen around the country. Police forces could be expected to cooperate with them, particularly as they were already working on a national cooperative system of criminal identification. The FBI saw data collection as an opportunity to extend their influence. Congress in 1930 passed legislation empowering the FBI to collect, compile and publish reports on crime from the various police forces.

The FBI was not a statistical agency, but a law enforcement one, and its director, J. Edgar Hoover, came to be a spokesman for police forces generally. Under the aegis of the FBI the statistics would have an ambiguous purpose, particularly as their existence depended on voluntary police cooperation. On the other hand, they would have to provide information the police felt they could use and it would have to be beneficial to the police. If they produced bad effects for police departments, like criticism from the public or cuts in funding, the departments would stop cooperating. The regular FBI publication with the statistics, the Uniform Crime Reports, would have to be billed very much as a house organ of the police. On the other hand, the report was obviously of interest to the general public, and to various kinds of analysts. They would want to know the technical qualities of the data and they would want figures reflecting the total crime patterns and not simply police activity. Unfortunately, technical difficulties with the data could reflect on the police who collected them, and social data was not worth the trouble of collecting.

The choice of agency was not uncontroversial, however. In 1930 the issue of crime was one which evoked intense public interest. Indeed it was this very interest that made it possible for the statistical effort to be mounted at all and for Congress to approve FBI participation and fund the work. Important statistical series seldom start without considerable impetus behind them. In any case, in response to public concern about crime, and in particular concern about crime associated with Prohibition, President Hoover appointed a Commission on Law Observance and Enforcement (the Wickersham Commission). Its real object was to stave off the problem of taking a stand on Prohibition, but in the course of the work some useful analysis was done, and some recommendations made about crime statistics.

Often in situations where broad societal questions are at stake which are difficult to grapple with, one of the first issues is the data. Are they adequate to the kind of analysis that is needed? Have they been defining the wrong kind of problems, or promoting the wrong solutions? Maybe after all the data is the main problem, or maybe at least we can put off dealing with the problem until we sort out the data a little more. In any case, the Commission assigned the job of assessing the quality of criminal statistics to a Harvard Law professor, who worked on the study for some months. His report (Warner, 1931) pointed up many of the problems with police statistics and the confusion in having several bureaus collect various types of criminal statistics and he recommended the transferral of the effort to the Bureau of the Census, as a professional statistical agency that would do a better job in the long run. The Commission echoed his words and recommendations (U.S. National Commission on Law Observance, 1931) to the indignation of police chiefs and others (Davies, 1931). The Commission even convinced the Attorney General to take a stand against having such inadequate statistics published under the aegis of his department. However, the police chiefs prevailed and the statistical responsibility remained with the FBI.

The problem, which was clear enough to many in 1930, has become painfully obvious now. Indicators for general public consumption should not be the responsibility of an operating agency, especially one charged with the alleviation of the problem to which they are relevant. The FBI has regarded its objective as providing a house organ for the police rather than a public information service (Lejins, 1966) giving, in great part, management information (although it is unclear that the crime index serves that purpose well). But it was also reasonable for them in that context to use the data to argue particular points. Time and again the official publication containing the data, the *Uniform Crime Report* (UCR), has been the forum for arguing against the abolition of capital punishment, leniency in the courts, or new rules about handling suspects.

Coupling this kind of political argument with data presentation has been found to be harmful to the credibility of even the best data. In this case, however, it was even more of a problem as there were some widely agreed-upon flaws in the data which tended to bias the trends upward (Bell, 1960). The inflation effect on the larceny category, the increased availability of cars for joy-riding, the natural population increases, the relative increase in the young, and regular improvements in police work and management all conspire to increase crime totals without necessarily reflecting an in-

162

crease in the percentage of criminals or the risk of being victimized. In fact the long term trend for much serious crime like homicide has been steadily down. The FBI, however, has not made much effort to alleviate the impression that crime is rapidly increasing, either by reformulating the data or explaining the issues, as an agency would whose prime concern was informing the public. They did begin to use more up-to-date population bases to compute crime rates after 1958, but at the same time introduced a crime clock which counteracted the modifying effect on the apparent rate of crime increase. The clock was a graphic and frequently reprinted illustration of the number of crimes committed in a particular time period. The number of course increases automatically with population growth. The widely held impression has been that the FBI has wanted to make it appear crime is high and increasing fast to strengthen its own position. Even if this is not true, the appearance undermines the credibility and therefore usefulness of the data.

FAILURES OF THE METHODS

Another reason that the FBI has been an inappropriate agency for the responsibility has been a lack of statistical expertise and incentive to produce high quality statistical work. It is difficult to separate intentions from ability, but it is clear that the FBI applied little of the available analytic work on crime measures in the original development of the crime indicators or later. Most of the important issues in measuring criminality were well known, at least to researchers, in the 19th century. They recognized, for example, that it would be most meaningful to look at crime in relation to the population capable of committing crime or to separate out serious crime to get a proper qualitative measurement. They recognized that knowing the characteristics of offenders was an important diagnostic tool. But the FBI did not even take up these elementary points. Even in 1974 the UCR confines its causal analysis to a one-page list of possible reasons like "economic status and mores of the population" and "relative stability of population" without providing any data that might help confirm or deny these. The FBI was apparently uninterested in the analytic uses of the data as a more technically oriented agency might have been, which produced statistics to serve a public client.

The Bureau did not apply the methodological caveats of the 19th century nor many of those of contemporaries when they began the crime statistics in 1930. They clearly did not feel their reputation would stand or fall on the basis of their statistical prowess. For example, the reports prepared for the Wickersham Commission pointed out that statistical publications of agencies like the Census Bureau always provided an explanation of terminology, of how figures were collected and compiled and of uses and limitations. The UCR, even today, contains little such explanation. This was particularly critical for the crime data in the thirties, as terms like "robbery" had a wide range of meanings in different cities, and there were different practices of classifying events. Warner (1931) pointed out that some cities show crime rates five or ten times those in similar cities whereas dissimilar cities may show identical rates. Seeking everywhere for explanation, he had to discount relative size of police force, differences in state laws and socio-economic characteristics. He concluded the problem lay with different practices.

The FBI, however, gave this problem only a cursory study (1939), considering just whether police were filling in the forms accurately. They neglected the issue of whether they followed different policies about offender treatment in the first place and concluded, against common sense and expert opinion, that actual crime varied by tremendous percentages. The variations have been cut somewhat today with stricter controls on record-keeping practices and more uniform laws. It is now recognized that different police forces respond differently in various kinds of communities to anti-social or illegal behavior (Wilson, 1963). So even with the best of record-keeping and most uniform laws, crime will be reported in unreliably different ways in disparate communities. The UCR has as yet given no explicit recognition to this problem, presumably because it can be interpreted as a police failure.

The FBI apparently ignored much of the classic paper on crime indices published in 1931 (Sellin), which has been the foundation of much of the later work, and beyond which current analyses are only beginning to go. The author pointed out the importance of planning the measures in relation to the policy analysis that would be demanded and the models that would have to be applied. Without crime data specific to areas or social groups, he said, it would be impossible to make studies relating crime trends to trends in other phenomena or to predict the effects of crime reduction policies. He also laid out many of the reasons that reported crime would not fluctuate with actual crime. People would tend to report crime in accord with prevailing customs, the victims' desire to have it known, attitudes towards the police, and expectations for the crime's solution. The reported rate might depend on police morale and standards of administration as well. All of these, of course, could change over time, and the implication is that one should interpret reported crime data in the light of information on these other matters. The UCR never did so and provided little guidance as to the limitations these problems made on the data.

They did use some portions of Sellin's argument, however. They accepted that the crime rate should be based on the data on those selected offenses which were most accurately reported. Once having selected these offenses, however, they apparently did little further study to assure themselves that the relationship of actual to reported crime in these categories was strong, or to tell how it might be related to other categories of crime. The FBI also used Sellin's famous precept that the value of a crime measure "decreases as the distance from the crime itself in terms of procedure increases". At the time this meant that reports to police on crimes were better than arrests, convictions or prison populations as crime indicators. It provided great justification for the FBI's methods. However, once the sample survey was developed a new possibility opened up to collect the data from a source much closer to the crime — the victim. The FBI, however, was tied to the police report as an approach and did not have the expertise to do a sampling. Such a survey is now finally in progress, but not at the instigation or under the supervision of the FBI. FBI methodologists continued to cite Sellin's precept in defense of their method despite the fact that it no longer applied.

None of this is to say the FBI was not honest in its work, but only that it was not suited for it. It made tremendous efforts to get accurate data from the police and painstakingly compiled monthly figures. It was certainly responsible for the existence of any data at all in the early thirties. Another agency would probably not have been able to produce results so quickly. The Census Bureau would have probably had far more problems organizing the system. However, they might have instituted a less costly and more representative sampling process and would certainly have made more imaginative efforts to check on the quality of the data and make its limitations clear to the public. It would have regarded the public as its client instead of the police forces. It would have found it possible, probably necessary, to look to outside support for their work and to keep up with the advanced thinking on methodology instead of ignoring it. A statistical agency has its reputation to uphold.

165

Although the crime index had patent inadequacies, the FBI continued to publish it, the press to report it in front page headlines, and politicians to point often and dramatically to the figures. It is possible that the data tipped the balance in some close elections, or helped to build the public climate for new legislation, but it was not specifically tied to any program or policy. People explained rises or declines in whatever way they wished, changes in public morality, changes in police deployment or changes in population composition. It was easy to disagree as the data left all these questions open. Thus, the indicator really did not have much effect as it carried little useful information. The users may have felt it fairly indicated rates were going up, but it did not tell anything about how or why.

Researchers and analysts often recognized the measure's failings but used it nonetheless. The public did not recognize the problem nor seem to care, and the FBI was not about to take the initiative to point out problems. They were not moved to action until a *Life* magazine article (Wallace, 1957) appeared, in which Thorsten Sellin, crime statistics expert, was quoted as saying U.S. crime statistics were the worst in the world. Just as with the unemployment statistics, the comparison with a foreign situation had an impact on public opinion. (This is a case of using other people's models in Pounds' sense, to define a problem. See Chapter I.) Moreover, situations recognized and described in specialized journals, like the faults of the crime statistics, often get no remedial action until their implications are spelled out in the popular press.

FBI director Hoover felt called upon to appoint a Technical Consultant Committee to help improve the image of the UCR. The Committee was favorably disposed to the FBI way of doing things and to the appropriateness of police statistics as an indicator of crime. However, they were not in total accord with the work and the pressure had built up enough for the FBI to recognize it should make some changes, at least at the margin. The Committee's report (U.S. Department of Justice, 1958) couched its suggestions in the argument that following them would make the data more helpful to police departments. Only hesitantly and secondarily did it mention ways which changes would make the measures more useful to the public. The FBI had given them a mandate to suggest certain changes, which they did and went somewhat further. Their report did not address directly most of the fundamental issues that so many analysts had been pointing out, though by implication it touched on them.

It is interesting to see how the FBI responded to the recommendations in terms of their function as a police agency. The committee recommended that the crime rates be based on up-to-date population estimates each year instead of the Decennial Population Census. Crime rates (crimes per person in a municipality) appeared to increase rapidly in fast growing areas and suddenly declined when new population figures were introduced. The Committee recommended use of the SMA (Standard Metropolitan Area) definition to identify urban and nonurban areas instead of the older method of using community size without relation to the character of activity or relation to an urban area. It seems likely that a statistical agency would have made these improvements automatically to assure that the data was meaningful and comparable to other data. The FBI, however, was only persuaded to make the change when it was pointed out how inconvenient it was for police to have erratic crime rates to explain and how rural areas would like to have the urban character of local crime identified. The latter could only be done, as a practical matter, by using the SMA criterion.

The Committee had less luck when it tried to tackle the basic problem of what the index meant conceptually, particularly to the public user. Crime rates had been given in two categories up to that time, Part I and Part II offenses, more or less separated according to seriousness. They were not completely consistent, however, as they were classified in ways police record them, according to objective type of activity. Some serious offenses were in Part II and some not so serious in Part I. This was confusing as Part I was used as a sort of serious crime index. The Committee recommended the elimination of various minor crimes from Part I and the creation of an index based on the remaining offenses in the group. The result would make the indicator more conceptually consistent. However, the FBI and police decided against eliminating auto joy-riding on the theory that doing so would somehow destroy the deterrent effect. Precisely how inclusion of a crime in the index would function to prevent kids from stealing cars was never made explicit.

The fact that the FBI made some changes after 28 years of little reexamination of the concept or method of the data, suggested that people were really beginning to care about the figures and to perceive that they could make a difference. For example, a popular article by ex-President Hoover in the *Reader's Digest* (1959) used the crime statistics to argue that we should be tougher in law enforcement. He used the figures in a simplistic way, saying an increase in arrests of young people showed a new problem and citing uncritically the increased crime rates generally. He went on, however, to say that the crime data was inadequate to determine such important things as whether crimes were being solved and offenders effectively dealt with. In other words, the data were inadequate for the most obvious kind of analysis. He proposed a census to get the information. Although no such census was then done (though something similar is starting now in the early seventies), it represented a breaking down of public acceptance of the crime data and the beginning of a critical and public look at the indices and evaluation of their usefulness.

WHEN THE DATA MAKE A DIFFERENCE

The sixties brought a new awareness and type of social analysis which was to ultimately cause great changes in the systems of crime statistics, as it has for other social indicators. A consciousness accompanied the Poverty Program that poverty was a problem with complex causes and effects and one with which it was the duty of an affluent society to deal. Riots and rising crime rates led to the establishment of a Presidential commission on crime, whose report (U.S. President's Commission on Law Enforcement, 1967) reflected the view of the Johnson Administration that crime was a byproduct of poverty and social unrest and therefore to be dealt with largely by social programs. As usually, accompanying such a basic reassessment was a hard look at the data, which was found wanting for these new objectives.

A particularly thoughtful Attorney General, Ramsey Clark, helped to educate the public and the Congress about the inadequacies of the FBI crime index in his testimony before Congress, his public statements and book (1970). The crime statistics gave so little information about suspects that they were virtually useless for social analysis. They provided no information about the effectiveness of the criminal justice system, as Hoover pointed out, in that one could not follow any suspect through the system to see how long his case took, how well courts dealt with different kinds of offenses, and whether the treatment resulted in repeated offenses or not. The UCR contained data on the numbers of arrests and numbers of offenses "cleared" by arrest. These two were

168

meant to be measures of police efficiency, but they failed on that score as well as they did as indicators of crime generally. It was impossible to find out how many offenders were associated with any crime or how many crimes with any offender. Arrests are a function of police practices, and their number is not necessarily related to the solution of crimes. The extent to which it is is never measured by police, as they do not collect data on the disposition of the cases — not even on whether they themselves had to release suspects for lack of evidence. The clearance figure is used for evaluation of police so there is great pressure to get good results on that dimension. Therefore, police may persuade people to confess to many crimes after arrest in order to be charged with a lesser offense than otherwise.

Most important, however, an increasingly wider circle of decisionmakers began to recognize the upward biases in the index which encouraged overreaction to the indicator and undue strengthening of police powers. It was clearly a case where the focus of the indicator was providing the wrong problem definition and promoting the wrong solutions. The data contained basically only the crime rates and nothing that would help in planning for prevention. The natural answer to rises in the index was to strengthen police forces.

Out of this discussion in the mid-sixties grew the Omnibus Crime Control and Safe Streets Act of 1968, which among other things, established a National Criminal Justice Information and Statistics Service in the Department of Justice, quite separate from the FBI. It is potentially in a position parallel to that of the BLS, with a certain degree of autonomy and no operating responsibility except over its statistical program. The legislation also set up a system of providing assistance to local law enforcement agencies under the new Law Enforcement Assistance Administration (LEAA) for virtually any kind of activity.

This combination of activities, getting underway as President Nixon took office, gave him just the opportunity he wanted to show his commitment to law and order. He had run on a platform greatly devoted to a pledge to lower the rising crime rates. His inclination was to propose legislation extending police powers and limiting a suspect's rights as did his District of Columbia crime bill with its controversial provision for police entry into suspects' homes without knocking. However, such legislation was difficult to pass, and he could show his commitment by proposing vast new appropriations for existing anti-crime efforts. These, of course, reflected to some degree the different perspectives of an earlier Administration, more concerned with social policy.

Tremendous sums of money began to flow into efforts to develop better criminal statistics, more than could reasonably be spent at first and probably more than a rational decision-making process would have allocated to these indicators over many others. It seems to be the case, however, that, given the many false starts, there must be a fairly sizable effort to produce worthwhile new indicators — an effort which might not be instituted under completely "rational" thinking. The WPA with its vast funding and its mandate simply to get people to work provided the opportunity to do the wasteful, inefficient work that may have been a necessary prerequisite to developing the unemployment indicator.

The Nixon Administration also stepped up LEAA funding to states and this too fed back into the thinking about criminal statistics. First it was becoming increasingly clear that the Federal government now had an anti-crime program even if much of its content was left to the local communities. This meant that Congress and the public would want to keep a much closer eye on the crime statistics to see if there was any improvement. Just as with the unemployment rates and budgets, crime indicators became more important because a national policy came into being. The indicators themselves, of course, contributed to the development of that policy in the first place. Once it existed, however, much more would be demanded of the indicators, such as causal analysis, uses for evaluation, and incorporation into the operation of programs. In particular, after the LEAA had been dispensing funds primarily to states for a period, a great complaint arose from big-city mayors that, while they had the majority of the crime problem, they were not getting a majority of funds. The answer, incorporated in an amendment to the legislation, was to dispense funds according to a formula which depended in part on local crime rates measured by the UCR. As millions of dollars in funding may depend on the rates, it seems certain that they will be undergoing increasing scrutiny, and serious flaws will not be permitted to remain.

Part of the Administration's massive new crime statistics program is an effort to improve the quality and reliability of the crime index. Another part is likely ultimately to supplant the FBI crime index — the National Crime Panel, an interview sample survey of household and businesses to find out how many crimes they have experienced. Preliminary reports (U.S. Department of Justice, 1974) show that crimes in the index categories (the most accurately reported) are seldom more than 75% reported and often as little as 25%. Although an indicator based on such a study is unlikely to fully replace the UCR figures, as it will never provide much detail on local areas, nor reflect police activity, it is liable to be considered far more accurate and representative. It is likely to raise questions about public confidence in the police and certainly cast doubts on the usefulness of UCR figures as analytic tools. Other studies will trace suspects through the criminal justice system, and examine court procedures and jail populations (Hall, 1972), finally answering some of the demands for analysis of the effectiveness of criminal justice systems.

Although the current statistical effort has been too rapidly mounted for the development of the necessary analytical capability to manipulate and use much of this data, there is promise for the future. The new agency is far more likely than the FBI to develop indicators that can be used and trusted by the public and researchers. Some of the important conceptual and methodological work does not appear as yet to have been put to use, though the possibility is far more open now than ever before. The current stage of the development of crime statistics is probably similar now to that of unemployment in the thirties. Out of the process, hopefully, there will eventually emerge a reliable, widely acceptable, and genuinely useful set of crime indicators for future decision-makers.

Chapter VII

Creating a Concept

By definition an indicator represents something, or purports to. This concept may have been the carefully planned basis for the indicator's design, it may have been ascribed to some existing statistic, or, most likely, it was partly formulated along with the measure. The important point is that concepts are our artifacts. We can choose and design them, or accept them by default. They can, however, affect the way we think and define problems, and they can provide opportunities or constrain our analyses. It seems reasonable therefore to exercise as much deliberate control as possible over the concepts behind indicators. One way to tackle this elusive task is to try to understand some of the ways in which concepts for various existing indicators have come to be created.

A key to thinking about concepts for indicators and understanding how to develop them or evaluate their appropriateness is to consider them in relation to our implicit models. In other words, the way in which we explain our environment and the values we assign to various situations should mesh with the concepts we measure and use. I use the term "model" in the broad sense defined in Chapter V (pp. 62—63), including the many formal and informal ways we abstract from our experience to make predictions and plan actions. A model, or several models are implicit in any policy or program or any definition of a problem. The measures will affect the kind of model and analyses we can use to define needed change and choose among policies. On the other hand, the analysis we intend to have can help determine what concepts we are likely to want to measure. Such an iterative way of defining models, concepts and measures is not only necessary but also beneficial to the whole process of making informed and appropriate public decisions.

GROPING FOR A CONCEPT

Often a major obstacle to developing a new indicator is the lack of a clear concept, which usually derives from the lack of a clear model of what is happening, what to do, or what is wanted. As the case histories in Chapter VI suggest, society and decision-makers may come to define some general problem for which they want an indicator, but without a model to put the idea in context it is difficult to decide precisely what to measure. For unemployment for example, by 1920 there was a consensus that people being without work was a bad thing. It was still not possible to measure the problem because it was not clear which people in which circumstances were to be considered unemployed. This in turn was only possible to settle as it became clearer that industrial failures and overheating in the economy would be blamed. Then it became clearer that the regular full-time worker was of main interest. A normative model of who ought to be able to have work would also help define the precise individuals to be included.

Numerous other significant concepts in public policy are either too vague or there is too little agreement on their outlines to measure them. Efforts have gone on for at least 75 years to define and measure poverty. The real obstacle is clearly the conceptual one rather than the technical one. The very basic decision has not been made whether poverty is a level of material well-being, a relative condition, or a state of mind. Even if that is decided, the concept is still too general to measure. The question of health is a basic policy issue in most nations and considerable money is spent to assure good health. However an index of health is still unavailable primarily because of the fundamental conceptual problem of deciding what good health is. Is it the absence of clinical disease, the absence of pain, peak physical and mental efficiency, or a personal sense of well-being? The technical problems of measuring any of these will of course not be easily solved, but the conceptual problem is the first obstacle. There has been a concentrated effort in the U.S. to develop an index of health (as opposed to one of illness or mortality) for at least the last 20 years and the conceptual problem is still unsettled. Housing quality is another example where we have not really been able to begin to tackle the technical measurement issues because we cannot really agree on even a general concept. Accessibility, amenity levels, social mobility, and discrimination are among the many other policy-relevant ideas for which we are seeking the concepts for measurement.

The process of formulating a concept is apt to be long, even if it is assigned a high priority. Most indicators examined here, which are among the most widely used, have required 10 or 15 years of concentrated effort just to get a workable concept. The standard budget concept took shape over 30 or 40 years depending on when you consider the idea to have begun, and the unemployment concept took close to 20 years. Many other concepts are even more subtle and do not promise to emerge any more quickly. The process takes a long time in part because it involves the exploration of basic values and assumptions and in part because the development of the concept is iterative with the development of the method of measurement. Developing a concept for a usable indicator is a process and not a one-time event. As we learn to define more precisely the phenomena that concern us, we also learn to specify our concerns better, redefine problems and in turn alter the way we define concepts.

An indicator's concept is good insofar as it works to distinguish a particular group, solve problems or aid in analyses. This perspective corresponds to the "instrumentalist" view of analysis described by Kaplan (1964) and seems appropriate where we are concerned with indicators (hence concepts) for policy-making. It follows that a concept is good not only if it fits our analyses, but also if it is unambiguously measurable. If it is not, it can only confuse analyses.

What then does one do to find such a concept? Part of the answer is that it requires a lot of trial and error, which is why the process takes so long. A process which produces a measure that stands the tests of time and use tends to be an open one with participation by experts in statistics, potential users, analysts and even the general public. If all these can let their reactions be known, as various concepts and measurement approaches are proposed and tried, they can help to assure the final result is something they can use. Such input is possible through formal advisory committees, direct consultation, professional conferences and publication of findings, testimony in Congress and public airing of issues of concepts and measures in the media. All these things have been done with varying degrees of success, and all have a role.

MODELS AND OBJECTIVES AS GUIDES

The most useful approach however is to let one's implicit models and the purposes of one's analysis be a way of narrowing down among the many alternatives to the most appropriate concepts. For example, if we believe that the reason to be concerned about housing quality is that poor housing promotes poor mental health or physical disease, then we would define housing quality in ways that could be relevant to those problems. Thus crowding and sanitation are obvious dimensions of a measure of housing quality. However, personal satisfaction, convenience, and comfort are other objectives for housing, and we still have poor models of how these relate to physical qualities of housing. Therefore we can do little to define these elements of housing quality. Measures of social mobility are being sought through theories about the causes of mobility or lack of it, and which changes in status are related to other changes in status (in say education, occupation, or income) and thus reflect a real move (Blau and Duncan, 1967) in the social system. Having done this it is then possible to choose an indicator of social mobility.

Economists have, since at least the forties, wanted a measure of job vacancies as an indicator of demand for labor to compare with unemployment as a measure of supply. The effort to make such a measure has only just begun in earnest, in part because of the difficulty of defining the concept of a vacancy. To know under what circumstances to decide a particular job is vacant, requires a model of how a firm operates. What is their reaction to the departure of an employee or the availability of new funds? Do they automatically declare an opening, restructure work assignments, or decide between hiring and other investment according to opportunities that emerge? Does hiring occur at the same level as quitting or retirement and does it occur without obvious vacancies? Without modelling some of these behavior patterns, the term job vacancy will be difficult to usefully operationalize.

Poverty is a particularly obvious example of a concept that cannot be reasonably defined without a model, and therefore not measured. If you believe that the reason poverty is bad is simply material want, the model and concept are simple enough. You simply find out what level of deprivation causes malnutrition, physical suffering or perhaps prevents participation in basic responsibilities like voting or attending school. This concept would probably be clear enough to permit one to decide precisely which goods and services would be required to prevent problems or allow participation. One may believe, however, that poverty is a problem in affluent societies less because of absolute deprivation than because of the relative position of some badly off groups or individuals (Townsend, 1973). This in turn may be a problem because these groups have a poor sense of self worth and are discouraged or

175

because the system closes out opportunities to such groups. In any case, the measure of poverty based on such a model has nothing to do with levels of living per se but is some measure of relative well-offness like half the median income, for example. If the problem of poverty is that some people have no opportunities, then one might want to conceptualize poverty as lifetime well-being and use a concept like Becker's human capital (1964). If the problem is that poverty generates a culture of its own which is destructive to the opportunities of poor individuals and harmful to society generally, then material well-offness would probably not be the only dimension of a poverty concept. Behavioral patterns would have to be part of it, as many with low incomes would not participate in the culture of poverty.*

If we look at indicators that have been proposed, we can see how various perspectives and values are implicit in the choice. A concept of health depending on sick days from work or activity days lost would fit into a model of health as a factor in the economy influencing the quantity and quality of labor. A concept based on self-reports of well-being fits more with a model of satisfaction in society and one based on clinical reports suggests that society is responsible primarily for objectively identifiable disease. A concept of school output based on student achievement tests fits into a model that says schools are to teach certain academic subjects. Opponents of such measures tend to believe schools' purposes are to teach certain behavior patterns or to encourage diverse forms of self-expression (Wynne, 1972). They are quite reasonable in the circumstances to oppose measures, as they don't fit their models.

To carry this line of thought to the next logical step, one can choose a model and concept with a view to the kind of public action one favors. If the object is minimal income support, one chooses the absolute concept of deprivation. If one is interested in income redistribution, the concept should be relative poverty. If one wants social work solutions, one chooses a behavioral definition. In health if the object is to increase the number of doctors, you would probably concentrate on the clinical signs of illness, while if you are more interested in physical fitness programs, you will define health in a more positive sense. If you are interested in changing the structure of work and opportunities for recreation, then you might work on a concept of a personal sense of well-

---

* Miller et al. (1969) covers many of these issues.

being. A concept of crime that deals with the morality of offenders will tend to suggest punitive or rehabilitative strategies to deal with the problem. One which deals with the costs to the community may suggest policies of insurance or other forms of reparation to victims. Architects tend to define housing quality in physical terms, while planners think of location and neighborhood characteristics because these are the aspects with which they can respectively deal.

We are always more equipped or inclined to apply one solution rather than another. The concept we choose to think about and measure will make it more or less difficult to justify a particular action. There should be nothing startling about this observation as those involved in policy analysis have often been acutely aware of the implications of accepting one concept or another in public discussion. In fact the principal reason that we have no generally accepted measure of poverty, despite considerable interest in the issue, is that proponents of various strategies are resisting each other's proposals for measures. Insofar as they cannot come to agreement on a policy, it is difficult to come to agreement on a concept and indicator.

In some sense it is circular reasoning to design one's concepts, models and indicators in order to get particular solutions. But not to do so is to let these solutions be chosen by default. In general the method one chooses inevitably predisposes to certain solutions or types of solutions. If you apply a regression analysis to a number of variables, you are at most going to conclude that some of them are a more important part of the problem than others and not that some of them interact with one another nor that they take effect in sequence. You are certainly not going to be able to conclude anything about variables you did not include in the analysis.

Measures are just part of the method one applies, whether one is talking of regression analyses, more complex forms of multivariate analysis, dynamic models, or the simple intuitive models we use every day. We cannot avoid the analytic and value decisions involved in choosing measures. It is only self-deception to think that by not making the choices explicitly we are somehow being objective. We are simply replacing our judgment with chance or someone else's judgment. The circularity is ultimately unavoidable in all analysis. It need not be a closed system however, where we do not let reality and new facts alter our choice of methods and models for the next iteration. The circular process can be an evolutionary one as we test measures and models against experience and try to alter each with the aid of the other.*

OPEN CONCEPTS

Even after one has applied some general analytic model and considered the kinds of solutions one is interested in, the concept is likely to remain somewhat open. That is, it may take on a precise meaning only in particular contexts or only after it has been measured. Before that it is likely to be vague or ambiguous at the margin (Kaplan, 1964). This is actually a useful stage of concept formation as it allows discussion and analysis and careful molding of the appropriate concept. It is important to avoid what Kaplan calls premature closure of the concept, which comes from too hasty efforts to make measurements and can result in some arbitrary decisions.

The idea that unemployment includes those willing and able to work but unable to find work is a good general guide for an indicator, but still is open, as it leaves many of the marginal issues unsettled. It does not say how willing someone should be or how able nor what criterion to use to decide. It does not say how hard people should be trying to get work or what to do if they are only looking for very specialized jobs. The idea of a national product began as a very open concept. It still is not clear how you combine, for example, government services and goods and services produced in the market to get a meaningful total. It does not tell you what to do about destructive activities like polluting the environment or nonmarket activities like housework. These decisions were made in defining the measure for reasons ranging from practicality and convenience to objectives of use and theories of the economy. A great many concepts that are the focus or potential focus of public policy remain very open, despite efforts to define indicators for them. Job satisfaction for example will require definition of particular attitudes and actions that represent satisfaction. Alienation is another concept that political scientists are trying to define precisely for measurement.

---

* Teitz (1974) has done a thought-provoking analysis of how methods and the paradigms they require evolve in part in response to their perceived usefulness.

The open concept will inevitably be specified more precisely in the measurement process. This specification clarifies the concept and aids communication. The process, however, may add values and models not in the original concept and may detract from its usefulness or destroy a previous consensus on the open concept. Much of this specification process cannot be done purely on the basis of the general purpose of the measure. Details and basic decisions will be settled because of the constraints which the measurement process imposes, and many may be decided purely arbitrarily. It may also be defined on an instrumental basis according to what definition will separate out a target group, and mesh with other data. A choice may be made for a less than ideal definition because it is reliably measurable. A certain element may be decided simply because it is necessary to decide something. It is important to recognize these influences on the concepts we do measure in order to apply the necessary qualifications when we use indicators.

The development of the unemployment concept for the monthly survey provides an example of the iterative process between attempts to measure and attempts to conceptualize. It illustrates how some of the solutions represent compromises between the pragmatic questions of how well it works and the more theoretical ideas about what to measure.

Much of the definition process took place in the thirties in surveys on unemployment designed and conducted locally in many sections of the U.S. These surveys seldom made a formal definition of unemployment, but defined it de facto through the procedures they followed (Webb, 1939). For example, they used various devices to select respondents of whom further questions would be asked. Questions on job seeking were often asked of gainful workers, and questions on gainful work were usually asked only of those above a particular age. This hierarchical structure of questions provided a de facto definition of unemployment as those over 14 with previous gainful work and looking for work. The experience in these surveys made clear how a concept would, in the final analysis, take its form from the actual questions and procedures that were followed in gathering data. The concepts applied in the nationwide survey later reflected this experience.

The distinguishing feature of the concept that was used in the monthly survey was its use of the activity criterion to classify respondents (see Table 4 for the description of the measure, and also U.S. Departments of Commerce and Labor, 1967). The criterion classified people according to their current activity, such as working, or job-seeking, rather than according to their attitudes like desiring work. It was selected largely because it was unambiguous. Without it the questions required subjective answers difficult to evaluate and compare. The activity criterion did not provide a perfect mesh, however, with unemployment concepts determined on other bases. Economists would like a measure of the effective labor supply at a particular moment in time, while public policy in the thirties clearly required the number of jobs the economy and government should supply to provide those in need with work. The activity criterion did give an approximate idea of the number actually putting pressure on the labor market, although this did not include available workers not actively job seeking, nor did it account for the amount of work needed as opposed to the number of jobs. It excluded the partially employed who were looking for work because the sorting mechanism already placed them in the employed category.

There was a modification to the activity criterion to include those who needed work but were not looking because they thought none was available. This inconsistency was introduced to make the measure conform with a social policy concern that those in declining areas also be recognized as unemployed. The questions about reasons for not seeking jobs had to be dropped in 1945 because of the difficulty of getting reliable responses. It was a clear example of the conflicts between defining a concept according to models, objectives and the practical requirements of reliable measurement.

The fuzzy edges of the unemployment concept were also determined in the measurement process partly according to the indicator's use and partly in an arbitrary way. Today, for example, to be counted as unemployed, one must have taken a specific job-seeking action in the previous four weeks. This criterion was required because the measure was being challenged as an exaggeration by interviewers of the number actually wanting work, to promote Administration anti-unemployment policies. The 4-week period was arbitrary, representing simply a need to be definite. The change from including to excluding the 14- to 16-year olds in the labor force in 1967 was again largely arbitrary and primarily done to avoid confusion. In addition, many detailed decisions about the concept can be found in the lengthy instructions to enumerators, indicating to them how, for example, to decide if an individual is unable to work. The concept only takes complete shape when all these decisions have been made, but not all of them follow logically from the original objective.

The process of operationalizing concepts plays an important role in giving them specific formulation. The level of living, measured by a standard budget, represents a general idea of meeting prevailing standards of health, efficiency, the nurture of children and participation in the community. In practice, however, the exact contents of the life style are determined by the choice of items and the way they are taken into account (see pp. 176—179). This in turn is guided by many practical considerations, as the concept itself is too vague to provide much guide. Many of the important policy questions for which concepts are fuzzy like amenity level or accessibility will very likely be given their particular form because of the constraints and opportunities of the measurement process if we try to develop indicators for them at this stage. While this may be a necessary compromise to get some kinds of measures to use before our models and objectives have fully crystallized, it should not be forgotten that it was a compromise. Some concept specification through measurement is inevitable, but it is unlikely to provide ideal concepts for the purposes. As our models and conceptions improve, so should the indicators be reformulated and sharpened.

PROCEEDING WITHOUT CONCEPTS

Many indicators represent an effort, in an empirical tradition, to bypass the problem of defining concepts or models. Some statistics exist because they were convenient to collect in the course of doing something else (like insured unemployment data), because they served some administrative function (the crime rates), or because someone thought, intuitively, that the statistic would represent something important without being able to formulate exactly what (like most of the measures we have). Such statistics may come in practice to be used as indicators of something and that something comes to be defined in detail by the measure itself. It is an extreme case of the measurement process defining the concept, without even an open concept to guide the indicator's design. The concept, by default, becomes whatever the indicator measures.

It is reasonable to make some kind of measures even when one's concepts and theories are so thin as to provide no useful guide. One can proceed without knowing exactly what one is trying to measure and hope that the measurement process and use of the measures may help one to find out. However, to accept the measurement operations as defining the full extent of the concept is more dangerous (see Chapter V). One tends to forget that the concept might have quite different characteristics. It is impossible to validate, improve, or even evaluate such a measure because one has no standard against which to compare it.

VALIDATION

Validation, or the process of determining whether or not a measure represents the phenomenon it is intended to, is an important consideration in the appropriate choice and use of indicators. To do this, of course, it is necessary to have an intended concept apart from the actual one. Moreover, if there is a concept apart from the measure, then it should be possible to get at this concept through a different set of operations, a parallel measure of some kind. All measures are likely to be somewhat imperfect in representing a concept, but looking at the behavior of several related measures provides one way of evaluating or validating any particular one. A complex and often redundant set of measures gives a perspective on interrelationships and provides important opportunities to expose flaws and peculiarities in individual indicators. (See Chapter VIII for further discussion of this point.)

Tables 7, 8, and 9 show the cluster of indicators surrounding the standard budget, crime, and unemployment rates, each of which reflects a different aspect of the problem. On numerous occasions one measure has revealed the failings of another. For example, movements in insured employment were at variance with CPS estimates in the 1940s, leading statisticians to begin the search for the problem. It was eventually uncovered when the CPS questions were changed to get a more accurate response from those who had part-time or irregular work. The budget is used to show the invalidity of the poverty line; help-wanted advertising and new job vacancy data are intended to reveal whether unemployment figures reflect a lack of jobs or an unwillingness or inability of job-seekers to fill them.

Measuring with no basis in a concept and only later ascribing one, has further drawbacks. The match between the indicator and the concept is likely to be indeterminate, or the concept remains vague. This means that the measure does not fit well into models and analyses, and it tends to be confusing to users. The U.S. crime rate, for example, is based on matters of presumably criminal nature which *happen* to come to the attention of the public and the police. Of these a subset that happens to be comparatively well-reported is combined into an index giving equal weights to each crime. It was never decided that the measure should represent the incidence of crime generally, serious crime, crimes of violence, or a representative set of crimes. The crime rate is neither more nor less than a measure of the crimes the police know about. It serves reasonably well as a measure of police activity and is not a bad indicator of needs for personnel. The concept, however, that the measure represents the trend of anti-social activity was ascribed later. Over the years it has become clear that the measure does not match the concept well, but it was not clear precisely in what ways it fell short. There were too many unknowns for analysts to use the crime figures in research that met any high standard. Although crime rates are frequently cited in political speeches as indicators of bad situations, they have seldom been used in any detail to analyze a problem or propose action. A simpler measure conceptually like the unemployment rate, whose relation to our models is easier to determine, is also easier to use and to trust.

The standard budget is also a measure with an indeterminate prior concept. It is therefore hard to communicate what the budget means without describing it in detail. This means that many potential users do not understand it and, even if they do, they cannot fit it into a conceptual model. Its level and composition are affected by many unknown influences, and it cannot be said to represent a particular variable which acts on other variables and is acted on by them in some comprehensible way. For analysis and research a conceptually simpler measure would be more usable, such as the median family income, the physical subsistence level, or the average family expenditure. The budget is the result of applying criteria based on each of these to varying, unknown degrees. Accordingly it is an unpredictable measure and concept.

The abortive effort to measure unemployment without a concept in 1930 (Van Kleeck, 1931) produced a measure that no one could use because it was unclear what it meant. The census classified people according to their activity on the day before the enumeration in seven categories such as "with a job but voluntarily idle" or "with a job but on layoff". The census designers did not decide which groupings were to be labeled unemployment, nor did they design the categories to fit along a single dimension of degree of unemployment. It proved impossible to identify unemployment from the categories, as several seemed to contain some individuals that should be classified unemployed and others that should not. The groups could never be disassembled and re-aggregated in a useful way, as the census designers somehow hoped. They had tried to avoid defining unemployment as a state of mind, an activity, or a question of need. Clearly, however, avoiding a definition was tantamount to making no measurement, and the census figures remained unused and unusable.

CONCEPTS ARE ROOTED IN TIME AND PLACE

If concepts must be fitted into particular formulations of problems and indicators must bear some relation to the concepts, then it follows that the appropriate indicators may be different for different times and places. The perceptions of problems and the problems themselves change over time, and, as they do, it may require changes in indicator's concepts. The values and perspectives that underlie the choice of a concept are likely, moreover, to be closely related to a culture and economy, and this suggests that indicators may not be directly transferable from one nation to another.

EVOLUTION IN TIME

Indicators that have been produced and used over a long period have been changed in response to evolving social realities. Certainly the fundamental concepts do evolve, as for example the definition of poverty has evolved through the centuries along with the class structure and views of the social order (Marshall, 1969). The standard budgets not only changed in their precise contents over the years, the standard of adequacy that they represented changed (Lamale, 1958). In the late 19th century the cost of living was included as a factor in production costs and was therefore

184

essential to economic analysis. It implied the measurement of a subsistence standard, resources just sufficient to maintain physical efficiency. However, after the turn of the century, the important issue became justice for workers, rather than maximum production. Accordingly, standard budgets tried to measure "decent" living, which was higher than subsistence and reflected the view that the worker deserved some self-respect. Postwar budgets in the twenties represented a more comfortable level of "adequacy", including provision for long-run as well as short-run needs. They reflected the desire to compensate for the deprivations of wartime and give all a share in the prosperity that had accompanied the growth of the period.

The Depression then provided a basis for yet a different meaning of adequacy. The perspective was that the hard times would not last, but that in the meantime, the government had a responsibility to maintain people at some essential level of consumption. WPA budgets used to set relief workers' pay reflected these views and represented needs for a family to maintain health (but little more) in the short-run. The concept of adequacy after the Second World War evolved to include social participation. Money for recreation, telephone, radio, and a wardrobe that was not only serviceable but also attractive, became necessities virtually equivalent to food and shelter. The change was in part due to the rising level of prosperity and with it the feasibility of achieving such a standard and, in part, to the development of economic theory in the thirties, which places a positive value on consumption as a force in the economy.

Finally, today, as our social policies become more complex and more specifically directed at particular problems, we want parallel concepts of adequacy for use in different contexts. Adequacy for a family living on welfare funds is one type, and adequacy for a working person's family is another. This double standard reflects the fact that we expect to deal differently with these classes of families and also that the welfare family's leisure time has a value for which the working person must be compensated.

Our concept of unemployment has also changed over time as the problem and understanding of it changed. The measure has responded to some degree but not fully, largely because it is more institutionalized than the standard budget. Its changes lag behind changes prevailing in concepts. Many indicators are built on the realities and goals of an earlier time, which may no longer be fully applicable. There is, of course, resistance to change in an indicator from those who want consistent measures over time for long-term comparisons. Nonetheless marginal conceptual changes have been made. The original concept in 1939 was of people fully unemployed but genuinely desiring work. These were the people towards whom policy would be directed and for whom jobs might be created. The decision to leave out the partially unemployed was partly due to measurement problems but also to the prevailing view that the fully unemployed were the immediate priority. Certainly this problem was large enough to distract attention from the problem of underemployment. Discouraged workers, not looking for jobs, believing none were available, were included because the numbers were significant and because it was considered that such discouragement was reasonable. They were excluded after the war in part because they were so few and there were so many jobs available that discouragement did not make much sense. The current move to reincorporate this group into the unemployed reflects new models and perspectives on individual behavior and the economy. It reflects beliefs that the economy has little place for certain unskilled workers, that barriers of racial prejudice and work habits make it difficult for many to get jobs, and that many are genuinely isolated from opportunities and correctly believe there is no work available for them.

The official concept has been changed as well in, for instance, the reclassification of those on layoff from employed to unemployed. This was done after a study of the movements of the data suggested those laid off were not being rehired. So new perceptions of realities or new realities change the concept. It can be argued that not to change the concept and its measure in the face of such changing situations and beliefs is to find oneself measuring a different concept in any case. In other words, the genuinely unemployed may behave or be treated differently in different times and circumstances. Those laid off may at one time represent people with strong basic attachments to jobs, but in poor economic times the layoff may be just another word for firing. The response to a question about why someone is not looking for work can clearly be interpreted in different lights according to the economic conditions and the opproprium attached to not working.

Today it seems likely that changing social and economic conditions call for a new concept of unemployment to fit with current views on who should be considered unemployed, and who considered part of the work force. Increasing affluence, we have noted, has not been equally distributed and our economy appears to have left behind a group of people who do not fit into it and are not included in the unemployment figures though they are not working and do need work. The original concept of unemployment assumed that all needing work would try to get it but this is only true if they have a chance of getting it.

Secondly, the value that women should not have to work and should not take jobs men could have, is beginning to disappear. It was strong immediately after the war in 1946, but is receding rapidly as more women look towards employment as a positive attraction. It is also receding as the reality changes and more women actually enter the regular labor force. The concepts and CPS questions do not account for this potential labor force, however. Women, accustomed to the role of staying at home may not find it necessary to say they are looking for jobs, or even to look for jobs as men might, but may enter employment directly without first being "unemployed". The greater female participation makes the labor force far more flexible than it was, as both husbands and wives feel freer to enter or drop out of it. Large fluctuations occur in the labor force size which are surely related to economic conditions, though it is unclear how. Those who happen to be counted as unemployed at a moment in time under the current system are not so obviously today a coherent group including most of those wanting or needing work. It may turn out that if we want to continue measuring this basic group we will have to change the unemployment concept. As currently defined it is not useful for such purposes as predicting the pressure for jobs in the economy. The statisticians' argument for continuity may be outweighed by a need for relevance and undermined by the fact that the times have changed what is being measured.

TRANSFERABILITY OF CONCEPTS

Just as unemployment concepts have changed over time in the U.S., the appropriate concepts differ among countries at different stages of development and with different cultures, life styles, and work patterns. It has been recognized for some time that the U.S. concept of unemployment could not be reasonably transferred to developing countries, though it has been tried often enough. This concept depends for its usefulness on the existence of a labor market in which there is information, a minimal level of common skills and capability, some interchangeability among workers, and motivation to work in impersonal business situations. It is only meaningful to think of the job seekers as being essentially equivalent to the unemployed if these conditions more or less hold.

In developing countries, however, a different model obtains. Taking work for pay and outside the family or village system is not always the normal expectation or objective. Moreover, people are not necessarily equipped either in terms of work habits, values, or skills to fill the conventional work roles of the developed countries.* There may be far less distinction between workers and nonworkers, as all participate. In such a context it makes little sense to think of unemployment as including those without paid work, actively seeking it. Even the substitute concept of underemployment introduced to analysis in developing countries to deal with the different situation, still depends far too much on a model of a developed economy and a particular kind of society to be appropriate. The concept was developed in England in the 1930s to account for the fact that there was a group that was working either less than they needed to or at a lower skill level than they could. Measurement of the amount of underemployment and unemployment would be necessary to calculate the amount of work that the economy should generate. In developing countries the objective of the measures is rather to estimate how much economic activity could take place if all the underutilized labor resources were put to work. Unfortunately, it was not clear that the individuals classified underemployed by this concept considered themselves underemployed and would welcome more work. Even though they might be living at bare subsistence, they were not necessarily motivated to work or to consume more.

Myrdal argued that not only were the concepts inappropriate in the context of a realistic model of at least South Asian societies, they were not even the right kind of concepts and measures to be looking for. To build the economies of these developing countries he argued, one should measure motivations, skills, and cultural values to see what needed to be changed to make a nation more productive. Moreover, it was not clear that the countries should be aiming at the same objectives as the Western nations had in the sense, for example, of making industrial development a primary goal. It would be highly capital intensive and not necessarily efficient, given the level of work force training. Certainly as an

---

* Much of this argument is taken from Myrdal (1968) but other relevant papers are in Jaffe and Stewart (1951), Jolly et al. (1973), and Moore (1953).

interim goal, improvement of agriculture might be more useful to build up the nation. With such an objective, however, it would be even less desirable to use a conventional unemployment measure, which has never worked well even in the U.S. for the poorly defined activities and hours of farm work. In short, the indicator concepts from Western developed countries were not transferable to or useful in certain developing countries because the appropriate models to analyse their problems and objectives were different.

The GNP indicator is another which has been transferred from the U.S. to most countries around the world (Myrdal, 1973). It is used in Third World countries as an indicator of development (in the form usually of GDP/capita) and often its increase becomes a national goal, as it has been in the U.S. In the U.S., however, the total worth of the goods and services can more or less reasonably be measured through the market prices available for most of them. However, in planned socialist economies, prices are often set through the political system so they may be less an indicator of output than of social policy itself. In largely subsistence economies much output never gets a price in money, and it is difficult to devise a reasonable way of combining various items in an index without such prices. Additionally, in developing countries the export business may be very large and a high GDP/capita can reflect a huge oil business, for example, and have little to do with social or economic development of the country.

Most important is the fact that GDP does not take into account the real value to a country's future of investments in such areas as education and health or other ways of building up the human resources. These expenditures are not valued in any market and so they appear as simply the cost of providing the service rather than the value to society. Using the index as a major goal, therefore, makes it difficult for a nation with little revenue to decide to allocate much to social programs, as their results will show up very little. Thus use of GDP can be dysfunctional in economies where the realities, goals, and problems are very different from the U.S.

The same kind of argument may be made for many other indicators, particularly against the effort to transfer from Western, developed countries to Third World nations or from capitalist to socialist ones. But the difficulty exists as well even among developed Western, noncommunist countries, to the extent that they hold different values and operate according to different patterns. It is a difficult enough assumption in the U.S., for example, that there exists a common consumption standard among all groups that can be measured through a standard budget. In any case, part of the budget is clearly determined by prevailing practices, opportunities and values in the local community. The level of deprivation in any area is certainly relative to what others have (Townsend, 1973). In detail, a radio for example, may only be a necessity if radio stations exist nearby, if information is given out over these stations, and if there is a social value placed on an informed public. The amount and quality of clothes that is a social minimum depends on climate, work patterns and life styles. More broadly, the total level of consumption considered a necessity will depend on how much the nation values material consumption. In the U.S., personal consumption has long been regarded as an important fuel to the economic system, while in the Soviet Union, public spending is a more important objective.

In the U.S. we have no official measures of social class. The closest approximation is a measure of income or occupation. But in Europe, where social stratification is a much more obvious fact of life and clearly affects the way society operates, there is a routine use of social class indicators. It is not clear that the transferral of such a measure to the U.S. would be appropriate. Even if it can be argued that the U.S. also has a class system, it is certainly a weaker one, and U.S. analysts and decision-makers are, in any case, averse to explicit use of any such concept, as it is not an accepted one in the American ethic.

Crime provides another example of how one may have to use a different concept to get at comparable things in different countries. The type and standards of acceptable behavior vary enormously according to a nation's history and style. Carrying guns, for example, is a fundamental right in the U.S. that dates back to the original Constitution and is founded in the conviction that government should be prevented from becoming the oppressor. In England, however, government is more trusted and accepted and people are not expected to carry guns. One might think that violence would be equally criminal in any modern, developed country, but in Italy and France crimes of passion are excusable, often even when they involve homicide. In other societies violent revenge for a crime like rape may be accepted or encouraged.

In short, the concepts behind indicators have, or should have, an integral relation to the environment and values in which they exist and will be used. This relationship is more subtle than many may recognize and the unthinking use of an indicator from one time or place in another may be dysfunctional. These observations have several implications. One is that the concepts used for indicators need to be constantly reexamined over time to assure their continued relevance and meaning. The second is that anyone proposing to transfer an indicator from one culture to another should have the burden of proof to show that it will work. It can distort one's understanding of a country where it is inappropriately used. Moreover, transferral will not necessarily allow cross-national comparisons, as the same indicator may reflect different phenomena in different countries (Davis, 1965; Deutscher, 1973).

INDICATOR CONCEPTS AND SOCIAL SCIENCE RESEARCH

Some of the concepts that we will use for indicators in the future are almost certainly going to emerge more or less full-fledged from social science research. The emergence of indicators through such studies implies a different process of concept creation, with different implications for the relationship of indicators to models and theories. The concept and the indicator emerge together, and emerge in a context and a defined relationship to other variables. Such indicators have great potential for use, but also can be constrained by the particular formulation the research has given them.

A major quantitative study on a subject of vaguely defined social concern can, if its findings are presented in a policy relevant context, focus public attention on a specific set of issues and definition of problems. Inherent in quantitative studies are indicators, which are relatively easy to pick out. These measures come ready-made with concepts and models and bypass many of the problems of definition. The only trouble is that this ready-made character can prevent meaningful discussion about appropriate problem definitions, as the researcher's definitions may simply be accepted. It can also mean unquestioning acceptance of a measure whose implications in dimensions not covered by the research are poorly understood. However, an intellectual controversy, if it occurs, can help to expose such issues at a more sophisticated level than for most ordinary measures.

The most notable example of a quantitative study producing indicators was the Report on Equality of Educational Opportunity, the so-called Coleman Report (U.S. Department of Health, Education, and Welfare, 1966). This was a massive study of the characteristics of schools, teachers, and students across the country, demanded by the 1964 Civil Rights Act to investigate the availability of equal educational opportunities for Negroes and other minority groups. The mission was vague, as no one provided the meaning of equal educational opportunity precisely enough to measure it. But Coleman and his task force defined new issues. At least one indicator has emerged from the work it set in motion, and others are beginning to appear.

Coleman's formulation of the problem, from a directly policy-oriented perspective, was to find out whether school inputs (teachers, capital investment, etc.) made a difference to the school outputs (student achievement). The conclusion that attracted particular attention was that, if one accounts for the differences in achievement associated with environment of the students, one finds that school inputs have very little additional effect on achievement. Further, the study suggested that schools which were largely black provided less opportunity for achievement than schools largely white.

It was out of this study and others on similar questions that emerged the argument against de facto segregation, that is the segregation of schools by race because of custom or neighborhood rather than by law. The implication of this study was that for blacks to have equal chances in school they would have to go to schools that were largely white. Additional investment in the schools would not compensate. Thus began a search for the critical indicator, the percentage of black that could be in a school and have it remain effectively white in educational environment. School systems were brought into federal courts charged with providing unequal opportunity because of de facto segregation, and the percentages of blacks in schools were cited as evidence. School systems were told to allow more choice, and to bus students from one part of town to another, and separate urban and suburban systems were told to merge to eliminate de facto segregation. The courts have resisted demands to give a precise figure to the concept of racial imbalance, but implicitly, they have accepted that the ratio of blacks to whites is in some way an indicator of harmful imbalance. Clearly this is the indicator that many others as well consider to reflect latent discrimination and segregation largely because of the analysis and models in the Coleman report and later studies.

On a lesser scale, the Moynihan Report on the Negro Family created a social indicator (Rainwater and Yancey, 1967). As an Assistant Secretary of Labor, Moynihan submitted a policy analysis to President Johnson which was a reformulation of some census data showing the preponderance of female-headed families among blacks compared to whites. He combined tables and charts with some carefully chosen words giving his theory that a deterioration of Negro society was due to deterioration of the Negro family.

Leaked to the press, it caused an unpleasant sensation among civil rights leaders after President Johnson had made use of it in mentioning the breakdown of Negro family structure in a speech at Harvard. The percentage of female-headed families among blacks has since become a regularly reported measure in the news, and a concept in the public mind. Certainly the breakup of families under the Aid for Dependent Children program, which has given welfare only to families without fathers, has been an important argument in favor of welfare reform. Moynihan's report, rightly or wrongly, established the view that "female-headedness" is a good indicator of family disorganization. The public was already inclined to have great faith in the conventional family, so the message did not fall into a vacuum. Moynihan crystallized a set of questions with the aid of numbers and convinced many.

Other indicators too have entered our thinking from a similar path. The key elements seem to be an existing, if vague, public concern, a study which formulates the issues clearly and provides some dramatic quantitative results, and a format of presentation which gives it some official sanction. It seems likely that the experimental studies of income maintenance, housing allowances, health insurance, and school vouchers currently in progress in the U.S. will produce some new indicators, particularly if the programs are implemented and the motivation for data gathering continues. The studies are quantitative and involve the thinking through of measurements within a model of social behavior. Possibly in the future we can hope for a process of finding the concepts for indicators in a more efficient way than in the past and in a way that will mean they are likely to fit into analytic models. The greater use of policy-oriented quantitative studies may provide that means.

SUMMARY AND COMMENTS

Concepts are the foundations of indicators and are essential to the effective use of an indicator. The process of choosing and creating them, however, is not a trivial effort, and it is important to understand it and to recognize that it takes time, expertise, and judgment. A concept should mesh with the problem definitions, values, and models one wishes to apply in various situations. The concept itself tends to begin as an amorphous, open idea which gains precision in the measurement process, though some of that precision may be arbitrary. Indicators may be designed without guiding concepts, but they tend to be misleading and difficult to understand, use or validate. Concepts and, therefore, indicators are dependent on the perspectives and realities of a particular place and time and therefore cannot be readily transferred or kept unchanged for long, if they are to be useful. The concept or method of measurement may have to change just to assure that the same phenomenon continues to be measured.

These observations suggest that first there should be a conscious effort to design not just an indicator but a process for creating a concept that will be relevant and mesh with the values and models that will or should be applied in particular situations. It seems likely that a process where the technicians, statisticians, sociologists, and economists and the informed public can interact with the policy analysts and policy-makers could permit the creation of practical and usable concepts. Secondly, a process for reassessing concepts of established indicators, considering new models, and ultimately changing the concepts is important if an indicator is to remain relevant. Such a process has operated for the unemployment indicator, but it has perhaps moved too conservatively. Finally, if one is interested in a policy change, one should examine the indicators that are implicitly or explicitly involved. Their concepts may be helping preclude against or predispose toward a particular analysis and policy and perhaps a basic first step will be to find other measures based on other concepts.

Chapter VIII

Collecting the Data

The choice of the method of collecting data is an integral part of designing any indicator. It should be done in the light of the models and concepts one wishes to use. The constraints and possibilities of the collection process may make one decide to alter the concepts, or these constraints may affect them de facto, as Chapter VII discusses. If it is difficult to get one kind of information through a data collection process, then one may settle on some slightly different information. This in turn may alter the other data needs so they can mesh with one another. A new definition of unemployment, for example, required by the limitations of the survey technique can entail parallel changes in the definition of employment. Moreover the model explaining why people become unemployed may also have to change somewhat if different categories of people are included in the group. Because the crime figures are collected by the police, they represent public crime. If they were collected from the victims they would include public and private crime, but leave out the crimes without victims, like gambling and prostitution, which police reports would include.

The intended use of the measure also is important in thinking about data collection strategy. Like most other elements in this process of indicator design the intended use both places some demands on the data and will, in turn, be affected by the character of the resulting data. Different procedures for collecting data have inherent in them different degrees of reliability, and types of bias. Some produce greater detail or speed in getting results. Cost varies widely. Every method will have some drawbacks, but the object is to find the optimal mix of qualities for the uses. If changes in a measure require prompt action and reflect rapid change, timeliness may be important, as it is for unemployment, and as it is not for standard budgets, which represent a slowly changing norm. If a major decision rests on the indicator and there is great cost in an error, then high reliability is important. It is worth a great deal to make the Consumer Price Index very accurate and reliable, as millions of dollars in wages are tied to its movements. Reliability is very valuable in an indicator of enemy missile placement as an error could set off war.

On the other hand the use of the measure is apt to be affected by its qualities. If it is given in great detail for example, it is likely that analysts will find models which make use of the detail. Moreover the existance and use of indicators seems to generate constantly escalating demands for detail, reliability, and timeliness.

DEFINITIONS

Some key terms should be explained at the outset. *Reliability* is a basic one. It refers to the quality in a measure of consistently reflecting a characteristic without wide variability due to peculiarities in the measurement instrument. The term *instrument* is used here broadly to include such things as a questionnaire, a person administering it or recording from it, the setting, the sample selection process, and whatever else may be part of the procedure for gathering the data. If this instrument responds in different ways at different times to the stimulus we are trying to measure, or somehow alters the stimulus, the data will be unreliable. We then cannot explain variations in the data in terms of the phenomenon we are trying to measure. The ideal is an instrument which provides a clear, passive, and predictable channel for information. The most obvious example of unreliability is a too small sample where results tend to diverge widely from the actual population mean. But subjective or ambiguous questions in a survey can produce unreliable results as we are unable to tell whether variations in answers are due to misunderstanding or to real variations in what we are looking for. If the enumerator is allowed to use discretion in phrasing questions, the answers can, by the same token, be unreliable.

Bias is the quality in a measure of consistently misrepresenting the underlying phenomenon. It may make it too large or too small, increasing too fast or too slowly, or with some component over- or underrepresented. Unlike unreliability it does not cause inexplicable fluctuations in the measure, but a steady error, and it is thus far more difficult to detect. Often the only way is to look at other, related measures collected by different methods to see that some group is undercounted or that changes may not be occurring so fast. Bias can occur because a sample is poorly chosen or because a question is poorly written. Some instruments are notoriously bad at getting at certain segments of the population. For example, a telephone survey misses the nonsubscribers and the people who are out a lot, both of which categories are likely to be very different from the remainder of the population. The social class or ethnic background of an enumerator can result in consistently wrong results for certain population groups either because of hostility or a desire to live up to some presumed standard. The results of forms that one must fill out oneself tend to be more incorrect for the poorly educated. Bias is particularly important to policy where it involves special target groups — which it frequently does — because the small population subgroups tend to be most severely affected.

A third indicator quality is *precision*. A precise measure is one given in great detail — a population down to the last individual or the national product down to the last loaf of bread. It is not to be confused with accuracy, which means lack of bias. A measure may not be precise, but it may be at least approximately correct if the method of getting it is appropriate. On the other hand, a measure may be very precise but entirely wrong. Carrying out the figures to great detail does not improve their quality if there is basic bias and unreliability. In fact such detail may be harmful in encouraging the user to ascribe more power to the measure than it has. Precision can be specious when the method of collecting the data almost certainly includes an error that would cancel out the detail. A census normally misses several percent of the population because we are not skillful enough at searching out everyone (U.S. Congress, 1970). So it is absurd to present the results in detail down to the last individual. Even if we missed no one, many people would have been born and died simply during the time of taking of census. It would be less misleading simply to round off the figure to a number that we are confident is approximately right.

COLLECTION METHODS

There are numerous techniques for eliciting and recording information, each of which has its strengths and disadvantages and each of which meshes differently with different objectives.* All have, in

---

* Two of the best books pertinent to this whole chapter are Morgenstern (1963) and Webb et al. (1966). Both are highly readable and accessible to the nontechnical reader.

one way or another, been used in the design of many indicators, though some less than others. They include observation, interview, selfreports, and archives.

INTERVIEW

The interview is the dominant technique as it is the most flexible. It is best, of course, for information that can only be elicited from people — opinions or topics that are poorly recorded elsewhere. This includes the great majority of information we are apt to want. However, the interview is the most expensive way of getting data, and it has some special problems. Most importantly it is far from a clear channel for information and considerable distortion may occur.

Moreover, the interview does place a certain form on information. To find out something from a person one must phrase questions to be understood unambiguously and not to offend. One must apply categories that fit the perceptions of the person being interviewed, which do not necessarily correspond to the ideal categories for research or the appropriate ones to mesh with program analysis. To get subjective information one must apply some objective correlate, which inevitably does not match precisely. For example instead of asking "Do you want a job?" in the CPS, the question is "Are you looking for a job?". The two do not necessarily identify identical individuals, however, and the concept of unemployment and its relevance to various models and policies are affected by the choice.

The analysis and policy implications would be very different for any of these concepts of unemployment. The idea of wanting a job fits into a model that says all who want work should be able to get it and we must find ways to keep generating jobs. The idea of looking for work is likely to conjure up, in addition, ideas of job information systems and encourage us to ignore those who want work, but have given up looking. Finally the concept of needing work is likely to suggest relief programs as the first two concepts never would, as need is hidden in them. So one's choice of data collection method can have important, often unseen, implications for policy. In the 30's it was reasonably clear that the desired concept of unemployment was to include those who wanted work, but it was the use of the interview method that demanded a change in the concept to "looking for work".

Self reports, where individuals or organizations provide data on themselves according to some established format, provide a less expensive means of getting some of the information otherwise obtainable only through interviews. They can be used to cut data gathering costs, with interviews as a supplement for hard-to-understand questions and people who are too poorly motivated or educated to provide the answers on their own. The 1970 Census consisted of forms which individuals filled out and mailed back and follow-up interviews when forms were not returned or answers had obvious discrepancies. Self-reports are obviously suitable for the simpler more unambiguous questions like age, sex, home-ownership or number of children, for the number of employees and size of payrolls in a firm.

However, for things which are hard to remember, like income over a year, or questions which need further explanation like "Where do you do your shopping?" self reports may be inadequate. One may not know how to answer if some shopping is done in one place and some in another, or if it varies by type of purchase or time of year. A good many questions could arise and an interviewer would be essential to assure a consistent set of answers.* Self reports may be appropriate for some delicate questions, say about sex or other topics where the personal relationship between interviewer and respondent may produce unreliable answers. Self reports used alone can, of course, be biased against those unwilling or unable to fill out forms. The competence of the target groups should certainly be a consideration in the choice of this method. It has been found that businesses tend to have both staff and expertise to respond well to many statistical inquiries. They can be trained to deal adequately with fairly subtle issues. A vast sample of employers for example provide monthly responses to questionnaires for the BLS series on employment statistics, wages and hours. The BLS is now working with some employers to develop a workable definition of job vacancies so they can provide this information also through self reports.

---

* Useful discussions have arisen on the comparative effectiveness of self reports and interviews and various specific methods of dealing with response and recall problems in the design of consumer expenditure surveys. (See Flueck et al., 1972, Pearl and Levine, 1972, and Sudman and Ferber, 1972.)

Observation implies getting information through watching, hearing or otherwise directly sensing something. It is the part of the caseworker's interview of the applicant for unemployment compensation, where he notes whether the applicant is neatly dressed and was on time for the interview. It was what Rowntree's surveyors (1901) did to check the validity of the income-based poverty line they developed, when they sized up the house, clothes, and life style of a family to decide if they were effectively poor. It is what we have done in the main to determine housing quality. Though we sometimes ask whether particular plumbing facilities exist, the determination of the existence of dilapidation is still something that can only be done through observation. It is also the taking of notes on behavior at bus stops or patterns of using a park.

Observation is often at least one element in any information gathering process, and it undoubtedly should be as it permits the absorbing of different data or data in a different form than the other methods allow. It is simple, comparatively cheap and can often help to uncover errors concealed in our other methods. A welfare applicant may be able to lie to the caseworker and falsify the forms they fill out about their poverty and inability to find work, but their clothing or freshly styled hair can provide a different perspective. For some things observation may be the only way of getting accurate information or information in the desired form. For example if you want to describe crowd behavior, those in the crowd are probably unable to understand what is happening to the group as a whole, and those controlling the crowd like the police are only concerned with the negative aspects and problems of violence.

Observation can have the special advantage of being a nonreactive way of gathering data in that the mere act of observing does not require any reaction from the observed. The opportunity and incentive for distortion is less than with the other methods, though it still exists. Of course one can look at trace information. In other words, to describe the use of parks, look at the footpaths that users have made rather than ask them where they go, or look for the best-thumbed books to determine their popularity. It is the Sherlock Holmes approach of using nicotine-stained fingers to find a smoker, recognizing that this is likely to be a more dependable indicator than his reply to a direct question, particularly if smoking is apt to carry some opprobrium. This is why observations of lifestyle, such as yachts or travel abroad are often used to uncover lies on income tax returns. It might be useful to uncover such observational measures for illegal activities like smoking marijuana or gambling.

The disadvantages of observation are first that interpretation can be particularly difficult and second, that it can produce a reaction in the observed. In observation, by definition one must more or less passively accept data as it comes, and it often does not come with any explanation. The heavy wear around a particular exhibit in a museum may reflect great popular interest or simply that people were getting tired at that point and shuffling their feet. Trace observations usually require supporting information to be properly interpreted. Secondly people can behave differently when they are being observed even when they do not know why they are. They would be likely to conceal illegal or anti-social behavior if they saw someone taking notes or they might simply become suspicious and develop an unnatural behavior.

DOCUMENTS

Documents or archives are another source of data which can be either passive or reactive depending on the situation and which do provide some opportunities which other techniques do not. Using existing documents is probably the simplest and least expensive way of gathering data. The birth and death rates, most crime rates, and welfare case closings are all common indicators that depend heavily on documents that are filled out primarily for other purposes. The kind of information is limited to those areas in which someone already provides some service or takes some action. The information is sorted into categories that are useful in performing the activity rather than analysing it.

The material may be historical documents or archives, in which case there is no problem of reactivity between data collector and subject, but there is often a problem of putting information into context for interpretation. There may have been some kind of reactivity between those making up the documents and their supervisors, which may mean there are hidden inaccuracies. Often, however, there is some reactivity in the keeping of documents as people are aware they will be examined, and often have an interest in how the results appear. If welfare becomes unpopular, reasons are soon found to close welfare cases in part so the indicators will look better (Piven and Cloward, 1971). It has long been clear that accounting practices change the way people do things as well as how they record them, as indeed they were intended to do. Police reporting of crime was partly instituted to change police behavior, although it also provided some incentive for lying when it was known that the crime rate would become a criterion for judging police efficiency or need for funds. Collecting data through documents can be a fairly passive way of getting information which may have the disadvantage of not being in the form one wants or covering all the topics one wants, but which is cheap and often easily available. It can however, change the behavior one wants to examine if one institutes a system of documentation to get an indicator. If, in turn, one judges the data collectors' performance by the outcome of the indicator, it can encourage falsification.

CHOICE OF POPULATION

The three major ways of choosing the people or items to be examined are a complete census, a sample, and a group served by some administrative process. Each procedure has been widely used and has advantages and disadvantages for various contexts of data use.

CENSUS

A census can have complete coverage, at least in theory. One can obviate the problems of bias by examining everyone. This was the first and only method until 1940 that was generally accepted as providing dependable results. Public discussion in the twenties and thirties on unemployment reflected the assumption that this was the only method of getting total figures. There is no substitute for a census in getting populations and some of their basic characteristics, to permit the drawing of samples. Its sheer size, in addition, permits detailed cross tabulations to be done with some reliability. However, it is no longer the only way to get other figures pertinent to the total population, nor is it even the best way. A census is slow and expensive, and it is now increasingly recognized to have serious bias in that certain hard-to-find groups may be missed altogether (Taeuber, 1969). The failure to count millions of black males in the 1960 census was only recognized after the study of the age structure of the population. The census apparently always undercounted unemployment partly because of this bias. Moreover, because every question on a census is so expensive, as it must be administered to everyone, cost considerations keep the questions to a minimum. As they are so expensive questions must be of interest to a number of agencies and groups. In practice, this means they are usually general background data and not directed at any issue or program. In addition the number of enumerators is so great for a census that control and training are difficult, and questions must be fairly simple.

For a census to be complete, it has often been necessary to make responses legally required. This places a further limit on the number of questions as it is politically unpopular to require any but the most obviously necessary information. Moreover, sensitive questions often must be avoided, which might be construed as invasions of privacy, or infringement on Constitutional rights. Questions on religion must be optional; political preference cannot be covered at all in the U.S. There was an extended discussion in the media and Congress of the propriety of asking, in the 1970 Census, whether a family shared a bath with anyone. Various government agencies felt it was essential as an objective measure of housing quality but some Congressmen and many public leaders felt the question was an invasion of privacy and refusal to answer should not be punished (U.S. Congress, 1969).

A census is appropriate to measure phenomena that change slowly, are of wide general interest, noncontroversial, and do not require immediate action. The limitation on the number of questions and on their complexity or subjectivity prevents the use of census for very penetrating analysis. The bias is sufficient to recommend against use of census data for policy questions which focus on population subgroups that may have been poorly sampled.

BYPRODUCT DATA

Administrative processes provide the least expensive and usually most rapidly available data. Some examples are the number of welfare cases opened or closed in a particular month, the number of offenses cleared by arrest, hours worked in industry, industrial accidents, unemployment based on insurance claims, and income figures based on tax returns. However the data was originally collected, the statisticians usually gather it from documents so the considerations described earlier in the chapter apply. There are many drawbacks to indicators based on most such data, but the cost is often so marginal that they are collected anyway. The data can be used well if their limitations are recognized and they exist in a complex of other measures that provide a perspective. Under some circumstances the data can be the best obtainable by any means.

Administrative byproduct data tends to be both biased and unreliable.* It is biased because most administrative processes involve only a segment of the population and an unrepresentative sample of that. Thus welfare in the U.S. goes to not the poorest, but to those among the poorest who happen to know about it, who request it, and who fit into eligible categories. Those who do not are likely to be different from those who do in some significant respects, such as intelligence or independence. Unemployment insurance usually goes to those who have worked before, and figures on insured unemployment do not include workers looking for a first job. In the U.S. it does not include domestics and many of the lower skill categories. Crime reported to the police is only that which people think it is worth the trouble of reporting or which they know about and want solved.

The data are unreliable primarily because they are not collected for statistical analyses, but usually for management and control. A new order on record-keeping can change the figures though the phenomenon is unchanged and the activity of the agency is unchanged. A change in the period of accounting or in a minor definition could be all that was needed. Moreover, the people who may record data are unlikely to be trained as statisticians and normally have other responsibilities. These record-keepers may make differing and inappropriate judgments about classifying many items that are marginal. The classification may make sense in terms of their activity but not in terms of consistent statistical analysis.

The gathering of police statistics on crime provides examples of many of these problems. Individual police officers have to make decisions as to whether a man who snatched a purse did so with force so his crime was assault, or without force so it was robbery, or whether the complainant simply dropped her purse.** The policeman has a lengthy manual, but ultimately has to rely on his

---

* Morgenstern (1963) gives the best general discussion of this kind of data.
** Beattie (1960) discusses many of the crime data collection problems, including the issue of judgment on classification and variations in police practices.

204

judgment. This judgment in turn may be colored by the likely punishment for a crime and whether he considers it too severe for the particular incident. The indicator, offenses cleared by arrest, is used as a management criterion for the efficiency of police forces. Therefore police may encourage someone caught for one crime to admit to others. Different practices in different cities can make results meaningless to compare (Warner, 1931). Evolving objectives of police forces can produce different record-keeping behavior, such as painstaking recording of all complaints when a crime wave might swing support behind the police, or low recording due to corruption or simply to have better percentages of clearances. It is well known that crime rates may rise after the introduction of a reform police chief. To use such data is to require a full understanding of the operations and motivations of a police force in particular environments (Wheeler, 1967).

None of these comments are meant as criticisms of the police. The same problem exists for staff of any operating agency keeping data. Their first responsibility is to some other job whose demands may conflict with good statistical practice. Studies of police behavior show that different communities expect different things from their police in the way they treat offenses and offenders (Wilson, 1968). Naturally this appears in the statistics as variations that have nothing to do with actual crime. Moreover, it is expecting a great deal to ask people to keep measurements of their own activity by which they will be judged and expect that no error, even subconscious, will be introduced.

Finally, byproduct data is based on definitions appropriate to the activity of which it is an output, which seldom corresponds to those required for broader analysis. Some effort may be made to standardize definitions, but one cannot change a program simply to get more useful statistics. The unemployment rate at the state level in the U.S., for example, is based on insured unemployment levels and does not correspond in definitions to the national rate computed through the CPS. For example, there is a one-week waiting period before one can apply for benefits, but no waiting period for the CPS version of unemployment, and a time limit to insured unemployment, but none to CPS classification (Green, 1971).*

---

* For a fuller account of the ways the various data series on employment relate to one another (or fail to) see U.S. Bureau of the Budget, 1955. It also suggests some of the difficulties and opportunities in looking at clusters of indicators rather than single ones to keep a check on validity.

There are occasional exceptions to these difficulties with by-product data. If an administrative procedure covers everyone, provides clear detailed instructions about records, and involves little or no interaction between the record-keepers and the subject and no direct service on which either may be judged, then the data may be among the best (most reliable, least biased, most detailed, and timely). One such example is the income data from the Internal Revenue Service. Although there is some incentive to lie, there is also considerable discentive. Record-keeping practices are standardized, and the record-keepers are expected as part of their job to be consistent. Vital statistics provide another example. The fact of birth or death almost always is recorded. Although the cause of death is a question of judgment, the fact of it seldom is, nor, usually, is the date. In the U.K., where coverage for unemployment is virtually universal, cheating or error is comparatively unlikely as each worker has to lodge an employment book either with an employer or with the unemployment office, reasonably complete unemployment statistics have been coming for years out of the insurance system. The data have been good enough so the British have not felt it necessary to do an unemployment survey like the CPS. As with so many techniques however, this may change as changing work patterns and analytic requirements reveal inadequacies in data for current interests. A working party recently concluded that the statistics failed to identify unused labor resources in some important ways, like concealing the employable and temporarily stopped, because both could be ineligible for compensation (U.K., 1972).

However, even when the data has many disadvantages, the low cost, timeliness and tremendous detail of byproduct data often make it worthwhile. Without such data we would be unlikely to have any sort of indicators at city and often state levels. Detailed characteristics even on a limited portion of the problem may be better than none. The important thing is to recognize the data's limitations so as not to misinterpret their movements but to be able to identify the bias and unreliability. Such indicators can be useful as part of a constellation of measures (see Tables 7—9, Appendix). One can then take advantage of the speed and detail of byproduct data, while recognizing the relation their movements have to other data, which are unreliable or biased in different ways.

The sample survey provides a middle way between the other two methods, cheaper and faster than the census though less complete, and more reliable than byproduct data though less detailed. It does have some special advantages of its own. The subject has been discussed in Chapter II, but to summarize briefly: stratified random sampling has opened up a range of possibilities. New kinds of information for new kinds of purposes are now feasible. One can choose topics and definitions having nothing to do with ongoing programs. Staff can be more experienced and better trained, and one can aim for more subtle information than in a census. The questions can be more numerous and need not be chosen for general interest or to be totally uncontroversial. Mistakes can be made and experiments can be done without the loss of vast investment. A sample can be repeated relatively reliably time and again. It can focus on the small population groups that are of particular concern.

The drawing of the sample does depend on an accurate population count, and its results may therefore be as biased as the census. But once some of the biases are recognized, a sampling design can cover missed groups, and enumerators can be trained to find them and given the time to do so, as they have in the subemployment surveys (U.S. Department of Labor, 1969). Samples can then give more accurate returns than full censuses. The evidence is that the CPS, for example, was more accurate than the censuses of 1940, 1950 and 1960 in measuring unemployment.

Some indicators are only feasible and useful for their purposes, with sampling, like unemployment, which requires frequency and accuracy, crime victimization, which requires sensitive, probing questions, and the consumer price data, which requires frequent and detailed information on retail prices, impossible to do except through a sampling of prices in a sampling of markets. Many possibilities have yet to be exploited, because sampling is not costless nor technically easy, and people tend to accept measures available from other sources. A sensible strategy might well be to have an indicator based on a sample as the central element in a cluster of related indicators as it is apt to be the least biased and best focused. Data from the census and from administrative activities can be better understood against the backdrop of such an indicator and can fill in information the sampling process did not provide.

PROBLEMS OF THE INSTRUMENT*

The data collecting instrument introduces many sources of error beyond those conventionally discussed in statistical textbooks or acknowledged in statistical publications. Sampling error is usually described, but the effect of such error is dwarfed by the other kinds in most social measurement. Most of this other error is not even measurable. The best we can do is to be conscious of its existence, and avoid using an indicator in a setting where the particular error could make a critical difference. Recognition of potential errors can also make it clear how and why it may be impractical to try to measure a concept and suggest ways one might reformulate it to get more reliable measurement.

MISTAKES

The measurement instrument inevitably involves human beings, and they are fallible, filling in the wrong blanks, counting or adding wrong, drawing the sample wrong or simply forgetting the answers to questions. The more steps in a data collection process and the more people involved, the more likely error is to occur. More complex and less recent information is also more subject to error. In general errors of this inadvertent kind tend to cancel out, so often one need not be greatly concerned about them. One should be conscious, however, if errors tend to occur more in one direction than another. In the case of unemployment measurement, for example, a large discrepancy between unemployment measured in an old and a new CPS sample was found due to error of which the effect was almost entirely to lower unemployment estimates. The enumerators for the old sample were not being supervised and were getting careless in the way they conducted the interviews. As it was more difficult to find out if someone was unemployed than employed, the error was mostly in the former category (U.S. Dept. of Commerce, 1954).

---

* Ducoff and Hagood (1947) and Bancroft and Welch (1946) describe how many of these sources of error were found in the early years of the Labor Force Survey (later the CPS) and discuss the remedies, many of which involved altering basic concepts. Dodge and Turner (1972) also discuss many of the problems like respondent recall and the volunteering (or nonvolunteering) phenomenon in connection with the experimental studies of interviewing to find crime victims.

208

A respondent or enumerator may fail to understand precisely what information the designer of the survey or study wants. The respondent may answer a different question than was asked or the enumerator may record a different answer than was intended because of misunderstanding (Stambler, 1969). This is a question of communication among those designing the instrument, those administering it, and those submitting to it. The self-report method is susceptible to this problem if the questions are complicated. This is one problem well-trained interviewers can alleviate, providing explanations or communicating meaning with an inflection in a way a passive questionnaire never can. Misunderstanding however, is a problem for any type of data collection. The clerks who fill out forms that become documentary sources of data can misunderstand them or the world on which they are recording information. Even direct observation requires interpretation.

LIES

There are many reasons for one of the participants in data collection to lie or at least choose a false role for himself. Such situations are apt to occur when questions are personal or concern matters about which there are strongly defined socially acceptable answers. For example the answer to the question "Are you looking for work?" asked in the CPS should obviously be yes if you are an able-bodied male without a job. The question (and concept as a result) had to be changed to "What have you done to look for work?" in part because of the great temptation to lie (Bancroft and Welch, 1946). In addition the incentive to lie may exist when there is a major difference between enumerator and respondent in ethnic group or class. The classic example is the middle-class interviewer and lower class respondent who does not want to admit to some socially unacceptable behavior. The desire to be liked or approved is pervasive and potent. The problem has been recognized more often now in such surveys as the BLS sub-employment surveys where interviewers are carefully selected to communicate with local people.

Another situation conducive to dishonesty, almost designed to produce false information, is where one of the participants in data gathering is going to be judged on the answer. Insofar as police are going to be judged on the numbers of clearances of crimes, or welfare workers on the numbers of families removed from welfare, one can expect these data to be unreliable and biased. During recent U.S. efforts to control wages and prices the word went out in the Cost of Living Council to use BLS price statistics as the starting point for locating offending forms. The idea was that firms reporting large price increases to BLS surveyors would get pressure put on them to cut back. The BLS resisted supplying the information, recognizing it would destroy the usefulness of the index and their good relationship with firms. Fortunately the effort was abortive because although it might have temporarily kept prices down, it would have encouraged wholesale lying about prices in future.

The method of payment of enumerators or respondents can be conducive of dishonesty. In the census enumerators have been paid something for each family they survey. The amount is not great, and it is the same for all no matter what the location. The incentive to invent the data on those who live in rough neighborhoods or who seldom answer their doorbells is great.

In the panel studies, which are often the most efficient way of surveying populations, members of the sample are repeatedly interviewed in a several-month period. This sets up a personal relation between the interviewer and respondent which may provide additional encouragement of one or the other to lie. For example in the 1940's it was found that enumerators were filling in themselves the reasons for not looking for work rather than offend the family they would have to see several more times by asking the question. The solution was to delete the question.

VOLUNTEERING

In any method bias is created by some people not being forthcoming or available. Even in the census where a reply is legally required, a small percentage is impossible to find, or does not cooperate. For other studies the nonvolunteering percentage is much larger. The problem is that those who do not fill out the forms or answer the questions are likely to be different from those who do. They may be more self-assured, more ignorant, or, worst of all for the statistics, may have some specific reason for not wanting to reply to the questions. They may have something to hide or some problem and be the very cases one most needs for analysis. For example in the Coleman study (U.S. Dept. of Health Education and Welfare, 1966) of inequality of educational opportunity a sizable percentage of schools did not return the question-naire. While the characteristics of these schools were not described in the report to permit some estimate of the type and amount of bias that may have occurred, it is likely the schools studied not only did not represent a cross-section of schools but also that those missing had special racial problems.

THE LEARNING PHENOMENON

The measurement process itself can serve as change agent and affect the phenomenon measured, defeating the purpose of mea-surement (though measurement can be a strategy explicitly de-signed to create change). The commonest type of change is learn-ing. In experimental science the researcher soon finds he has to apply a learning curve to interpret results on a series of retests of the same experiment. As he becomes more expert at setting up the experiment and at taking the measures this alters results. Similarly as enumerators gain experience they may be able to elicit more and more accurate answers and exercise better quality control. While this is certainly desirable, it does create difficulty in com-paring indicators over time.

In panel studies or simply cases where the same individuals are subject to questioning, they too may become more experienced and better able to understand and explain themselves. But more difficult to deal with is the problem that they may actually change their behavior or reactions because of being measured. The first time you ask someone about their perception of the ambient noise level they may reply that it is low. The second or third time their perceptions may be so awakened that they are very bothered by the same level of noise they did not notice before. In the con-sumption surveys where families give weekly or monthly reports on expenditures to enumerators, there is considerable danger that this unaccustomed process of keeping track limits total expendi-ture or curtails some types of expenditure.

GUINEA PIG EFFECT

Another way measurement can act as change agent is to cause people to behave differently because they are being observed. The problem exists for any data collection process where a participant is conscious of being observed. It is a version of the Hawthorne effect demonstrated in a management study in a plant where workers produced more output under all test conditions, including those which involved more adverse working conditions. The conclusion was that the experimental situation itself provided the conditions making people work harder. Any effort to take social measures is likely to have a similar effect. For example, it has recently been found that in the rotating panel of the CPS where families are interviewed for four-month periods, dropped for several months and then interviewed again for four months, unemployment rates are higher for families when they are interviewed in the first month of the period. While as yet I have not seen an explanation of this, it seems likely that the mere awareness of being under scrutiny is enough to encourage some individuals to try harder to find work.

PASSAGE OF TIME

A major objective of social indicators is to trace the direction and patterns of change over time. But the passage of time creates problems for the collection of good statistics. Enumerators and survey designers learn over time. The individuals and their styles change over time. The meaning of questions evolves in new social contexts as do behavior patterns. An unchanging instrument does not always bear a constant relation to the phenomenon over time if the phenomenon changes in fundamental ways.

CLASSIFICATION

In every data gathering process someone must look at an amorphous or complex reality and decide what is important and how to classify it or some portion of it. Sometimes it is the respondent who must sort out among his own array of reactions to decide if he is happy or unhappy with his neighborhood. Sometimes it is the enumerator who must decide if a sagging porch is dangerous or just potentially dangerous and if therefore a house should be classified as deteriorating or dilapidated. In doing so enumerators can come to widely varying conclusions (U.S. Dept. of Commerce, 1967).

A policeman must decide if a broken store window represents vandalism, breaking and entering or attempted burglary. In regular, professional surveys a large handbook of instructions aids the enumerators, as the crime reporting manual aids police in making some of these decisions. However, the decision often rests on the

212

judgment of enumerator or respondent. Because of this it is important to measure concepts with unambiguous meanings, which are generally accepted. It is more likely that marginal or unusual answers will be classified consistently and as the analyst would like them to be if the enumerator has a clear grasp of the objective of the classification process.

COPING WITH THE PROBLEMS

Most of these problems are never going to be fully soluble. We can find ways of minimizing them and guarding against them. We can make some compromises in the concepts. We can use several related measures with compensating types of error to help us recognize the extent of bias or unreliability. Most of all we can make the problems explicit whenever we present data for public interpretation and use, and we can do more research and testing for the existence, extent, and character of the errors. In general we should always, in designing indicators or choosing data to use in analysis, think through whether the drawbacks of the data collection method could be critically harmful to our purpose. We may well find that use, concept, and collection method all have to be adjusted to mesh with one another.

Chapter IX

Structuring the Data

Once data are gathered they must be organized and summarized for presentation. We must select, aggregate and reformulate the numbers, as long lists of raw data would be of little use and inaccessible to most people. As a minimum one must classify and tabulate, but for indicators that are to focus on particular problems more structure is required. This involves making judgments and applying normative and analytic models. To many it implies cynical manipulating of data, but to stop with classifying and tabulating is not to avoid the ultimate responsibility for making the choices. Raw data is only more neutral than structured data insofar as it is more incomprehensible. The mere choice of questions in a survey already defines the possibilities. However, to go a step further and try to formulate the data so it can communicate a message clearly is only to be more explicit, and, in many ways, more honest. If we recognize some basic principles and rules for structuring data for indicators, then the "manipulation" cannot be too dishonest. Not just any impression can be created, but some facts will come through.

CRITERIA FOR CONSTRUCTING INDICATORS

The structuring of data for indicators can involve a wide variety of things — the choice of a representative figure like the median level or one which combines all of the data, like total national income. The process can be simple, just adding items, or complex, transforming, selecting and combining different elements of the data. One can create various impressions and point up different issues. While there are no rules to define specifically how the choices should be made in individual cases, some things are clearly wrong and deliberately misleading (Reichard, 1974). Moreover, there are some positive criteria one can apply. These criteria ultimately rest on our concepts and models of the phenomena and the uses to which we wish to put the indicator. It is possible to structure data to create a deliberately deceptive result using the same principles as required to give an informative result, but that problem is not at issue here. The defense against lying with data is interested people and groups who understand how the indicator is constructed and why, and the implications. But this is an institutional and political issue which we will address elsewhere. We proceed on the assumption here that the interest in designing an indicator is to inform rather than to conceal.

VALIDITY

The most important criterion for an indicator is its validity, but this is unfortunately an elusive concept and difficult to test for. It means the extent to which the measure reflects the phenomenon or concept it is intended to. No phenomenon is immediately and directly accessible to us without the mediation of instruments of perception or measurement, and the results of our observation are only interpretable in the light of a model and set of expectations. As Chapter V discusses, to measure anything we make assumptions about how our perceptions work, and we have types and characteristics in our minds to classify what we observe as well as some idea of our purpose to help sort out the relevant material from the noise.

There are three basic approaches to estimating the validity of an indicator. We often forget the most obvious — to look at the way it is designed and decide if, intuitively and in the light of all one knows about the phenomenon, the particular measure sounds reasonable. This probably means thinking through and evaluating the model connecting the measurement with the reality.

The second possibility is to see if the measure behaves the way you would expect the phenomenon to. This of course implies that you have some model of how the phenomenon relates to a set of other variables and you have some idea whether it should be moving up or down or fast or slow with respect to these other variables. The trouble is that in looking at behavior in the past, we still do not necessarily have a good way of knowing whether the indicator will be valid for future situations. A related approach is to see whether the measure helps to predict some situation that would be caused by or coincident with the phenomenon we are trying to measure.

A third approach to measuring validity is to look at the behavior of other measures of the same or related phenomena, collected by other means or structured in different ways. If all of these seem to move in approximately the same direction or the directions one would expect, it tends to confirm the validity of the particular measure. Of course, it does not do so with any detail or precision nor tell us how to resolve the problem if two do diverge widely.

It is sensible to use all three approaches jointly, however, as each is likely to give additional information. If the results all converge, we can perhaps accept the validity of a measure. In practice with indicators that are a regular part of public discussions of policy there is a kind of testing of the validity of the measure against public perceptions and understanding. A public perception for example that the poverty line no longer represented the cost of a socially acceptable minimum standard was a reason that this line is now being redesigned.

The problem of determining validity is one reason to avoid indicators of the black-box variety, which are designed operationally rather than on the basis of a prior concept. It is meaningless to even think about validity without a precise concept against which to match a measure. Not to have any feeling about validity of a measure is to be unable to use it with confidence and expect it to behave predictably in new situations.

SENSITIVITY

A second criterion for choosing and structuring a measure is its sensitivity to changes in the phenomenon. Does it respond quickly and noticeably when the phenomenon changes or do its movements mask the real problems? A classic example is the mortality rate, which, though it has been used as an indicator of health, is very insensitive to health. For one thing it may reflect the age composition of the population rather than the general level of health. Since a large part of the rate is made of old people in a developed country then even a serious epidemic will not change the rate much. Most importantly, the majority of disease is non-fatal, in any case, and does not show up in mortality figures.

Infant mortality is a somewhat more sensitive health index, as infants are more susceptible to disease and more likely to die than most other groups. Thus this rate will more quickly reflect health changes. However, it is a very insensitive health index in developed countries where communicable disease and nutrition are only a

216

small part of the health problem. In such cases, infant mortality rates reflect mostly genetic difficulties and accidents, and have virtually no sensitivity to the principal health problems of chronic disease among the middle-aged and elderly. Life expectancy as a health indicator does, to some extent reflect this, but it moves slowly and shows little about nonfatal disease. Sensitivity is not a quality that inheres in a particular measure. It depends on the character of the phenomenon at a particular time and place and the relation of the measure to it, both of which are subject to change. To evaluate a measure's sensitivity, as its validity, requires clear concepts and models.

DECISIONS IN STRUCTURING DATA

The problem of manipulating data to create useful indicators is one for which there is no simple solution strategy. The possibilities are only limited by one's imagination, time, and technical capacity. The object is to simplify and impose some order on a complex reality, to make it easier to comprehend and analyze. One can focus on a small piece of this reality, or combine several pieces. One can emphasize the effect of the passage of time or the distribution of some goods or characteristics. The choice is ultimately dependent on one's purposes and understanding of reality, but we can structure the way we address the problem to help us find a strategy for making choices. There are various options open, which have different potential in different situations. Moreover, it is possible to define some things which should not be done as they are deceptive or confusing. As a minimum it is worthwhile to recognize the array of options to find those which may be most useful.

CHOICE OF UNITS

A starting point is to decide on the units for measurement. This is a step which is often bypassed as it seems self-evident what the units are. For example, if you are interested in unemployment, you count people or if income, you count dollars. If education is the topic, you examine qualities of schools, if social interactions are involved, you look at neighborhoods. However, these formal, obvious units into which our experience happens to be divided do not necessarily correspond to the conceptual units that are the subject of our indicators, nor fit into the models we wish to apply (Etzioni and Lehman, 1969). If the quantity of unemployment is an issue, we may want to count units of time or productive work lost (Perry, 1970). If need is the issue, then income might be counted in some units corresponding to need satisfaction. If you are looking within cohesive educational environments, the proper unit may be internal to schools, tracks or even classrooms, or external, school systems with common educational styles. Neighborhoods may not be the relevant definition of the social universe for many types of people whose community is of the nonplace variety, extending from London and Paris to Washington, Cambridge and Berkeley and touching down nowhere in between (Webber, 1964).

SCALES

Related to the problem of units is the question of finding a scale for the indicator. If we do not use the obvious units, how do we assign numbers to our observations? The basic strategy is to find some other unit that does correspond approximately to the phenomenon of interest like Perry's measure of estimated productivity foregone to replace number of individuals out of work. This measure would permit accounting for variations in the type of labor involved in unemployment and fit better with policy models of economists to determine how much new economic activity is required to employ people. One can continue to count the formal, recognizable units, but use a weighting scheme based on a valuation of the units along some other scale. Sellin and Wolfgang (1964) experimented with this concept to weight crimes so they could be combined more meaningfully in an index than they are in the UCR, where all crimes are equivalent. They asked a panel of opinion leaders to evaluate on their subjective scale the relative gravity of index crimes. The crimes could then be weighted and combined in a measure which would represent the quantity of crime according to some social valuation of harmfulness (so long as the opinions did represent a social consensus).

It is important in planning a scale for an indicator to recognize the wide range of choice one has in the qualities of the scale. It is not absolutely necessary to find one which is the equal-interval, ratio scale to which we are accustomed. We can also settle for simpler scales, which may be less powerful, but are also more

218

appropriate to the amount of information we can extract from the data. The possible scales range from a classification of items into different categories (nominal scale) to ordering of the items (ordinal scale), ordering the items and specifying the distance between them (interval scale), and finally, specifying in addition a zero point (ratio scale) (Torgerson, 1958). We can perform whatever kind of operation we want with the latter scale, and most importantly, compare the absolute values of different things. Often however, all we can realistically say is that one item is more than another. For example it is not clear an additional thousand dollars of income is worth the same to someone with $20,000 a year as it is to someone with $3,000. We can apply an ordinal scale to such a situation, however, saying that we know at least that $4,000 is more than $3,000 and $21,000 is more than $20,000. The important thing to do is to apply a scale which preserves the information one needs without imposing structure the data cannot support.

CONSTRUCTING A RATE

Most measures are more useful if they are given as rates or percentages rather than as simple totals. The absolute magnitude of a phenomenon or of a change normally means little if we do not have a basis for comparison. For example, is an extra 500 million dollars a large or small addition to GNP? The answer will depend on the total GNP in the previous year at least, so you might use the percentage increase of GNP or compare the amount with the usual annual increment, or you might look at the change in GNP/capita if you thought population was increasing. The choice depends on the assumptions one will make in using the measure and one's understanding of reality. It is likely that more than one indicator will be necessary for a perspective.

One basic principle to follow is simple, but amazingly often ignored — the base for a rate should be the population-at-risk, the group or phenomenon which is capable of the kind of change being measured. The population-at-risk varies according to what one is trying to measure. Insofar as the FBI crime index is a measure of the risk of exposure to crime, it makes sense to cite rates in terms of cities where crimes occur. Insofar however, as the object is to measure trends in criminality, the base is wrong as many crimes are committed by people from out of town. However, if one were to try to develop an indicator of criminality by location, one would not be able to use the total local population as the base for the rate, but rather population old enough to be at risk as criminals according to legal definitions. After the 1930 census on unemployment, one of the great mistakes which caused the furor to arise over the reported results was the failure to compute the rate on the basis of population-at-risk though the principle was well known (Hogg, 1930). The first figures gave unemployment at 2% of the total population. As a sizable portion of the population would in no case go to work, the figures seemed irrelevant. The gainful worker base was later used and eventually the labor force concept. If the proper base is not used, irrelevant factors can change the indicator. A baby boom, for example, could decrease the unemployment rate at some later date. The current labor force concept is becoming increasingly unsatisfactory as it no longer includes most of the population likely to be either employed or unemployed. This makes interpretation of changes in unemployment rates difficult, as they are as likely to reflect changes in the labor force as in the amount of unemployment.

TIME PERIOD

The time period used for a rate can also have significant effects, and should not be an arbitrary choice. If a phenomenon fluctuates widely and erratically or if there is little one can do about it on short notice, a long time period may be appropriate, and vice versa. An indicator of life styles, like the standard budget, is probably changed often enough every 5 or 10 years unless war or severe inflation hastens the gradual process of change. School achievement indicators might make sense on an annual basis, but surely not less, as school programs are structured around annual curricula. Crime rates on a quarterly basis may be too frequent as they may fluctuate meaninglessly around rashes of crime which could probably be little influenced by policy change. This is not to suggest that for police programming more frequent data is not necessary, but rather that for broad consideration of crime prevention policy it may be counterproductive, or at least not worthwhile. Basic policy change in crime prevention strategies, in, for example, laws on treatment of suspects or punishment of offenders or in the development of new social programs, all require time to create, implement, and have effect. This is very different from economic policy, where fiscal and monetary tools can be put to work on a few hours notice and take visible effect within weeks or even days. For unemployment frequent data collection therefore has some value.

THE AGGREGATION PROBLEM

Reality has many facets and we are often reluctant or unable to ignore any of them in our measures. We seek a composite measure of housing, air, or even life quality which will somehow incorporate all the important elements in a single, summary figure. This is sensible to do when two conditions hold. The first is that we have an acceptable model which says that it does make conceptual sense to add the elements together, that the resulting index will correspond to an idea we can use and understand. The second is that we have a reasonable method to transform unlike things into a common scale so they may be added together. To combine units of dilapidation with units of crowding we need to transform them both into units of housing quality.

Unfortunately it is not clear that there are many other cases where both conditions can be met. Price indices are a major exception. The idea of some overall level of price rise makes some intuitive sense and certainly is relevant to questions of wage increases. Moreover, it is possible to add the price increase in one time to that in another by weighting them according to their relative value in the total array of goods chosen by an average family. This was reasonable because the price index would reflect some effective price increase for families. This weighted index is probably the most satisfactory of any we have, but it has problems because the model is too simple and does not account for everything. It does not deal with the problem of rising prices' changing people's tradeoffs (there is no feedback in the model) nor with quality changes in goods. An additive model is, after all, a simple one, and we would be unusually fortunate if it were to be sufficient. The best one can say is that the index works reasonably well when life styles are fairly constant.

GNP is another index which is fairly satisfactory and involves adding different things together. Again the idea of a total national product seems conceptually satisfying, and it is an idea fundamental to Keynesian economic theory. It is possible to add disparate kinds of things in this case because it is reasonable to measure most of them on a common scale of money value. However, it, like the CPI, took twenty or thirty years to develop from original concept to satisfactory index. Even for this relatively straightforward concept the additive model turns out to be oversimplified. Many elements in the GNP should perhaps not be added, but subtracted, like pollution cleaning up activities. Moreover the linear money scale may well not correspond to social valuations of many goods and services. Doubts about the GNP as an adequate measure of national output are rapidly growing (Olson, unpublished; Myrdal, 1973).

The fact that the GNP and CPI, which involve summing up relatively similar things, took years to evolve and still have serious conceptual drawbacks, should be fair warning to those who seek aggregated indices for housing quality, accessibility or other fuzzier concepts. It is unclear that these are unitary ideas that can be measured along a single dimension. For example, housing quality is an issue, at least, of physical deterioration, existence of plumbing or other facilities, size relative to occupancy, and environment. To create an aggregate index from these you need first to find a way to measure each component and to do so on a common scale. Conceivably one could find a social consensus on the relative seriousness of various housing problems by some opinion testing like Sellin and Wolfgang's effort in scaling crime. It seems unlikely however, as housing preference varies according to one's stage in the life cycle, class and cultural background. It is unclear there would be a consensus on the proper mix of public and private space, or how to make tradeoffs between plumbing facilities and deterioration. Moreover, for this type of index of housing quality to make sense the characteristics must contribute independently and additively to the problem. A very good case could be made that deterioration and overcrowding create a synergistic effect so that the existence of the two in combination is worse than the simple sum of their separate effects would indicate.

In other words, to develop an aggregate index you need a model of the phenomenon which says its components are additive. However ideas like noise pollution or accessibility have components that are on dimensions that it may make no sense to add together. Noise, for example, can be measured in decibel level, annoyance quality, time of day, and persistence. These, in different combinations, could vary widely in their disturbing effects. Accessibility, on the other hand, is a question of distance, ease of travel, and time for trip. These variables have different values to people of different ages, incomes and life styles. To combine them on some

222

average scale would be meaningless. It would tell us about neither an individual nor the group.

In England a weighted index was devised (Little and Mabey, 1972) to identify educational priority areas that should be targeted for special aid. The index included such diverse measures as occupation, overcrowding, immigrants and teacher turnover. Not surprisingly the weighting was a conundrum resolved in an ad hoc way. The only way to test whether the measure was a valid way of identifying the underprivileged areas was to test the results against the intuitive impressions of local officers. There was a reasonable agreement, which suggests that the effort might have been dispensed with all together, except perhaps that allocating government funds often requires an apparently objective index.

An additional problem with an aggregated index of something like housing quality or social deprivation is that even if it does more or less correspond to a consensus view of the totality of the problem, it has virtually no diagnostic value. To say that certain areas get high scores is not to give any idea what to do. Such aggregate indices normally have to be broken down again into their components to get a handle on whether to deal with housing problems, for example, through community organization, code enforcement, subsidies to landlords, or subsidies to tenants.

OTHER APPROACHES TO SUMMARY MEASURES

The weighted additive index is only the best recognized of many ways for getting a single measure for a complex problem. Many other methods are being experimented with which involve more subtle models and different ways of transforming data or extracting the significant elements. A notable example is the effort to measure social phenomena in terms of a production function. The object of measurement, like poverty or health, becomes the output of a production process and can be measured in terms of some relationship between the inputs which are usually more readily measurable. Morgan and Smith, for example, use such an algorithm to measure economic well-offness (1969). This is a very popular approach because the economists' production model is well developed and understood. However, other types of indicators can emerge from other kinds of models. The important thing is to recognize that we need not be limited by simple formulations for indicators. The only drawback to other approaches may be the difficulties of explaining them to users.

223

In collapsing various dimensions into one a great deal of information is lost. Information about the movements of the individual dimensions and their relation to one another may be critical to one's analysis. There is often an advantage, of course, in a single measure, particularly to call public attention to a problem. However, such a measure may be neither a valid nor a sensitive indicator of the problem, and not adequate as a basis for action. Frequently it will be less deceptive and less of a conceptual problem to keep dimensions separate, letting decision-makers apply their own value judgments and models to make the tradeoffs. This is the argument many make for the use of an alternative to a simple cost-benefit criterion to sum up the value of projects which have many different impacts and values for different groups. One of course must keep the number of measures of different dimensions as few as possible, as even sophisticated analysts have trouble dealing with too many variables. The ordinary member of the public or local leader may be less equipped to do complicated analyses. But certainly they would understand better what the amenity level in an area was if they had one measure of park space, one of indoor recreation and one for shopping facilities than they would with only one mysterious measure combining all three.

Any indicator usually can be a measure of central tendency or the dispersion. For social policy, which is primarily concerned with the allocation of resources to problem groups in society, measuring the distribution of some quality or good is often more important than identifying the median or average. Depending on why one wants to know about the question or on the quality of the distribution, a central tendency figure may be utterly meaningless. If a man is standing with one foot in ice and the other in boiling water, it makes no sense to say he is, on the average, comfortable. The measure of average income in an underdeveloped, oil-rich country is not very useful, as virtually everyone is probably well above or below that average.

There are numerous alternative ways of measuring distributions, inclusing summary measures like the Gini index of inequality. Alker and Russett (1968) summarize many of the other possibilities. We can compare the average values for upper quintile with those for lowest quintiles, the median with the average in the lowest quarter, or total shares of some good held by those at the bottom with shares of those at the top. As one might expect, the choice is not insignificant, but tends to influence the way one looks at a problem and finds its solution, or even decides whether there is a problem. For example, if the figures on overcrowded housing are given in the categories of more than 1.5 people per room, more than 1, and then all the rest, they suggest a policy of upgrading the bottom levels of the distribution to some acceptable crowding minimum for everyone by adding housing for the least fortunate. If however, the distribution figures also showed the number of units with less than 0.1 person per room, the policy implications might involve redistributing existing housing. Similar examples could be cited for almost any policy question. This should suggest one reason for planners and decision-makers to be in on the structuring of indicators in the first place.

THRESHOLD INDICATORS

Often the design of an indicator includes not only its content and structure, but also its level. One decides what are the elements of the consumption standard that should go into an index, and also, for the standard budget or poverty line, one makes the further step of deciding what level of the measure should be the norm. This involves another order of magnitude of value judgments, but it may be essential if an indicator is to have any meaning. To give someone's score on a math test is not very useful unless you know the passing grade. Determining that passing grade is part of designing the indicator.

A good many social indicators require a decision about the threshold level above or below which something significantly different and important begins to occur. Health, for example, exists on a continuum from critical illness to in condition for the Olympics. To measure the prevalence of ill health it may be necessary to find a way to define the threshold between adequate functioning and something less. For unemployment one kind of threshold was determined in saying no one with over 1 hour of work a week was unemployed. Another kind is involved in the use of the 4% unemployment level to define full employment. In view of the additional judgments involved it may be most appropriate for a target value to be settled upon through a political process. However, ultimately these values will depend on the models one applies.

Most of the social indicators under discussion involve macrodata — data about collectivities. There is an alternative, however, which is more difficult to get, but which for many objectives may be far more productive. This is microdata, data on individuals or other units, in which the history of the units is retained. The important element becomes not so much the character of a place, society or group, but the paths and processes by which individuals make decisions, evolve or are affected by the system. In other words, instead of measuring the quality of housing in a city at various points in time, one would follow the course of individual units as they are improved, altered, or allowed to deteriorate.

This kind of effort is expensive, but it is increasingly recognized that macrodata conceals the mechanisms and processes which we need to understand if we are to take remedial actions. The criminal transaction statistics effort, for example (Kolodney and Wormeli, 1972), traces individual suspects as they pass through the criminal justice system through arrest, trial, jail and parole and rearrest to see how the system is working. Are there delays? Does rearrest occur more often for individuals who have had a particular course of experience? It is the same principle on which cohort studies are based, following a group of individuals through time to find sources of change in their history rather than in aggregated social patterns. The paths followed by various age cohorts may provide more useful explanations of social change than periodic snapshots of a population. For example to understand why high school students may be doing poorly, it may not be enough to know the characteristics of the school and the children. It may also be necessary to know where the children went to school before. If programs are designed to change or influence individual decisions, they can only be properly tested with microdata, as were OEO programs and the Graduated Work Incentive Experiment (Watts, 1972).

ADJUSTED DATA

Social phenomena tend to have sources of fluctuation which are unrelated to the issues in question. It has been suggested that crime data would represent the trend in criminality more meaningfully if it were adjusted to a population standardized with respect to age (Wolfgang, 1963). Since the young are more likely to be involved in crime than older people we may get the impression that our tendency to criminal behavior as a society is increasing when it is simply that the youth population is growing relative to the rest. Unemployment increases each year in the summer, when students flood the labor market and in winter when construction work declines. The figures can be affected also by bad weather. These are temporary interruptions in an overall trend and can be confusing if one is interested in the state of the economy. They may be useful to recognize for some purposes, like the planning for unemployment relief, but, on the whole, such short-term variations make interpretation complicated.

Economists have chosen to "purify" the unemployment indicator by a seasonal adjustment (U.S. Department of Labor, 1971). This is a kind of smoothing process, which purports to transform the data to what it would look like without temporary aberrations. The variation in rates is separated into three components representing seasonal, trend, and random variations. This is done with the aid of a moving average of previous years' experience. The method depends on the assumption that the present is similar to the past. A causal model of variation that took explicit account of the factors we know to exist would probably allow a better prediction and adjustment for unusual circumstances (Kaplan, 1972). For example, in June 1971 the method apparently over-adjusted for the students normally joining the labor market, who, apparently recognizing its poor state, never even entered it. The effect was to depress unduly the announced rate which then unduly bounced back in September. An alternative way of doing an adjustment that might not have such peculiar aberrations is to use a more explanatory model. One could account for actual weather patterns instead of assuming the present resembles the past. One could take account of the effect of particular strikes or model the response pattern of seasonal work to various weather conditions. The result could then be trend data far more effectively cleaned of irrelevant variation.

There are obvious pitfalls to such manipulations. Most important, users are often not conscious of the difference between the adjusted figures and the actual figures, or, if they are aware of a difference, they may not be aware of the assumptions they must accept to use the data — particularly if they are going to ascribe meaning to their every movement. One can get aberrations in results when the adjustment model is too simplistic. However, adjustments to eliminate variations that are meaningless in terms of the analysis can make indicators more accessible to a wider public. Not only could the crime rate be advantageously adjusted to age distributions, but also, for some purposes, health indices, literacy rates, family income and many others. All of them vary with age distributions, and the focus of social programs on one or another group means that their effect may be obscured without standardization. In a country for example where there are many old people the effect of a program of educating children might be lost in unadjusted data on literacy rates. Only adjustment might make it possible to compare the efforts of two different countries. Data may be adjusted for a range of other sources of variation besides population and seasonal factors. It can be done for anything which occurs without relation to the problem under consideration, and either predictably or unpredictably. When adjustment is done, however, it should be made clear what its assumptions and objectives are and what kind of variation has been eliminated and why. Variation which from one perspective appears uninteresting and worthy of discarding may be important from another. Real totals usually continue to have a value.

THE IMPORTANCE OF PRIOR MODELS

It is possible to make decisions in the design of an indicator without a clear, specific model of the phenomenon, or why one wants to know about it. As discussed in Chapter VII, an indicator may well take a particular form in part because our theory is not good enough to tell us how to deal with every marginal issue. However, the less guidance one has from a model connecting a measure with a phenomenon, the more difficult the measure will be to interpret and use. An ad hoc operational measure is virtually impossible to validate, and can therefore be hard to use in informing public discussion. The standard budget is one example which is not atypical of many indicators that are now being proposed to measure some still amorphous concept. It is worth learning something about how such an indicator was constructed, to understand the contention that the design of an indicator without a clear measurement model can be a major cause of difficulties in gaining acceptance.

The concept that the BLS defined for the City Worker's Family Budget (CWFB) was a living standard providing for the "maintenance of health and efficiency, the nurture of children, and participation in community activities... not a 'subsistence' budget, nor... a luxury budget; it is... a modest but adequate standard of living". A "standard of living", according to the BLS, refers to the "goals we set for ourselves as consumers of goods and services and as users of leisure time and to our norms for conditions of living. Standard budgets measure the total costs of maintaining these levels and manners of living".

Their measurement model says that there is a consumption scale established by society, which can be discovered through observations of society's ratings of existing levels of living. These ratings are expressed in the judgments of scientists, such as medical and public health authorities (Kellogg and Brady, 1948) and in the behavior of individual consumers.

Theirs is a descriptive model, though a sketchy one, of family preferences or utility for goods. It states that there is a set of preferences common to the social group. It posits that this utility is ordered on a (presumably) linear scale and that it derives in some way from socially determined values. Finally, it relates observable data to this underlying preference set in saying that consumer behavior and scientific judgments reflect it. Unfortunately, the nature of this relationship between observable data and the underlying standard is not spelled out, nor is the method of selecting a level. The model provides only the most general framework for making measurements. "Scientific" and consumer criteria may be in conflict with each other and, in any case, even if we can agree that the two do reflect society's values, we still have no theory with which to draw the implicit values out of masses of data on consumption or the varying testimony of experts. The sketchiness of the model testifies to the empirical tradition from which the budgets emerged and in which they are still steeped.

The budget items are in practice selected according to whatever convenient criteria may be found. Most selection processes combine judgmental, consumer, and scientific criteria in their own ways, and differently for each category of goods or services. For certain consumption items it is assumed there is a desirable level that may be determined on *a priori* grounds by evidence apart from actual preferences. Even these items are not, in practice, limited to the physical efficiency level, which seems the only scientifically definable one. The excess is usually the result of some consumption-based criterion. The nutrient standards are the official ones promulgated by the National Research Council, which Department of Agriculture home economists translated into specific food plans at different costs. The BLS chose the moderate cost plan, modified by data from the USDA Household Food Consumption Survey so it would include items actually used in various regions by families in the income class containing the median income. They also devised weights for the food items on the basis of the same consumption patterns.

The result of this process is a hybrid standard. It is not a minimum cost way of achieving good nutrition. If nutrition were the only value involved, the diet would probably be 50% soybeans. So the scientific standard is only part of the criterion. Realism is also a value, but the modifications made for consumer preferences still do not make the food plan realistic. Many families with the moderate budget level income do not have nutritionally adequate diets — much less the diets prescribed by home economists. They would not be able to calculate out the requirements the way a home economist does, even if they were motivated to. The result may be an approximate indicator of a socially defined norm, but it is clearly not one that is actually practiced.

The housing standard too was a similar blend of scientific, ad hoc, and consumer standards. The scientific element is provided by official standards of public groups, the American Public Health Association and the U.S. Public Housing Administration. It called for an unfurnished five-room unit, in sound condition with a private bath, hot and cold water, access to public transportation, stores, and play-space for children, in a hazard-free residential area. The price was the average rent for the middle third of the distribution of rents for actual housing fitting these requirements. This procedure is likely to produce an unrealistic result in the sense that such standard housing may be a small percentage of total housing and cannot represent usual housing. It also may not represent even a possible choice, which makes the indicator of dubious value as a normative guide to benefit levels.

The empirical basis of the measure in the 19th century has proved a hindrance in other ways. In that period the consumption categories were more or less arbitrarily determined according to the functions these items served, such as clothing, housing, heat, or food. The categories more or less remain unchanged, and all analysis for quantities is done within them. However, they are not functionally cohesive categories in contemporary terms the way they may have been at first. Many items now serve double functions which the existing classification system provides no way of accounting for. Sports clothes, for example, are for clothing and

230

recreation. Even food expenditure is partially for other purposes than nutrition. For example, processed foods save time but the processing portion of the cost cannot be attributed to needs for eating. Food expenditures for entertaining would fit more reasonably into a recreation category if one wanted to analyze the reasons for increases or decreases in such categories. In the near subsistence economy of the turn-of-the-century industrial worker these options were not open.

The resulting measure is difficult to explain, describe or use in a model as it has no precise conceptual analogue. It involves too many decisions made on different bases. It is not surprising that this indicator has had little use in social science research. It is possible that a simpler, clearer measure that did not try to approximate anything so hard to get hold of as a consumption standard would be preferable. The solution is probably to measure something different but related, that would be easier to formulate clearly and unambiguously, and easier to use in a model. For example, one could substitute the median income for the moderate level budget. The two figures are close to one another and undoubtedly there is a causal relation. The income level that, in the opinion of a cross-section of Americans is sufficient for a decent living, could be another substitute. It would not be precisely the same concept, but it would certainly be easier to use and understand because it represents a concept that people can refer to and use in relation to other ideas.

Chapter X

Institutionalizing Indicators

If an indicator is to play an effective role in public decisions, it must have an existence apart from the immediate issues. If it is created by an advocate of one view specifically for the discussion, it can be suspect rather than informative. Moreover, if the existence of an indicator depends on the awareness of and readiness to act on a particular issue, it cannot call attention to new problems. The alternative is to institutionalize the collection, dissemination, and use of measures so that they will be produced, accepted, and made part of decisions no matter what they show or whose side they benefit. There are drawbacks to institutionalization, such as a lack of flexibility, and there are different degrees of institutionalization. The object here is to understand how, in practice, an indicator may become institutionalized and what are the implications of the various steps.*

The term institutionalization, in this context, means the setting up of procedures and practices which ensure the continuing existence of an indicator and which legitimize and formalize its methods and concepts. An institution is not only an organization, but it is also a pattern of behavior and interrelationships which is sanctified by time and well accepted norms. The setting up of procedures is one step in institutionalization and the winning of public assent for the measure and its uses represent further important elements. This acceptance and the incorporation of the measure and its applications into the routine of public activity gives an indicator the viability that is required if it is to be anything more than the source of one more argument.

Institutionalization may be a prerequisite for an effective indicator but it is a double-edged sword. It is possible for unsatisfactory concepts, methods, and uses to become permanent. Just as the creation of norms and institutions takes time and resources, so

---

*For a view of how the use of information and expertise is institutionalized, yet in a political context, see Lyons (1971).

does their evolution or replacement. Sometimes we become so habituated to thinking in terms of particular measures that we stop looking for where they fall short. This is a serious problem in view of the changes that occur in society and its perception of problems over time, as Chapter VII discusses. One answer may be to work on ways of institutionalizing change processes. Experience shows that some of the strongest and best indicators have evolved in concept and method through routine, accepted patterns. It seems very likely that measures which cannot bend in response to change will break.

ELEMENTS IN INSTITUTIONALIZATION

Although there is no single path for institutionalizing measures for public decisions, there are some factors which contribute. Existence of one or two features implies a weakly institutionalized measure, and of all of them implies a strongly institutionalized one.

— The concept of the measure (or at least the presumed concept) meshes with a public perception, whether it changes the perception or is changed by it.

— The agencies that collect and manipulate the data are respected and not subject to immediate political control.

— Long-term financing and regular production of measures can be depended upon.

— The data are presented in a nonpolitical context.

— There are informed, active interest groups who use and support the continuance of the data series.

— The media and the public are conscious of the measure's existence and its role.

— There are processes established and followed for orderly change in concepts and methods.

— The indicator is tied into particular programs as a criterion for funding or a trigger for its operation.

— The indicator is tied into the analysis and conduct of policy to which government is committed.

— Institutional arrangements exist to use and analyze the measure in connection with policies.

THE INSTITUTIONALIZATION OF UNEMPLOYMENT RATES*

To look at some of these let us start with one of the most fully institutionalized of U.S. measures, the unemployment rate. This measure had a good start in 1940 as its concepts and methods were the results of long discussions and the generation of considerable consensus. The process of institutionalization could probably be said to begin in 1942 when the data became a regular responsibility of the Census Bureau, a well-established and respectable statistical agency with no policy affiliation or operational responsibility. At the same time, the Budget Bureau set up an interagency task force on concepts and methods in the labor force survey in recognition that the user agencies might find problems and need changes. The task force would provide a forum for discussion and decision on changes.

The key event was the passage of the 1946 Employment Act, which represented a public commitment for the first time to the objective of high employment. The legislation clearly made the indicator a criterion of the policy's success and set up a situation in which policy-makers would have opportunity, competence, and incentive to use the measure.** Unemployment rates became a prominent feature in the annual Economic Reports of the President from their start. These reports gathered increasing public attention over the years as they became known as the vehicle through which Administrations laid out their economic policy. Today it receives prominent, detailed attention in the press and is studied extensively by Congressmen, businesses, analysts, and students. As the Act requires a report on and prediction of employment levels, linked with a program for remedial action, the statistics moved to center stage. Eventually the Administration would have to account to the public for every adverse move of the unemployment rate. Because of public awareness it would not be possible for any Administration to wish it away or ignore unemployment as an issue.

The Council of Economic Advisors (CEA) not only included the measure in their report, they used it prominently in their discus-

---

*This story is given in fuller detail in Chapter VI. Here some factors are simply highlighted.

**General references on the role of information in this system of policy-making are Flash (1971) and Wilensky (1967).

sions and analyses. They discussed whether there should be a target level of unemployment and, if so, what it should be and how it should be calculated. They and other economists interested in national policy developed models which explained or predicted unemployment. This technical use meant that there was close scrutiny of the quality and composition of the measure and that an important group of economists developed a considerable stake in the continuance of the measure.

The Joint Economic Committee (JEC) also had functions which strengthened the measure. First it had the responsibility of examining the report, drawing further public attention to it and focusing Congressional attention as well. They had to examine economic policies in the light of this report and of measures of unemployment. Their hearings were to become a forum for education of the Congress and the public as they called on expert witnesses and administration officials. The Congressmen soon decided that a special subcommittee on economic statistics was needed to keep watch on the statistical system. This group by 1961 had become sophisticated about the nature and uses of a wide range of statistics. This development may have been partly due to the fact that there were at least two professors of economics on the committee, but the process was unlikely to have happened without the forum the subcommittee provided.

The committee also, by its adversary position with respect to the Administration, helped create a demand for a measure that was unbiased, reliable, and insulated from political manipulation. While CEA economists might have been equally anxious for such a measure, they were in a less appropriate position as servants of the President than the committee to criticize effectively. Outspoken members of the CEA have often been reprimanded by the Administration. In any case, the committee held hearings whenever there were problems with the measure in concept, method, or interpretation and found the Administration responsive.

Meanwhile, a base of support from informed users was growing in a variety of ways. The JEC in 1950 sent out questionnaires to union leaders, businessmen and government officials to understand their views on the meaning of unemployment figures and included them in 1954 and 1955 hearings on the methods and concepts. The Federal Statistics Users Conference, organized by the Budget Bureau, provided an opportunity for two-way education of statisticians and users of many statistics. The JEC began to publish a descriptive supplement to the economic indicators publication

(U.S. Congress, annual), and in 1959 the Administration began to hold regular press conferences with the monthly release of the figures. In short, a public information and public relations campaign was launched for the data, and some processes set up for interaction of users and producers, which ultimately involved users as supporters of the data.

By the late forties, rival unemployment estimates had virtually disappeared as labor and management organizations accepted the official statistic instead of their own. They became important defenders of the measure when it came under attack in 1961 (pp. 80—83). This confidence was unshaken by the transferral of the analytic responsibilities for CPS from the Census to the BLS. The latter had a nonpartisan professional reputation equivalent to the Census, and with its greater sensitivity to economic and social issues it could produce more information, structured in more useful ways. Moreover, the Bureau had set up Labor and Business Research Advisory Councils made up of analysts working for user groups. Though they had no formal powers, they were kept informed of proposed changes in methods or concepts and could bring pressure against developments they did not like. Meanwhile, however, these groups felt they were being consulted and in some sense became part of the decisions.

Thus an important element in the institutionalization of the unemployment measure was the public flow of information about the measure and an alliance of interest groups, individuals, and groups within Congress and the Administration. It was partly the result of a government policy to provide public information on the data and to involve users in the decision-making processes of the BLS. It was also partly due to the existence of experienced research staff in major labor unions and manufacturers' organizations like the National Industrial Conference Board, who could play the intermediary role between users and designers of measures. In all sectors professional staff and policy-makers were working cooperatively, BLS statisticians with the Labor Department and Congressional staff and outside economists with the JEC.

In the forties and fifties then, orderly processes of change developed. The elimination of ambiguous questions on reasons for not looking for work were adopted by the interagency task force in 1945, subcommittees of the task force reported to the JEC in their analysis of needs for changes. The JEC in turn examined the issues and made recommendations. They also heard from the expert committee which studied the 1954 sampling discrepancy (U.S. Dept. of Commerce, 1954) and based recommendations for changes and funding on these reports and on the comments of users. Although the changes made in 1957 did not correspond exactly to the committee's recommendation (technically the committee had no jurisdiction over the agency's funds), they did correspond approximately (U.S. Dept. of Commerce, 1958). The legitimacy this process lent to the changes would become important later when they were questioned. Moreover, the establishment of the possibility of change and laying out of the routes to change would also provide an outlet to criticism made at various times.

The extent to which the unemployment rate had become an institution was revealed when James Daniel's *Reader's Digest* article (1961) attacked the concept and methods of the measure. There was no dissenting voice among economists, industrial users and Congressmen, who hastened to defend the measure. The calling of a Presidential Committee to study the statistics was not an overreaction, but a recognition of the critical role they had come to play in public decisions. The extent of support for the indicator from both political parties, the academic world, and business, labor and management was a hallmark also of the acceptance the indicator achieved (U.S. President's Committee, 1962, U.S. Congress, 1963). Although it was not perfect, as would become increasingly obvious in the ensuing years, all had participated in its creation and legitimation and had agreed to agree on it. The response to Daniel was strong because users greatly valued the consensus they had achieved.

CONSUMER PRICE INDEX (CPI)

Many of the same features characterize the CPI as the unemployment rate, and it is the only measure that rivals it in the degree to which it has become an institution. The process began when the CPI became an important element in decisions on wage increases during World War I. Wage changes thereafter were implicitly compared to the index, and unions came to have a vested interest in its continuance. In 1948 the first wage contract was actually tied to the CPI, and since then its direct impact on wages has mushroomed, to a point in 1974 where it is a fully accepted principle that wages should keep pace with the index. A price index has been an integral part of the systems of wage and price control in the U.S. and U.K. in the seventies. Its rapid increase is accepted as prima facie evidence of a situation requiring reaction, and its movements at this writing are the central issue in a British national election.

In the U.S. CPI production is the responsibility of the same well-respected agency as the unemployment figures are — the BLS. It has had the benefit of input from non-government experts. In fact, the important methods of designing the index were developed outside of government, in the NBER. The public explanation of the measure is considerable. There have been regular press briefings on the monthly figures, and its methods have had as careful scrutiny as the unemployment figures (for example, U.S. Congress, 1951). The Employment Act strengthened the index's role just as it did the unemployment measure because it also established the goal of maintaining purchasing power. Eventually, rates of unemployment became associated with rates of inflation represented by the CPI and the policy became one of balancing off the two. Therefore, the CPI became part of policy in a way similar to the unemployment rate and additionally institutionalized in wage analyses.

The measure was, like unemployment figures, seriously challenged, and the response was parallel in an investigatory Presidential Committee (Sayre, 1946, and Arnow, 1951). The measure was found in need of revision, but its basic methods and integrity of its designers remained unscathed. During the Second World War in the U.S. a rule was adopted to allow a maximum percentage wage increase equivalent to the rise in the cost of living index in a particular period. Workers felt this was an inadequate recompense for increased costs. The natural target was the measure, and they claimed it did not actually represent living cost increases.

A committee of the American Statistical Association was called, headed by an eminent statistician, and when their ambiguous report failed to stifle criticism, Roosevelt appointed a Presidential Committee with business and labor members. There was much dispute, but the Committee was able to conclude that the index did understate price rises considerably (U.S. President's Committee, 1944). The principle of the index involves getting monthly prices on a set of goods corresponding to usual purchases of a working class family. The quantities of goods provide the weights for these prices which are combined in an index. But during the war, the mix of goods in the market changed radically. Although the BLS took cars, nylon stockings, and other unavailable items out of the index, they were not able to account for the downgrading in quality of many goods, the disappearance of low-priced items from stores, and relative changes in prices which meant that the array of index goods was no longer representative of actual choices. Moreover, the index took no account of the unavoidable life style changes under war conditions, like the necessity of eating in restaurants to supplement rationed food.

The result of this dispute was that the allowed wages in the postwar stabilization period were increased, and the index was named the Consumer Price Index instead of "cost of living index" in recognition that it did not measure living cost changes, but price changes. More significantly, however, the whole affair brought home how important was an accurate measure based on proper weights and how difficult it was to make any decisions without a measure that all could agree on. The war period was marked by constant industrial dispute. Before this, expenditure surveys to provide weights for the index were erratic, but now they are done routinely every ten years or so, and the index is under close public scrutiny.

THE STANDARD BUDGET

The standard budget has never become fully institutionalized in the sense of the first two measures, although it has become considerably more since 1966. It has not been accepted as the official measure of income adequacy, and its position is so precarious that it was nearly abolished by a hostile Administration in 1971.

Despite the aura of respectability lent it by the BLS, the budget's methods and concepts were never fully explainable and this detracted from its acceptability. The users were administrators at all government levels, managers, and union leaders with little in common, and they never came together as an interest group. Until 1966 budgets were only collected at the request of Congress whenever they recognized a need for a perspective on changed life styles. Most important no policy incorporated an unambiguous objective of income adequacy. While the measure was tied to such things as welfare benefits or payment formulas, it did not have the visibility and Congressional attention that involvement in a national policy would have given it.

The situation began to change in 1966 when the budget became part of the regular BLS program and when it entered into the debate on the Family Assistance Plan. Notably the changes in method and expansion from one to three standard budgets at that time were suggested by a group of outside technical advisors on the budgets, in 1963 (U.S. Dept. of Labor). However, welfare reform has not passed Congress and even if it does, there is no guarantee that it will depend on a budget criterion. So the measure remains in jeopardy. While it is sufficiently well understood and professionally designed not to be readily manipulated by politicians, its existence is in doubt, now that it has come to provide an unwelcome policy criterion.

THE POVERTY LINE

The U.S. poverty line is an example of an abortive effort to institutionalize a measure. The Administration selected a measure of poverty based on Orshansky's definition (1965) and made every effort to institutionalize this measure. It became the "official" poverty line, and census tabulations were presented in terms of it as well as many analyses. But it represented no consensus, and many agencies continued to use their own poverty criteria. Academics had plenty of other suggestions, and the general public soon found that it did not correspond to its views of poverty.

In 1973 it went back to the drawing boards, and it has few to mourn it. Hopefully, out of the discussions will eventually emerge a measure that is more representative of a consensus among users. Internal agency discussion is a reasonable beginning, but it seems likely that there will have to be an open process of design if any measure is to gain wide acceptance. There are those who fear institutionalizing a measure of poverty may help to institutionalize poverty. This is a recurrent issue as an established measure creates an established presence of a problem.

CRIME RATES

The Uniform Crime Reports also represent an institutionalized data series, though one that has solidified in the wrong form. However, the data is not nearly as pervasive and widely accepted as the CPI, for example. The crime rates have been respected not because of the reputation of the sponsoring agency for professional statistical work, but because of the FBI's independence of

240

partisan politics. It seemed that any data the FBI produced would be free of taint. To say the FBI was nonpartisan was not to say it was apolitical, however, as it had causes to promote, particularly the strengthening of crime-fighting activities. This potential bias would prevent the data from ever being fully accepted. Moreover, as the FBI did not provide information about the quality and character of the data, researchers would be prevented from making much use of it or serving as an interest group or spokesmen for it. The data did have support among police, but this kind of support did not give it intellectual respectability nor a group of experts to work on improving it.

Politicians and police chiefs made use of the data to demand funds or criticize city executives. President Nixon made use of the rising crime rates in his 1968 campaign, and the media and the public seemed prepared to accept the measures as adequate. However, no policies have been established to hinge directly on the rates. The closest to a policy use is that LEAA funds are distributed in part according to local crime rates. But as Congress spends more time discussing crime and its prevention, it also becomes more knowledgeable about the inadequacies of crime figures and demanding of more reliable data.

RACIAL BALANCE

An indicator of racial balance in schools could suddenly become institutionalized in the courts, but judges have thus far shied away from taking any step that could lead to a fixed measure. Numerous court cases in recent years on whether de facto segregation existed in a particular school system have confronted the problem of defining the percentage of black in a school which makes it imbalanced. There is some theory on ideal ratios for best educational environments and there has been pressure on the courts to find a simple definition and avoid endless future litigation. However, the theory is poor, and judges have preferred to use both the results of research and existing percentages as a guide and sources of information but not institutionalize a particular ratio.* Most

*For example, a judge in Norfolk, Virginia in a decision (302 F. Supp. 18, May 19, 1969) which drew heavily on social science research concluded there was insufficient evidence to decide what percentage black marked the critical dividing line between a good and a harmful educational environment. He was quite willing however to accept in principle the notion that there was a
(cont. on p. 190)

decision-makers, however, cannot take time to contemplate each situation and often settle for some compromise measure of imbalance just to make action possible.

PROPOSALS FOR INSTITUTIONALIZING SOCIAL INDICATORS: AN EVALUATION

It seems indisputable that if a system of indicators is to have an impact on public decisions, it must be to some extent institutionalized. That is, there must be some kind of tacit consensus on the acceptability of the measures, concepts, and methods, and the measures must have sufficient viability that they cannot simply be summoned up or ignored, as suits the politicians. They should have some kind of an accepted place in policy-making processes, rather than depend for their use on chance. If not, indicators serve as little more than partisan tools of those in power and not vehicles for communicating information nor forces for positive change.

There are dangers in overinstitutionalization or fixing inappropriate measures into the system of public analysis and action. It has its drawbacks when basic change is needed in the way we measure something, as it retards such change. For the measures in which we have less confidence we may wish to avoid the full range of moves that would harden a particular form and use into the measure. However, as the next chapter illustrates, when needs and uses develop for which existing measures are inappropriate, basic forces come into play to change the measure.

Concrete efforts in the U.S. to set up and institutionalize social indicators are of two kinds. One is the official publication of a book of measures pertinent to areas of social concern (U.S. Executive Office of the President, 1974). This is the step several governments have already taken and it is unquestionably important. However, it should be clear by now that it is only one of many needed moves, and in itself is not sufficient to make the indicators

---

percentage which was too high. A Massachusetts law passed in 1965 declared any school unbalanced and ineligible for state subsidies if it contained over 50% black students. This abrupt institutionalization of a firm figure into the policy has proved somewhat counterproductive as it has made compromise difficult and no one has been prepared to stand behind the figure as ideal. The controversy over this legislation has continued at a high pitch since then.

used or used effectively. Although the choice and design of measures for these publications has not been divorced from political or pragmatic considerations, the process has not been a particularly open one, nor has it generated the consensus that is likely to be required for people to take the measures seriously. While the existence of these compilations may give visibility to new measures and new combinations of measures and be the catalyst for essential debate on what we should be measuring and why, they are unlikely in themselves to change the quality of public decisions or the way they are made.

An effort has been made in the United States, however, to deal with some of the other institutionalization problems. This is the legislation repeatedly proposed by Senator Mondale since 1967 to establish a Council of Social Advisors and an annual Social Report. (See the hearings, U.S. Congress, 1968, 1970, 1971.) The proposal is tailored to a U.S. political structure and is not in detail necessarily applicable elsewhere, but the principle is general. If social indicators are to play a role in decision-making, there must exist a capability and machinery to use them, as well as an incentive. The bills have taken different forms, but they all contain the basic provisions that first the President shall be required to submit to Congress an annual social report charting the progress of policies in such areas as health, education, and housing, and second, there shall be a Council of Social Advisors in the Executive Office to prepare the report, gather data, develop indicators on broad social goals, appraise programs in the light of the goals, help set priorities, and conduct or sponsor special research.

The legislation is explicitly modeled on that most successful of systems of indicator use and sophisticated analysis of public issues and policies, the system set up by the Employment Act of 1946 with the CEA and the annual Economic Report. It was this system which firmly institutionalized the use of unemployment rates and inflation indices. However, there are some differences in the situations. While the legislation clearly represents constructive thinking toward implementing not just the creation, but also the use of indicators, some important elements are missing. It is not clear that the analogy with economic policy can be carried so far.

First, analysis machinery for economic policy was launched in connection with a specific and overriding concern — the avoidance of massive unemployment — and came into being in spite of considerable opposition to any kind of central planning and control. That opposition still exists to some extent, but the incentive to

243

overcome it in terms of a well-defined, urgent policy goal is not there. Moreover, the field of social policy is far broader than economic policy, which is routinely defined largely in terms of purchasing power, employment, and possibly two or three other goals. It is difficult to work up public support or Congressional enthusiasm for a measure designed not so much to affect a particular public problem, but rather to influence the way in which problems are dealt with across the board. The question of processes seldom gathers the same sort of attention as the question of end products, despite the fact that changing processes can create far more fundamental long-term changes. The Senate has passed the legislation in several sessions, but the House has yet to consider it. The difference reflects their perspectives, as the senators' longer terms and broader constituency allow them to think in terms of long-range objectives and of processes. The House takes a more pragmatic view and is more interested in legislation with identifiable impacts on their constituencies.

This objective of using social indicators as part of an effort to set some basic priorities leads to the most significant obstacles to the passage of this type of legislation. Essential to the operation of the Employment Act machinery is the existence of an equivalent function to that of the CEA for the Administration in the Congress. The JEC serves this function reasonably effectively, but to provide Congressional machinery to do formulation of national priorities like the Council of Social Advisors is not a simple matter. Congress has never been organized to do this and subject matter committees have run their own fiefdoms without interference from above in decision-making. This power is not easily wrested from those who have it.

Recent developments in Congress, however, may provide the machinery necessary to make use of social measurements. In fact they may create a demand for such data. The legislation has recently passed to reform the process by which Congress considers the budget and set up, in the House and Senate, budget committees to make recommendations about the array of national priorities, policies, and programs as a whole. Although both houses do have appropriations committees, neither meets as a whole, but normally approves recommendations of their subcommittees, which specialize in the appropriations for various agencies. Specialized committees tend to favor their particular areas and no one in Congress has had a mandate or opportunity to consider major tradeoffs.

The effect of the previous arrangement was to give the Executive Branch with its vast staff to prepare and analyze budget alternatives far greater power than Congress in determining the basic budget. This is a matter of no small significance as the budget is the closest we come in the U.S. to making any sort of a national plan. It is the unique forum for significant choices about the future. Policies and programs are argued individually, often on broad societal and philosophical terms, but the critical decision remains with the final distribution of funds among competing demands for education, health, defense, and so on, which occurs in the budget-design process. Wildavsky (1964, 1973) has argued that budgeting is at most an incremental process, that decision-makers have little to choose among basic priorities as so much of budgets is committed years in advance. He argues that all the tradeoffs are at the margin and that, in any case, it is just as well because no one could handle the complexity of such vast decisions any other way. I do not contend that our command of social and political phenomena is sufficient to make very different kinds of decisions with any confidence that they will produce their intended outputs. However, in current circumstances, some tradeoffs are made either deliberately or de facto, and Congress has little opportunity or capacity to judge most of them. The Administration, on the other hand, with its centralized analytic function in OMB can make overall policy decisions about spending. It can decide to increase spending in domestic programs for minority groups at the expense of agricultural subsidies, emphasize experimental studies, or insist on evaluation with all new programs. Congress has not been in a position to do the equivalent.

Despite the constraints on the budgetary process it is virtually certain that if Congress has an opportunity to confront it as a whole they will make some different decisions, if only because the committee considering it will have no special interest in one subject, but rather in the total package. In this process the legislators will have to justify basic value judgments with as much objective information as possible. They will have to come to agreement among themselves and account to colleagues with widely differing views. One very likely approach they will take will be to simplify the problem by using indicators as proxies for some parts of the issues. The monthly unemployment rate and the 4% unemployment level defining full employment have come to simplify economic policy discussion for example. Before the existence of the unemployment measure, policy discussion was hopelessly bogged down in arguments over what was actual and desirable unemployment. The numbers proved helpful in getting to the next step of choosing among policies.

Moreover the Congressional committees will be in an adversary position to OMB on these broad issues. They are likely to demand and use regularly produced public data to get a handle on whether the Administration's arguments for particular priorities are reasonable and to give them weapons in the discussion. This is certainly the reason for the existence of some of the more successful indicators. They were demanded by Congress in part as a protection against secretiveness and the argument that Administration experts know best. Thus it seems probable that a system for demanding and using indicators will emerge as the budget committees try to do their work. If this is what happens, it will help confirm the notion that use of new kinds of information in public decisions is likely to be possible only if decision-making processes are restructured, and, in turn, that the restructuring of the processes may create new demands for information.*

There remains a need for more thinking about the strategy for assuring a greater use of social measurement. The measures that have been comparatively successfully institutionalized for public decision-making, have all been closely tied to specific, significant public questions at at least some point in their history. Moreover, the measures have had strong support from informed interest groups, and great care has gone into, not only the choice of measure but also of agency to collect and present it, into the form of presentation and the effort to inform the potential users about the character and limitations of the measures.

These observations suggest that an interim strategy may be to develop and institutionalize indicators piecemeal rather than as a system. Thus one can opportunistically append to legislation relating to poverty or manpower training the requirement for some type of indicator whose ultimate implications may extend beyond that legislation. One could set up machinery for publically evaluating what such measures may imply. Congress is likely to have to take the lead in such actions, as experience has shown that Administrations seldom freely choose to measure their own performance.

---

*Two worthwhile references on information processes and decision-making in Congress are Schneier (1970) and Beckman (1971).

The coherent overall program for design and use of social measurement generally may take a long time to develop — if it is a feasible goal. However, considerable progress can be made toward improving the information system we now have and developing new and more pertinent measures by developing several kinds of efforts. Congressional committees can be encouraged to take a greater interest in the nature and quality of statistics pertinent to their subjects. There are various methods of raising their consciousness on this matter, like reports from bureau statisticians and testimony of expert witnesses. There can be a more positive effort both within and without government to build a base of informed support and criticism for the measures, as this can ultimately strengthen them.

A more positive statistical policy could be demanded by Congress and implemented by the Office of Management and Budget (OMB) to, for example, insist that each Department provide two or three indicators that it is prepared to accept as representative of the issues with which it deals. Most agencies now produce masses of data but make little, if any, effort to select or focus it on particular problems. As a result most data has little impact and little use. It is likely that Congress, social analysts, and the public may disagree with the Department's choice of measures, and heated discussion may ensue. But such airing of views is likely to be beneficial in the long run as it provides the opportunity for those concerned with public decisions to find common grounds of discussion and common definitions of problems. It would be one possible path to the development of key indicators that could play important roles in public perceptions and understanding. But whatever strategy is followed, it must be remembered that the design and use of indicators for policy will require legitimation and wide support as well as formal institutional arrangements and quite possibly legislation not only to set up systems to produce measures, but also systems to use them.

Chapter XI

Indicators in Use

Some of the vast quantities of data that government produces does play a role in public decisions. While the precise impact of a measure on a public action is seldom possible to determine, one can see how certain patterns of use predispose to particular ways of dealing with issues. Some indicators have been more used than others or more useful in some situations than others. These differences are related to the characteristics of the measures — the quality of the methods and appropriateness of the concepts. Some kinds of uses demand more than others, when, for example more is at stake or more consensus is required for action.

The study suggests that uses or attempted uses of measures in public decision-making place great pressure on them to fulfill the demands of their task. Indicators which are basically inadequate are either not used or are gradually altered and improved until they fulfill some minimal requirements. Though there may be a lag in which some misguided decisions are made on the basis of measures which do not represent well the concerns and conceptions of decision-makers, it is remarkable how the public scrutiny and use of an indicator help to sharpen and improve it. The inadequacies of many policies lie with the failures of the underlying analyses rather than in the data. Experience suggests that once the conceptions and commitments exist, the data can be generated, though some data is of course needed to help start the process.

Designers of indicators are often concerned about misuse of indicators, usually meaning that someone is using them in a way *they* (the designers) had not intended. However, once an indicator becomes a public institution (which by definition it must) its designers' intentions are not particularly important. So long as the user understands the measure and its implications, it is legitimate for him to use it in any way commensurate with these. Misuses of indicators are those based on misunderstanding or involving a deliberate attempt to deceive. Neither lasts long if public decisions hinge on the measure because an important group of those affected soon becomes informed and exposes the problem.

The usual categories defining types of indicator use are description, prediction, analysis, and evaluation, but these are rather scholarly in perspective and do not provide a useful breakdown of indicators' public roles. They have affected the whole range of decision-making, from problem formulation to policy and program design, administrative procedures and negotiations. They have pointed up comparisons to define problems, set standards and goals, identified target populations, set criteria for resource allocation, provided estimates for the scale and feasibility of proposals and been incorporated into models accounting for the relationships of societal variables.

CONTEXTS OF USE: SOME DEFINITIONS

Indicators play different roles and have different demands placed upon them depending on whether they are part of policy-making, program design or administrative procedure. Although these are part of a continuum, and the distinction between them is often blurry, it is useful to recognize some differences. A policy is a statement of objective and often the approximate means to reach it. A policy is, for example, the statement "We must improve educational opportunity for blacks by integrating them into white schools" or the statement "We must set limits on the growth of wage rates and prices to avoid runaway inflation and depression". The policy depends on a theory of cause and effect which may, of course, be wrong. Its effects are likely to be wide ranging and it can be the subject of much public discussion (Moynihan, 1970).

A program is a specific set of measures often designed to implement a policy. It too depends on a theory connecting the goals to the actions. A program is, for example, a plan to bus black students from black city schools to white suburban ones on a voluntary basis. Programs do not, however, necessarily grow out of a policy nor relate to explicit goals. In that case a program is simply defined by a certain level of generality of planning, specifying actions in some, but not complete, detail. In the U.S. a government program tends to be created more significantly through a legislative process than in many other countries, where the bureaucracy does the program design. This affects the kind of measurement used.

Administrative procedures are the detailed rules for carrying out the program. These might be, for example, the rules for choosing the schools and students, and the dates of the exchange. Some of these choices might be explicit in the original program and others left to administrators. These details are usually presumed to be in implementation of a program and ultimately a policy, but the motivations of administrators tend to be different from those of policy-makers and program designers. They are answerable to their immediate superiors more than to the general public. The procedures must appear to be impartial, but tend to get little public exposure.

PREPOLICY USES

The best recognized role for indicators is what might be called a prepolicy use, and is akin to what many mean by "descriptive" uses. When no policy exists on a subject, one can look at data on a topic in a general exploratory way to define problems or get a perspective. The idea is in the empiricist tradition. It is probably a necessary prerequisite to many more structured analyses and uses of data and undoubtedly does influence the ways these will develop.

Data on employment in the twenties and family expenditures and crime in the 19th century was partial and imperfect but was used in this kind of prepolicy way. There was no clear idea of what the problem was, but it was gradually being formulated. Today data on IQ differences associated with race are used in this prepolicy way, as are figures on many other subjects. The official publications on social indicators in the U.S., U.K., and France present measures that will presumably play such a role. Nothing is specifically at stake, however, and the uses are often intuitive and inexplicit. The indicators tend to be more or less accepted in whatever form they appear.

THE UNEMPLOYMENT RATE: AN INDICATOR FOR POLICY

The monthly unemployment figure based on the Current Population Survey (CPS) became, in part because of its subject and in part because of its design, an indicator of primary relevance to policy. As an aggregate measure of a simple concept, it is easy to understand and apply to broad national issues, although virtually impossible to use for detailed planning. Until the early sixties, it

250

was generally adequate for the policies under consideration. Economists, administrations, Congress, the media and the public have used its movements to point up the need for action. It soon became accepted that governments could and should keep this indicator at an appropriate level, and high rates of unemployment brought heavy criticism onto any government. This visible use of the measure contributed to its firm institutionalization, just as its institutionalization made it possible for it to have influence. The extensive use of the measure also contributed to its high quality.

AN UNEMPLOYMENT NORM

Faced with the Employment Act requirement to maximize employment, production, and purchasing power, the Council of Economic Advisors (CEA) and Congress sought a standard by which to gauge success. A model connecting employment with GNP and the rate of change in the CPI which could provide subtle guidance to policy would not be operational for 10 or 15 years. Instead simple norms of acceptable inflation and unemployment would substitute. Some frictional unemployment was inevitable if there was to be any job mobility and more than that would have to be accepted for other reasons.

There were numerous ways to select the full employment level of unemployment (Gordon, 1967) and numerous motivations to make it higher or lower. The primary one was a liberal-conservative conflict over government spending levels. A low unemployment standard would have made public employment programs more likely. In fact the term "full employment" was eliminated from the legislation to allow it to pass with the modified objective of maximizing employment. The decision about what specific levels of employment should be maintained was so difficult that it was deliberately left for later political discussion or technical determination.

It turned out that the unemployment norm was determined through a complex intermingling of political and technical issues. Despite a conflict in the CEA about whether a specific number should be selected and various theories defining full employment, the effort was all to find a simple guideline. The simplest and the one that was ultimately most influential was to look at past levels in what seemed typical years as a guide to the lowest unemployment that could be reasonably expected.

Economic theory would suggest for example that full employment occurs "when individuals work as much as they would be willing to work at a given wage." Unemployment is the difference between this and actual employment (Nixon and Samuelson, 1940). It is a measure of the short-run supply of labor and might be the difference between the total manhours per month, for example, which people wish to work and the total hours actually worked. The unemployment measure was a count of individuals, not hours, and of actions, not wishes, so it could reflect in only the most approximate way on the economist's concept of full employment — which, in any case provided no guidance to the levels of frictional unemployment. Economists would learn to make do with the measure in their models later, but it did not completely mesh with theory.

Beveridge (1944) suggested, to deal with the frictional issue, that employment was full when the number of vacant jobs equalled the number of job seekers. Job vacancy data, however, were very sketchy. The problems of collecting them on an equivalent basis to unemployment figures have still not been solved as it is difficult to define when a job is open and what its characteristics are before it has been filled.

The Joint Committee on the Economic Report (1950) tried to find a consensus norm by sending out questionnaires to business and labor leaders and government officials. They asked what level of unemployment is "alarming", what level "serious", and what level "normal". The consensus was hard to generate. The Secretary of Commerce replied as one might expect a representative of business to, that the existing level of unemployment, 3,400,000 was "not abnormal". The Secretary of Labor took issue with the question, saying the level was not important, only its rising or falling tendency and pointed out that a simple level cannot indicate what ought to be done.

Although the CEA in its early years implied that 3% unemployment was the full employment level, it later stopped talking in terms of precise norms because of the controversy this generated. Tacitly, however the target became accepted as being somewhere between 3 and 4% in the ensuing years, depending on one's political leanings. The figures represented the lowest levels reached in peacetime years and were, presumably, practical goals. It was a historical model for defining the problem, in the sense Pounds discusses (see pp. 5—7) and differed from the effort to use other people's models to define a consensus like the Joint Committee had. It was not a subtle approach, but it had the advantage of providing unambiguous policy guidelines.

252

The influence of this norm has been great over the years and has become increasingly obvious in the early seventies. The Administration has tried valiantly to redefine it at a higher level, in recognition of the criticism it was getting because it could not meet the 4% goal (Business Week, 1971; Oliphant, 1972). Though public officials have recognized the oversimplification, they keep coming back to the summary statistic. However, while gross unemployment rates might guide the direction and level of public action, they revealed little of the causes of unemployment and the types of remedial action that might be most effective.

AN EMPIRICAL MODEL

The most influential rationale for the unemployment norm was the empirical law known as the Phillips curve, relating the level of unemployment to the inflation rate. Given a rule of thumb about inflation, based on experience with runaway rates in various countries, one could locate an unemployment level that would correspond to safe inflation. There was clearly some causal connection between heating up the economy to provide jobs and inflation. However, the model was not based on an analysis of what were the exact causal links between inflation and unemployment — certainly if you could find a way of decreasing unemployment without heating up the economy there might be no link at all. The relation was rather a descriptive one. An economist (Phillips, 1958) did an analysis of British wages, prices, and unemployment for the previous fifty years and plotted the relation of the change in wage rates to the unemployment level for each year, to get this now well-known relationship:

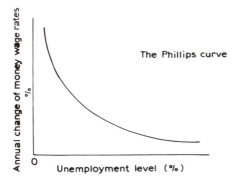

253

The relationship in recent years has come to be regarded as somehow immutable. Its origin in empirical observation in a foreign country in the past did not seem important since the pattern more or less continued to hold until the late sixties. However by 1971 it was clear that even the high target level of 4% unemployment no longer corresponded to a "safe" inflation level. One explanation was that the curve had shifted upward, and obviously the fiscal and monetary tools to stimulate or depress the economy could no longer be relied upon.

It was this conviction that led to the remarkable step taken by a Republican Administration to institute the first peacetime economic controls in the U.S. Both price and wage increases were to be limited by public authority to keep inflation down without adversely affecting unemployment. The concept was described by one analyst as one of pulling down the top end of the curve. It might be added that by 1974 most agreed the policy had failed, for reasons that have yet to be analyzed. It is interesting, however, how long it can take for analysts and policy-makers to stop trying to force an inadequate model to suit their purposes, after they have become accustomed to thinking in the terms it poses.

CAUSAL ANALYSIS

The problem is that this model shed no light on the causes of the unemployment/inflation relationship, and accordingly, obscured the likelihood of or reasons for the shift. So long as unemployment was solely explained by economic conditions its connection with inflation seemed self-evident and the aggregate national indicators were satisfactory. However, when policy directed at those conditions failed to alleviate unemployment, more subtle causal analysis was sought which put increasing demands on the indicator to provide more detailed information. The public level of discussion of issues of causality dates back to a major dispute on the reasons unemployment remained high after the recession of 1957. Economists, administrators and Congressmen debated whether the unemployment was due to structural changes in the labor market or the inadequacy of total demand for goods (U.S. Congress, 1959, 1961a, 1961b). On the one hand, there might be plenty of jobs for all who wanted them, but the job hunters might not be qualified or, on the other, the economy might be balanced at the low consumption level Keynes described so that it could not provide enough jobs without some stimulus.

The policy implications of the two analyses were far reaching but vastly different, and there was tremendous Congressional interest. Acceptance of the structural notion implies that the remedial emphasis must be on training and providing job information. The inadequate demand theory implies that fiscal measures should be taken to stimulate the economy. The former is far less expensive than the latter, and the latter implies the use of an unbalanced budget. This meant that the argument boiled down to a partisan political dispute, as spending levels were always a factor separating Republicans and Democrats. Major efforts based on both types of theories were undertaken such as the Kennedy tax cut and the Manpower Development and Training Act of 1962. The structuralists came to see the data as a hindrance to their analyses, and pressed for changes and improvements.* The CPS sample was not large enough to provide geographic detail or analysis of the comparatively small problem groups. Even a major expansion of the sample to 52,500 households made no basic change. More important was the fact that the indicator involved arbitrary dividing lines between unemployed and the near-unemployed, like those with only a few hours work a week or those who would work the moment a realistic opportunity appeared. The reasons for the size of the unemployed group could not be understood and dealt with unless the statistics took account of these marginal groups who floated in and out of the labor force.

It was this kind of thinking that led to the Manpower Administration's commissioning of surveys in poverty areas to find "hidden unemployment" and develop some useful categories (U.S. Department of Labor, 1969a, b). While the Nixon Administration was not very interested in such surveys which tend to blow up unemployment estimates, it is likely that the failures of macroeconomic policy and the aggregate unemployment measures appropriate to it, will encourage the development of a different kind of unemployment policy and measure in the long run.

EFFECTS OF USES AND PERCEPTIONS ON THE INDICATOR

The unemployment measure has evolved in many ways over the years as a result of its use. The discovery of the inadequacy of

---

* Two good accounts of manpower analysis and programs are Ruttenberg, 1970, and Wolfbein, 1965.

questions on employment in the 1940s resulted from the effort to find more workers (p. 77). The expansions of the sample resulted from the increasing demands on the data as policy analyses grew more complex and required increasing assumptions of accuracy. The seasonal adjustment was introduced in 1959 to make the indicator's movements more sensitive to economic trends as we become more adept at the fine tuning of the economy. When unemployment became high and policy-makers were confronted with the need for response there was often a reexamination of the statistic, as in 1950, 1954, and 1961. This was usually followed by changes, though with a five- or six-year time lag.

The changes in definition in 1957 and 1967 were the result of new perceptions of problems, a changing character of unemployment, and efforts to improve the reliability of the measure. The application of the indicator to problems created, in great part, the new perceptions and needs. The changes resulted from the recommendations of expert committees who considered prevailing views of what employment and unemployment *should* mean and the size and nature of the *actual* problems. The committees looked at, for example, the movements of the data on various groups of the population that were not obviously classifiable to decide with which group (employed, unemployed, or not in the labor force) their behavior would best place them. Implicitly they accepted the principle that the concepts are valid only in a time and place.

The 1954 committee's technical report (U.S. Executive Office of the President, 1955) noted that there was continuing criticism of the inclusion in the employed category of those on short-term layoff and waiting to start new jobs. They therefore concluded that excluding these two groups (from the unemployed) did "not conform to general public or economic conceptions". They checked and found that the numbers on temporary layoff usually increased just before a period of rising unemployment. Apparently employers were using the layoff as a modified form of firing, but workers tended not to look for new jobs because of a stronger sense of attachment to work than they once had, perhaps because of union agreements.

Thus changing social realities had affected public conceptions, and these were translated into changes in the measure. The committee recognized the interrelationship of concept, measurement method, and uses, saying, "for many situations there are no inherently correct definitions and, given a set of definitions there may be differences of opinion in their application of specific cases". The report clearly acknowledges that concepts are not given truths, but rather ideas grounded in realities and adds that the "intent of measurement cannot be separated, for practical purposes from the questions of the success of measurement".

The 1967 definitional changes, eliminating from the unemployed those who took no action to seek work and eliminating from the labor force all under 16, resulted from the publication of a *Reader's Digest* article (see p. 80) criticising the concepts and methods and accusing the government of deliberate falsification of results. The ensuing investigations concluded that there was ambiguity in the definitions. To protect against future implications of dishonesty, the answer was to make the definition less ambiguous even at a cost to relevance. The elimination of 14- and 15-year olds was a reflection of the fact that child labor laws effectively barred their participation in economically significant work and thus confused economic accounting and led to criticism of the figures. In the 1970s with higher unemployment levels there would be criticism that the changes represented a deliberate effort to minimize the number of unemployed. But this inevitable time lag in changing indicators while ideas are formulated, discussed, agreed upon, tested and gradually implemented confused perceptions of the dynamic of change. In the mid-sixties when the change was proposed, unemployment was low and little incentive existed to push the figures still lower. The elaborate interactive process of design and use of indicators moves very slowly, and the reasons for developments may be obscured before they actually take effect.

Other changes in the sixties also reflected the effect of feedback from experience with the measure. The fact that users demanded increasingly greater detail in the data reflects the fact that the existence and application of reasonably good data like unemployment figures seems to generate a constantly escalating demand for more and better data. Some of the demand for increasing precision is absurd and cannot be put to good use or would be unnecessary given the crudeness of models we can apply (Alonso, 1968). Some of it, however, represented an increasing sophistication in our understanding and analytical capabilities. The expansion of information on persons not in the labor force was in recognition of the existence of hidden unemployed, in need of work, but not looking, and of the need for a greater understanding of the labor force and the causes of its fluctuations, which were at first assumed to be readily explainable. As the Gordon Committee recognized, the problem was historically based in that "policy determinations in the 1930s required a count of unemployment — particularly a measure that would suggest the minimum number of jobs necessary to take care of the jobless. Very little effort seems to have been devoted to establishing an independent concept of the labor force or to indicate its relation to labor supply. It was apparent then there was more than sufficient labor supply to meet all needs" (U.S. President's Committee, 1963, p. 63). The new social concern was not jobs for the average person but for the disadvantaged, who were often missed by the conventional unemployment concept.

THE STANDARD BUDGET: AN ADMINISTRATIVE INDICATOR

The standard budget has followed a pattern that sharply contrasts with that of unemployment rates, in that its countless uses have primarily been in administrative processes.* Only in the last few years has it begun to play a role in policy or program design. Its uses have been less public and the measure less scrutinized. There has always been some doubt about its methods, assumptions and the appropriateness of the basic concept. The specificity of the budgets and their obscure complexity made them difficult to apply in particular situations, and limited in applicability. Accordingly, the uses and users have been widely separated, and never formed pressure groups that might defend, analyze or press for improvements.

The budget is an indicator of a norm for acceptable income levels, but it is not used to keep track of changing norms. Its principle use is as criterion for equitable public decisions on wages, benefits, and payments. Though its users do not necessarily claim it is an objective standard, it is an impersonal one. In administrative decisions it is important to operate by uniform rules, avoiding appearance of favoritism. The budget is useful as an exterior criterion of equity. The adequacy of income is a fundamental issue in many administrative decisions, and, as the standard budget is the only real effort to measure this, the demand for it has been sustained. The hundreds of budgets produced over the years testify to this.

---

* A summary of principal uses is contained in U.S. Department of Labor, 1963.

The adequacy of income is an issue of central importance to public policy, but budgets have played little role in the discussions of questions like the design of the Social Security Act in the U.S., the setting of the minimum wage, or the National Insurance program in Britain. There are two kinds of explanations for this. One lies in the nature of the measure and the other in the fact that income adequacy may not always have been so important a goal as one might assume.

First, for policy one is often concerned with the status of particular population groups, but the budget is difficult to use in this context. It is a micro measure applying to particular family types. If an analyst wishes to use the budget to identify groups in the population whose incomes are low, a great deal of data is required — more than has been available until quite recently. In particular, data is required on family incomes by family size. Moreover, until equivalence scales were issued, it was impossible to classify the vast majority of households. The budget did not apply to other than a four- or five-person family.

Secondly, policy discussion involves the setting of priorities and goals. As such, basic values come into conflict. Moreover, the discussants of policy are largely laymen — not experts in statistics or budgets — Congressmen, administrators, journalists, business and labor groups. The values hidden in the mysterious processes of budget design make them suspect to almost all, particularly those who do not like the result of their application — the income level they define, or the people they identify as beneficiaries of policies. As a result, though budgets are frequently offered in policy discussion, they are seldom decision criteria. Instead the goal of income adequacy often recedes.

A prominent example of the problem is found in the discussions over Roosevelt's Economic Security program during the Depression, the program that produced Social Security and Unemployment Insurance, and federal aid for public assistance. The President's Committee on Economic Security declared:

"The one almost all-embracing measure of security is an assured income. A program of economic security, as we vision it, must have as its primary aim the assurance of adequate income to each human being in childhood, youth, middle age or old age. . ." (U.S. Congress, 1935, p. 1312).

The policy statement seems to demand the use of budgets as the

259

only available income adequacy criterion for different types of families. However, the Committee goes on to cite figures about the percentage of employed with annual earnings of less than $1000 and less than $1500. They appear to be arbitrarily chosen round numbers without much bearing on actual welfare levels. Senator Wagner, author of much of the legislation, did appear to have used budgets in making his recommendation of benefit levels. One Senator questioned him closely on the source of his figures and how precisely he measured a decent living standard. Wagner could not explain his estimates nor claim they were "official" figures. The Senators seemed to doubt that any such standard could be measured objectively (U.S. Congress, 1935).

The Administration bill in January 1935 clearly depended on a concept of income adequacy and would have required a quantitative indicator for implementation. It said that any old-age pension shall provide an amount sufficient (with other income) for "a reasonable subsistence compatible with decency and health". The language is reminiscent of the 1920 BLS Health and Decency Budget. Its purpose was to permit benefits to vary with circumstances, rather than be fixed. States could be denied federal funds if they did not provide an adequate benefit level, so an adequacy measure would be essential. Conservative Senators were dubious about the principle, fearing that without objectively determined standards, the Administrator of the program would have arbitrary power. They did not have confidence in a budget to serve the function.

The discussion revealed that there was interest in measuring a standard of living in some objective way. It seems likely that if an accepted, institutionalized measure had existed, it would have been used in the discussion. It might well have meant that variable standards for states according to local conditions would be acceptable to the Congress, so long as they had a criterion that was not politically manipulable. The bulk of the hearings instead was devoted to the costs of the program. As largely insurance programs, the focus was on the limitations on benefits imposed by ability to pay into the fund and fairness of benefits in relation to previous wages rather than need. As the programs were to apply only to short portions of the working person's life, individuals were expected to draw on other resources than the insurance. In any case, no adequacy standard was even implicit in the legislation and actual benefits lagged behind the most minimal estimates of need through the years.

260

This case of the nonuse of budgets in a situation where they were the apparently logical criterion, is testimony to the low priority of adequate incomes as a public goal and the failure of the budget to mesh with policy-makers' views. It was repeated in the discussion of the minimum wage law. In theory this was supposed to provide an adequate floor on wages but, in practice, the debate had to do with who should be covered and what effect the level would have on the viability of various industries. Many felt that those earning minimum wages were likely to be extra workers in a family, rather than breadwinners so the budget criterion would be inappropriate. But this simply reveals the ambiguity of discussing "adequacy" of minimum wage. If that could have been resolved, a budget might have had a role.

One major Congressional discussion on wages, the so-called "White-Collar Hearings" (U.S. Congress, 1944) did depend on budgets. The wartime limitations on wage increases, coupled with rapidly rising living costs had put white-collar workers in a severe bind. Unions were able to organize cases before the National War Labor Board, but most white-collar workers were not unionized, and accordingly, were on essentially fixed incomes. The Senate held hearings to ascertain the quality of life for those on fixed incomes. They were for policy. No specific legislation prompted them; rather it was an effort to define the problem and search for causes. The Board would allow wage increases if the wages were substandard by an arbitrary criterion they chose of $0.40 per hour. But this standard was not well accepted, and the budget criterion was brought in to suggest its inadequacy.

The Committee questioned the BLS Commissioner about a budget the BLS had helped the Steelworkers to develop for wage arguments. Senators compared the budget costs and costs of WPA budgets with average wages for the white-collar groups. Wages were often below even Depression subsistence standards. The Senators felt this was a prima facie case for higher standards, but Chairman Davis of the Board replied the country could not afford such standards and that, in any case, he could not define subsistence. The Committee however, seemed convinced that budget standards were sufficiently objective, and the Chairman retorted that the subsistence level was not a matter of opinion but one of fact. Legislators, who must make value judgments daily do not seem uncomfortable using value-laden measures. The Committee's report concluded that millions of white-collar workers had substandard incomes. It went on to criticize the cost of living index as a measure of living cost changes in wartime. It recommended stronger price controls, an end to the wage increase formula based on the index, an exemption from wage control for wages up to $0.80 an hour, higher wages for state employees and higher public assistance. Little of this had much effect, as the war was winding down, but these hearings did call public and Congressional attention to a need for a generally acceptable measure of a standard of living. They undoubtedly contributed to Congressional desire to develop and use a new budget standard.

The standard budget found its way into important policy discussion in the early seventies in connection with welfare reform proposals. If a policy is enacted and the budget is a criterion for it, then the budget could become as firmly institutionalized as the unemployment rate.

BLS issuance of the lower level budget in 1969 coincided closely with Nixon's announcement of his Family Assistance Plan, which would provide guaranteed income maintenance to families according to a formula whereby they would receive basic grants if their incomes were low enough and have a gradually increasing tax on additional income. Nixon described the purposes of this plan as to raise benefit levels in the states where they were lowest, provide assistance to the working poor, and to avoid family dissolution caused by current welfare systems. Notably, income adequacy was not on the list, though it may have been implicit in other goals.

Nonetheless, the ensuing discussions in Congress (U.S. Congress, Senate, 1970, 1971) thrust the budget into the limelight and made far more people aware of the existence of the budgets than ever before. They came into play largely as a defense against Administration efforts to keep benefits low by using the official poverty line (equal to $3721 in 1969) as their benchmark. Though they did not assert the line meant an adequate lifestyle, they counted potential benefits in terms of the number who would be pushed over the line, as if it did represent a meaningful division. When the Administration focused so much argument on the poverty threshold, it was to be expected that the line itself would become an issue and have to be as much a product of public understanding and consensus as the whole program. The hearings produced a rising chorus of complaints about the poverty line. Many witnesses accepted it as an immediate, though unsatisfactory goal, and they went on to cite the BLS lower level budget as a more appropriate target. The fact that it was almost twice as high as the poverty line was the reason for the preference rather than any methodological consideration, but it is clear that it comes closer to a consensus view of income adequacy.

This view became obvious also in other policy debates. Witnesses critical of the poverty line before McGovern's Hunger Committee proposed the substitution of the BLS Budget level (U.S. Congress, 1969). A panel of the White House Conference on Food, Nutrition and Health (1970) demonstrated their contention that the poverty line was too low by comparing it with the BLS lower and intermediate budgets. The National Welfare Rights Organization and the National Tenants Association, among the most organized and vocal representatives of the poor, attempted to have the idea of a $6500/year guaranteed income (BLS budget level with modifications) adopted as a plank in the Democratic Party platform in 1972. Increasingly, too, the budget appeared in the editorial pages of newspapers, usually in criticisms of existing levels of welfare.

The BLS budget is popular with Administration critics not only because it is higher than the poverty line, but because, in addition, it draws on a long tradition and is the product of a respected, nonpolitical agency. Users of the budget always hasten to point out that it is an official BLS statistic.

The budgets are gradually picking up adherents and gaining a public. Many do not understand how the budgets are constructed, nor what their implications and weaknesses are. These will undoubtedly become clearer as opponents of their use as poverty criteria try to pick them apart. Whether the budgets will survive this intense scrutiny is unclear. Meanwhile, they are beginning to gain a life of their own. The Administration producing them cannot keep rein on their use and impact. People use the lower level budget to criticize or alter Administration programs. Congress was undoubtedly somewhat swayed by the evidence of the budgets to raise the income floor in the welfare legislation above levels the Administration considered practical. However, the dispute continues, and consensus on the measure is still far away.

ADMINISTRATIVE PROCESS: BUDGETS AS "OBJECTIVE"
STANDARDS

The basic reason standard budgets continue to be produced over the years, despite the problems, is their role as impersonal and presumably equitable criteria for administrators. While budgets have never found full acceptance in public discussion, administrative actions usually require a somewhat lower degree of consensus. They require primarily that the administrator or agency be seen as even-handed and fair. To do this one must apply uniform standards to all situations, preferably standards externally derived. The administrator avoids personal judgments to keep his job without controversy.

The administration of innumerable policies and programs in public and private sectors involves a question of comparative welfare or need. When the decision-maker has to answer to the public in some way an exterior criterion can become essential. Thus meeting some standard of adequacy is important in wage negotiations, particularly when one of the negotiators is the government. It is equally critical to the administration of public welfare programs that benefits be paid out, if not according to some absolute measure of need, at least without favoritism, or the appearance of it, and without obvious inequities. Increasingly public programs in developed countries depend on a scale of comparative welfare among families of various incomes to set payment or benefit levels, as in taxation or in sliding fee scales for child care. Implicit is a measure, not just of minimum need, but of a socially accepted, moderate standard. Even administrators of charitable activities have an incentive to refer to outside standards, and management often wants to offer wages that are seen as fair in the community to gather support for its position.

The fundamental nature of this need for a standard of income adequacy should not be discounted. It is pervasive, and if no measure exists, one will be invented. It is particularly important that an indicator used to directly affect the money in people's pockets should represent some consensus. Most administrative uses have been so discreet that they have not stirred up the necessary interest to generate improvements and, finally, consensus on the measure. There are exceptions, but, unfortunately, the circumstances when it was important fade after a time and interest in the measure with it.

Many public decisions are made on the basis of implicit standards which purport to represent equality, justice, or some other value, but the standards are little examined. Though many contend that government agencies should not design norms or standards and that social indicators are not properly used as such, the facts remain that agencies *do* set standards and that indicators *will* be drafted to the purpose. In the U.S., we have had a standard rate of unemployment (4%), a standard rate of inflation (2%), and a standard of overcrowded housing (more than 1 person/room) that have guided policy. If public agencies must use standards, they should be ones that the society understands and agrees on.

WAGE SETTING

A budget is frequently part of wage discussions, but causes great controversy because its basic concept is itself a bone of contention (Blackman, 1947, Sibson, 1953). It purports to represent satisfactory consumption patterns for some "normal" family, working man, housewife and some average number of children. To use such a budget as a wage standard is appropriate to the extent wages represent payment according to need. But capitalism and most of its associated economic theory demands payment according to the value of work done. Even if it is accepted that need should be a component of the wage structure (which it usually is), then how can you decide what family type should be the target? And in any case, how could you in a capitalist economy differentiate wages for family circumstances?

Budget use in wage disputes is most common when government gets involved, as when government pays its own employees or when it takes control of the labor market in a war or economic crisis. Either for justice to workers or the assurance of uninterrupted production, the Federal government has considered the adequacy of wages. Arbitration boards or the equivalent have been frequent users of budgets. In fact some of the earliest U.S. budgets were designed expressly to submit to such boards. The Railroad Labor Board and arbitration commissions for miners used budgets during the First War in their analyses, but they were not the decisive factors. Budgets formed part of the evidence in disputes over municipal workers' wages in numerous cities in the same period (Bureau of Applied Economics, 1920; Stecker, 1921).

Although both employers and workers agreed that a living wage should be paid, they could not agree on a measure of it, and this fact hampered budget use by arbitration boards. Employees felt the budgets offered by employers were too low, providing only an "animal existence" and employers objected to the higher level "comfort" budgets that began to appear in 1917 and 1918. They called these "theoretical" budgets saying they were based on a view of what a group *ought* to have rather than what they actually *did* have (National Industrial Conference Board, 1921). All were replete with value judgments, and inevitably became a source of controversy, rather than a helpful aid to decisions. Only where wages fell below minimum subsistence budgets, did these apparently provide some floor for wage awards.

During three major wars and again in 1971, the Federal government set up boards to control wage increases and adjudicate wage disputes. The basic issue of substandard wages has arisen each time, and each time budgets have played a substantial role in resolving it. The boards limited wage increases to some percentage related to a change in the cost of living index, but the rule imposed an unequal hardship on the lowest paid, whose absolute increases would have to be very low. If their earnings did not provide a decent living before controls, they could never improve them after controls. Moreover, the disparity between higher and lower paid workers would widen rapidly. Therefore advocates before the boards, the boards themselves or Congress sought an objective criterion to define the substandard level wages which would be free from controls. Budgets seemed to provide the only possibility.

For example, the National War Labor Board, established in 1913, stated as its policy:

1. The right of all workers, including common laborers, to a living wage is hereby declared.

2. In fixing wages, minimum rates of pay shall be established which will insure the subsistence of the worker and his family in health and reasonable comfort (U.S. National War Labor Board, 1918).

They had the longer concept of a budget in mind and ordered that a study of the existing budgets be submitted. After examining the budgets, the Board's labor joint chairman introduced a resolution declaring that the living wage was $1760.50, equal to the cost of a budget representing a level of living "above minimum subsistence" for a shipyard worker's family of five. The proposal produced protracted debate with employer groups opposing designation of any fixed sum. The Board resisted applying a formal decision rule based on the measure, preferring case by case decisions. Many of the ensuing decisions were based on a lower level budget however. The budget was a hidden criterion in the Board's analyses, although it was too controversial to be used freely.

There is a constant tension between those who would set up automatic decision standards in terms of indicator levels and those who want to avoid such formalization and loss of opportunity to make judgments. Often it is the weaker party to the argument, the suppliant, who wishes to use an indicator as a kind of barrier to protect him against public inaction. If those with the power to decide things can reserve the right to discuss and determine things according to their own internal criteria, they potentially have arbitrary power. This explains why the labor and liberal groups fought for a minimum unemployment standard and why poverty groups seek a formally defined poverty line. The fight in the courts of civil rights groups to get a firm quantitative definition of a *de facto* segregated school in terms of percentage black is similarly motivated. Judges thus far have resisted such a definition as they could not find a good rationale for any figure as opposed to another. They have preferred the more flexible, and probably more rational, approach of considering in each case the whole situation of the school and its environment, social and political. The process, however, also reserves for them the right to make the decision in whatever direction they choose.

A formal standard is not necessarily beneficial to the suppliant groups in the long run, though it may be a useful protection in the short run. If the standard is defined too ungenerously or if it does not match their needs it can be harmful. It is not necessarily rational or ideal to operate by such fixed standards, but it may be necessary to reduce complexity and the extent of the open areas for individual judgment in public decisions, and prevent the exercise of arbitrary power. Such standards are likely to continue to be frequently applied.

The National War Labor Board (NWLB) in World War II adopted the principle of allowing a maximum 15% wage increase corresponding to the rise in the cost of living index, as a general wage control yardstick.* A presidential order amended this, authorizing approval of wage increases where necessary "to eliminate substandards of living". The Board arbitrarily chose a criterion of $0.40 an hour, below which an increase would be automatically approved. In 1944 however the Textile Workers (TWUA) demonstrated that $0.40 an hour would not cover even the WPA Emergency Budget at prices prevailing in five communities where workers lived. The budget represented a low level of living, perhaps hazardous to health over an extended period, according to the WPA. The Board was impressed and raised its definition of substandard to $0.55 an hour.

---

* The story is best documented in U.S. President's Committee, 1945 and Sayre, 1946.

The employers were not satisfied with the standard but not because it represented too high a level of living but because once again they did not accept the four-person family as the norm. Moreover, the Union had done something which would invariably destroy the usefulness of an indicator for settling public disagreements. It had quite reasonably added a sum to the food component to compensate for the inability of workers to purchase as efficiently as nutritionists who planned the diet. While the employers did not necessarily disagree with the idea, they could claim the union had "manipulated" the indicator and destroyed its "objectivity" (Blackman and Gainsburgh, 1944). If they had presented it exactly as it came from the WPA, the Union would have been in a stronger position.*

The controversy over substandards recurred in 1971 and 1972 bringing budgets more firmly into public view. In the face of rapid inflation and high unemployment, President Nixon invoked the economic controls in mid-1971. When Congress reexamined the enabling act a few months later, testimony from the Distributive Workers of America and some Congressmen indicated that there was no special consideration for poorly paid workers. Accordingly, they amended the Act to read that substandard wages should be exempt from controls. The Committee Report specified that the BLS Lower Level Budget (used in the testimony) was the criterion. The budget was priced at $6960 for a family of four. Using this level would have meant an exemption from control for all wages under $3.50 an hour, and excluded about half the work force from controls.

The Cost of Living Council went back to the familiar objection about the representativeness of the size of the budget family and the number of workers. They proposed to exempt wages up to $1.90 an hour on the basis of the fact that the average number of workers per family is 1.7 rather than 1. This decision led to great publicity and bitter controversy between labor, Congress and the Administration, and it was one of the factors that led to the labor members' decision to quit the Pay Board in March of 1972. In

---

* A set of volumes (U.S. National War Labor Board, 1947), which documents the decision-making process of the NWLB in tremendous detail provides an unusual insight into the role of the budget indicator in the Board's decisions. Most agencies do not terminate definitively, and if they do, it is seldom with a complete official history of this sort. For students of the process of the creation of government policy this history is a remarkably good example.

July a federal court declared the Council's decision to be contrary to the intent of Congress, and the Council responded by raising its cutoff for "substandard" wages to $2.75.

The budget was once again influential, though not decisive. Because it was an "official" statistic, it helped it win sympathetic attention to labor's cause, but it caused as much dispute as it settled. The question of whether it actually measured adequate living levels was never raised. Tacitly it seemed accepted. The issue was rather one of whether adequacy was ever meant to be the criterion, and how one would apply the concept if it were.

In the U.K. where a similar incomes policy has been in force since 1965, the formally stated policy of exempting substandard wages has not been implemented. The reason offered by the Chairman of the Prices and Incomes Board (Jones, 1973) is the practical problem of applying any general standard of income adequacy to a population of varying family composition. Notably, he does not say income adequacy is unmeasurable or irrelevant. To deal with the necessity of an objective standard, the Board used other quantitative criteria, like parity with comparable workers. In fact, they relied so heavily on such measures that a tremendous scandal arose when it was discovered that the refusal to raise coal miners' pay in late 1973 was apparently based on faulty calculation of pay levels of comparable workers. It is indicative of how significant such measures can be that the coal miners strike that ensued was the proximate cause for the nation's going on a 3-day work week, and ultimately it precipitated a general election.

CRITERIA FOR COMPARATIVE WELFARE

Budgets in combination with equivalence scales provide the only means for comparing, even approximately, the living levels of families of different sizes and incomes and locations (for example, Stecker, 1937). Theory in welfare economics falls far short of providing a better guide and it is unlikely ever to do otherwise. The problem of aggregating welfare levels of individuals into a common measure or comparing them on a common scale is unlikely ever to be solved. The budgets provide an approximate ad hoc way of doing this which is as good as any other. The need for making the comparison is implicit in many programs.

Charities and government agencies who provide services have made wide use of budgets to determine the fee for a particular individual according to need (Orshansky, 1959). Several united charities like the Community Council of New York (1963) have found a budget important enough to design their own, specifically tailored to the area and client group. College scholarship levels are frequently determined with the aid of budgets to take into account family size and income.

Congress authorized the original City Worker Family Budget in 1946 to evaluate post-war tax reform proposals in terms of their effect on the welfare of families of different sizes. The concept of calculating tax on this basis dates back at least to the Civil War, when an income tax law was passed with a $600 personal exemption. The Report of the Commissioner of Internal Revenue said, "It was, of course, the purpose of the law to exempt so much of one's income as was demanded by his actual necessities" (1866). In 1920, a British Tax Commission declared there were three income levels where taxable capacity might be held to begin: the minimum income necessary for bare subsistence; the level necessary for health and efficiency; and an income sufficient to provide conventional comforts and luxuries of working people.

During the Second World War, the Senate Finance Committee (1943) and the Administration disagreed on the best way of raising war revenues. The Treasury Secretary proposed additional income taxes, and the Committee was more inclined toward a sales tax. The latter used a budget indicator to estimate how much of a $5000 a year income would go to necessities and thus how much there would be left for a tax.

Many public programs like the Supplemental Benefits in the U.K. or Public Assistance in the U.S. which purport to provide incomes at some decent level, match neither the level nor the scale provided by budget analyses. It is difficult to sort out whether adequacy was lost as a goal in part because the measure did not define adequacy in the way that subjectively corresponded to public view.

RESEARCH USES

The budget has been little used in research, largely because it does not represent a well-defined variable and therefore does not fit into the models social scientists design. It is difficult to relate changes in so complex a variable to changes in any other variable. The methodological imperfections alone could provide the explanation. The problem is due largely to the lack of theory in the indicator's design and it has important consequences. Since the measure cannot be used in theory, it is difficult to use in policy analysis, which also requires models of social or economic change. The failure of the theoreticians to support it or attempt to solve its conceptual problems may mean the budgets will never meet the tests of relevance and rigor that would make them widely acceptable. The difference between this and the unemployment rate is that the latter is to a much lesser degree operationally defined and that unemployment is a concept (moderately well measured by the indicator) that fits into a major theory relevant to public policy. Perhaps when social scientists develop theories about adequate living standards, some measures of income adequacy may emerge with a more significant role.

FEEDBACK

The standard budget was not continuously collected by a single agency until a few years ago so one cannot speak of feedback and deliberate processes for orderly change as one can with the unemployment measure. The budgets have been produced by many different groups at different times almost always in response to particular demands. The passage of time, however, and the budgets' uses have produced some evolution.

For example, budgets over the years have not only evolved in content to reflect life styles, they have represented different levels of living to reflect policy concerns, with comfortable budgets after wars and frugal ones during the Depression. Just as the WPA unemployment survey was an obvious improvement on all private estimates and soon displaced them, the CWFB in 1946 soon replaced the many other budgets that had been in vogue. By now the budget indicator is mildly institutionalized. It has become a regular line item in the BLS annual Budget and has a fairly vocal group of supporters. Its use seems to be more widely known and accepted than it once was. It fulfills a useful function, obviously, as the demand for it recurs constantly. And clearly so long as no other income adequacy measure is developed and accepted as much as this one it is probably better to use it than to use nothing and make no effort to assure an adequacy criterion in public programs.

POLICY USES OF INDICATORS INSTIGATE IMPROVEMENTS

It is generally true that once an indicator begins to be bound up

271

with a policy its deficiencies are revealed publicly and there is considerable impetus for improvement, provided by both supporters and detractors of the policy. It becomes essential to find some common terms of discussion.

The Uniform Crime Reports existed for some 35 years without substantial public complaint or even recognition of the deficiencies which researchers had recognized from the start. When, however, in the mid-sixties actual legislation to deal with crime was under consideration, Congressmen began to take a greater interest in the meaning of the data. Ramsey Clark, Attorney General under Johnson, was sophisticated about the data and anxious to prevent responses by Congress to drastically rising crime rates, preferring more orderly improvements in social conditions. He pointed out in testimony that the figures misrepresented the rate of increase in crime and Congressmen listened (U.S. Congress, 1967). The Nixon Administration, running on its law and order platform, wanted to show how much worse crime was than suspected and proposed a regular survey of crime victims on the model of one done some years earlier. Congress was voting to change laws on dealing with suspects and voting large sums to the LEAA. Suddenly the data seemed important and they acquiesced to a massive crime statistics effort.

Housing quality data has been collected in the census since 1940 but has been well recognized as inadequate — too subjective and not covering the significant elements (U.S. National Commission on Urban Problems, 1968). In the mid-sixties when the official commitment came to provide a "decent home" for all Americans, along with it came an impetus to improve the measure which would define that decent home and chart progress toward the goals. The measure as it stood missed many inadequate homes and was too subjective as well. But research is increasing to find better housing indicators in great part as a result of policy efforts and their failures (Marcuse, 1970).

The Consumer Price Index was revised and renamed as a result of its use during the war and the problems that it raised. A Presidential Commission and several technical committees recommended changes in methods. By 1951, when it became evident that wage agreements would regularly be tied to the measure, Congress scrutinized it carefully (U.S. Congress, 1951) and placed its collection on a regular basis.

The official poverty line fell into disrepute when it was used to identify the poor for analyses for the Poverty Program. It seemed too low and too crude to identify the poor in a way that was precise enough for the analyses. It seemed too low to Congressmen and witnesses when the Administration tried to use it to set standards for the Family Assistance Plan. Finally, the Administration also became dissatisfied with the measure when, in 1970, it showed an increase in poverty for the first time. Although social analysts had been working for some years on improved poverty indices, the effort to apply the measures seemed prerequisite to a commitment to improvement.

INDICATORS IN PROGRAM DESIGN

It is a short and natural step from using an indicator in policy to incorporating it into the design of a program of the operation of a wage contract. For example, states having more than 6% unemployment (based on insured figures) were eligible for funds from the 1971 Emergency Employment Legislation which was in turn enacted because of the high levels of the indicator. Workers argue that wages should increase because the cost of living has increased and, accordingly add a clause to their contract requiring wage increases automatically when the CPI increases. The argument that millions are poor because they have incomes under the poverty level leads almost inevitably to a program whose participants must have incomes below that line or whose benefit levels are no higher than the line. Such uses of indicators are pervasive and often have tremendous and far more identifiable impact than indicators used in policy.

Vast sums of money can change hands because of indicators used in various ways in the design to programs. They turn into eligibility criteria for individuals or localities to participate in programs. They can become the ingredients in allocation formulas for federal funds or help to define the operation of programs in many ways. Program designers may use the indicators to identify target groups and then calculate funds for budget requests, based on the size and presumed needs of these groups. They also often end up being criteria for the evaluation of program success, though this is seldom an appropriate use as an indicator is usually not designed to match the timing and impact of the program.

Despite the importance of indicators in this context, they tend to be far less closely examined and to represent less of a consensus than indicators used in the more public arena of policy analysis.

There is often little concern with arbitrariness in such measures until particular groups feel an impact. Then a dispute over the measure, reflecting many of the underlying unresolved issues will erupt into the public arena and ultimately becomes a question of policy. The U.K. operates many programs on the basis of the indicators, perhaps because of the degree of economic control the government exerts. Indicators provide a seemingly impartial and open way to administer such programs and help to reduce the complexity of decision-making. Wages are tied to productivity increases, price indices and other measures. In fact the British worker stood to gain 40p a week in May of 1974 if the retail price index was 7% above that of October of 1973.

The extreme reliance the British place on such measures became obvious during the 1974 election, which was called largely because of the difficulties of coming to a settlement with the coal miners, who were striking for more pay. A major reason the Government would not approve the increases was a perception that their average wage rates were higher than those in comparable industry. The perception of course was based on indices of wage rates computed in some complex way to account for hours of work and various benefits. Despite the fact that the perception flew in the face of the more dramatic fact that miners were leaving the pits for other work at the rate of 100 per day, the reliance on the index remained. Almost inevitably a Pay Relativities Board was set up to look at wage comparability, and they discovered that the computation of the indices was wrong. The furor this created was tremendous in view of the possibility that the strike and its severe consequences may have been unnecessary. It turned out that a number of analysts were well aware of the errors, but somehow the type of discussion that had prevailed seemed not to provide the opportunity for them to impress this point on decision-makers. The Relativities Board seemed a necessary group to do such a public reanalysis, and get some change in the indicator.

Local unemployment rates are factors in the allocation formulas for Economic Development Assistance in the U.S. The numbers in poverty and the percentage of housing which is substandard are often used to determine eligibility for levels of funding for social programs. Crime rates were added as a criterion to allocate Law Enforcement Assistance funds after the big city mayors complained that states had not passed along funds to localities in relation to the size of their problem. These formulas can be the subject of dispute in Congress, as the choice of an indicator can determine who gets

274

what. Revenue sharing funds given to states on a population basis will have an entirely different distribution than those given on a poverty population basis. Program designers often feel free to choose almost randomly among possible measures for those that will select the localities they wish to favor. For example, the official poverty line has seldom been used in these formulas (usually the data on family size and income is not available locally in any case to apply it), but some other convenient income measure. For example, the formula to designate poverty areas for special funds under Title II of the 1964 Elementary and Secondary Education Act used a flat figure of $2000 annual family income rather than the poverty index in order to spread the amount of available money appropriately throughout the desired districts (Jeffrey, 1972). It seems likely that such political favoritism could be avoided and funds directed in the way the legislation intends if more public and institutionalized measures are used.

CONCLUSIONS

This account covers only some of the many uses of indicators in public discussion. Hopefully it conveys some idea of the range of possibilities. An important conclusion seems to be that, although indicators may well be imperfect for many of their uses, use itself does result in reassessments, changes and improvement in the measure. Once a reasonable measure comes into use there is constant escalation of demand for more detailed and more accurate data to meet increasingly higher standards.

Of the various uses that measures may have, that in policy discussion is the most conducive to public understanding, institutionalization, and improvement of the indicator. The fact that a measure represents a norm or contains value judgments does not appear a great obstacle to its uses in public decisions as such decisions inherently depend on even greater levels of value judgments. Problems seem to arise rather because there is no agreement on the value judgment or no understanding of the measure's design.

Indicators have fulfilled some basic needs for tidy, unambiguous, readily communicable information resolving endless disputes over the numbers of unemployed or the rise in living costs. They have permitted more complex analysis than would be possible without the measures, especially where they have been clear and meshed well with theory and analysts' needs. Designers of indicators should not neglect, however, to think about their other likely roles in simplifying the increasingly complex job of public administration and providing a way of making administrative or program design decisions that will be both fair and in keeping with policy objectives. It should be clear by now that we are talking about an interactive process between designing measures and using them. We may define and solve some problems in terms of measures we have, but we also redefine measures to fit problems we perceive and solutions we want.

Chapter XII

Politics and Indicators

Mini-Jabberwocky

Most people would find rising unemployment
A source of unenjoyment.
Not so the anonymous presidential advisor
Whose comment might have been wiser.
He has informed the nation
That rising unemployment is merely a statistical aberration.
I don't want to argue or squabble,
But that gook I won't gobble.

Ogden Nash*

In the early 1970s many statistical operations in the U.S. have moved to the center of a political arena under circumstances disturbing both to producers of statistics and users in and outside of government. Statistical series revealing unsatisfactory situations were cancelled, statisticians removed for explaining data in a way that did not correspond to the political interpretation, and men whose qualifications were more political than professional were appointed to head statistical agencies. The series of events, which has evoked an angry response from Congress and the academic community, is detrimental to the potential of indicators to elucidate and inform public discussion.

The situation is not simply caused by a manipulative and unscrupulous Administration (though this is not an unusual characterization of the Nixon Administration). The problem is inherent in the nature of politics and the nature of indicators. Once indicators become relevant to and influential on policy, they become part of politics by definition. Similar efforts to manipulate statis-

---

* From *The Old Dog Barks Backwards*, Little, Brown, Boston, and André Deutsch, London. Copyright © 1971 by Ogden Nash. Reprinted by permission.

277

tics and their interpretation for political ends have often occurred and are entirely to be expected.

Politicization of data is the opposite of institutionalization, and the latter is the protection against the former. It is the attempt to make data no more than tools for immediate political ends, usually by interfering with their regular patterns of collection and analysis. Politicizers of data are not interested in them for their information content, but for propaganda. Such data lose much of their value for analysis and discussion. To forestall the problem, it is worthwhile to look for the opportunities that may exist for politicization in particular situations and the ways in which an environment can create pressures for it to occur. For a start, pressures become great whenever basic decisions and resource allocations depend on the measures.

The answer, however, is not to isolate statistics from politics completely, because that is to make them irrelevant. It is not to try to develop "value-free" indicators because there is no such thing. The values and implicit models may be those of the statisticians or of the politicians, but they influence our analysis nonetheless. Our goal should be to insulate, but not isolate, the statistics from the immediate vagaries of day-to-day politics and to set up institutions which will permit change in indicators to occur in an orderly fashion, with public scrutiny and public assent, and in a way relevant to changing concerns and perceptions. The purpose should be to strike a balance between political and technical considerations, allowing neither to dominate and to permit long-term political goals to influence the statistics, but not short-term.

TOO MUCH POLITICS

For an extreme example of what can happen if immediate political pressures are allowed to dominate statistical practice, we can look at the experience of Communist China (Li, 1962). Ironically, part of the reason this happened was that in the beginning statistical activities were too isolated from politics. During the "Great Leap Forward" the Chinese attempted to politicize statistics and statisticians with disastrously counterproductive results. Agricultural progress statistics played a critical role in the plans for publicity and stimulating effort. The idea was that each level of government would provide the next level above with two sets of targets, one which they guaranteed to meet and a second some-

278

what higher as a hoped-for goal. To create an incentive the higher target would become the guaranteed one for the next lower level of government. This systematic inflation of targets was perhaps not unreasonable in view of Pounds' observation (1969) that planning targets tend to be safely lower than what is possible. However, it led to a continuous upward revision of production targets, but not output. This placed tremendous pressure on the statistical system to produce good figures. The pressure came close to destroying the statistical system.

In 1958 this system was relatively centralized, professional, and apolitical. Provincial offices collected harvest and sowing data several times a year using indicators, methods, and schedules provided by the central office. Like the Census Bureau and other U.S. statistical agencies, it was not very responsive to political demands or local interests. Local government units, however, had become the basic operating groups under a decentralization plan, and suddenly local statistics took on new significance. Weekly and even daily figures on progress were essential to local leaders to make policy and to stimulate effort, but the statistical service claimed not to have time for such work. Continued pressure led the Director to agree to do some local progress data work but he insisted that the methods should continue to be designed at the national level. This produced even more protest as local leaders felt the national procedures did not take into account local needs in timing or ways of dealing with these special conditions. The complaint took shape that the statistical agency by its apolitical stance was impeding the revolution. Statistics would have to be collected and published by those with commitment.

The answer was to decentralize the statistical agency and give over control to the local governing groups. Statistical activity was largely at the local level where party leaders often took virtually complete charge of the work. To get cooperation in collecting data and confidence in it when it came out, mass participation was introduced. Finally, on the view that statistics operate by no special rules that differ from those of politics, many local groups reduced statistical personnel or eliminated statistical units.

The result was that in April of 1959 Premier Chou announced fantastic increases in output, and in August he had to back down, admitting exaggerations and errors of one third to one half. This was embarrassing to the government, but, more importantly, the incorrect figures had distorted planning and purchasing operations of the economy generally. An important rule had been broken.

279

The statistics gatherers were the ones who would benefit or be blamed for the results, and the temptation was tremendous to make sure the results were good. Deliberate, direct falsification was, interestingly enough, only a small part of the problem. Falsification is risky and probably seldom done as it is usually unnecessary. There are other ways of getting the same effect. In particular one can employ methods which depend on heavy doses of judgment.

In China for example, the "model survey" provided the opportunity. Instead of a complete census one simply looked at one farm in detail and multiplied its yield by the number of acres under cultivation in the area. The choice of a productive farm would make the estimated total very high. A professional statistician would be disinclined to make such a calculation because it is so obviously against rudimentary statistical precepts, and because he has less incentive to produce figures which are conducive to any particular conclusion. His job depends (normally) on the quality of his statistical methods, not the results of it.

In any case, the debacle apparently convinced the authorities of the necessity of accurate statistics, both for planning and for public confidence. Checks of statistical quality were introduced, and centralized control of methods were reintroduced. Some kind of party review of the statistics was added, which did keep statisticians under pressure not to produce discouraging data (they often produced two sets of statistics, more and less optimistic). Publication of data suggesting failures or reverses was cut back. However, the complete subservience of statistics to politics was gone. At least the government decided *it* needed adequate indicators, whether or not it was prepared to publish them.

DUAL PURPOSE INDICATORS: PLANNING AND CONTROL

High quality, publically acceptable indicators are particularly critical to a controlled social or economic system. Decision-makers have to decide for the whole collectivity rather than simply for themselves, and indicators often provide the only way of getting a perspective. The statistics must be accurate, however, as an error can have far-reaching effects. And yet error is made peculiarly likely by the very situation and the difficulty of keeping measurement and political pressures separate. In the U.S. under economic controls some examples of this problem were evident. The Consumer Price Index (CPI) in the U.S., for example, has been a prominent indicator of the success (or failure) of economic controls, as well as a guide to wage increases. The Price Commission in its effort to keep prices down demanded to know from the BLS which specific prices in which areas were driving the index up. The BLS, whose function has been to supply impersonal statistics rather than to participate directly in operational activities such as controlling prices, was reluctant, but not in a position to refuse. Inspectors were sent out to a selection of firms in the offending groups. While the firms reporting to the BLS were not identical with those inspected, the danger was that the whole procedure could encourage lying in future surveys. Equally likely was a spurious decline in the index due to enforcement procedures focused on the index components. When one wants to measure change with the same tools one is using to create the change, the tools themselves are affected.

Another type of problem arises when a government owns a considerable share in some industries or determines the prices directly. The French Government, for example, sells all the cigarettes and sets the prices, but only one of the two kinds is included in the index. The price of the other can (and does) move freely without affecting the indicator.

Moreover, under controls fairness and apparent objectivity are important. Indicators become the criteria for decisions to replace individual judgments partly because so many would be required and partly no one wants direct responsibility for far-reaching decisions personally affecting many individuals. Thus in the British system of economic controls, statistical criteria were set up to determine the amount of wage increases, like the worker contribution to increased productivity, or wages out of line with remuneration for comparable work. These indicators have been taken seriously to a point where an election hinged in part on them (see p. 217). Errors which suddenly appeared in one of the indicators caused considerable criticism, as the effort to control wages would completely collapse without indicators in which there was confidence.

DETACHMENT IN STATISTICIANS AND STATISTICAL AGENCIES

The pattern established by Carroll Wright in the early days of the BLS (Chapter III) seems to have been a comparatively successful compromise between serving policy and politicians and maintaining a reputation for professional integrity. It did involve abdicating the design of some statistics that were particularly pointed or presenting indicators in a framework directly relevant to policy. The statistical agency had time and incentive to do a good job on the statistics. Agencies like the Census Bureau and BLS have been directed by professionals rather than politicians and allowed some autonomy. They have direct relationships, not filtered through the Secretary, with Congress, the users, and the public through the press and their own publications. The situation has encouraged them to serve that public rather than simply the political leadership of the moment.

Reputation and public confidence are valuable assets, which can take years to build, but only a short time to destroy and, along with them, the credibility of the statistics. The appointment by Nixon in 1973 of administrators to run the Census Bureau and oversee Commerce Department statistics, neither of whom was a statistician or economist, and one of whom was a paid Nixon campaign worker, represents a break with tradition that has backfired. Some Senators took the then unusual step of opposing the appointments, the American Statistical Association (ASA) president made public his dissatisfaction, as did the Federal Statistics Users Conference (FSUC). Articles in weekly journals and editorials in the daily newspapers described this move as a threat to the integrity of the statistics. While the individuals concerned may well be entirely professional in their approach, a loss of public image in itself diminishes the effectiveness of the agency's work.

One means of maintaining this confidence has been in the past to make sure that professional organizations, like the ASA or the American Economic Association, support the appointments. A Joint Subcommittee of the ASA and FSUC produced a report (1973) on problems of integrity of federal statistics and recommended specifically that statistical agency heads should be in the career (not political) service and be statisticians of publically recognized capability, with publications, professional honors, and previous experience and that they should have direct control over personnel, budgeting priorities, publications and planning programs. The importance of this last point has been reaffirmed several times in connection with reorganizations proposed by the Administration (and partially implemented) of statistical services within various departments designed apparently to undermine this partial autonomy. It is understandable that a political leadership does not wish any of its agencies to be beyond its control. However, in the interests of efffective government, and, indeed, of informing itself, it may be necessary to stand back a little and allow statistical agencies to march according to their own drums.

The Nixon Administration, however, tried to maintain tight control over statistical efforts through reorganization in most departments. The effect has been to consolidate statistical and analytic work under a policy-oriented Assistant Secretary and to separate long-range from short-range analysis. The precise rationale for the change remains fuzzy though its ostensible purpose is to make statistical and analytic work more efficient and responsive to policy. The additional effect is to keep the more thoughtful and analytical functions separate from the press and public relations activity that goes with short-range work. Newly appointed statisticians in charge of short-range analysis presumably have to make it their business to keep in close touch with policy-making and remain relevant. The long-range studies can cover almost any topic under these circumstances without having much impact.

One of the important ways the government statisticians have in the past been encouraged to act apolitically has been that, in the more autonomous agencies, they have been able to think of themselves as part of the larger community of professional statisticians (or economists or demographers). They have been able to do comparatively challenging work and publish their findings in official and professional journals. The findings of the experimental period of the labor force survey in the 1940s are documented, for example, in the journal of the ASA. Census publications have appeared reporting on studies of such sensitive questions as interviewer reliability in housing surveys (U.S. Department of Commerce, 1967). Although such studies are feared by politicians as leaving statistical programs vulnerable to criticism, they seem to increase confidence among users, who feel they are being told the truth and that they can use the data, making allowances for its limitations. The lack of such commentary and analysis in connection with crime statistics has made many analysts shy away from it. As these are the people who vouch for the data to the layman, their good opinion is essential.

So publications about methodological problems gain public confidence for the statistics and helps the statistician to maintain status with a professional reference group. The latter is important as it gives him the incentive to do work of good technical quality and gives him someone else to please besides his political superiors. He will try to meet some standards of work that are accepted in the field. The President's Economic Advisors, for example, have frequently given unpopular advice or made gloomy predictions, rather than simply tried to please the President because their reference group values were economists'. It was from this group they came and to which they would have to return.

It is not that such advisors or statisticians do not modify their views to fit political realities and the policy predictions of their political superiors. Most do and should. There is no proof that economists' values are better than politicians', nor that taking a stand simply to please one's professional colleagues may not be as dishonest as taking one to please a politician. However, there are rules of good and bad practice in economics or statistics or sociology. They may not be the only rules to operate by, but over the years they have grown up and been accepted by a discipline. Operating by them is one way to win the essential confidence in indicators and the analyses that go with them. It is a method of agreeing to agree on something. Unfortunately this practice of encouraging publication and professional reference groups for government statisticians in the U.S. appears to be declining. Morale is currently low among the statisticians and early retirements have thinned the ranks of the most competent. Ultimately it can lead to a merger of statistical and political activities that can be damaging to any hope of using measurements to inform rather than distort public discussion.

SAYING IT IS SO MAKES IT SO

One reason that public consensus on concepts, measures and norms is important is that it prevents confusion when someone changes the name of an indicator or definition of a norm. There is considerable incentive when an indicator brings bad news to rename it or redefine its implications. For example, in 1971, the numbers in poverty increased, and the poverty line was used as an indicator of subsistence income to undermine Administration proposals to provide a lower minimum in the Family Assistance Plan. As a result, the Administration renamed the poverty line "the low-income line". They could not actually abolish it, as it was too firmly institutionalized, but they could name it something less evocative and perhaps convince many that it represented some different level.

A recession has never been formally and quantitatively defined, but has occurred when the National Bureau of Economic Research (NBER) said it did. In practice it has usually had something to do with a percentage decline in GNP over some period, but the criteria in the past have apparently varied in detail and depended on judgments particularly at the margin between recession and no recession. It is possible, therefore, for the NBER and government spokesmen to refuse to call a great variety of unsatisfactory economic conditions recessions, at least until they are over. It may seem unimportant what an economic situation is called, as surely everyone is aware of a problem. The term recession has far more pejorative connotation, however, than a confusing set of indicators. An agreement on even an arbitrary description of a recession would prevent the policy-makers from declaring one or not as it suits their purposes.

The argument over the unemployment level that corresponds to full employment represents a more acceptable approach as it is public. The norm has been tacitly accepted as somewhere between three and four percent for some time, but Nixon economists have been asserting that the full employment level is more like 4½ percent or 5 percent now due to structural changes in the labor force. They provide an argument for the change and a rational means of deciding, though certainly their motivation for moving the norm upward was that they could not move the indicator downward.

PRESENTATION OF INDICATORS

The method of presenting indicators to the public is important to their credibility and the quality of public understanding. The rules about this are well-defined after years of experience and yet it seems necessary to learn the lessons over and over. Data should be presented in an apolitical context by comparatively disinterested statisticians and any conclusions should be based on the soundest of statistical principles. That is, no matter how politically charged the results of a survey may be, these political implications must be left for others to draw and not tied to the presentation of indicators. Of course the indicator may have been designed in great part to point up a particular problem or issue. This does not mean, however, that there is the same degree of consensus on the problem definition or policy implication of a measure that there is on the measure itself. If the two are tied, then a disagreement with

285

the policy interpretation may cause a distrust of the measure, and make it a natural target for attack.

In 1930, for example, the presentation of the unemployment figures from the census was disastrous and gave the entire effort a bad press from the start (Van Kleeck, 1931). The Commerce Department eagerly announced a preliminary unemployment figure of 2% based on partial returns and only one of the several categories of people that might be considered unemployed. It was obvious that the government was hoping to show the figure was not as high as claimed. It was equally obvious that the partial returns were not representative, as they were heavily weighted with rural figures. The popular press lashed out at the effort to "pass" underestimates as good currency. A former BLS commissioner said the statistics "invited misunderstanding" and the expert on unemployment hired expressly for this census resigned and made very public his objections to the data. The furor was in part due to the conceptual problems in the design of the census, but it would have been unlikely to blow up so publically if the statistics had been presented with proper qualifications and explanations.

There is a fine line between explanation of measures in statistical terms and interpretation in political terms. There is no clear criterion for it. Unfortunately statistics without explanation are liable to be meaningless to most, particularly when they have been carefully structured for a specific purpose on certain assumptions. But the statisticians' explanation can run counter to the policy implications that were hoped for. Such a conflict caused the cancellation in March 1971 of press briefings on the release of unemployment figures and the eventual removal of two official statisticians from the responsibility for press relations and explanation of the data.

In early 1971 unemployment was sticking at the high level of about 6% and the Secretary of Labor was anxious to find some sign of improvement. When the figures came out in three different months, the Secretary's optimistic public statment about the figures was incompatible with the statistician's explanation in the press briefing. The Secretary claimed, for example, that a small decline in one month was of "great significance" while the statistician said it was "marginally significant". The statistician's comment referred to the technical concept of statistical significance and the Secretary's to economic significance. The first, however, is clearly a prerequisite for the second and is only likely to be known to someone who handled the calculation. The seasonal adjustment provided another source of disagreement over how far statisticians' explanations should go. The method involves the assumption that the present resembles the past. If this is not true, the adjusted data can be subject to quirks that are artifacts of the method rather than reflections of changing realities. The technical press release for June 1971 explained the drop in seasonally adjusted unemployment as not significant for technical reasons. Statisticians felt it represented an over-adjustment for students entering the labor market that year, as breakdowns of the figures suggested a much lower number of such student job-seekers than in previous years. It was widely reported that the President made known his displeasure with this commentary.

The consensus seems to have been among academics, interested Congressmen, and in the FSUC report that policy officials were unjustified in their criticisms and the statistician's comments were necessary. In fact, the course of events so alarmed many that the Joint Economic Committee (JEC) (1972, 1973) took the step of holding hearings each month to replace the public briefings and assure that the statistician's explanation was publicly available. The Census and Statistics Subcommittee of the House Post Office and Civil Service Committee (1972) did a study of politicizing federal statistical programs, partly prompted by this well publicized conflict of BLS statisticians and the political officers (see also Hauser, 1973).

The conflict won much publicity, most of which pictured the political officials as trying to conceal "facts". Even given the relativity of "facts" to understanding and perspectives, the criticism seems fair in these cases. The facts had to do with the details of the calculations to which only the statisticians were privy. The statistician's role should be at least to account for the assumptions that went into his part of the work so the public can judge the results appropriately. But what else should he explain and how? The idea of giving the breakdowns of unemployment figures and the components of change is more or less accepted, though it has considerable implication to point out that teenagers or blacks are the largest growing group of unemployed, for example. Forecasting has been officially ruled out, as has any explanation of causes apart from this limited sense of describing the components of change. The presentation of data by a policy level official rather than by a statistician or in a technical press release is also normally avoided. Labor Secretary Goldberg's presentation of CPS data in connection with his policy proposals in 1961 made of the indicator a political weapon rather than carrier of information. It apparently provided a considerable impetus to the criticisms that began with the *Reader's Digest* article and finished with the Presidential Committee on measuring unemployment (the Gordon Committee). J. Edgar Hoover's coupling of recommendations about capital punishment and crime control measures with his release of crime data has also been much criticized.

Timing of the presentation is equally important to interpretations as the Gordon Committee and many others have noted over the years. A date should be set well in advance for the publication of the current indicator, and it should not be leaked ahead of time or delayed for political reasons. The temptation is strong, however, not to follow this rule. For example, it is widely thought in Britain that the required release of disastrous balance of trade figures shortly before the 1970 election contributed to the government's fall. Elections, close votes in Congress, agreement in wage negotiations, can depend on figures being released or not. Often an early release of a figure in conjunction with some policy announcement can draw attention to that policy. But it detracts from public faith in the measure.

IF THE NEWS IS BAD, TURN IT OFF

Governments in power are not very interested in publishing measures that reflect badly on their programs (or lack of programs). The U.S. Government is no exception. When the urban employment survey, for example, began to suggest that unemployment, according to its definitions, could be as high as 20 or 25% in some areas, the Administration abruptly cancelled the survey. The reason given was that the sample was out of date as it was based on the 1960 census. The excuse was rather lame as other surveys based on such samples continued. The standard budget, which had become a thorn in the Administration's side was harder to eliminate as it was a line item in the Department's budget. It could not simply cease to produce the budget as the proposal to do so brought fire from users, particularly labor unions. Its existence is precarious but continues, because of interest group support. Other new studies however, done by government analysts on special problems such as discrimination will not be published in the first place.

An abrupt halt to a statistical series is of course possible where the series' only reason for existence was an Administration move. In general, it is not desirable for indicators to be eradicable when they bring bad news. Some are not. The poverty line was renamed, but not actually abolished, and the CPI and unemployment rates have been allowed to irritate administrations for years. They keep them going because they have to because the measures have become institutionalized, in the sense discussed in Chapter X. The opportunities and incentives exist to prevent data from being eliminated. Congress holds hearings when unemployment press conferences are stopped. The proposal for elimination of the standard budget is routinely presented to the Labor and Business Research Advisory Committees and promptly stirs up strong opposition. The media understand and publicize many of the issues. Many people depend on the figures, and they are widely understood and scrutinized. Such factors provide the greatest protection against arbitrary exercise of executive authority in turning off the bad news.

NEW SYSTEMS OF INDICATORS: POLITICAL OBSTACLES

In the U.S. administrative efforts to establish a regular social report and to legislate a system of social reporting have met many obstacles. The problems are quite predictable. The efforts which began in 1966 with the institution of a group in the Department of Health, Education, and Welfare (HEW) to produce a preliminary report have partly been slowed by indecision of the experts. But gradually also as White House staff came to recognize the political potency of some measures being proposed, they began to veto one after another. The book which finally did emerge from a five-year effort in the Office of Management and Budget (OMB) contains virtually no text, in response to pressures against any form of interpretation (U.S. Executive Office of the President, 1974). An earlier "social report" on the other hand, contained almost no figures (U.S. National Goals Research Staff, 1970). Either way emasculates the effort.

The problems with the passage of legislation for indicators are more complex, but a major part of the difficulty is Administration opposition, which is apparently inherent in the mere fact of being in power. Executive Staff testifying against the Mondale legislation for a social reporting system returned in later years to testify in favor of it, on the basis of their personal views. The passage of such legislation may well depend on the entry of a new Administration with no feeling of responsibility for past events.

The story suggests some rules that can be followed for governments to assure that data cannot be used against them:

— Keep tight control of the presentation of data, to assure that technical interpretations mesh with political ones.

— Remove technicians who fail to suppress data that has bad implications or whose public explanations of data are indiscreetly frank.

— Make all data to be published subject to prior approval by a political official. Suppress data revealing bad situations or data which might raise hard new questions.

— Discourage academic and professional ties for government statisticians, economists, and other analysts. Discourage professional publication.

— Provide as little information as possible about the methodology to users.

— Politicize statistical bureaus by appointment of loyal leadership.

— Present data in conjunction with policy proposals and keep control of the timing of their release.

— Keep long-range analysis separate from short-range.

— Use indicators whose methods leave room for judgments so the results can be manipulated. Make methodological changes in the indicator to get the desired results.

The trouble is that most of these precepts are self-defeating. While data under these circumstances cannot be used against policies, it also cannot be used for them. Moreover, those who must make the decisions are deprived of information that they themselves can depend on. In any case, in the U.S. an administration is prevented by a whole structure of institutions from doing many of these things or from doing them easily. Methods cannot be changed in practice without following some open process of decision. Data presented in the wrong way is greeted with prompt and vocal criticism. However, to keep governments from overindulging in the natural tendency to control arbitrarily the nature and use of information, those interested in well-informed, open decision-making will have to keep up their efforts to protect the indicators.

Chapter XIII

Conclusions and Policy Implications

Quantification of social phenomena is a fundamental response of a society when it must make collective decisions. It is a way of reducing uncertainty and extracting simple ideas out of complex ones. It creates a sense of security about some facts amid otherwise shifting grounds of discussion and provides a way of improving communication and reaching agreement on some portions of problems. Evidence of interest in quantification in relation to many kinds of issues goes back well into the 17th century. It has grown with the complexity of society and the functions of government. Decision-makers often seek out numbers to give them bearings on a problem which they cannot grasp with simply their own experience. They may not use the numbers in any subtle analytic way. The numbers may not even tell them much they did not already suspect, but they do provide a way of identifying problems and a foundation for discussion. Most importantly, numbers are useful for communication to the broader public who must participate in either the decisions or their implementation. Finally they help cut down judgmental elements and thus the personal responsibility of decision-makers.

Statistics, however, are often not used or not used definitively in many situations where they would appear to be potentially useful to settle discussions and permit more subtle analyses. Instead policy makers apply personal experience, anecdotes and purely political considerations. While all successful policy choices are in a sense political in that they must satisfy many different interests, the purely political are determined without any regard for the presumed policy problem of, for example, helping the poor or improving the opportunities for recreation. Students of public decision-making often point to such cases as evidence that we have a basic resistance to using numbers in analyses of public issues. Closer inspection, however, often reveals that one of two things is true. The data at hand may not be chosen or structured to be pertinent to the issues as the participants really see them or they may not be technically adequate to support the necessary decisions. It is also likely that if better data exist, there is no system to assure their recognition, acceptance and use in actual decisions.

If indicators are to fill any needs at all, their design must be integrated with the processes of analysis and public perceptions of problems. However, much public decision-making has not been set up to consider data or the findings of research. There have not been people with training, opportunity, incentive, and legitimacy to think about public problems in such a context. Merely producing better indicators will fall far short of assuring that public decisions are better informed. Any effort to find better data for public policy necessarily involves a restructuring of the way public decisions are made so they can and will take account of data. Such reorganization is desirable, as taking account of data is integrally connected with better planning in the sense of recognizing alternatives, finding ways to distinguish among them, and assessing outcomes. However, reorganizations are disruptive to established distributions of power and, therefore, are politically difficult to achieve. They normally only occur when there is an overriding issue. Unemployment was such as issue after the war, but even then the reorganization established by the Employment Act did not directly redistribute decision-making power but merely set up advisory systems. The reorganization of the Congressional process for considering budgets has been recommended for years, but only the Watergate scandals and extraordinary Presidential encroachment on Congressional powers made this reform feasible. Reform of decision processes does not often have high priority and almost never is attempted without some substantive output as a goal.

Design processes for indicators cannot be done as technical exercises and ignore prevailing public conceptions of the issues. While indicators often give specific form to problem perceptions, they have to be somehow related to the existing views to begin with. If the experts understand the issues differently and want indicators to be used which are unlike public conceptions, they will have to plan strategies to change those conceptions, through, for example publicizing research findings and focusing on their policy implications. The design of an indicator which is both relevant and practicable to collect or apply is highly interactive. Methodologists and users have to be able to communicate their requirements and concerns to one another, at least indirectly.

This interaction may affect both concept and methods, as users have particular formulations of issues and varying priorities about reliability, bias and detail in the data. Time horizons, the nature of the populations, and the desired policies will all have considerable bearing on the way the indicator should be structured and presented. The methodologist who structures data according solely to the requirements of some social science theory is unlikely to find it useful elsewhere. In addition the methodologist who designs the ideal measure of the ideal concept will find that when he tries to implement it, there will have to be many modifications of the concept because of practical difficulties of accurate or reliable measurement.

By the same token the indicator users can be well served by letting the methodologists help them formulate the concepts and their measures. The purely operational measures, put together in an ad hoc way without the aid of well-defined concepts and no relation to models often tend to be more trouble than they are worth. When an indicator's meaning is too fuzzy, it is difficult to apply or interpret and it seldom leads to further understanding of problems.

Therefore it takes a long time to get a useful indicator, and requires a system in which many linkages exist between participants. It also requires flexibility in the sense that decisions about concepts, data collection methods, structuring data or using them are not considered permanently fixed at any time. Moreover processes should be built into the system for changing these as testing and use suggest new problems and opportunities, as methods evolve, and reality itself takes on new forms.

FINDINGS

This study of indicator design and application suggests a number of things that are likely to be true for indicators that achieve some usefulness. A retrospective study cannot of course predict the future, nor tell us anything definitive about the causes and effects in the past. However, it can give us some possible scenarios and some ideas about the pathologies that we can try to avoid, and opportunities we can try to take. It can also provide hypotheses for further study and some basis for the next steps in planning for the production of more and better data for public decision-making.

— A great deal of time goes into the evolution of a satisfactory concept, then the production of a practical measure, and finally into assuring that the resulting indicator is understood and used. Existing indicators have required twenty or thirty years, or longer, if one considers the effort to have begun when the first public demands and theoretical analysis emerged.

— A great deal of money and effort had been spent in the process of developing indicators and much of it was wasted. Technically competent unemployment measurement was made possible by WPA efforts to find ways to spend money. The standard budget was made possible by consumption surveys for price indices. Even price index surveys were only done at first in connection with major upheavals like wars or depressions, and the methodology for the index was developed because economists wanted it.

— Indicators which are grounded in the models and concepts of users and in the best theory available about a problem tend to be more useful than operationally defined measures. They are better understood and accepted and fit with more analyses. Without clear underlying concepts the design of the indicator may be arbitrary, and it is virtually impossible to determine whether it actually represents the idea it is being used for. A measure however, that meshes not only with public conceptions of issues but also with economic or social theory is likely to get considerable methodological attention and improvement. It also makes it more possible to consider public issues in the light of such theory. If it does not mesh with such theory, as standard budgets and crime rates have not, it is both possible and reasonable for it to be disregarded at critical decision-making junctures.

— A useful indicator is not fixed over time in concepts, methods, or uses. The concepts evolve because reality and perceptions and understanding of reality change. A concept of unemployment in a depression is bound to be different from the concept in a war, and different again from the concept in prosperous times. The methods evolve because we learn how to do things better and because use of the measure itself creates demand for better methods, as defects appear. Additionally, the use generates an escalating demand for greater quality and detail in the data. Accordingly in unemployment measures, concepts and methods have evolved whereas in crime rates and standard budgets they have been relatively fixed. But the latter are not especially useful because of their continuity. On the contrary, they are regarded as primitive in methods and conceptually poorly related to current thinking. The main criticism of the unemployment rate today is that it has not evolved enough to capture the essence of modern unemployment. Formal continuity in an indicator's method may mean a lack of continuity with reality.

— A successful indicator's method, concept and use all evolve interactively among themselves. The method constrains and helps give precision to the concept. The use helps determine the choice of data collection techniques and particular ways of formulating the indicator. The concept itself takes its form in part because of the intended use.

— The use of an indicator to formulate policies, allocate resources, or judge participants in public actions places great pressure on the indicator. The measure may be attacked by the opponents of a proposed policy. There may be attempts to subvert or distort the measure so it will appear to show some desired outcome. But also in this process the indicator is apt to be much improved, as its methods and concepts undergo scrutiny. Moreover, inadequate indicators are often rejected at this point and really unsatisfactory measures are seldom used definitively in public decisions.

— If indicators are to be accepted and trusted by various sides of a discussion, they require an institutionalized life, somewhat removed from the immediacy of day-to-day politics. They also seem to require a basis in some consensus about their concepts and methods and the appropriateness of their use in particular contexts. Moreover, if they even appear to be manipulable by those in power, they will not serve as neutral information carriers in a policy discussion, but will rather be ignored. Institutionalization of a measure's production, design and dissemination can be the essential ingredient for its success in use. Such indicators can be powerful weapons to attack those in power and reveal inadequacies of policies that could otherwise be ignored. The main drawback of institutionalization is that it is a source of inflexibility and may prevent indicators from changing as often as they should.

POLICY IMPLICATIONS

These observations have implications for those who want to improve the information content of public decision-making through better data.

— Plan in terms of *systems* of production and use of data. Though individuals may work on designing particular measures, someone should be guiding the development of a system for appropriate indicators to be regularly produced, used and improved. Such a plan should take account of the way decisions are made and include strategies for changing processes which provide neither opportunity nor incentive to consider information. The system should involve dependable funding for basic research into concepts and methods within a variety of disciplines which continues after a measure is developed, nonpolitical statistical agencies with ties to policy makers, specialized users, the public and the professional groups, the organization of user groups, and the involvement of legislative bodies in statistical issues. In general the system should have plenty of linkages and opportunities for communication among users and producers of data, particularly at times when there is some question about the data. Create incentives for each to take into account the other's concerns and opportunities for constructive interaction. Plan ways to assure the use of information in public decisions by creating expectations for its use and integrating requirements for its inspection and analysis into substantive legislation.

— Count on the creation of an effective new indicator taking a long time. Because of the iterative quality of concept formation and measurement efforts and the difficulty of pinpointing the precise nature of public concerns before producing a measure, it is difficult to shorten this period. Moreover, if a new method must be worked out, time has to be allowed for trial and error. Even if there is some background research and consensus on the problem, it is likely to take at least 10 years between the desire to have a measure and its actual production.

— Allow for a massive effort to develop a new indicator. The amount of money necessary to spend will be far from rational in terms of immediate results. The effort may also require considerable duplication and waste before something usable emerges.

— In view of the scope of the effort, it will be advisable to link the development of systems for indicator production and use to the implementation of new policies and programs. One should be opportunistic about this because the issue of social indicators will never be potent enough by itself to assure the necessary funding nor make possible reorganization of decision-making.

— Look to Congress for the impetus for indicator production and use or possibly to a new Administration in its first wave of activity. New indicators are unlikely to be developed and produced willingly by an existing Administration because they can be too potent as weapons against them.

296

— Encourage a style of statistical agency that is professional yet linked to and conscious of policy issues without having direct responsibility for them. Encourage the statisticians to respond to a professional reference group by encouraging and rewarding publication, selecting well-trained individuals and encouraging interaction with the academic community. Motivate the agency also to respond to the public and users' views. The BLS provides in many ways a good model.

— Regularize the methods and standardize concepts. Assure that methods allow as little room as possible for judgment. Set up some patterns to legitimize the methods and concepts and to consider and legitimize change. Publish clear descriptions of techniques which can be duplicated and of the concepts they are meant to represent. Never make changes without open public consultation with outside groups such as users or professional nongovernment technicians.

— Encourage the development and maintenance of a set of measures related to important public policy concepts. Each will offset bias or errors in the others and the interpretation of all as a group is more dependable than of any one alone. The set should contain at least one measure derived from a sample survey and precisely focused on the topic of concern.

— Emphasize public relations. A public consensus is important to assure that an indicator can have an impact, and use itself tends to improve and legitimize an indicator. An open process of indicator design and use is important to assure confidence in it. Various levels of recognition and understanding of an indicator are involved, each requiring a different kind of effort. Press releases and press conferences with explanations of technical issues and implications may be important for the general public. Readable compilations of data with clear explanations are important for the nonspecialist user and detailed accounts of methods for the specialist. These are important not only so the indicator is known and used properly, but also so it has an informed group with an interest in its continued existence, capable of explaining it to others.

— Mobilize and organize users and potential users and set up systems for regular communication and consultation between them and the producers of the data. Give them legitimate roles in making decisions about change, involving them in the indicator design process.

— Plan a way of institutionalizing the measure's production and use so it cannot be arbitrarily stopped or ignored by those in power. This means a regular source of funding, tying the indicators clearly and publicly into the implementation of relevant legislation and creating institutionalized forums for considering data.

These are the general suggestions that emerge from the study. The specific way of implementing these will depend on the particular situations. Whether, for example, linkages between users and producers can be best produced by setting up special expert committees at important moments, by publication in professional journals, or broad media coverage will depend on the type of problem and the style and readership of the publications.

FUTURE POLICY

It is not clear, however, that we can transfer the experience from the U.S. to other countries directly. Many of the successful styles of indicator development and use depend on particular institutional arrangements for public decision-making. In France planning is not subject to much public scrutiny except at specified intervals and has little legislative review. Moreover the centralized educational system and the fact that many of those in key government positions have attended the same school means that indicators, to be useful and credible to the relevant users, may not need as much institutionalization and legitimation as they do in the U.S. In England, where public participation is less of a tradition than in the U.S., where more confidence is placed in the civil service and central government, and where there is no separation of executive and legislative powers, indicators are less likely to emerge because of an adversary process. They are more likely to be developed as part of an effort by government either to reassure the public or to find formal guides by which to operate. The overall lessons however, are surely relevant for any nation. Development of usable indicators takes time and money. Assuring indicator use requires an interactive process of design and application, and a system of opportunities and incentives for policy-makers to consider what the indicator shows. The best strategy to get indicators is one of opportunism, attaching this effort to others of more widely recognized importance.

THE FUTURE OF SOCIAL MEASUREMENT

Quantification for social issues and analysis can only expand in the future. Policies of governments steadily grow more complex and more ambitious. The public grows more aware and more demanding of an accounting for the money spent. Schools are rapidly turning out policy analysts and practitioners of planning in health, housing, social work and many other areas who are not only equipped but also motivated to use numbers in support of analyses and proposals. These are the people who will increasingly be formulating the public policy issues and identifying the solutions. The role of such policy analysis is rapidly expanding already at the Federal and in some of the larger U.S. state and city governments.

Moreover, increasingly, built into legislation, there are requirements for the production and analysis of quantitative information, whether it is in the form of output data, evaluations or environmental impact statements. These requirements are based on the assumption that data can and should influence what is done. They are all efforts to institutionalize the production and use of quantitative information in decision-making. As such, the work on social indicators can be usefully applied. These required activities can provide one institutionalized base for indicator research and development. Moreover, those designing and implementing such social programs are usually not specialists in measurement and social science, so they can well use the work that has gone into indicators. There is also a great need for more institutionalized measures to use in such analyses so that the figures can have an accepted, common meaning and so that it is more difficult for measures to be produced to create whatever impression may be desired by a single, unrepresentative interest. The trends in legislation suggest, in any case, how pervasive is the conviction today that data are powerful and useful to making decisions for society.

References

CHAPTER I

Bowles, S. and Gintis, H. (1973). "IQ in the U.S. Class Structure", Social Policy, Nov./Dec. 1972, Jan./Feb. 1973, 65—96.

Cartwright, T.J. (1973). "Problems, Solutions and Strategies: A Contribution to the Theory and Practice of Planning", Journal of the American Institute of Planners, 39, 179—187.

Cohen, W.J. (1968). "Social Indicators: Statistics for Public Policy", American Statistician, October, 11—16.

Duncan, O.D. (1972). "Federal Statistics, Nonfederal Statisticians", American Statistical Association, Proceedings of the Social Statistics Section, 151—153.

Herrnstein, R. (1971). "IQ", Atlantic Monthly, September, 43—64.

Jencks, C., Smith, M., Acland, H., Bane, M.J., Cohen, D., Gintis, H., Heyns, B. and Michelson, S. (1972). Inequality: A Reassessment of the Effect of Family and Schooling in America. New York: Basic Books.

Jensen, A.R. (1969). "How Much can we Boost IQ and Scholastic Achievement", in Environment, Heredity and Intelligence, Reprint Series No. 2, Compiled from the Harvard Educational Review. Cambridge: Harvard College.

Li, C.M. (1962). The Statistical System of Communist China. Berkeley: University of California Press.

Marris, P. and Rein, M. (1967). Dilemmas of Social Reform. New York: Atherton Press.

Moynihan, D.P. (1969). Maximum Feasible Misunderstanding. New York: The Free Press.

Moynihan, D.P. (1970a). "To Solve a Problem, First Define It", New York Times, Annual Education Review, 49, January 12.

Moynihan, D.P. (1970b). "Counsellor's Statement", in U.S. National Goals Research Staff, Toward Balanced Growth: Quantity with Quality. Washington, D.C.: U.S. Government Printing Office.

Pounds, W.F. (1969). "The Process of Problem Finding", Industrial Management Review, 11, 1—20.

Rittel, H.W.J. and Webber, M.M. (1973). "Dilemmas in a General Theory of Planning", Policy Sciences, 4, 155—169.

Vickers, G. (1973). "Values, Norms and Policies", Policy Sciences, 4, 103—111.

Wickens, A.J. (1953). "Statistics and the Public Interest", Journal of the American Statistical Association, 48, 1—14.

U.S. Department of Health, Education and Welfare. (1966). Equality of Educational Opportunity. Washington, D.C.: U.S. Government Printing Office.

CHAPTER II

Duncan, O.D. (1969). Toward Social Reporting: Next Steps. New York: Russell Sage Foundation.

Glass, D.V. (1973). Numbering the People. Farnborough (England): D.C. Heath Ltd.

Rein, M. (1970). Social Policy. New York: Random House.

Stigler, G.J. (1954). "The Early History of Empirical Studies of Consumer Behavior", Journal of Political Economy, 62, 95—113, No. 2, April.

Williams, F. and Zimmerman, C.C. (1935). Studies of Family Living in the United States and Other Countries: Analysis of Material and Method. Miscellaneous Publication 223, U.S. Department of Agriculture. Washington, D.C.: U.S. Government Printing Office.

Zimmerman, C.C. (1932). "Ernst Engel's Law of Expenditure for Food", Quarterly Journal of Economics, 47, 18—101.

CHAPTER III

Clague, E. (1968). The Bureau of Labor Statistics. New York: Praeger.

Hansen, M. and Hurwitz, W.N. (1944). A New Sample of the Population. Washington, D.C.: U.S. Bureau of the Census.

Hilton, J. (1923). "Statistics of Unemployment Derived from the Working of the Unemployment Insurance Acts", Journal of the Royal Statistical Society, 86, March, 154—205.

Kendall, M.G. (1968). "On the Future of Statistics — A Second Look", Journal of the Royal Statistical Society, Series A 131, 182—192.

Kruskal, W. (1973). "The Committee on National Statistics", Science, 180, June 22, 1256—1258.

Leiby, J. (1960). Carroll Wright and Labor Reform: The Origin of Labor Statistics. Cambridge: Harvard University Press.

Lock, G.F. (1971). "Statistics for Politicians", Statistical News 12.9—12.12, February 1971.

Mills, F. and Long, C. (1949). The Statistical Agencies of the Federal Government, A Report to the Commission on Organization of the Executive Branch of the Government. New York: National Bureau of Economic Research.

Stephan, F.F. (1948). "History of the Uses of Modern Sampling Procedures", Journal of the American Statistical Association, 43, 12—39.

Taeuber, C. (1969). "Counting the Invisible Americans: The Inner City and the 1970 Census". Census Tract Papers Series GE-40, No. 5. Washington, D.C.: U.S. Government Printing Office.

Torgerson, W. (1958). Theory and Methods of Scaling. New York: John Wiley and Sons.

U.K. House of Commons, Estimates Committee (1967). Government Statistical Services, Parliamentary Papers H.C. 246. London: Her Majesty's Stationery Office.

U.S. Congress, Joint Economic Committee (1967). The Coordination and Integration of Government Statistical Programs, Hearings. Washington, D.C.: U.S. Government Printing Office.

U.S. Congress, Joint Economic Committee (1969). Review of Federal Statistical Programs, Hearings. Washington, D.C.: U.S. Government Printing Office.

U.S. Department of Commerce, Bureau of the Census (1967). Measuring the Quality of Housing: An Appraisal of Census Statistics and Methods. Working Paper No. 25. Washington, D.C.: Bureau of the Census.

U.S. Department of Commerce, Bureau of Census/U.S. Department of Labor, Bureau of Labor Statistics (1971). The Social and Economic Status of Negroes in the United States, 1970. Special Studies, Current Population Reports, Series P-23, No. 38, Bureau of Labor Statistics Report No. 394. Washington, D.C.: U.S. Government Printing Office.

U.S. Department of Labor, Bureau of Labor Statistics (1922). "The Bureau of Labor Statistics: Its History, Activities and Organization", Bureau of Labor Statistics Bulletin, 319, October.

U.S. President's Commission on Federal Statistics (1971). Federal Statistics. 2 Volumes. Washington, D.C.: U.S. Government Printing Office.

CHAPTER IV

American Academy of Arts and Sciences, The Committee on Space Efforts and Society (1963). "Space Efforts and Society. A Statement of Mission and Work", reprinted in R.A. Bauer (1969). Second-Order Consequences. Cambridge: MIT Press.

Barker, A. and Rush, M. (1970). The Member of Parliament and his Information. London: Allen and Unwin.

Bauer, R.A. (1966). Social Indicators. Cambridge: MIT Press.

Bauer, R.A. (1969). Second-Order Consequences. Cambridge: MIT Press.

Beckman, N. (1971). "Congressional Information Processes for National Policy", Annals of the American Academy of Political and Social Science, 394, 84—99.

Campbell, A. and Converse, P.E., eds. (1972). The Human Meaning of Social Change. New York: Russell Sage Foundation.

Canada, Office of Senior Advisor on Integration Statistics Canada (1974). Perspective Canada: A Compendium of Social Statistics. Ottawa: Information Canada.

Carter, R.E., Jr. (1958). "Newspaper Gatekeepers and the Sources of News", Public Opinion Quarterly, 22, 133—144.

Crain, R.L., Katz, E. and Rosenthal, D.B. (1969). The Politics of Community Conflict: The Fluoridation Decision. Indianapolis: Bobbs Merrill.

Dewhurst, J.F. and Associates (1947 and 1955). America's Needs and Resources. New York: The Twentieth Century Fund.

Duncan, O.D., Schuman, H. and Duncan, B. (1973). Social Change in a Metropolitan Community. New York: Russell Sage Foundation.

Flash, E.S. (1965). Economic Advice and Presidental Leadership: The Council of Economic Advisors. New York: Columbia University Press.

Flax, M.J. (1972). A Study in Comparative Urban Indicators: Conditions in 18 Large Metropolitan Areas. Washington, D.C.: The Urban Institute.

France, Institut National de la Statistique et des Etudes Economiques (1973). Données Sociales. Paris.

Germany (1973). Gesellschaftliche Daten 1973. Bonn: Presse und Informationsamt der Bundesregierung.

Gross, B. (1966). "The State of the Nation: Social Systems Accounting", in R. Bauer, ed. Social Indicators. Cambridge: MIT Press.

Gross, B., ed. (1969). Social Intelligence for America's Future: Explorations in Societal Problems. Boston: Allyn and Bacon.

Hale, J.E., Jr. (1968). Newsmen and Government Men. Dissertation, State University of New York.

Henriot, P.J. (1970). "Political Questions About Social Indicators", The Western Political Quarterly, 23, No. 2, June, 235—255.

Henriot, P.J. (1971). "Political Implications of Social Indicators", Paper prepared for the 1971 Meeting of the American Political Science Association, Chicago.

Japan, Economic Planning Agency (1974). Whitepaper on National Life 1973: The Life and its Quality in Japan. Tokyo Overseas Data Service Co. Ltd.

Jones, M.V. and Flax, M.J. (1970). "The Quality of Life in Metropolitan Washington (D.C.): Some Statistical Benchmarks", Working Paper 136-1, Washington, D.C.: The Urban Institute.

Kacser, P.H. (1972). A Progress Report on Social Indicators in the United States and Internationally, Proceedings of the 25th Annual Meeting of the Industrial Relations Research Association, 106—111.

Land, K.C. (1971). "On the Definition of Social Indicators", The American Sociologist, 6, No. 4, 322—325.

Land, K.C. (1972). "Social Indicator Models: An Overview", Paper presented at the American Association for the Advancement of Science Meeting, Washington, D.C.

Lyons, G. (1971). "The President and His Experts", Annals of the American Academy of Political and Social Science, 394, 36—45.

Morgan, J.N. and Smith, J.D. (1969). "Measures of Economic Well-Offness and their Correlates", American Economic Review, 59, No. 2, 450—462.

Olson, M. (manuscript). The Evaluation of Collective Performance.

Organization for Economic Cooperation and Development (1973a). The OECD Social Indicator Development Program. "List of Social Concerns Common to Most OECD Countries". Paris: OECD.

Organization of Economic Cooperation and Development (1973b). "How to Measure Well-being, OECD's Programme to Develop a set of Social Indicators", OECD Observer, No. 64, June.

Parke, R. and Sheldon, E.B. (1973). "Social Indicators One Year Later: An Overview", Paper presented at the Second Annual Social Indicators Conference, Washington, D.C.

Rainwater, L. and Yancey, W. (1967). The Moynihan Report and the Politics of Controversy. Cambridge: MIT Press.

Sheldon, E.B. and Moore, W.E., eds. (1968). Indicators of Social Change — Concepts and Measurements. New York: Russell Sage Foundation.

Sheldon, E.B. and Freeman, H.E. (1970). "Notes on Social Indicators: Promises and Potential", Policy Sciences, 1, 97—111.

Sheldon, E.B. and Land, K.C. (1972). "Social Reporting for the 1970's", Policy Sciences, 3, 137—151.

Shonfield, A. and Shaw, S., eds. (1972). Social Indicators and Social Policy.

Social Science Research Council. London: Heinemann Educational Books Ltd.

Springer, M. (1970). "Social Indicators, Reports, and Accounts: Toward the Management of Society", Annals of the American Academy of Political and Social Science, 388, 1—13.

Terleckyj, N.E. (1969). "Measuring Progress Towards Social Goals: Some Possibilities at National and Local Levels", Paper presented at the Annual Meeting of the American Association for the Advancement of Science, Boston (Mimeo).

U.K. Central Statistical Office (1973). Social Trends, No. 4. London: Her Majesty's Stationery Office.

U.N. (1954). International Definition and Measurement of Standards and Levels of Living. Sales No. 1954, IV:5.

UNESCO, Department of Social Sciences (1972). Synchronic and Diachronic Approaches in the UNESCO Project on Human Resources Indicators. Wroclaw Taxonomy and Bivariate Diachrome Analysis, SCH/WS/209, Paris.

UNESCO, Department of Social Sciences (1973). Report of the Workshop on Indicators of Human Resources Development, SHC/WS/303, Paris.

UNRISD (1973). A Proposal entitled "The Measurement of Real Progress at the Local Level", UNRISD/73—18, Geneva.

U.S. Department of Commerce, Bureau of the Census (1963). Methodology and Scores of Socioeconomic Status, Working Paper No. 15. Washington, D.C.: U.S. Department of Commerce.

U.S. Department of Health, Education and Welfare (1969). Toward a Social Report. Washington, D.C.: U.S. Government Printing Office.

U.S. Department of Health, Education and Welfare, Committee to Evaluate the National Center for Health Statistics (1973). Report, portions reprinted in Statistical Reporter, 73—11, 169—179.

U.S. Executive Office of the President, Office of Management and Budget (1973). Social Indicators 1973. Washington, D.C.: U.S. Government Printing Office.

U.S. National Goals Research Staff (1970). Toward Balanced Growth: Quantity with Quality. Report, p. 9 and p. 11. Washington, D.C.: U.S. Government Printing Office.

U.S. President's Commission on National Goals (1960). Goals for Americans. Englewood Cliffs, New Jersey: Prentice-Hall.

U.S. President's Research Committee on Social Trends (1933). Social Statistics in the U.S. A report by S.A. Rice and collaborators. Ann Arbor: Edwards Bros.

U.S. President's Research Committee on Social Trends (1933). Recent Social Trends. New York: McGraw-Hill Book Company.

Wilcox, L.D., Brooks, R.M., Beal, G.M. and Klonglan, G.E. (1972). Social Indicators and Societal Monitoring. An Annotated Bibliography. San Francisco: Jossey-Bass Inc. and Amsterdam: Elsevier Scientific Publishing Company.

Wilensky, H.L. (1967). Organizational Intelligence. New York: Basic Books.

Wynne, E. (1972). The Politics of School Accountability: Public Information about Public Schools. Berkeley: McCutchan Publishing Company.

CHAPTER V

Blalock, H.M., Jr. (1961). Causal Inferences in Nonexperimental Research. Chapel Hill: University of North Carolina Press.

Blalock, H.M., Jr. and Blalock, A.B., eds. (1968). Methodology in Social Research. New York: McGraw-Hill Book Company.

Burns, A.F. and Mitchell, W.C. (1946). Measuring Business Cycles. New York: National Bureau of Economic Research.

Campbell, D.T. (1966). "Reforms as Experiments", American Psychologist, 24, No. 4, 409—429.

Coombs, C. (1967). A Theory of Data. New York: John Wiley and Sons.

Etzioni, A. and Lehman, E.W. (1969). "Some Dangers in 'Valid' Social Measurement", in B. Gross, ed. Social Intelligence for America's Future: Explorations in Societal Problems. Boston: Allyn and Bacon.

Kaplan, A. (1964). The Conduct of Inquiry. San Francisco: Chandler Publishing Company.

Koopmans, T. (1947). "Measurement Without Theory", Review of Economics and Statistics, 24, 161—192.

Morgenstern, O. (1963). On the Accuracy of Economic Observations, 2nd revised ed. Princeton: Princeton University Press.

Torgerson, W.S. (1958). Theory and Methods of Scaling. New York: John Wiley and Sons.

Townsend, P., ed. (1970). The Concept of Poverty. London: Heinemann Educational Books Ltd.

Webb, E.J., Campbell, D.T., Schwartz, R.D. and Sechrest, L. (1966). Unobtrusive Measures: Nonreactive Research in the Social Sciences. Chicago: Rand McNally and Company.

CHAPTER VI

UNEMPLOYMENT

Arner, G.B.L. (1933). "The Census of Unemployment", Journal of the American Statistical Association, 28 (suppl.), 48—53.

Bailey, S.K. (1950). Congress Makes a Law — The Story Behind the Employment Act of 1946. New York: Columbia University Press.

Bancroft, G. and Welch, E.E. (1946). "Recent Experiences with Problem of Labor Force Measurement", Journal of the American Statistical Association, 41, 304—312.

Beveridge, W. (1945). Full Employment in a Free Society. London: George Allen and Unwin and New York: W.W. Norton & Company.

Daniel, J. (1961). "Let's Look at these 'Alarming' Unemployment Figures", Reader's Digest, September.

Dedrick, C. and Hansen, M. (1938). The Enumerative Check Census, Vol. IV, Census of National Employment, Unemployment and Occupations: 1937, Final Report on Total and Partial Unemployment, U.S. Department of Commerce, Bureau of the Census. Washington, D.C.: U.S. Government Printing Office.

Ducoff, L.J. and Hagood, M.J. (1947). Labor Force Definition and Measurement. Bulletin No. 56. New York: Social Science Research Council.

Feldstein, M. (1973). "The Economics of the New Unemployment", The Public Interest, No. 33, 3—42.

Flash, E.S. (1965). Economic Advice and Presidental Leadership: The Council of Economic Advisors. New York: Columbia University Press.

Gross, B. and Moses, S. (1972). "Measuring the Real Work Force: 25 Million Unemployed", Social Policy, 3, No. 3, 5—10.

Hansen, M. and Hurwitz, W.N. (1944). A New Sample of the Population. Washington, D.C.: U.S. Bureau of the Census.

Lindley, E.K. (1940). "White Rabbits", The Washington Post, March 18.

Myers, H.B. and Webb, J.N. (1937). "Another Census of Unemployment?" American Journal of Sociology, 42, 521—533.

Nathan, R.R. (1936). "Estimates of Unemployment in the United States, 1929-1935", International Labor Review, 33, 49—73.

National Bureau of Economic Research (1923). Business Cycles and Unemployment, Report and Recommendations of a Committee on Business Cycles and Unemployment, NBER No. 4. New York: McGraw-Hill Book Company, Inc.

National Bureau of Economic Research (1929). Recent Economic Changes in the U.S. Vols. I and II, Report of the Committee on Recent Economic Changes of the President's Conference on Unemployment. New York: McGraw-Hill Book Company, Inc.

Thompson, D. (1940). "In Reply to Critics", The Washington Post, March 18.

U.S. Congress, House Committee on Labor, Subcommittee Hearings (1937). To Provide for a U.S. Unemployment Commission, 75:1. Washington, D.C.: U.S. Government Printing Office.

U.S. Congress, Joint Economic Committee (1959). Employment, Growth and Price Levels. 10 vols. Washington, D.C.: U.S. Government Printing Office.

U.S. Congress, Joint Economic Committee, Subcommittee on Economic Statistics (1954). Economic Statistics. Hearings. Washington, D.C.: U.S. Government Printing Office.

U.S. Congress, Joint Economic Committee, Subcommittee on Economic Statistics (1955). Employment and Unemployment Statistics. Hearings. Washington, D.C.: U.S. Government Printing Office.

U.S. Congress, Joint Economic Committee, Subcommittee on Economic Statistics (1961). Higher Unemployment Rates, 1957-60, Structural Transformation or Inadequate Demand, J.C. Print 87:1. Washington, D.C.: U.S. Government Printing Office.

U.S. Congress, Senate Committee on Education and Labor (1929). Hearings. Washington, D.C.: U.S. Government Printing Office.

U.S. Department of Commerce, Bureau of the Census (1958). Concepts and Methods Used in the Current Employment and Unemployment Statistics Prepared by the Bureau of the Census, Current Population Reports, Series P-23, No. 5, May.

U.S. Department of Labor, Bureau of Labor Statistics (1969a). "Employment Situation in Poverty Areas of Six Cities, July 1968-June 1969", BLS Report No. 370. Washington, D.C.: U.S. Government Printing Office.

U.S. Department of Labor, Bureau of Labor Statistics (1969b). "Pilot and Experimental Program on Urban Employment Surveys", Report No. 354. Washington, D.C.: U.S. Government Printing Office.

U.S. President's Committee to Appraise Employment and Unemployment
Statistics (1962). Measuring Employment and Unemployment. Washington, D.C.: U.S. Government Printing Office.
U.S. President's Conference on Unemployment (1921). Report. Washington,
D.C.: U.S. Government Printing Office.
U.S. Works Progress Administration, Division of Research, Labor Market Research Section (1941). "Sampling Procedures and Method of Operation of
the WPA Monthly Report of Unemployment", Mimeo.
Van Kleeck, M. (1931). "The Federal Unemployment Census of 1930", Journal of the American Statistical Association, 26 (suppl.), 189—200.

STANDARD BUDGET

Brady, D.S. (1948). "Family Budgets: A Historical Survey", in U.S. Department of Labor, Bureau of Labor Statistics, Worker's Budgets in the United
States: City Families and Single Persons 1946 and 1947, Bulletin No. 927,
pp. 41—45. Washington, D.C.: U.S. Government Printing Office.
Brady, D.S. (1949). "The Use of Statistical Procedures in the Derivation of
Family Budgets", Social Science Review, XXII, No. 2, 141—157.
Bureau of Applied Economics (1920). Standards of Living: A Compilation of
Budgetary Studies. Washington, D.C.: Bureau of Applied Economics, Inc.
Kellogg, L.S. and Brady, D.S. (1948). "The City Worker's Family Budget", in
U.S. Department of Labor, Bureau of Labor Statistics, Worker's Budgets in
the United States: City Families and Single Persons 1946 and 1947, Bulletin No. 927. Washington, D.C.: U.S. Government Printing Office.
Lamale, H.H. and Stotz, M.S. (1960). "The Interim City Worker's Family
Budget", Monthly Labor Review, 785—808.
Moore, G.H. (1971). "Improved Program for the BLS Family Budget Estimates and Interarea Indexes of Living Costs", Memoranda, Office of the
Commissioner of Labor Statistics. Washington, D.C.: U.S. Department of
Labor, Bureau of Labor Statistics.
National Industrial Conference Board (1921). Family Budgets of American
Wage-Earners, A Critical Analysis, Research Report No. 41. New York:
The Century Company.
Orshansky, M. (1965). "Counting the Poor: Another Look at the Poverty
Profile", Social Security Bulletin, 3—29.
Rainwater, L. (1974). What a Money Buys: Inequality and the Social Meanings of Income. Chapter 6. New York: Basic Books.
Rowntree, B.S. (1901). Poverty: A Study of Town Life. London: Macmillan.
Textile Workers Union of America (1944). Substandard Conditions of Living:
A Study of the Cost of the Emergency Sustenance Budget in Five Textile
Communities in January-February 1944. New York: Textile Workers
Union of America.
U.S. Bureau of Labor (1891). Cost of Production, Iron, Steel, etc., 6th
Annual Report of the Commissioner of Labor for 1890. Washington, D.C.:
U.S. Government Printing Office.
U.S. Bureau of Labor (1892). Cost of Production: Textiles and Glass, 7th
Annual Report of the Commissioner of Labor for 1891. Washington, D.C.:
U.S. Government Printing Office.
U.S. Congress, House of Representatives, Committee on Banking and Cur-

rency (1971). Report on Economic Stabilization Act Amendments, House Report 92—714, December 7. Washington, D.C.: U.S. Government Printing Office.

U.S. Congress, Joint Committee on the Economic Report (1949). "Low Income Families", Hearings. Washington, D.C.: U.S. Government Printing Office.

U.S. Congress, Joint Committee on the Economic Report, Subcommittee on Low Income Families (1955). Low Income Families, Hearings, Washington, D.C.: U.S. Government Printing Office.

U.S. Congress, Joint Economic Committee (1959). "The Low Income Population and Economic Growth", by R.J. Lampman, Study Paper No. 12 prepared for the Study of Employment, Growth and Price Levels. Washington, D.C.: U.S. Government Printing Office.

U.S. Congress, Senate Committee on Finance (1970). "Family Assistance Act of 1970", Hearings. Washington, D.C.: U.S. Government Printing Office.

U.S. Congress, Senate (1911). Report on the Condition of Women and Child Wage-Earners in the United States. Senate Document No. 645. Washington, D.C.: U.S. Government Printing Office.

U.S. Department of Agriculture (1957). Family Food Consumption and Dietary Levels, Miscellaneous Publication 452. Washington, D.C.: U.S. Government Printing Office.

U.S. Department of Commerce, Bureau of the Census (1970). 24 Million Americans — Poverty in the United States: 1969. Current Population Reports, Consumer Income, Series P-60, No. 76. Washington, D.C.: U.S. Government Printing Office.

U.S. Department of Commerce, Bureau of the Census (1971). Characteristics of the Low Income Population, 1970. Current Population Reports, Consumer Income, Series P-60, No. 81. Washington, D.C.: U.S. Government Printing Office.

U.S. Department of Health, Education and Welfare, Social Security Administration (1948). "A Budget for an Elderly Couple", Social Security Bulletin.

U.S. Department of Labor (1959). How American Buying Habits Change. Washington, D.C.: U.S. Government Printing Office.

U.S. Department of Labor, Bureau of Labor Statistics (1919). Tentative Quantity and Cost Budget Necessary to Maintain a Family of Five in Washington, D.C., at a Level of Health and Decency. Washington, D.C.: U.S. Government Printing Office.

U.S. Department of Labor, Bureau of Labor Statistics (1920). "Minimum Quantity Budget Necessary to Maintain a Worker's Family of Five in Health and Decency", Monthly Labor Review, 10, No. 6, p. 1307.

U.S. Department of Labor, Bureau of Labor Statistics (1948). Bulletin No. 927.

U.S. Department of Labor, Bureau of Labor Statistics (1963). "Report of the Advisory Committee on Standard Budget Research", Washington, D.C. Mimeo.

U.S. Department of Labor, Bureau of Labor Statistics (1969). 3 Standards of Living for an Urban Family of Four Persons, Spring 1967. Bulletin 1570-5. Washington, D.C.: U.S. Government Printing Office.

U.S. Department of Labor, Bureau of Labor Statistics (1971). Minutes of the

Meeting of the Committee on Consumer and Wholesale Prices of the Labor Research Advisory Council, November 2. Mimeo.

U.S. President (1964). Economic Report of the President 1964. Washington, D.C.: U.S. Government Printing Office.

U.S. Treasury Department, Division of Tax Research (1947). "Individual Income Tax Exemptions", Washington, D.C. (Mimeo).

U.S. Works Progress Administration, Division of Social Research (1936). "Quantity Budgets for Basic Maintenance in Emergency Standards of Living", Research Bulletin Series 1, No. 21. Washington, D.C.: U.S. Government Printing Office.

Williams, F. and Zimmerman, C.C. (1935). Studies of Family Living in the United States and Other Countries: Analysis of Material and Method. Miscellaneous Publication 223, U.S. Department of Agriculture. Washington, D.C.: U.S. Government Printing Office.

CRIME

Bell, Daniel D. (1960). "The Myth of Crime Waves", Chapter 8 in The End of Ideology. New York: The Free Press of Glencoe.

Clark, R. (1970). Crime in America. New York: Simon & Schuster.

Davies, A.M. (1931). "Criminal Statistics and the National Commission's Report", Journal of Criminal Law and Criminology, 22, 357—374.

Hall, G.W. (1972). "The Program of the Statistics Division of the Law Enforcement Assistance Administration", American Statistical Association Proceedings, Social Statistics Section, pp. 106—110.

Hoover, H. (1959). "Do We Have a Duty to Get Tough? " Reader's Digest, 75, 143—146, July.

International Association of Chiefs of Police, Committee on Uniform Crime Records (1928). A Uniform Classification of Major Offenses. IACP.

International Association of Chiefs of Police, Committee on Uniform Crime Records (1929). Uniform Crime Reporting: A Complete Manual for Police. IACP.

Lejins, P.P. (1966). "Uniform Crime Reports", University of Michigan Law Review, 64, 1011—1030.

Robinson, L.N. (1911). History and Organization of Criminal Statistics in the U.S. Montclair, New Jersey: Patterson Smith (reprinted 1969).

Robinson, L.N. (1933). "History of Criminal Statistics (1908—1933)", Journal of Criminal Law and Criminology, 24, 125.

Robison, S. (1966). "A Critical View of the Uniform Crime Reports", University of Michigan Law Review, 64, 1031—1054.

Sellin, T. (1931). "The Basis of a Crime Index", Journal of Criminal Law and Criminology, 22, 335—356.

Sellin, T. (1967). Systems of Reporting "Crimes Known to the Police" in Selected Foreign Countries. U.S. President's Commission on Law Enforcement and Administration of Justice (Multilith).

U.S. Department of Justice, Federal Bureau of Investigation (1939). Ten Years of Uniform Crime Reporting 1930—1939. Washington, D.C. (Mimeo).

U.S. Department of Justice, Federal Bureau of Investigation (1958). "Uniform Crime Reporting", Report of the Consultant Committee, in Uniform

Crime Reports for the U.S., Special Issue. Washington, D.C.: U.S. Government Printing Office.

U.S. Department of Justice, Law Enforcement Assistance Administration (1974). Crime in the Nation's Five Largest Cities: National Crime Panel Surveys, Advance Report (Multilith).

U.S. National Commission on Law Observance and Enforcement (1931). Reports, Vol. 1, No. 3, Criminal Statistics. Washington, D.C.: U.S. Government Printing Office.

U.S. President's Commission on Law Enforcement and Administration of Justice (1967). The Challenge of Crime in a Free Society. Washington, D.C.: U.S. Government Printing Office.

U.S. President's Commission on Law Enforcement and Administration of Justice (1967). Field Survey No. 1. Report on a Pilot Study in the District of Columbia on Victimization and Attitudes Toward Law Enforcement. Washington, D.C.: Bureau of Social Science Research, Inc.

Wallace, R.F. (1957). "Crime in the U.S.", Life, September 9, 49—70.

Warner, S.B. (1931). "Crimes Known to the Police — An Index of Crime", Research Report No. 17, U.S. National Commission on Law Observance and Enforcement (Mimeo).

Wilson, J.Q. (1968). Varieties of Police Behavior. Cambridge, Massachusetts: Harvard University Press.

Wolfgang, M.E. (1963). "Uniform Crime Reports: A Critical Appraisal", University of Pennsylvania Law Review, 111, 708—738.

Zeisel, H. (1971). "The Future of Law Enforcement Statistics: A Summary View", in U.S. President's Commission on Federal Statistics, Vol. II. Washington, D.C.: U.S. Government Printing Office.

CHAPTER VII

Bancroft, G. (1958). The American Labor Force: Its Growth and Changing Composition. Appendix: Some Problems of Concepts and Measurement. New York: John Wiley and Sons.

Becker, G. (1964). Human Capital. National Bureau of Economic Research, No. 80 General Series. New York and London: Distributed by Columbia University Press.

Blau, P. and Duncan, O.D. (1967). The American Occupational Structure. New York: John Wiley and Sons.

Davis, J.S. (1945). "Standards and Content of Living", American Economic Review, 35, No. 1, March, 1—15.

Davis, K. (1965). "Problems and Solutions in International Comparison for Social Science Purposes" (Mimeo).

Deutscher, I. (1973). "Asking Questions Cross-Culturally: Some Problems of Linguistic Comparability", in D.P. Warwick and S. Osherson, eds., Comparative Research Methods. Englewood Cliffs: Prentice-Hall Inc.

Durand, J.D. (1947). "Development of the Labor Force Concept, 1930—1940", Appendix A in L.J. Ducoff, and M.J. Hagood, eds., Labor Force Definition and Measurement. Bulletin No. 56. New York: Social Science Research Council.

Franklin, N.N. (1967). "The Concept and Measurement of Minimum Living Standards", International Labor Review, 95, No. 4, 271—298.

Jaffe, A.J. and Stewart, D. (1951). Manpower Resources and Utilization: Principles of Working Force Analysis. New York: John Wiley and Sons.

Jolly, R., de Kadt, E., Singer, H. and Wilson, F., eds. (1973). Third World Employment: Problems and Strategy. London: Penguin Books.

Kaplan, A. (1964). The Conduct of Inquiry. San Francisco: Chandler Publishing Co.

Lamale, H.H. (1958). "Changes in Concepts of Income Adequacy Over the Last Century", American Economic Review, 48, No. 2, 291—299.

Marshall, T.H. (1969). "Poverty and Inequality: Changing Conceptions of Poverty and Stratification". Paper prepared for Conference on Poverty and Stratification. American Academy of Political and Social Science, Chestnut Hill, Massachusetts.

Miller, S.M., Rein, M., Roby, P. and Gross, B.M. (1969). "Poverty, Inequality, and Conflict", Chapter 12 in B.M. Gross, ed., Social Intelligence for America's Future: Explorations in Societal Problems. pp. 283—329. Boston: Allyn and Bacon, Inc.

Moore, W.E. (1953). "The Exportability of the 'Labor Force' Concept", American Sociology Review, 18, 68—72.

Myrdal, G. (1968). Asian Drama: An Inquiry into the Poverty of Nations. Vol. 2. Chapter 21 and Vol. 3, Appendix 6. New York: Pantheon.

Myrdal, G. (1973). "Growth, Gross and Net", Social Policy, Nov./Dec. 4, 23—26.

Rainwater, L. and Yancey, W.L. (1967). The Moynihan Report and the Politics of Controversy. Cambridge: MIT Press.

Rein, M. (1970). "Problems in the Definition and Measurement of Poverty", Chapter 21 in Introduction to Social Policy: Issues of Choice and Change. New York: Random House.

Stein, R.L. (1967). "New Definitions for Employment and Unemployment", in U.S. Department of Labor, Bureau of Labor Statistics, Employment and Earnings 13, No. 8. Washington, D.C.: U.S. Government Printing Office.

Teitz, M.B. (1974). "Toward a Responsive Methodology: The Future of Planning Methods". in D. Godschalk, ed., Planning in America: Learning from Turbulence. Washington, D.C.: American Institute of Planners.

Townsend, P. (1970). The Concept of Poverty. London: Heinemann Educational Books Ltd.

Townsend, P. (1973). "Poverty as Relative Deprivation. Resources and Style of Living", Chapter I in D. Wedderburn, ed., Poverty, Inequality and Class Structure. Cambridge (England): Cambridge University Press.

U.S. Departments of Commerce and Labor, Bureau of the Census/Bureau of Labor Statistics (1967). Concepts and Methods Used in Manpower Statistics from the Current Population Survey, BLS Report No. 313, Current Population Reports, Series P-23, No. 22, June.

U.S. Department of Health, Education and Welfare, National Center for Health Statistics (1964). Health Survey Procedure. Concepts, Questionnaire Development, and Definitions in the Health Interview Survey, Public Health Service Publication No. 1000-Series 1, No. 2. Washington, D.C.: U.S. Government Printing Office.

U.S. Department of Health, Education and Welfare, National Center for

Health Statistics (1966). Conceptual Problems in Developing an Index of Health. Public Health Service Publication No. 1000 - Series 2, No. 17. Washington, D.C.: U.S. Government Printing Office.

U.S. Department of Health, Education and Welfare, Office of Education (1966). Equality of Educational Opportunity. Washington, D.C.: U.S. Government Printing Office.

U.S. Department of Labor (1959). How American Buying Habits Change. Washington, D.C.: U.S. Government Printing Office.

Van Kleeck, M. (1931). "The Federal Unemployment Census of 1930". Journal of the American Statistical Association, 26 (suppl.), 189—200.

Webb, J.N. (1939). "Concepts Used in Unemployment Surveys", Journal of the American Statistical Association, 34 (suppl.), 49—59.

Wheeler, S. (1967). "Criminal Statistics: A Reformulation of the Problem", Journal of Criminal Law, Criminology and Police Science, 58, No. 3, 317—324.

Wilkins, L.T. (1965). "New Thinking in Criminal Statistics", Journal of Criminal Law, Criminology and Police Science, 59, No. 3, 277—284.

Wynne, E. (1972). The Politics of School Accountability: Public Information about Public Schools. Berkeley: McCutchan Publishing Company.

CHAPTER VIII

Bancroft, G. and Welch, E.M. (1946). "Recent Experience with Problems of Labor Force Measurement", Journal of the American Statistical Association, 41, 303—312, September.

Beattie, R.H. (1960). "Criminal Statistics in the United States — 1960", Journal of Criminal Law, Criminology and Police Science, 51, 49—65.

Dodge, R.W. and Turner, A.G. (1972). "Methodological Foundations for a National Survey of Victimization", Proceedings, American Statistical Association, Social Statistics Section, 111—117.

Ducoff, L.J. and Hagood, M.J. (1947). Labor Force Definition and Measurement: Recent Experience in the United States. Bulletin 56. New York: Social Science Research Council.

Flueck, J.A., Waksberg, J. and Kaitz, H.B. (1972). An Overview of Consumer Expenditure Survey Methodology. Proceedings, American Statistical Association, Business and Economics Section, Washington, D.C., pp. 238—246.

Green, G.P. (1971). "Measuring Total and State Insured Unemployment", Monthly Labor Review, June, 37—48.

Morgenstern, O. (1963). On the Accuracy of Economic Observations. 2nd ed. Princeton: Princeton University Press.

Pearl, R.B. and Levine, D.B. (1972). "A New Methodology for a Consumer Expenditure Survey", Proceedings, American Statistical Association, Business and Economics Section, Washington, D.C.

Piven, F. and Cloward, R. (1971). Regulating the Poor. New York: Vintage Books.

Rowntree, S.B. (1901). Poverty: A Study of Town Life. London: Macmillan and Company Ltd.

Stambler, H.V. (1969). "Problems in Analysing Urban Employment Survey Data", Monthly Labor Review, 92, 51—54.

Sudman, S. and Ferber, R. (1972). Some Experimentation with Recall Procedures and Diaries for Consumer Expenditures. Proceedings, American Statistical Association, Business and Economics Section, Washington, D.C.,
pp. 247—253.

Taeuber, C. (1969). "Counting the Invisible Americans: The Inner City and
the 1970 Census". Census Tract Papers Series GE-40, No. 5. Washington,
D.C.: U.S. Government Printing Office.

U.K., Secretary of State for Employment (1972). Unemployment Statistics.
Report of an Inter-Departmental Working Party. Cmnd. 5157. London:
Her Majesty's Stationery Office.

U.S. Bureau of the Budget (1955). Differences in Concepts and Measurement
Procedures and How They Affect Current Series of Employment and Unemployment Statistics. Washington, D.C.: U.S. Bureau of the Budget.

U.S. Congress, House of Representatives, Committee on Post Office and Civil
Service (1969). 1970 Census and Legislation related thereto. Hearings,
Parts I and II. Washington, D.C.: U.S. Government Printing Office.

U.S. Congress, House of Representatives, Committee on Post Office and Civil
Service (1970). "Accuracy of 1970 Census Enumeration and Related Matters", Hearings. Washington, D.C.: U.S. Government Printing Office.

U.S. Department of Commerce, Bureau of the Census, Special Advisory Committee on Employment Statistics (1954). Report. "The Measurement of
Employment and Unemployment by the Bureau of the Census in its Current Population Survey". Washington, D.C.: U.S. Department of Commerce.

U.S. Department of Commerce, Bureau of the Census (1964). Evaluation and
Research Program of the U.S. Census Population and Housing, 1960: Accuracy of Data on Housing Characteristics, Series ER 60, No. 3.

U.S. Department of Commerce, Bureau of the Census (1967). Measuring the
Quality of Housing: An Appraisal of Census Statistics and Methods, Working Paper No. 25. Washington, D.C.: Bureau of the Census.

U.S. Department of Health, Education and Welfare (1966). Equality of Educational Opportunity. Washington, D.C.: U.S. Government Printing Office.

U.S. Department of Labor, Bureau of Labor Statistics (1969). Pilot and Experimental Program on Urban Employment Surveys, Report No. 354.
Washington, D.C.: U.S. Department of Labor.

U.S. Department of Labor, Bureau of Labor Statistics (1971). BLS Handbook
of Methods for Surveys and Studies. Bulletin 1711. Washington, D.C.: U.S.
Government Printing Office.

Warner, S.B. (1931). "Crimes Known to the Police — An Index of Crime",
Research Report No. 17, U.S. National Commission on Law Observance
and Enforcement (Mimeo).

Webb, E. Campbell, D.T., Schwartz, R.D. and Sechrest, L. (1966). Unobtrusive Measures: NonReactive Research in the Social Sciences. Chicago:
Rand McNally and Company.

Wheeler, S. (1967). "Criminal Statistics: A Reformulation of the Problem",
Journal of Criminal Law, Criminology and Police Science, 58, 317—324.

Wilson, J.Q. (1968). Varieties of Police Behavior. Cambridge, Massachusetts:
Harvard University Press.

CHAPTER IX

Alker, H.R., Jr. and Russett, B.M. (1968). "Indices for Comparing Inequality", Chapter 16 in R.L. Merritt, and S. Rokkhan, eds., Comparing Nations — The Use of Quantitative Data in Cross-National Research, pp. 349—372. New Haven: Yale University Press.

Clay, P.L. (1972). National Housing Goals and Measures of Progress, Working Paper No. 14. Cambridge: Joint Center for Urban Studies of M.I.T. and Harvard University.

Etzioni, A. and Lehman, E.W. (1969). "Some Dangers in 'Valid' Social Measurement", Chapter 2 in B.M. Gross, ed., Social Intelligence for America's Future — Explorations in Societal Problems. pp. 45—62. Boston: Allyn and Bacon.

Hogg, M.H. (1930). "Sources of Incomparability and Error in Employment Unemployment Surveys". Proceedings, American Statistical Association, Supplement, 25, 284—294.

Kaplan, B.D. (1972). "Needs For Seasonal Adjustment Research". Proceedings, American Statistical Association, Business and Economics Section, pp. 59—62.

Kellogg, L.S. and Brady, D.S. (1948). "The City Worker's Family Budget", BLS Bulletin 927, U.S. Department of Labor, pp. 3—40.

Kolodney, S.E. and Wormeli, P.K. (1972). "Computer-Linked Transactional Records for Criminal Justice Statistics". Proceedings, American Statistical Association, Social Statistics Section, pp. 118—123.

Little, A. and Mabey, C. (1972). "An Index for Designation of Educational Priority Areas", Chapter 5 in A. Shonfield, and S. Shaw, eds., Social Indicators and Social Policy. pp. 67—93. London: Heinemann Educational Books Ltd.

Morgan, J.N. and Smith, J.D. (1969). "Measures of Economic Well-Offness", American Economic Review, 49, 450—462.

Myrdal, G. (1973). "Growth: Gross and Net", Social Policy, Nov./Dec., 4, No. 3, 23—26.

Olson, M. (unpublished). The Evaluation of Collective Performance.

Perry, G.L. (1970). "Changing Labor Markets and Inflation", Brookings Papers on Economic Activity, No. 3, 411—441.

Reichard, R. (1974). The Figure Finaglers. New York: McGraw-Hill.

Sellin, T. and Wolfgang, M. (1964). The Measurement of Delinquency. New York: John Wiley and Sons.

Torgerson, W. (1958). Theory and Methods of Scaling. New York: John Wiley and Sons.

U.S. Department of Labor, Bureau of Labor Statistics (1971). BLS Handbook of Methods. Bulletin 1711. Washington, D.C.: U.S. Government Printing Office.

Watts, H.W. (1972). "Microdata: Lessons from the OEO and the Graduated Work Incentive Program", Annals of Social and Economic Measurement, 1/2, 183—191.

Webber, M.M. (1964). "The Urban and the Nonplace Realm", in M.M. Webber, ed., Explorations into Urban Structure. Philadelphia: University of Pennsylvania Press.

Wolfgang, M.E. (1963). "Uniform Crime Reports: A Critical Appraisal". University of Pennsylvania Law Review, 111, 708—738.

CHAPTER X

Arnow, K.S. (1951). The Attack on the Cost of Living Index. Washington, D.C.: Committee on Public Administration Cases.

Beckman, N. (1971). "Congressional Information Processes for National Policy", Annals of the American Academy of Political and Social Science, 394, 84—99.

Daniel, J. (1961). "Let's Look at Those 'Alarming' Unemployment Figures", Reader's Digest, September.

Flash, E.S., Jr. (1971). "Macro-Economics for Macro-Policy", Annals of the American Academy of Political and Social Science, 394, 46—56.

Lyons, G.M. (1971). "The President and His Experts", in Annals of the American Academy of Political and Social Science, 394, 36—45.

Orshansky, M. (1965). "Counting the Poor: Another Look at the Poverty Profile", Social Security Bulletin, January, 3—29.

Sayre, R.A. (1946). "A Cost of Living: A Five Year Controversy", Management Record (National Industrial Conference Board), September, 291—296.

Schneier, E. (1970). "The Intelligence of Congress: Information and Public-Policy Patterns", Annals of the American Academy of Political and Social Science, 388, 14—24.

U.S. Congress, House Committee on Economics and Labor (1951). Consumers' Price Index, Hearings. Washington, D.C.: U.S. Government Printing Office.

U.S. Congress, Joint Economic Committee (annual) Economic Indicators, Historical and Descriptive Supplement. Washington, D.C.: U.S. Government Printing Office.

U.S. Congress, Joint Economic Committee, Subcommittee on Economic Statistics (1963). Measuring Employment and Unemployment, Hearings. Washington, D.C.: U.S. Government Printing Office.

U.S. Congress, Senate Committee on Government Operations, Subcommittee on Government Research (1968). "Full Opportunity and Social Accounting Act", (S-843), Hearings 1967, Parts I and II. Washington, D.C.: U.S. Government Printing Office.

U.S. Congress, Senate Committee on Labor and Public Welfare, Special Subcommittee on Evaluation and Planning of Social Programs (1970). "Full Opportunity Act", (S-5), Hearings. Washington, D.C.: U.S. Government Printing Office.

U.S. Congress, Senate Committee on Labor and Public Welfare, Special Subcommittee on Evaluation and Planning of Social Programs (1971). "Full Opportunity and National Goals and Priorities Act", (S-5), Hearings. Washington, D.C.: U.S. Government Printing Office.

U.S. Department of Commerce, Bureau of the Census, Special Advisory Committee on Employment Statistics (1954). Report. Measurement of Employment and Unemployment by the Bureau of the Census in its Current Population Survey. Washington, D.C.: U.S. Department of Commerce.

U.S. Department of Commerce, Bureau of the Census (1958). "Concepts and Methods Used in the Current Employment and Unemployment Statistics, Prepared by the Bureau of the Census", Current Population Reports, Series P-23, No. 5. Washington, D.C.: Bureau of the Census.

U.S. Department of Labor, Bureau of Labor Statistics, Office of Prices and Living Conditions (1963). Report of the Advisory Committee on Standard Budget Research. Washington, D.C.: Bureau of Labor Statistics.

U.S. Executive Office of the President, Office of Management and Budget (1974). Social Indicators. Washington, D.C.: U.S. Government Printing Office.

U.S. President's Committee on the Cost of Living (1944). Report, Office of Economic Stabilization. Washington, D.C.: U.S. Government Printing Office.

U.S. President's Committee to Appraise Employment and Unemployment Statistics (1962). Measuring Employment and Unemployment. Washington, D.C.: U.S. Government Printing Office.

Wildavsky, A. (1964). The Politics of the Budgetary Process. Boston: Little Brown.

Wildavsky, A. (1973). "The Annual Expenditure Increment or How Congress can gain Control of the Budget", The Public Interest, No. 33, 84—108.

Wilensky, H.L. (1967). Organizational Intelligence — Knowledge and Policy in Government and Industry. New York: Basic Books.

CHAPTER XI

Alonso, W. (1968). "Predicting Best With Imperfect Data", Journal of the American Institute of Planners, 34, 248—255.

Beveridge, W. (1944). Full Employment in a Free Society. London: George Allen and Unwin.

Blackman, J. (1947). "The Heller Budget in Wage Negotiations", Studies in Personnel Policy No. 82. New York City: National Industrial Conference Board.

Blackman, J. and Gainsburgh, M.R. (1944). "Subsistence Budgets: 1944 Model", Conference Board Management Record, 6, No. 10.

Bureau of Applied Economics (1920). Standards of Living: A Compilation of Budgetary Studies. Washington, D.C.: Bureau of Applied Economics.

Business Week (1971). "Living with a Higher Jobless Rate", December 25, 36—38.

Community Council of Greater New York (1963, revised 1970). 4 Family Budget Standards. New York: Budget Standard Research Department.

Gordon, R.A. (1967). The Goal of Full Employment. New York: John Wiley and Sons.

Great Britain, Royal Commission on the Income Tax (1920). Report. London: His Majesty's Stationery Office.

Jeffrey, J.R. (1972). Doctoral Dissertation. Houston: Rice University.

Jones, A. (1973). The New Inflation. The Politics of Prices and Incomes. Middlesex (England): Penguin Books.

Marcuse, P. (1970). Housing Policy and Social Indicators: Strangers or Siblings? Working Paper No. 130. Berkeley: Institute of Urban and Regional Development, University of California.

Moynihan, D.P. (1970). "Policy vs. Program in the 70s", The Public Interest, No. 20, 90—100.

National Industrial Conference Board (1921). Family Budgets of American Wage Earners: A Critical Analysis. Research Report No. 41. New York: The Century Co.

Nixon, R.A. and Samuelson, P.A. (1940). "Estimates of Unemployment in the United States", Review of Economic Statistics, 22, 101—111.

Oliphant, T. (1972). "Minimum 5% Unemployment Accepted Reality in Washington", Boston Globe, January 30.

Orshansky, M. (1959). "Family Budgets and Fee Schedule of Voluntary Agencies", Social Security Bulletin, 22.

Phillips, A.W. (1958). "The Relation Between Unemployment and the Rate of Change of Money Wage Rates in the United Kingdom 1862—1957", Economica, 25, 283—299.

Ruttenberg, S.H. (1970). Manpower Challenge of the 1970s: Institutions and Social Change, Policy Studies in Employment and Welfare No. 2. Baltimore: Johns Hopkins University Press.

Sayre, R.A. (1946). "The Cost of Living: A Five Year Controversy", Management Record, 291—296.

Sibson, R.E. (1953). "Budget Approach in Wage Determination", Labor Law Journal, 4, 624—631, September.

Stecker, M.L. (1921). "Family Budgets and Wages", American Economic Review, 447—465, September.

Stecker, M.L. (1937). Intercity Differences in Costs of Living in March 1935, 59 Cities. Research Monograph XII. U.S. Works Progress Administration, Division of Social Research. Washington, D.C.: U.S. Government Printing Office.

U.S. Commissioner of Internal Revenue (1866). Report. Washington, D.C.: U.S. Government Printing Office.

U.S. Congress, House of Representatives Committee on Banking and Currency (1971a). Report on Economic Stabilization Act Amendments of 1971. H.R. 92—714.

U.S. Congress, House of Representatives, Committee on Banking and Currency (1971b). "Economic Stabilization", Hearings, Parts I and II. Washington, D.C.: U.S. Government Printing Office.

U.S. Congress, House of Representatives, Committee on Education and Labor (1951). Consumers Price Index, Report, House Document 404. Washington, D.C.: U.S. Government Printing Office.

U.S. Congress, House of Representatives, Committee on the Judiciary (1967). Anticrime Programs, Hearings. Washington, D.C.: U.S. Government Printing Office.

U.S. Congress, Joint Committee on the Economic Report, Subcommittee on Unemployment (1950). "Employment and Unemployment", Report pursuant to Senate Resolution 26. Washington, D.C.: U.S. Government Printing Office.

U.S. Congress, Joint Economic Committee (1959). Employment, Growth, and Price Levels, 10 volumes. Washington, D.C.: U.S. Government Printing Office.

U.S. Congress, Joint Economic Committee, Subcommittee on Economic Statistics (1961a). Higher Unemployment Rates, 1957—60, Structural Transformation or Inadequate Demand. Washington, D.C.: U.S. Government Printing Office.

U.S. Congress, Joint Economic Committee, Subcommittee on Economic Statistics (1961b). Unemployment Terminology, Measurement and Analysis. Washington, D.C.: U.S. Government Printing Office.

U.S. Congress, Select Committee on Nutrition and Human Needs (1969). "The Food Gap: Poverty and Malnutrition in the U.S.". Interim Report. Washington, D.C.: U.S. Government Printing Office.

U.S. Congress, Senate Committee on Banking, Housing and Urban Affairs (1971). "Economic Stabilization Legislation", Hearings. Washington, D.C.: U.S. Government Printing Office.

U.S. Congress, Senate Committee on Education and Labor (1944). Wartime Health and Education. Hearings, Part 3 "Fixed Incomes in the War Economy", Washington, D.C.: U.S. Government Printing Office.

U.S. Congress, Senate Committee on Finance (1935). "Economic Security Act", Hearings. Washington, D.C.: U.S. Government Printing Office.

U.S. Congress, Senate Committee on Finance (1943). Revenue Act of 1943. Hearings. Washington, D.C.: U.S. Government Printing Office.

U.S. Congress, Senate Committee on Finance (1970). Family Assistance Act of 1970, Hearings. Washington, D.C.: U.S. Government Printing Office.

U.S. Congress, Senate Committee on Finance (1971). Social Security Amendments of 1971, Hearings. Washington, D.C.: U.S. Government Printing Office.

U.S. Department of Labor, Bureau of Labor Statistics, Office of Prices and Living Conditions (1963). Report of the Advisory Committee on Standard Budget Research. Washington, D.C.: Bureau of Labor Statistics.

U.S. Department of Labor, Bureau of Labor Statistics (1969a). Employment Situation in Poverty Areas of Six Cities, July 1968-June 1969. Urban Employment Survey, Report 370. Washington. D.C.: Bureau of Labor Statistics.

U.S. Department of Labor, Bureau of Labor Statistics (1969b). Pilot and Experimental Program on Urban Employment Surveys. Report 354. Washington, D.C.: Bureau of Labor Statistics.

U.S. Executive Office of the President, Committee on Labor Supply, Employment, and Unemployment Statistics (1955). Report of the Review of Concepts Subcommittee. In U.S. Congress, Joint Economic Committee "Employment and Unemployment Statistics", Hearings. Washington, D.C.: U.S. Government Printing Office.

U.S. National Commission on Urban Problems to the Congress and to the President of the United States (1968). Building the American City. U.S. Congress, House Document 91-34. Washington, D.C.: U.S. Government Printing Office.

U.S. National War Labor Board (1918). Memorandum on the Minimum Wage and Increased Cost of Living. Submitted by the Secretary at the Request of the Board at its Meeting July 12.

U.S. National War Labor Board (1947). Termination Report: Industrial Disputes and Wage Stabilization in Wartime January 12, 1942-December 31, 1945 (3 vols.). Washington, D.C.: U.S. Government Printing Office (Issued by the Department of Labor, Chapter 19 "Substandards of Living", pp. 211—225 and Appendices J-21 and J-22, pp. 659—664).

U.S. President's Committee on the Cost of Living (1945). Report. Office of Economic Stabilization. Washington, D.C.: U.S. Government Printing Office.

318

U.S. President's Committee to Appraise Employment and Unemployment Statistics (1963). Measuring Employment and Unemployment. Washington, D.C.: U.S. Government Printing Office.

U.S. White House Conference on Food, Nutrition and Health (1970). Final Report, 1969. Washington, D.C.: U.S. Government Printing Office.

United Steelworkers of America (1944). The Steelworker in 1943. Pittsburgh: United Steelworkers Union.

Wolfbein, S.L. (1965). Employment, Unemployment and Public Policy. New York: Random House.

CHAPTER XII

American Statistical Association (1973). "Maintaining the Professional Integrity of Federal Statistics", The American Statistician, 27, No. 2.

Hauser, P.M. (1973). "Statistics and Politics", The American Statistician, 27, No. 2, 68—71.

Jones, A. (1973) The New Inflation: The Politics of Prices and Incomes. Harmondsworth, Middlesex (England): Penguin.

Li, C.M. (1962). The Statistical System of Communist China. Berkeley: University of California Press.

Pounds, W.F. (1969). "The Process of Problem-Finding", Industrial Management Review, 11, No. 1, 1—19.

U.S. Congress, House Committee on Post Office and Civil Service, Subcommittee on Census and Statistics (1972). Investigation of Possible Politicization of Federal Statistical Programs. Washington, D.C.: U.S. Government Printing Office.

U.S. Congress, Joint Economic Committee (1972, 1973). Current Labor Market Developments. Hearings. Parts I, II, III, and IV. Washington, D.C.: U.S. Government Printing Office.

U.S. Department of Commerce, Bureau of the Census (1967). Measuring the Quality of Housing, Working Paper No. 25. Washington, D.C.: Bureau of the Census.

U.S. Department of Labor, Bureau of Labor Statistics (1971). Minutes of the Committee on Consumer and Wholesale Prices. Washington, D.C.: Labor Research Advisory Council.

U.S. Executive Office of the President, Office of Management and Budget (1974). Social Indicators. Washington, D.C.: U.S. Government Printing Office.

U.S. National Goals Research Staff (1970). Toward Balanced Growth: Quantity with Quality. A Report. Washington, D.C.: U.S. Government Printing Office.

Van Kleeck, M. (1931). "The Federal Unemployment Census of 1930", Journal of the American Statistical Association, 26 (suppl.), March, 189—200.

Appendix

TABLE 1
Origin and Evolution of the Unemployment Rate

Year	Environment and Key Events	Developments in Concepts	Methods	Intended and Actual Purposes
1921	Post war depression and unemployment. President calls National Conference on Unemployment.	Fuzzy ones only.	Guesswork and estimates based on employment in a limited group of industries and union data. Voted on final figure.	To aid business planning, and help avoid recessions. No government policy foreseen.
1928	High unemployment. Media agitation about data quality. Senate Committee hearings on unemployment.		Estimates based on movements in partial employment data.	
1930	Depression begins. Census covers unemployment.	Gainful workers: those with previous paid jobs. Unemployed: indeterminate subset of seven categories of those idle on day before interview. Employed: unspecified.	Census interviews.	To evaluate effects of Depression. To provide benchmark for later estimates.
1931	Special follow-up survey on unemployment.	Same.	Same.	To check the census results.

Year	Event	Concept/Definition	Method	Purpose/Use
1929–1937	Experimental surveys of unemployment in various cities, by private groups, states and WPA.	Gainful workers: over 14, willing and able to work.	Gradual application of theories of stratified, random sampling. Schedule design and interviewing improved. Widely differing national estimates.	To plan unemployment relief. For political discussion on relief policy and economic measures.
1937	Congress authorizes National Unemployment Census.	Seven categories ranging from totally unemployed to fully employed.	Postcard self-registration of unemployed. 70% returns.	For Congress and public to evaluate policy and appropriations.
1937	Enumerative Check Census.	A category equivalent to labor force: employed or available. Unemployment: boundaries still undecided.	Canvass of families and sampling of postal routes. More complete and less bias than registration.	To check completeness of registration.
1939	War. WPA begins monthly unemployment survey.	Classification on basis of current activity. (a) with a job = employed. (b) without a job and seeking one = unemployed. (c) either (a) or (b) = labor force.	Stratified random sample of 41 counties, 25,000 households.	Congress, media and public use traditional and conflicting estimates to argue over WPA appropriations and to equate with number of jobs needed. Little use of new survey.
1940	Decennial Census covers unemployment. Unemployment declines.	Same.	Complete coverage. Same questions.	
1942	Census takes over sample survey.	No change.	Improvement in sampling method for accuracy and less bias with same sample size.	Interest in survey results to locate workers for war industry.

323

TABLE 1 (continued)

Year	Environment and Key Events	Developments in		Methods	Intended and Actual Purposes
		Concepts			
1945		Change in employment concept to include all with any work.		Discovery of 2,500,000 employed by change in schedule. The only major discontinuity in series.	
1946	The Employment Act. Monthly Survey becomes CPS.	No change.		No change.	Unemployment data to be used to evaluate the new policy.
1950	Decennial Census. Congress refuses funds to update CPS sample.	No change. Search for consensus on full employment, level in range of 3 to 4% unemployed.		Unemployment 24% higher in CPS than in census. Reinterviews support CPS methods and results.	
1954	New sample shows 20% more unemployment than old. Expert committee studies reasons for discrepancy. Congressional hearings on Economic Statistics. Subcommittee created.	No change.		New CPS sample: 230 areas, no size increase. Reliability as if sample doubled. Discrepancy with old sample due to interviewers. New sample most reliable.	Increasingly to help set monetary and fiscal policy.

Year				
1955	Subcommittee hearings.	Minor changes recommended.	Introduction of seasonal adjustment.	
1956	Congress provides funds for bigger CPS sample.		Sample expanded to 330 areas and 35,000 households.	Detail needed as economic policy more complex and responsive.
1957			The "30 day lay-off" and "waiting for a job" categories switched from employed to unemployed.	Structure versus inadequate demand controversy requires increasing detail and sensitivity in data.
1959	BLS takes over analysis and presentation of data. High, stable unemployment level.			Development of Phillips curve and analysis of unemployment-inflation tradeoff.
1961	Democrat Kennedy assumes Presidency after laissez-faire Administration. Kennedy appoints Gordon Committee to investigate charges. Congress holds hearings on the charges. Users defend the measure.		Reader's Digest article challenges methods and concepts of CPS as incompetent and deliberately distorted to exaggerate unemployment and justify massive public spending.	The structural theory suggests manpower programs and requires data on the characteristics of the unemployed.
1962	Gordon Committee Report. Congressional hearings on Report. Enactment of MDTA.	Concepts supported. Minor changes recommended to make concepts unambiguously measurable and develop more independent labor force concept.	Methods supported. Integrity and objectivity asserted. Unrelated improvements suggested in sampling and seasonal adjustment.	For research, analysis, and economic and manpower policy planning.

TABLE 1 (continued)

Year	Environment and Key Events	Developments in		Intended and Actual Purposes
		Concepts	Methods.	
1964	War on Poverty.	Marginal changes in concept to meet recommendations of Gordon Committee. Net effect: slight decrease in unemployment.	Sample size increased to 52,500 households, 449 areas. New questions on hours of work, duration of unemployment, etc.	Data on deprived groups to plan programs and evaluate policy for poverty.
1967	New funds for CPS.			
1967–1970	BLS conducts Employment Surveys in urban poverty areas for Manpower Administration.	The regular concepts do not provide comparable results in poverty areas. They undercount those desiring work.	BLS and Census use exploratory questions on special employment problems, cultural differences, reasons for nonparticipation.	To get accurate and detailed enough data on the poor and black to plan manpower programs.
1969	Nixon Administration enters. Job vacancy statistics begin. Decennial Census includes low-income area employment surveys.			
1970	BLS low-income area data suggests unemployment rates of 15 to 20% by some definitions.	New concepts gain currency; subemployment, hidden unemployment, discouraged workers. Definitions still fuzzy.	Specially trained interviewers use new techniques to find those usually missed.	

| 1971 | Rising unemployment and inflation. Nixon invokes economic controls. Controversy over unemployment data and interpretation of findings and cancellation of low-income area surveys. | Administration tries to redefine full employment level as 4.5% unemployment. Elasticity of labor force recognized widely. | Economists point to upward shift of Phillips curve. Tradeoff of unemployment and inflation at higher level of both. | If full employment norm can be shifted, it decreases criticism of Administration. |

TABLE 2
Origin and Evolution of the Standard Budget

Year	Environment and Key Events	Developments in		Intended and Actual Purposes
		Concepts	Methods	
1850—1900	Growth of laboring class. Intermittent depressions. Social and labor reformers and concern for poverty.	Basic consumption categories (food, shelter, fuel).	Method and practice of family expenditure survey developed in Europe and U.S. Engel develops law of expenditure.	To describe living standards among workers, evaluate wage adequacy and interpret social behavior. To determine whether wage increases would be wasted or well used.
1884	Congress sets up Bureau of Labor Statistics (BLS).	The "normal" family, the working man and wife of moderate to low income, 4-5 children.		
1888	Congress orders first Federal family expenditure survey.	"Real wages", implicit in comparisons of consumption levels at zero saving. An index for price change.	Equivalence scale, to transform budget levels from one family size to another. Survey method. Weighting for price indices.	To resolve dispute over impact of tariff reduction.
1899	First budget, by B.S. Rowntree.	The poverty level, meaning "subsistence level".	Selection of consumption quantities and grouping into annual list for a family type.	To quantify the poor in York, England and precisely define their level of living.

Year	Events	Budget Standard	Purpose/Use
1902	The "American Standard of Living" cited as wage argument to Anthracite Coal Strike Commission.		To evaluate wages of the lowest paid groups and set relief payments. To set wages for government employees, and by arbitration boards to settle wage claims.
1903–1920	Many standard budgets designed by public and private groups in U.S.	Minimal, but above subsistence, standard, followed by comfort budget for the average worker family.	
1911	The first federally designed BLS standard budget published as part of a Congressional study.	Different standards for different classes and ethnic groups.	To evaluate the conditions of women and child wage earners.
1914–1919	The War. Inflation. Price and wage control. Federal family expenditure studies.	"Substandard" wages should not be subject to controls. Complete quantity budget, which can be priced anywhere.	War Labor Board uses budgets in wage settlements.
1920	Congressional Commission on Reclassification of Salaries requests new standard budget.	Health and Decency Budget for white-collar family.	To determine salaries for civil service and other white-collar jobs after war changed living patterns.
1929	Depression begins. New life styles. Massive work relief.		Increasing use to set fees based on income and determine grant levels.

TABLE 2 (continued)

Year	Environment and Key Events	Developments in Concepts	Methods	Intended and Actual Purposes
1934–1936	Vast family expenditure survey.	WPA Emergency budget for temporary sustenance and Maintenance Budget for life without comforts.	Not documented.	To set wages for emergency workers.
1939	War begins.			
1944	Inflation. Wage and price controls.	"Cost of Living" index recognized as a price index only not reflecting life style changes. Renamed Consumer Price Index (CPI).		Textile workers use budget to demonstrate substandard wages to War Labor Board.
1945	War ends. Congress directs BLS to design new, higher budget to replace WPA versions.	The City Worker Family Budget (CWFB) "modest but adequate" for a family of four. Similar budget for elderly couple.	Fully reproduceable methods, including expenditure/elasticity curve. Based on 1934 data.	To help fix new income tax rates and allowances to take into account the effect of changed life styles. For Social Security Administration to analyse benefit adequacy.
1950–1951	Expenditure survey to get new weights for CPI.			
1959	Interim Revision of CWFB.		Based on 1950-51 data.	

Year				
1960–1961	Expenditure survey for CPI.			
1964	War on Poverty begins.	Poverty line becomes an official statistic.	An arbitrary income level, the same for any size family.	
1965	BLS initiates first request for funds to redesign budget.	Poverty measure should reflect same levels of living for different families.	New poverty line, the Orshansky index, a multiple of the cost of an adequate diet for a specified family size.	To analyse the composition of the poor and plan anti-poverty programs.
1966	BLS requests funds to design two budgets. Congress approves three in permanent program.	The "low", "moderate", and "higher" level budgets.		The low budget is an alternative to poverty line. Moderate budget for union wage arguments. High budget for business location and salary decisions.
1969	President proposes Family Assistance Plan (FAP).			
1971	Inflation and high unemployment. Controls on wages and prices. Congress declares substandard wages exempt. BLS Commissioner proposes discontinuance of budget.	Implicit dispute over whether wages are payment for work or to support family and whether single breadwinner is the norm.	Cost of Living Council adjusts budget income to account for average number of workers per family (1.7).	Congress and interest groups use lower budget to argue for higher FAP minimum. Congress uses lower budget as definition of substandard wages. Cost of Living Council uses a lower figure.
1972	Court declares Council acted against intent of Congress. Exempt wage level raised. Budget continues.			

TABLE 3
Origin and Evolution of the Crime Index

Year	Environment and Key Events	Developments in		Intended and Actual Purposes
		Concepts	Methods	
17th century	Political Arithmeticians call for a measure of criminality.	Crime as immorality.	Count the number punished for crimes.	To measure moral health of society.
1778	Bentham urges compilation of crime data.		Conviction data as crime index.	To evaluate legislation.
1827	France initiates annual crime statistics report.		Data from the court system.	To find causes of crime and test theories behind crime reduction policies.
	Other countries and some U.S. States follow suit.		Data from penal systems.	
1856	England begins publishing police statistics.		From police records, includes acknowledgement of limitations of data.	
1871	U.S. Police Convention declares purpose of procuring and analyzing statistics.	Major conceptual and practical questions of measuring crime have been recognized by some analysts, including unrecorded criminality, selection, and weighting of crime in an index, choice of population base, and the pros and cons of various data sources.		For police departments.

Year	Event	Note	Purpose
1907	Census Bureau tries and fails to collect judicial criminal statistics.	Failure due to inadequate preparation.	
1909	U.S. Conference on Criminal Law and Criminology calls for Census to collect police and judicial statistics.	Few researchers working on concepts or methods.	
1911	24 states by now collecting judicial and prison data.	Data is poor in all but one state.*	
1920–1930	Visible crime and gangsterism. Many state crime surveys. Census Bureau does prison census.	Methodological studies of police statistics by the Department of Justice.	
1927	IACP sets up Committee on Uniform Crime Reports.	Crimes known to the police.	A basis for national crime statistics.
1929	Uniform Crime Reporting Manual published. Growing fear of lawlessness and opposition to Prohibition. President Hoover appoints Wickersham Commission.		For police departments in producing crime reports. To study causes of crime and relation to Prohibition and put off a decision about it.
1930	FBI begins to collect, compile and publish police statistics. Part I crimes become the crime index.	Part I crimes: largely the most serious and regularly reported: homicide, burglary, rape, aggravated assault, larceny, robbery, auto theft. Many local police departments voluntarily alter record-keeping practices and submit monthly reports to FBI.	Management tool for police chiefs. To argue to public for police funding and support.

333

TABLE 3 (continued)

Year	Environment and Key Events	Developments in		Intended and Actual Purposes
		Concepts	Methods	
1931	Wickersham Committee Report.		Recommends Census collect statistics. Criticizes FBI methods and reliability of its statistics.	Statistics for public information about crime.
	Sellin publishes classic article on crime indices**, detailing fundamental concepts and methodological caveats.	Index should be based on selected crimes which are public and "injurious to social welfare" to assure good reporting.	Police statistics are tampered with and other factors make them unreliable. The "value of a crime rate for index purposes decreases as distance from the crime itself in terms of procedure increases".	Criticizes use of most crime data as indices to crime. Wants crime index to do broad social analysis and gauge the effects of social reforms.
1957	Life magazine article says U.S. crime statistics worst in world. FBI appoints technical Consultant Committee.			To suggest marginal changes in crime data and satisfy critics.
1958	Consultant Committee Report published by FBI.	Recommends Changes: Substitute crime index for Part I offenses. Eliminate larceny under $50, auto joyrides, statutory rape and negligent manslaughter.	Recommends Changes: Update population base. Use census metropolitan area definitions for separating urban and rural. Get more complete coverage, provide more explanation.	Stresses importance for police information. Secondary is public use.

Year	Event	Detail / Recommendation	Finding / Response	Purpose
	FBI revises UCR.		Accepts most of recommendations except: Did not eliminate joyrides. Did not provide much explanation of data.	
1959	H. Hoover article in Reader's Digest.	We are not tough enough on criminals and our data is inadequate.	We need a census of crime and data on effectiveness of corrections system.	To be more effective in treatment of offenders and cut crime.
1961	Crime Factors list included in UCR.	A 1-page list of possible causes of crime.	Not followed up with data.	To absolve police of ultimate responsibility.
1964	The Great Society period. New social awareness. Riots and visible lawlessness.	Two opposing concepts. Crack down on criminals or more social programs. Social programs dominate.		
1965	President appoints Commission on Law Enforcement and Administration of Justice.			To look at social causes of crime and determine if the popular picture of crime corresponds to actuality.
1967	Commission's Report appears.	Recommends: Separating crimes of violence from crimes against property. New indices for non-indexed crime. Measuring social costs of crime. Promoting social and psychological conditions conducive to law-abiding conduct.	Findings: Surveys of victims show actual crime several times the index. Actual crime increasing, but so is reporting. Misleading information dissemination is unduly alarming the public. Recommends Federal crime statistics center.	To inform the public and measure the effectiveness of anticrime measures.

TABLE 3 (continued)

| Year | Environment and Key Events | Developments in | | Intended and Actual Purposes |
		Concepts	Methods	
1968	Omnibus Crime Control Act establishes LEAA and National Crime Data Service.			To give block grants to state governments for law enforcement. To begin research on new crime statistics.
	Nixon wins campaign using rising crime rate in speeches.	Crime as problem of enforcement.	Strengthen police to reduce crime.	
1969–1972	Legislation to give police more power. Increasing funding for crime statistics and block grants.		No-knock entry, wiretapping, preventive detention, increased penalties for some crimes.	
1973	Change in formula for LEAA grants.	More funds to high-crime areas.	Crime index becomes one of criteria for a city's level of LEAA funding.	To meet complaints of big-city mayors that states were distributing funds unfairly.
1974	Preliminary reports of victimization survey.	Crime as known to victims.	Interviews of households and businesses.	To get a more complete, reliable index of actual crime than the UCR and get some estimates of the cost of crime.

* Massachusetts, according to I.N. Robinson (1933), "History of Criminal Statistics (1908-1933)", Journal of Criminal Law and Criminology, 24, 125.
** T. Sellin (1931), "The Basis of a Crime Index", Journal of Criminal Law and Criminology, 22, 335.

TABLE 4

The U.S. Unemployment Rate: Concept and Methods.

Concept Represented	The unfilled demand for jobs.
The Measure	The unemployed/the labor force in a given week, seasonally adjusted. The labor force is the total of unemployed and employed. The employed includes all over 16 doing any paid work in the week, 15+ hours of unpaid work in a family enterprise, or temporarily absent with or without pay from jobs due to strikes, illness, weather, or vacation. The unemployed are those over 16 without paid work in the week, actively seeking work, waiting to start a job within 30 days, or waiting to be called back to a job after being laid off.
Purpose	To measure the number of jobs needed to keep those desiring work employed and to evaluate the performance of the economy.
Source	The Current Population Survey, a sample of about 50,000 families interviewed directly.
Collector	Census Bureau
Analysis and Presentation	BLS
Frequency	Monthly
Geographic Unit	Nation
Principal Users and Uses	The media, interest groups, unions, and high level political leadership to get a general picture of the direction of the economy and of the amount of hardship, and accordingly to praise or criticize policy. Economists, in government and private and public research, along with other data, to analyze the structure and predict the future of the economy. Economic advisors to formulate national monetary and fiscal policy. Analysts and politicians to advise on manpower policy. All groups for setting targets for national policy. Breakdowns of data by population groups used by government, independent analysts and interest groups to suggest and evaluate specific policy proposals.

TABLE 4 (continued)

Principal Problems	As aggregate measure for the nation not useful on characteristics of unemployment locally, though many remedial programs at state and city level. The concept of unemployment has left out the discouraged and the underemployed, toward whom programs have increasingly been directed. Did not provide a large enough sample of the urban poor for analysis. Use of aggregate figure as national target masks problems of individual groups which may persist though target reached. Fluctuations in the labor force hard to explain and confuse interpretation of changes in unemployment rates.

TABLE 5

The U.S. Standard Budget: Concept and Methods.

Concept Represented	A societal norm for the consumption standard of a typical family at a low or moderate level.
The Measure	A list, with prices, of the goods and services required by the family to live at the specified standard for one year. Level of components selected by a variety of methods, varying from fixed standards determined by other government departments or professional organizations to elaborate calculations of break-even points.
Purpose	To measure the adequacy of income.
Sources	(a) Sample survey of 17,000 families about expenditures in various categories. Either direct interview or self-administered questionnaires over a period of months. (b) Surveys of retail prices in stores across the country.
Collector	For household survey — Census Bureau. Prior to 1970 was BLS. For price survey — BLS field agents.
Analysis and Presentation	BLS
Frequency	New list produced at 10- to 15-year intervals. Normally repriced annually.
Geographic Unit	Nation as a whole. Individual large cities, small cities as a group.
Principal Users and Uses	Federal, state and city agencies to provide services on basis of need. Unions for wage demands, arbitration boards, businesses and governments in salary setting. Government agencies for evaluating equity in taxation. Congressmen and interest groups for evaluating and pricing income maintenance policies.
Principal Problems	Misunderstanding of concept, obscurity of methods of design and lack of unifying model make it easily discounted in public discussion.

TABLE 6

The U.S. Crime Index: Concept and Methods.

Concept Represented	Crimes known to the police.
The Measure	Combines all crimes in each of seven categories, murder, forcible rape, robbery, aggravated assault, burglary, larceny of $50 and over, and auto theft. Each crime is weighted equally.
Purpose	To show the trend of crime and provide a measure of police activity.
Source	Complaints to police, later confirmed. Observations of police or crimes found through investigation.
Collectors	State, county and city police forces.
Analysis and Presentation	FBI.
Frequency	Quarterly press releases and annual bulletins.
Geographic Units	Individual large cities, by region, by rural, urban and suburban location, SMSA's and groupings of cities of various sizes.
Principal Users and and Uses	The media and political leaders use it to argue for anti-crime measures and support of police; or as indicator of good or bad management of the nation or city. Media and social analysts use it as indicator of moral health of society. All use it to compare cities. Individuals use it to estimate safety in the streets. Used in formula dispensing LEAA funds and general evaluation of anti-crime efforts.
Principal Problems	Poor indicator of total crime representing at most 70% of only a selected set of crimes. Biased in ways not yet fully explored. Unit weighting of crimes does not correspond to societal valuation of relative seriousness. The rate of increase is exaggerated as definitions have not changed to adjust for inflation or other factors. Record-keeping practices and laws vary by city and over time, so comparisons are of dubious value. The FBI has designed and presented the data for police departments rather than the public.

340

TABLE 7

Measures Related to Unemployment in the U.S.

Measure	Agencies and Survey Name	What it Measures and How	What it Does Not Measure	Drawbacks	Advantages
Monthly unemployment rate	Census and BLS. CPS.	The number out of work and looking by home interview.	Those not found at home, discouraged from looking or inadequately employed.	Some interaction effects with interviewers and misunderstanding. Not enough detail for local figures or much analysis of problem groups.	Reliability and frequency good for unemployment prediction and fiscal and monetary policy.
Monthly employment rate	Same.	The number at paid work for more than 1 hour in a given week by interview and the number in unpaid family work for 15 hours or more.	Those not found at home. Those in unpaid work.	Same.	High reliability, good cross-section, little local detail.
Labor force participation rate	Same.	The employed and the unemployed in relation to the population 16 and over.	Those fully prepared to work though not actually looking.	Same.	Permits consideration of long-term trends in work patterns.
Subemployment index	Census and BLS. UES.	The number desiring or needing some work in certain low-income areas, by interview.	Those in other than designated areas.	Depends on up-to-date census and designations of poverty areas. Interaction difficulties with interviewers remain.	Detail on low-income groups and motivation. Broader view of unemployment, useful to manpower policies.

TABLE 7 (continued)

Measure	Agencies and Survey Name	What it Measures and How	What it Does Not Measure	Drawbacks	Advantages
Insured unemployment	U.S. and State Employment Services.	The number registering for benefits and work. By Employment Office Records.	Those in first week of unemployment, not covered by insurance, with expired benefits, not choosing to register, or who quit previous job.	Hard to analyze if rules change. Some estimating done for missed categories. Not reliable in detail.	Geographic detail and speed (weekly figures by city and state).
Insured employment	Same.	At work and paying for insurance through payrolls.	Uninsured workers.	Same.	Geographic and industrial detail. Speed.
Employment totals	BLS.	The number on payrolls in a month, by self-reporting survey.	Many self-employed, and double counts individuals on two payrolls or fired and rehired.	Employer cooperation and understanding of forms necessary. Fairly high level achieved.	Same. Good general economic indicator.
Help-wanted advertising	Conference Board.	An index of the help-wanted ads in a sample of newspapers.	Jobs not advertised for (the great majority).	Bias in types of jobs. May not move as do vacancies generally.	An indicator of trends in demand for workers.
Registered vacancies.	U.S. and State Employment Service.	Job openings voluntarily listed with services.	Jobs not listed (the great majority).	Jobs are mostly lower level.	A readily obtained indicator of trends in demand for workers.

| Job vancancy rate | BLS | The number of vacant jobs in industry, by occupation in comparison to total jobs. By questionnaire to sample of employers. | Jobs in selfemployment. Jobs open internally in a company. | The definition of vacancy not fully objective. Requires large sample to give useful detail. | The best measure of demand for workers to compare with unemployment or supply. |

343

TABLE 8
Measures Related to Levels of Living in the U.S.

Measure	Agencies and Survey Names	What it Measures and How	What it Does Not Measure	Drawbacks	Advantages
Standard budget	BLS and Census CES.	Societal consumption norm. Combination of actual patterns and accepted standards for a target type of family.	Ideal or average consumption. Actual living levels. Norms insofar as consumption is only one part.	Difficult to understand. Unconnected to theory and models, easy to misuse.	The only measure that attempts to reflect the norm implied in public action. Allows comparison by location and family size.
Low-income lines	Census and Social Security Administration.	The income levels just above deprivation for families of various sizes. A multiple of the cost of an adequate diet.	Special needs, assets, future income, changes in relationship of food to other expenditures.	Has not moved up with living standards, nor changed with life styles.	Simple to construct and use. The only accepted poverty standard. Necessary for much public action.
Public opinion on living costs	Gallup Opinion Poll.	Estimates of costs of living at various standards, by families of different income classes. Interview.	Actual living costs and standards families feel they have achieved.	Lack of knowledge or poor calculation by respondents to unknown degree.	Gives a rough approximation to norms, a general perspective.
Median family income	Many agencies in different contexts.	The middle income of the total range, through tax forms, census and other surveys.	Assets, expected income, special needs.	Not adjusted to family size.	A comprehensible benchmark for a perspective on incomes.

Per capita income	Many agencies in different contexts.	Total income divided by total population.	Same.	Not an indication of income actually available to individuals.	An index of a society's capacity to pay.
Income and wealth distribution	Many public and private groups.	The way income and wealth are distributed through overall indices of inequality and comparisons of amounts and percentage of resources available to rich and poor.	Wealth or income in relation to needs distribution.	No consensus on the best measure. Income and wealth hard to relate, as a practical matter.	To evaluate social and economic justice.

345

TABLE 9
Measures Related to Crime in the U.S.

Measure	Agency	What it Measures and How	What it Does Not Measure	Drawbacks	Advantages
Crime Index	FBI and local police departments.	Selected well-reported crimes, known to the police, gathered from uniform reports sent to FBI.	Poorly reported types of crimes. Crimes without victims. White-collar crime. The unreported part of index crimes.	Weighting does not correspond to public view of seriousness. Poor presentation. Built-in upward biases. Police may misclassify crimes.	The only direct measure of crime until 1970's. Allows data for small areas.
Arrests	same.	Individuals arrested by type of crime and previous arrest. From police reports.	Guilt of individual or of further disposition of case. Crimes for which no miscreant is found.	Can be biased according to local police practices.	A measure of police activity.
Clearances	same.	Crimes "cleared" by arrest or other identification of a suspect.	Whether individual is found guilty.	Practice of getting "confessions" to numerous crimes from one offender in return for leniency. Clearances cannot be matched with arrests or offenders, and data is often misinterpreted.	A measure of police efficiency, though an unreliable one.

346

Convictions and acquittals, judicial statistics	Department of Justice	People convicted and acquitted of crimes from court records.	Crimes for which there is no suspect or indictment.	Bias in the types of cases getting to court.	Accurate unbiased records with correct classification of crime.
Prisoners	Census Bureau	Number of people in prisons at a point in time, or committed to prison in a particular year.	Number on parole, types of crime.	Not a good indicator of crime, due to lags and biases from sentencing practices.	Good indicator of the work load of penal treatment institutions.

347

Glossary of Abbreviations

ASA	American Statistical Association
BLS	Bureau of Labor Statistics
CEA	Council of Economic Advisors
CES	Consumer Expenditure Survey
CPI	Consumer Price Index
CPS	Current Population Survey
CWFB	City Workers Family Budget
FAP	Family Assistance Plan
FBI	Federal Bureau of Investigation
FSUC	Federal Statistics Users Conference
GDP	Gross Domestic Product
GNP	Gross National Product
IACP	International Association of Chiefs of Police
JEC	Joint Economic Committee
LEAA	Law Enforcement Assistance Administration
MDTA	Manpower Development and Training Act
NRPB	National Resources Planning Board
OEO	Office of Economic Opportunity
SMA	Standard Metropolitan Area
SMSA	Standard Metropolitan Statistical Area
UCR	Uniform Crime Reports
UES	Urban Employment Survey
UNCTAD	United Nations Commission for Trade and Development
UNESCO	United Nations Educational, Social and Cultural Organization
UNRISD	United Nations Research Institute for Social Development
WPA	Works Progress Administration or Work Projects Administration

Subject Index

Index of Names

National Center for Education
Statistics 83
National Center for Health
Statistics 83, 311
National Commission on Law
Observance and Enforcement 162,
310
National Commission on Urban
Problems 272, 318
National Crime Data Service 336
National Criminal Justice
Information and Statistics
Service 169
National Goals Research Staff 98,
289, 304, 319
National Industrial Conference
Board 236, 265, 307, 317
See also Conference Board
National Institute of Health 78
National Resources Planning Board
93
National Science Foundation 103
National Tenants Association 263
National War Labor Board 261,
266–8, 318
National Welfare Rights
Organization 263
Newton, Sir I, 119
Nixon Administration 170, 255, 272,
277, 283
Nixon, R.A. 252, 317
Nixon, R.M. 82, 150, 151, 153, 169,
241, 252, 268, 282, 336

Office of Economic Opportunity 226
Office of Education 61, 191, 210, 312
Office of Management and Budget,
see Executive Office of the
President
Oliphant, T. 253, 317
Olsen, M. 45
Olson, M. 102, 222, 303, 314
Organization for Economic
Cooperation and Development
100–154, 303
Orshansky, M. 148, 240, 269, 307,
315, 317
Osherson, S. 310

Parke, R. 303
Pay Relativities Board, U. K. 274

Pearl, R.B. 199, 312
Peattie, L. 37, 47
Perry, G.L. 218, 314
Peters, M. 39, 46
Petty, Sir W. 63, 156
Phillips, A.W. 253, 317
Piven, F. 202, 312
Potter, T. 69
Pounds, W.F. 57, 58, 166, 252, 278,
300, 319
President 309
President's Commission on Federal
Statistics 77, 80, 83–4, 86, 302
Law Enforcement and
Administration of Justice 168,
310, 335
National Goals 304
President's Committee on Economic
Security 259–60
Cost of Living 238, 267, 316, 319
To Appraise Employment and
Unemployment Statistics
134–5, 237, 257–8, 287–8, 307,
316, 319, 325–6
President's Conference on
Unemployment 123–5, 307, 322
President's Research Committee on
Recent Social Trends 92–4, 304
Price Commission 280–1
Prices and Incomes Board, U.K. 269
Public Health Association 145
Public Health Service 78
Public Housing Administration 230

Quételet, A. 91, 156

Railroad Labor Board 265
Rainwater, L. 106, 192, 303, 307, 311
Reader's Digest 132–5, 168
Reagan, R. 19
Reich, R. 43, 47
Reichard, R. 214, 314
Rein, M. 13, 42, 47, 58, 176, 300–301,
259
Rittel, H.W.J. 54, 300
Rivlin, A. 9, 47
Robinson, L.N. 309, 336
Robinson, S. 309
Roby, P. 176, 311
Rokkan, S. 314